"God Alone Knows
Which Was Right"

"God Alone Knows Which Was Right"

The Blue and Gray Terrill Family of Virginia in the Civil War

RICHARD L. ARMSTRONG

McFarland & Company, Inc., Publishers
Jefferson, North Carolina, and London

FRONTISPIECE: Warm Springs, Virginia—1859. Drawing of the village of Warm Springs (then called Bath Court House). In the foreground is the rear of the courthouse and jail. Beyond that is the Warm Springs Hotel. Drawn by E. Albert Ludwig, professor of Modern Languages at Washington College, for Mary Jane Wise (courtesy Evelyn Lee Moore)

LIBRARY OF CONGRESS ONLINE CATALOGUING DATA
Armstrong, Richard L.
 "God alone knows which was right" : the blue and gray Terrill family of Virginia in the Civil War / Richard L. Armstrong.
  p. cm.
 Includes bibliographical references and index.

 ISBN 978-0-7864-4622-3
 softcover : 50# alkaline paper ∞

 1. Terrell family. 2. Terrell family—Correspondence. 3. Terrill, William Henry, 1800–1877—Family. 4. War and famillies—Virginia—History—19th century. 5. War and famillies—United States—History—19th century. 6. Virginia—History—Civil War, 1861–1865. 7. Virginia—History—Civil War, 1861–1865—Personal narratives. 8. United States—History—Civil War, 1861–1865—Personal narratives. 8. Bath County (Va.)—Biography.
 E605.A765 2010
 973.7'81—dc22   2009049593

British Library cataloguing data are available

©2010 Richard L. Armstrong. All rights reserved

No part of this book may be reproduced or transmitted in any form or by any means, electronic or mechanical, including photocopying or recording, or by any information storage and retrieval system, without permission in writing from the publisher.

Front cover, left to right: Colonel James Barbour Terrill (*The Confederate Soldier in the Civil War*); William Henry Terrill, 1856, and Lieutenant William R. Terrill (both courtesy Bath County Historical Society). Background ©2010 Clipart.com and Shutterstock

Manufactured in the United States of America

McFarland & Company, Inc., Publishers
 Box 611, Jefferson, North Carolina 28640
 www.mcfarlandpub.com

First, I would like to dedicate this book to God, Creator, Master and Preserver of all things. Without His constant guidance, His placing source material in my path (or vice versa), and His blessings, this story could not have been written.

Second, this book is dedicated to the memory of the Terrill family of Bath County, and to the Porterfield family. Through it, their lives are remembered.

And lastly, to the late Virgil Howell, who loved the story of the Terrills and loved Bath County.

Acknowledgments

Where to start? In the course of the years spent researching the Terrill family, I have encountered many interesting people. Sadly, many of them are no longer with us.

Among the first individuals I wish to thank are the staff members of the National Archives, in Washington, D.C. Between 1972 and 2007, these wonderful people endured many questions and requests, and they suggested potential source material.

Then I must thank the descendants of the Terrill family that I was fortunate enough to correspond with or personally meet. Miss Mercer Terrill Vaden, of Richmond, was a granddaughter of Brigadier General James B. Terrill. In the latter part of the 1970s, while living in Lubbock, Texas, I contacted her by phone. After telling her what I was looking for, she informed me that she did have some material about her grandfather. Several days later I received a medium sized manila envelope from Miss Vaden by regular mail. Imagine my surprise when I opened it and a tintype photograph of her grandfather dropped out. It was so clear that one could see the hairs of his head.

Another Terrill descendant contacted by phone was Miss Elizabeth Jackson Morton, also of Richmond. She provided me with valuable details and photographs. Regrettably, these two dear Southern ladies are now deceased. I shall forever be grateful to them for their kindness and generosity.

One of the Terrill descendants that I was fortunate enough to meet on several occasions in the 1980s was Annie Terrill Yount Thomas. She was a great-granddaughter of Doctor George Parker Terrill, of Salem, Virginia. She was most helpful, providing many details about her family during those meetings and subsequent correspondence.

Another distant relative of the Terrills, through the Pitzer-Wise family, deserves special mention. Miss Evelyn Lee Moore, of Lynchburg, Virginia, was for many years the family historian. Through her efforts, many wonderful stories of the Terrills and of Bath County in the 1850s and 1860s have been preserved.

Howard R. Hammond, of Greenville, South Carolina, deserves mention for his contribution to this work. He is connected to the Terrills through William H. Terrill's second wife, Rachel C. Hamilton Scott. He provided access to correspondence between William and Rachel in the last days of their lives. Thank you, Howard, for your generosity.

Finally, I must thank Mr. and Mrs. Philip Terrill Porterfield III of Charles Town, West Virginia. The Porterfields shared their collection of Porterfield and Terrill items with the Bath County Historical Society and with me. Through the generosity of this family, the fine horsehair sofa from Colonel Terrill's Rose Hill home returned to Bath County, along with a number of photographs and stories.

To the staff members of the many local libraries, university, colleges, historical societies, and military academies consulted in the quest for Terrill material, I say thank you. The staff of the Bath County Public Library deserves special thanks for processing the many interlibrary loan requests. Your assistance was most valuable and appreciated.

I wish to mention the contribution of The Homestead Preserve, of Hot Springs, Virginia. Their generous financial assistance helped complete the work necessary for this manuscript.

There remains one very special person to thank — Becky Armstrong, my wife. She not only read (and reread) this manuscript, but listened to and encouraged me as I obsessed about the Terrills time and again. Thank you, from the bottom of my heart. I am reminded of a meeting between local historian Hugh Gwin and Becky at a social event in the fall of 2005. Upon seeing her, Mr. Gwin took her hand and inquired, "Are you sick of the Terrills yet?" All had a good laugh.

Among the many others to whom thanks are due is Mark Johnson, author of *That Body of Brave Men*, who shared the fruits of his research with me.

If I have neglected to thank anyone by name, I now apologize for that oversight, and say thank you. Thank you everyone for your generosity, encouragement, and help.

Richard L. Armstrong • Hot Springs, Virginia

Table of Contents

Acknowledgments — vii
Introduction — 1
Military Terminology — 3
Operation of a Light Battery — 4
Terrill Family Tree — 8

I — William Henry Terrill — 9
    Including Jeremiah Morton Terrill, Sarah Jane Terrill McDannald and John Allen Terrill

II — George Parker Terrill — 36
III — Emily Cornelia Clay Terrill (and George Alexander Porterfield) — 47
IV — William Rufus Terrill — 85
V — James Barbour Terrill — 172
VI — Philip Mallory Terrill — 218

Appendix I: Address at the Burial of Brig. Gen. William R. Terrill — 241
Appendix II: Terrill Burial Monument Myth — 245
Chapter Notes — 249
Bibliography — 271
Index — 283

*"Lord, it seems that truth and honor
Sure can come at an awful price"*
— From "Laughlin Boy," by William Jolliff

Introduction

This is the story of Colonel William H. Terrill, of Bath County, Virginia, and his family during the Civil War. His family was one of those tragically divided by loyalty, duty, and the politics of war. Three of his sons and a son-in-law fought for the Confederacy, and one son fought for the Union.

Colonel William H. Terrill served the citizens of Bath County for more than thirty years as prosecuting attorney. During the Civil War, he was briefly attached to the staff of Confederate Brigadier General Arnold Elzey, and later served as Provost Marshal in Bath County.

William Rufus Terrill, a graduate of the U.S. Military Academy, served in the U.S. Artillery. After serving for a year as Assistant Professor of Mathematics at the Military Academy, Lieutenant Terrill went to Florida and took part in the Third Seminole War. He was later assigned to duty with the U.S. Coast Survey, and was on duty in Florida just prior to the beginning of the Civil War. When Colonel Terrill learned that his son (Lieutenant Terrill) intended to remain loyal to the United States, he tried to entice him to resign and come home. Failing to persuade his son to turn his back on the government, Colonel Terrill disowned his son, telling him that he could never come home again, regardless of the outcome of the war.

Lieutenant Terrill soon became Captain Terrill, and commanded Battery H, 5th U.S. Artillery. His gallant actions at the Battle of Shiloh, Tennessee, in April 1862, led to his promotion to Brigadier General of Volunteers in September 1862. Within a month, General Terrill was killed at Perryville, Kentucky.

James Barbour Terrill, a graduate of the Virginia Military Institute, served the Confederacy in the 13th Virginia Infantry. Appointed Major in May 1861, he advanced to the rank of Colonel by the spring of 1863. While leading his brigade against the Federal fortifications at Bethesda Church, Virginia, on May 30, 1864, James was shot through the head and killed. His confirmation as Brigadier General was passed the following day.

Philip Mallory Terrill was a student at the University of Virginia when the

Civil War began. He left his studies and returned to Bath County, where he was appointed First Lieutenant in Company G, 25th Virginia Infantry. Captured at Rich Mountain in July 1861, Philip remained a prisoner of war until the fall of 1862. Resigning his commission in the spring of 1863, he joined Company B, 12th Virginia Cavalry as a private. He was killed near Winchester in November 1864.

Doctor George Parker Terrill graduated from the Virginia Military Institute and Jefferson Medical College. During the Civil War, he served as Colonel of the 127th Virginia Militia, commanded the Roanoke County home guards, and provided medical services to the Confederate Hospital at Salem, Virginia. He was the only one of four brothers to survive the war.

Emily Cornelia Clay Terrill, a daughter of Colonel William H. Terrill, married George Alexander Porterfield in 1849. Porterfield was a graduate of the Virginia Military Institute, and a Mexican War veteran. When the Civil War started, he was commissioned as a Colonel of Virginia Volunteers, and sent to Grafton, in Western Virginia. He retreated from Grafton, and was routed from Philippi, resulting in a court of inquiry. Failing to be re-elected as Colonel of the 25th Virginia Infantry in the spring of 1862, Porterfield retired from active duty. Returning to his home in Jefferson County, (West) Virginia, he was arrested by Union authorities, and allowed to remain at home on parole.

According to folklore, William H. Terrill had the phrase "God Alone Knows Which Was Right" inscribed on a monument to honor two of his fallen sons—Generals James B. Terrill and William R. Terrill. Like many similar stories, this monument is only a fable.

The author of this book uses family letters, wartime letters, official records, and many other sources to tell the story of this old Virginia family. At last, the lives of these gallant soldiers are recorded for the enjoyment of Civil War enthusiasts everywhere.

Military Terminology

To help readers who are not familiar with military organization and terminology, the following guide is given.

Corps—an organization usually consisting of two or more divisions

Division—a tactical unit composed of a headquarters and usually three to five brigades

Brigade—a tactical and administrative unit composed of a headquarters, one or more infantry units, and support units

Regiment—a military unit consisting usually of two battalions

Battalions—a military unit composed of a headquarters and two or more companies, batteries or similar units

Company—a military unit consisting usually of a headquarters and two or more platoons. A company usually had 100 men in it.

Platoon—A subdivision of a company of troops consisting of two or more sections and usually commanded by a lieutenant.

Section—An army tactical unit smaller than a platoon and larger than a squad.

Squad—The smallest tactical unit of military personnel.

Battery—a grouping of artillery pieces for tactical purposes equivalent to a company with up to 152 men.

Enfilade—a military term for gunfire (or artillery fire) directed from a flanking position along the length of an enemy battle line, such as a trench or column of troops.

Adjutant—a staff officer who assists the commanding officer and is especially responsible for correspondence.

Operation of a Light Battery

The operation or drill of a properly trained battery of light artillery is a remarkable sight. During the Civil War, it was not uncommon for officers and men to stand and watch the operation of a battery during battle or at practice. Every man had a job to do and a sequence to follow. Once put into motion, the men performed their duties like parts of a well-oiled machine.

A battery of artillery usually consisted of six guns, divided into three sections of two guns each. The sections were referred to the right, left and center sections. Each gun had a limber, a two-wheeled cart, which carried a chest of ammunition and equipment needed to work the gun. The limber could hold up to 50 rounds of ammunition, along with fuse, tools, sights, friction primers, haversack, lanyard, etc. The limber also supported the trail of an artillery piece, allowing it to travel. An additional limber, attached to a two-wheeled cart called a caisson, carried additional chests of ammunition. A team of six horses pulled the gun and limber, while a similar team pulled the caisson and its limber. The battery was accompanied by a battery wagon, a mobile forge, and several supply wagons. A captain commanded the battery, which required up to 152 men and 154 horses to operate.

The captain of the battery had a very responsible and demanding job. A very high degree of competence was needed, as well as a good background in mathematics and applied physics. Regular artillery officers were selected by their standing at graduation from the United States Military Academy. The top quarter of the class became engineer officers, while the second quarter became artillery officers. Cavalry and infantry officers came from the lower half of the class.

The duties of each rank in the battery are as follows:

Captain— has command, control and responsibility for training, serviceability, discipline and combat operation of the battery. He serves also as the recruiting officer, procures horses, equipment, and supplies through the regular channels as well as outside them.

Lieutenants—two first lieutenants and two second lieutenants are assigned to the battery. Three of them—the first lieutenants and the senior second lieutenant, each have command of a section of the battery, along with four limbers and two caissons. The junior second lieutenant is responsible for the caissons and ordnance (ammunition), and has command of the chiefs of caissons (junior corporals), drivers, and extra men. He frequently serves as adjutant of the battery, which means that he helps the captain with administrative affairs.

1st Sergeant (Orderly Sergeant)—answers directly to the captain and oversees the entire battery. He is responsible for the administration of the battery, preparing reports, holding roll call, maintaining rosters, etc. In battle, he remains near the captain and carries orders. If necessary, he will take up the duties of the chief of the line of caissons.

Quartermaster Sergeant—receives his orders from the captain or first sergeant, and is responsible for drawing and issuing clothing, personal gear, rations and sometimes small arms ammunition, and keeps records. In battle, he sometimes remains near the captain to carry orders, but most often remains with the wagons to keep them secure.

Commissary Sergeant—a position found in Union six gun batteries. He takes care of drawing and issuing rations to the men of the battery instead of the quartermaster sergeant.

Sergeant (Chief of the Piece)—has charge of the equipment and men of a gun: a gunner, cannoneers, the chief of a caisson, and the drivers. This usually consists of one gun, nine to thirteen horses, their harness and saddles. He is also responsible for training the men in each position of the crew that serves the gun. During battle, he is dismounted and stands in the rear of the gun, where he can oversee the operation of it.

Senior Corporal (Gunner)—has responsibility for the men and equipment of the gun: six to ten cannoneers, and a limber. In battle, he aims and orders the firing of the gun.

Junior Corporal (Chief of Caisson)—has charge of a limber and caisson, and has to insure the ammunition is properly packed and in good condition. He has limited authority over the drivers.

Drivers—this duty is performed by privates, whose main duty is to care for the horses and harness.

Cannoneers—the duties of the cannoneers is performed by privates, whose duty it is to carefully load the gun for firing. It is hazardous duty at best.

Buglers—one musician, and sometimes more, stand by the captain to sound his commands during battle. When not in battle, the buglers are often detailed as clerks.

Color Bearer (Guidon)—carries the battery flag, and stands by the captain during battle.

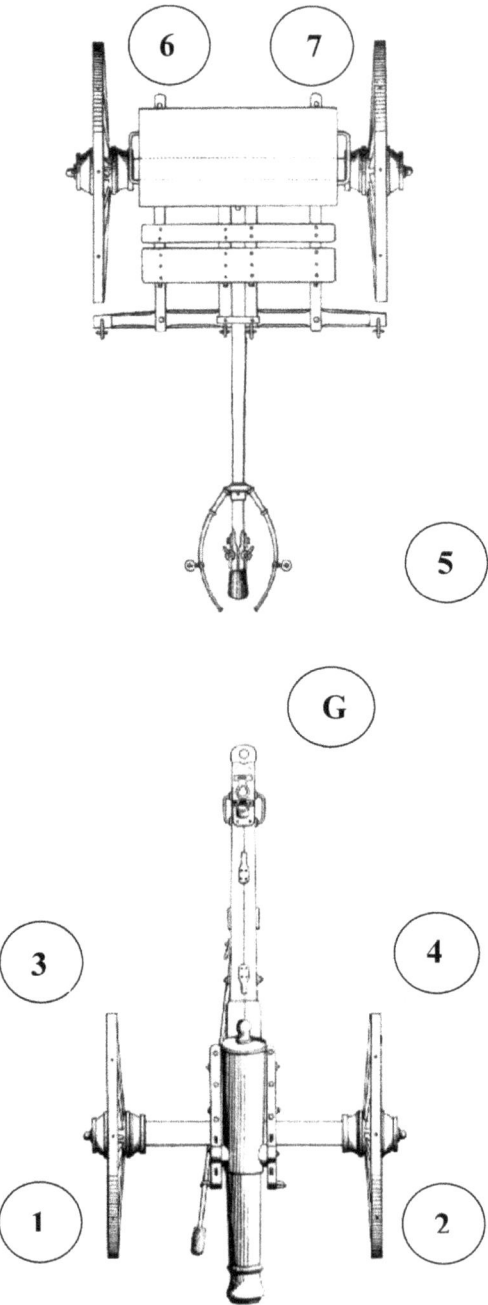

Diagram showing positions occupied by a gun crew while working a piece of artillery (based on a diagram by Charles TenBrink). Explanations are on the facing page.

Now that the duties of the men have been explained, we look to the operation of a gun and the chorography necessary to perform it.

After the gun is un-limbered (detached from the limber) and wheeled into position, the men take their stations about the gun and limber.

The **Gunner** gives the command "load" to set the crew into motion. While they are performing their duties, the gunner sights the gun, assisted by the cannoneers in position **Number 3**.

Cannoneer **Number 1,** using a wet sponge attached to the end of a pole, swabs the tube (barrel) to extinguish any remaining sparks, while Cannoneer **Number 3** places his thumb (protected by a leather thumbstall) over the vent of the gun.

Cannoneer **Number 6 or Number 7** removes a round from the limber chest, prepares the round by cutting the fuse (if necessary), and passes the round to Cannoneer **Number 5**.

Cannoneer **Number 5** accepts the round from Cannoneer **Number 6 or Number 7**, places it in his haversack, and carries the round to the front of the gun, where he hands it to Cannoneer **Number 2**.

Cannoneer **Number 2** takes the round from Cannoneer **Number 5**, and places it in the muzzle of the gun.

Cannoneer **Number 3** places his thumb on the vent of the gun, while the round is rammed into position by Cannoneer **Number 1**.

Cannoneer **Number 1** reverses the pole with the sponge on it, and rams (pushes) the round into position at the rear of the tube (barrel).

Cannoneer **Number 3** inserts a vent pick (a metal pin, sharpened on one end) into the vent, puncturing the paper or cloth bag containing the powder charge.

Cannoneer **Number 4** steps forward and attaches the lanyard (a length of heavy cord) to a friction primer, and inserts it into the vent.

Cannoneer **Number 3** holds the friction primer in place as Cannoneer **Number 4** steps back from the gun, pulling the lanyard taunt. When in place, he gives a signal that the gun is ready to fire.

Everyone now steps clear of the gun. The **Gunner**, who has sighted the gun, and set the elevation, assisted by Cannoneer **Number 3**, who moves the trail of the gun as directed by the **Gunner**, now gives the command to fire the gun. Cannoneer **Number 4** pulls the lanyard, igniting the friction primer, which in turn ignites the powder charge, firing the round.

After the firing of the gun, the cannoneers wheel the gun back into position, and the whole process begins anew. A well trained gun crew can fire two rounds in a minute's time. The cycle would continue until the command to cease fire is given.

Terrill Family Tree

William Henry Terrill — Elizabeth Pitzer
(1800–1877)   (1805–1858)

Sarah Jane (1828–1850)	George Parker (1830–1884)	Emily Cornelia Clay (1832–1906)	William Rufus (1834–1862)	Jeremiah Morton (c. 1835–c. 1840)	James Barbour (1838–1864)	John Allen (1839–1858)	Philip Mallory (1842–1864)
--	--	--	--	died young	--	died single	died single
William H. McDannald	Sarah Brent Dold	George Alexander Porterfield	Emily Drennen Henry		Charlotte Eucbia Drury		
Charles T.	Francis Heath	William Terrill	No Children	No Children	James Mercer	No Children	No Children
	Elizabeth Dold	Elizabeth Morton			Emily Barbour		
	William H.	John Moler					
	George Morton	George Terrill					
	Mary Louisa	Mary Jane					
	Anna Carter Johnston	Charles Alexander					
	Samuel Miller Dold	Katherine Seton					

Chapter I

William Henry Terrill

Including Jeremiah Morton Terrill, Sarah Jane Terrill McDannald and John Allen Terrill

William Henry Terrill
1800–1877

Pre-War, 1800–1860

William Henry Terrill, the fourth generation of his family to be born in the United States, was born July 16, 1800,[1] in Orange County, Virginia, to William Terrill, Jr., and his wife, Jane Morton. On his mother's side, he is a cousin to Confederate General James Ewell Brown "JEB" Stuart. Rumor has it that General Robert E. Lee and Governor John Letcher are among his distant relatives. Genealogical research has proven the connection to Stuart, however the Terrill–Lee–Letcher connection cannot be substantiated.

Family tradition tells that William received a good English education. His parents instilled a strong sense of frugality in young William, which he tried to impress upon his children. One family historian described him as being "tight as a tick."[2]

Evelyn Lee Moore, a grand niece, described William as "an individualist with outstanding characteristics, a most noticeable one being his forthrightness. He was a cultured, courteous gentleman with a fine touch of humor." His niece, Cornelia H. Wise Moore, referred to William as a "cultivated, scholarly man."[3]

Deciding to make a career as a lawyer, William graduated from the Needham Law School at Farmville, Virginia, in the early 1820s. By 1824, William commenced his practice in Covington, Alleghany County, Virginia. The circuit court of Alleghany County granted him permission to practice in that court on October 18, 1824, after taking the required oaths.[4]

While practicing law in Covington, he met Elizabeth Pitzer,[5] the daughter of Bernard and Jane Kyle Pitzer, and began to court her. William and Elizabeth were married in Botetourt County on October 26, 1827, and set up housekeeping on Bath (now Main) Street in Covington.

William's ability as an attorney soon gained him the office of prosecuting attorney for Alleghany County, serving one term in 1827. He spent the next three years (1828–1831) as a delegate to the Virginia Legislature from Alleghany County, dividing his time between Richmond and Covington.[6]

Sarah Jane Terrill, the first of William and Elizabeth's eight children, was born in 1828. Two years later, on February 23, 1830, their second child — a boy — was born. The Terrills named him George Parker Terrill, in honor of William's brother George, who was a surgeon in the U.S. Navy. Like his namesake, George became a doctor.

Following his service in the House of Delegates, William resumed his law practice in Covington. Looking for ways to increase his business, William turned to the nearby county of Bath. On September 26, 1831, William qualified and took the required oaths to practice law in Bath County.[7]

The third child born to the Terrills was a daughter named Emily Cornelia Clay Terrill, who was born at Covington on July 10, 1832. Two years later, on April 21, 1834, William Rufus Terrill was born, also in Covington.

Following the pattern of a child every two years, the Terrills' fifth child arrived in 1836, and was named Jeremiah Morton Terrill. Unfortunately, Jeremiah did not survive to adulthood, dying before 1840.

With at least a dozen years' experience in practicing law, William's fees brought him a comfortable living. He supplemented the income from his legal practice by hiring out his slaves in the salt works in Kanawha County, Virginia. In a December 1837 letter to his kinsman, Dr. George Morton, William described his practice and his plans for the future:

Daguerreotype of William Henry Terrill (c. 1856) (courtesy Bath County Historical Society).

> My practice since the 1 of September last has been worth three thousand Dollars, Eleven hundred of which accrued on the defense of prisoners. If it should continue in the same ratio for a very few years I should then be willing to retire from the Bar, but that

good fortune I do not anticipate. My estate is now worth twenty thousand Dollars. I shall be content to retire on forty thousand.[8]

By March 1836, William moved his family to Warm Springs, in Bath County, Virginia, purchasing two tracts of land and a house adjoining the Warm Springs Hotel property in January 1838. The Terrill home was situated in the Germantown section of the Warm Springs Valley, near the Presbyterian Church. Across the road from their home was the residence of Elizabeth's sister, Mary Jane Pitzer (Mrs. David G.) Wise. Miss Evelyn Lee Moore described the Terrill home as a low, rambling frame house, set high above the road to the Warm Springs Hotel. The family named the home Rose Hill because

Portrait of Elizabeth Pitzer Terrill (courtesy Mr. and Mrs. Philip T. Porterfield).

The horsehair sofa salvaged from the Terrill home "Rose Hill" as it burned. Scorch marks are visible on the back of the sofa (courtesy Bath County Historical Society).

Dr. George Terrill, brother of William H. Terrill and former Navy surgeon, who lived in Alabama and Rhode Island. Photograph taken in Charles Town, West Virginia, in the 1890s (courtesy Elizabeth Jackson Morton).

of the large growth of roses on the hill. One unusual feature graced the home, as the Terrills piped water to their back porch from a nearby spring.[9]

A suspicious fire destroyed Rose Hill in early 1873, leaving only the foundation stones and a few bricks. A convicted felon is thought to have set the fire, seeking revenge against Terrill for sending him to prison. Only a few possessions were salvaged from the burning home, among them a horsehair sofa. In 1907 only the smokehouse, icehouse and outside kitchen stood as a reminder of the location of the Terrill home. There are no visible traces of the home today.

Soon after moving into the new home, another child was born into the family. The sixth child, named James Barbour Terrill, was born on February 20, 1838.

Following a brief stint as a special prosecutor for Bath County in the summer of 1838, William soon found himself serving as prosecutor for Pocahontas County (now in West Virginia). He held this position until May 1852.

The Bath County Court appointed William to the position of prosecutor in 1839, to complete the term of John H. Peyton, who had resigned. From then until 1869, William served as prosecuting attorney. After a brief absence, the court re-appointed him to fill the position until the next regular election. In all, William H. Terrill served as prosecutor in Bath County for 33 years.

The last two of the Terrill children, John Allen and Philip Mallory, were born on October 1, 1839, and June 6, 1842, respectively.

During 1845, William began to have trouble with his eldest daughter, Sarah Jane, who was then about 17 years of age. In September 1845, William's brother George wrote from Pensacola, Florida:

> I regret to hear that, up to the date of that letter, you had not seen your daughter. I will not undertake to say that your course in this matter is reprehensible — but I will say that it is unwise, and ill judged.[10]

It was not until December 1845 that a clue to the difficulty between father and daughter appeared. In a letter to his youngest daughter, Emily, dated December 5, William informed her that Sarah had given birth to a son about two weeks before.[11]

While there is no record of Sarah Jane's marriage in Bath County, she did marry by October 1847.[12] She chose as her husband William H. McDannald, a merchant at Warm Springs. There are no additional details about the son born to Sarah Jane in the fall of 1845.

In the spring of 1848, on May 19, Governor William "Extra Billy" Smith appointed William to the Board of Visitors at the Virginia Military Institute. The appointment was for one year, during which time William served on the committees for the Quartermaster and Stewards Department.[13] The board met on June 22, 1848, and continued in session until July 4. Among their many duties was the examination of cadets (including his son George), examining

Bath County Courthouse and Jail. Built in 1843 and closed in 1907, when a new complex was built. The building is now known as the Warm Springs Inn (courtesy Bath County Historical Society).

the condition of the buildings, inspecting the arsenal, cadet quarters, and mess hall. While serving on the board, William formed a relationship with such notable figures as Philip St. George Cooke, Charles James Faulkner, John B. Floyd and George W. Mumford.[14]

Census records in 1850 list William's personal fortune as $4,200 in real estate, and an unspecified amount of personal property. The Slave Census, taken for the first time in 1850, revealed that William owned 23 slaves.[15]

The census records also reveal that Sarah and her husband, William H. McDannald, were living in the Terrill household. Interestingly, the census does not list any young children in the home. Other records indicate that a son, Charles T. McDannald, was born to the couple in 1850. What became of the child born nearly five years before?

Only a few months after the taking of the 1850 Census, Sarah Jane Terrill McDannald became ill. She suffered from the ravages of some malignant disease and died on August 9, 1850, aged 22 years.[16]

More than a year later, William wrote Emily about Sarah's illness and her last moments:

> Oh how often do I behold with the minds eye my poor suffering child, with her eyes directed to me with a supplicating cast of countenance, as much as to say "Father I have disobeyed you, I am sorry for it. I am paying the penalty of my disobedience, won't you forgive me and take care of my dear little boy." Yes my dear child I have long since forgiven you, others misled you and a just God will avenge the wrong. Your little boy would be a comfort to your parents, but you were scarcely committed to the silent grave before he was unfeelingly torn from us and our eyes have never beheld him since. I can never forget the closing scene of her life. I was reading aloud to her at her bed side, not thinking that death was so near, when she turned her eyes upon me and remarked please Father don't read any more. It was manifest that she knew her minutes were numbered and she wished to spend them in taking leave of those around her and poor thing she had scarcely time to accomplish that wish before her spirit took its everlasting flight.[17]

It appears that William and his son-in-law did not get along, despite living in the same household in 1850. By the time of the taking of the 1860 Census, William H. McDannald and his son, Charles, were living in the household of George Mayse, owner of the Warm Springs Hotel. Charles T. McDannald must have died before 1870, as he does not appear in the census records for that year. There is no record of his death, nor is there any mention of any interaction between William H. Terrill and his grandson.

As Colonel Terrill gained prominence, more and more of his time was spent doing something other than practicing law. During the 1850s and 1860s, William served as commissioner and superintendent of the Bath County school system, as well as a term on the University of Virginia Board of Visitors.

In July 1853, Elizabeth Terrill visited the White Sulphur Springs, in Greenbrier County, Virginia. While there, she wrote her sister Martha Ann Pitzer Smith on the 20th:

> I am again as you will perceive from the date of my letter at this place in search of health. I still labour under an affliction of the throat. I am now under the care of the resident physician, Dr. Lake, of this place. He has been using very prompt measures, with costic in burning the ulsers in my throat. He thinks he can cure it. The operation is very severe, but I submit to it very willingly if it is to cure me. My general health is not very good. My nervous system is very much deranged.[18]

After speaking of her health, and the health of their various friends, Elizabeth proceeded to update her sister on the accomplishments of her children.

> My son George has graduated in medicine and has settled in Salem near to our brother's. He thinks he will do very well, has been there but a short time. He is married to a Miss Dole of Lexington, Va. William has graduated at West Point and will be home in a few days. My daughter Emily is now at my house. She has 2 children, a son and daughter. She still resides in Washington City. She calls her daughter Mary Elizabeth. She goes by Bettie all the time. They are very sweet little children.[19]

Daguerreotype of woman and child, identified as Elizabeth Pitzer Terrill and probably a grandchild (courtesy Bath County Historical Society).

Elizabeth then spoke of her husband:

> Mr. Terrill left me on Monday to go to his court in Highland. He has taken Randolph County in his Circuit which makes it much more laborious. He now weighs nearly 3 hundred.[20]

According to family lore, William was at least six feet two inches tall, weighing over 300 pounds at one time in his life.[21]

After thirty years of practicing law, William's skill and reputation was widely known. In addition to practicing in Alleghany (1824) and Bath (1831) counties, he extended himself to the counties of Greenbrier, Pocahontas (1839), Highland (1847) and Randolph. Because of his extended practice, he was frequently absent from home, leaving Elizabeth with only the smaller children for company. Elizabeth's niece, Cornelia H. Wise Moore, recalled:

> Aunt Betty always wanted one of us girls to stay with her, all of her children being off at school except the two youngest boys who had a tutor. It was the delight of my life to be allowed the privilege. Young as I was I recall the pleasure of listening to my Uncle's sonorous, beautiful voice as he read aloud after supper as we sat around the great fireplace, and there I imbibed a deep love for the British Poets. He would always keep one of us as long as possible on his return; [he] was a great lover of children.[22]

During the mid–1850s, the Terrills seemed to have traveled about quite a lot, mostly in search of a cure for Elizabeth. She was quite sickly during that time, usually suffering with a sore throat. Family lore states that the Terrills sometimes spent the winter in Richmond. Elizabeth, however, did not always remain away from home for the entire winter.

A November 1855 letter to his son John Allen Terrill reveals a few interesting habits of William H. Terrill. William smoked a pipe, and is pictured smoking a cigar. That same letter continued:

> Knowing that I must be lonesome here by myself you [John] ought to write to me more frequently. It is now after 12 o'clock at night and I am setting by the fire with pipe in mouth and pen in hand writing to one of my Dear children who is in all probability in the land of dreams.... I have been feasting for the last three or four days upon wild game, such as turkey, pheasants, squirrels, &c. Lewis is my Huntsman. He goes out everyday and never fails to bring in a bountiful supply. The game always falls at the crack of his gun. He wastes no ammunition. Only think of it—for Breakfast boiled squirrels, swimming in nice butter—& for Dinner wild turkey or pheasant roasted and squirrels stewed!!! Don't it make your mouth water to think of such good eating.[23]

By April 1857, William had earned the title of Colonel. This was not a military title, but one of honor and respect. The governor usually bestowed this title, practiced particularly in Virginia, Kentucky and Georgia. In Georgia, lawyers automatically held the title of colonel—perhaps the reason for William's receiving it.

John Allen Terrill became ill with typhoid fever in December 1857 while attending the University of Virginia. He succumbed to the effects of the fever on January 14, 1858, with his parents by his side. He was just eighteen years of age. He spoke to his mother before he died, repeating a prayer that he learned as a child. To his grief-stricken father, he with difficulty said, "*Father, I am not afraid to die!*"[24]

The family had John Allen's remains laid to rest on the Terrill estate Rose Hill in Warm Springs, beside his younger brother Jeremiah. All trace of the two graves has been lost. These graves may have been the source of the enduring legend of the burial of James and William R. Terrill at Warm Springs.

William noted in a letter to his sister Jane Pilcher in February 1858 that Elizabeth was now sick, but the doctor thought she would soon recover. In a letter written the same day to his kinsman, Dr. George Morton, William confided his fears:

John Allen Terrill. Died of typhoid fever at the University of Virginia in January 1858. Note the Mexican War period military style cap he is wearing (courtesy Elizabeth Jackson Morton).

> My poor wife, heart broken under our bereavement, is now & has been for the last three days confined to a sick bed with symptoms not unlike those that marked the case of our son.[25]

Philip, writing to Emily Porterfield the same day, added his own concerns over the state of their mother's health.

> Mother is not so well now as she was when I commenced this letter, her fever seems to have increased. Doctor [Alexander G.] McChesney is now in her room. I will keep this letter open until tomorrow evening, I hope that mother will soon be better, but since Johns death, we all feel timid in regard to fever. Mother seems to think that she has Typhoid Fever, but I suppose her sickness was brought on by her distress.[26]

A month later, William again wrote his sister Jane, giving her an update on Elizabeth's condition.

> My wife is still unable to leave her bed to which she has been confined just five weeks, but her Physician thinks she is now out of danger. She is still very feeble & unable to set up in her bed more than a few minutes at a time, but I hope she will soon be restored to health and strength.[27]

Elizabeth Pitzer Terrill lost her battle with typhoid fever at 11 P.M. on April 20, 1858, at the age of 52 years. William had his beloved wife laid to rest in the nearby Warm Springs Cemetery. Her obituary noted that she was the mother of six sons and two daughters, and that one son had recently died at the University of Virginia. Her sister, Mary Jane Wise, acted in her place whenever the children (the youngest was 14) needed a mother's advice.

The summer and fall undoubtedly was a difficult one for William. In October 1858, while attending court in Highland County, he wrote his beloved daughter Emily.

> I feel unusually sad this evening.... Your Dear mother & Brother are rarely ever absent from my mind and my bereavement becomes more and more oppressive every succeeding day. The intensity of my grief is agonizing in the extreme. I don't know what it may lead to. Our dear and once happy home has a deserted appearance. She who was always there to make it cheerful and to greet my return with the smiles of affectionate welcome is not there now and the place that she so much loved will know her no more forever. I am overwhelmed with sorrow, inconsolable sorrow whenever I think or talk or write about your dear mother.[28]

Several weeks later, William again wrote Emily:

> When I am alone and happen to be unemployed I get to thinking about your dear Mother and Brother until it seems as if my heart would burst. I very often imagine that she is sitting near me.... I love her memory more and more every day.[29]

A year later, William began to think about getting married again. His intended was a widow from Covington named Rachel Hamilton Scott.[30] Not everyone was thrilled at the prospect of his taking a new wife. William Rufus, it seems, had some misgivings about his father's pending nuptials. Writing on June 30, 1859, to his brother-in-law George Porterfield, William commented:

> I have never yet by word or deed given any one to understand that I approve of Fathers marriage, *but just the contrary*. To approve of a matter, and to cease to oppose it are two things *entirely different*. I went home and stated to Father my objections. He thinks that he is about to promote his own happiness and comfort by the step.[31]

Although William Rufus and his siblings disapproved of their father's intention to marry again, he said that he would give the woman the respect and consideration due her as his father's wife. William H. Terrill and Rachel Hamilton Scott were married in Covington, Virginia, on February 16, 1860.

By the summer of 1860, William and Rachel were living in Warm Springs, along with sons James and Philip. The census that summer reported that William owned thirty slaves, while Rachel owned twelve.[32] William and Rachel had little need of other than a few house servants. As a result, they continued to hire out most of the slaves to the salt-works in western Virginia, or to other businesses.

The War Years, 1861 to 1865

With the war clouds swirling about and many Southern states severing their ties with the Union, the Virginia Legislature called for a state convention to decide what course the commonwealth should take. The legislature ordered the election of delegates held throughout the state on February 4, 1861, and ordered those elected to assemble in Richmond on the 13th. A single delegate would represent the counties of Alleghany and Bath at the convention. William H. Terrill was one of three men considered for the position. Thomas Sitlington, a Bath County farmer, and Covington attorney Henry H. Robertson were the other candidates.

The results of the election in Alleghany and Bath Counties were as follows[33]:

Candidate	Bath County	Alleghany County	Total
William H. Terrill	207	93	300
Thomas Sitlington	262	345	607
Henry H. Robertson	6	123	129

Why did the citizens of the two counties in which William had spent more than half of his life, in business and public service, choose someone else to represent them in the forthcoming convention? It seems that both Sitlington and Terrill opposed secession, while Robertson's inclination is not known.

The records of the election list William as a Union candidate. This seems odd, especially in light of future behavior. What happened between February and April to change his mind?

William's feelings concerning the outcome of the election are unknown. Judging from vague comments found among the family correspondence, William believed he would become the delegate without difficulty. He must have been very disappointed and disheartened by the results of the election.

William's son James voiced his displeasure of the election results to his brother-in-law, George A. Porterfield. On February 8, 1861, James wrote:

> I have been annoyed ... by the state of politics especially in this section of the state. Father received the nomination of the [conservative] convention to represent the united *Kingdoms of Bath & Alleghany* in the state convention, the defeated aspirant Col. Thos. Sitlington not only refused to abide by the decision of the nominating committee, but violated his solemn word given to Father, that if Father was nominated that he Col. S. would give him his support, it is only necessary to add that so flagrant a breach of honor on the part of Col. S. seconded by the dishonorable conduct of his friends in falsifying the position of Father as a candidate at a time when it would have been impossible to have canvassed the two counties the time before the election being too limited, has resulted in Fathers defeat.[34]

After the Virginia Legislature passed the Ordnance of Secession on April 17, 1861, it was necessary to bring it before the people of Virginia for ratification.

The people cast their votes on May 23, 1861, upholding the ordnance by a large majority.[35] William's name does not appear on the list of those voting that day.

When it became clear that war was inevitable, William received a severe blow — the first of several that beset him during the war. His son, William Rufus, who was then serving with the U.S. Coast Survey in Florida, informed his father that he intended to remain loyal to the Union.

When the decision to secede was passed in mid–April, a wave of excitement swept across Virginia. Colonel Terrill had his normal business matters to attend to, but out of excitement and patriotism devoted a portion of his time to encouraging the local volunteers. When the Bath Cavalry went to Staunton in April 1861, the 60-year-old attorney accompanied them as commissary officer. Upon reaching Staunton on the 22nd, the governor ordered the company to return home. Colonel Terrill immediately telegraphed John Letcher, asking the governor to assign him to "some position in which I may be useful. I am subject to your orders at a moments warning."[36] William returned to Warm Springs by stagecoach the following day, anxiously awaiting the governor's reply.

Several weeks later, before the Bath Cavalry again marched to Staunton on May 14, William delivered a stirring speech. Following their departure, William turned his attention to helping organize two additional companies of volunteers.[37]

The day after the Bath Cavalry left Bath Court House, William took the opportunity to answer his son's letters. The letter, while very formal, contained strong patriotic language, most likely caused by the previous day's excitement. He proceeded to denounce William R. Terrill, to the point of referring to him as Benedict Arnold.

William continued to do what he could to support the local troops. After the disaster at Philippi on June 3, in which his son-in-law Colonel George A. Porterfield was involved, he went to Richmond.

The depth of William's feelings toward the South must not have been general knowledge in the county. In the days following the retreat of the Virginia forces from Philippi, Charles B. Hopkins addressed a letter to President Jefferson Davis, calling for an investigation into Porterfield's actions. Hopkins wrote on June 10 from Healing Springs:

> As we all believe that his [Porterfield's] appointment was through the persuasion and influence of his Farther [sic] — in — law Wm. Terrill of this County, in whom the people generally has no kind of Confidence, he being too slow in taking sides with the South, and having expressed his opinion at different times too freely in opposition to the intrusts [sic] and actions of the South, and at this time has a son an acting officer in the Northern Army, the people being generally very suspicious of his motives.
>
> Mr. Terrill having returned home in this County, equipped in Uniform claiming to have an appointment from you it is the general opinion of those who know him that you could have made much better selections than to have appointed him to any office.[38]

Hopkins concluded his letter with the words, "I have been prompted by no unkind feelings not the slightest to either of these gentlemen in writing to you, but wholly for the good of my country."[39]

Although he claimed not to have unkind feelings in writing the letter, the words show otherwise. Undoubtedly, this letter had some impact upon William's later efforts to obtain an appointment in the government, as well as upon the career of Colonel Porterfield.

The reference to William receiving an appointment from Jefferson Davis or being in uniform seems to be only a rumor. As to his influence with the government and securing an appointment for his son-in-law, that too seems to be rumor. William is clearly in favor of the Southern cause. True, at some point in his life, he may have been solidly in favor of the Union, but that changed in early 1861. Perhaps the old man was embarrassed to have a son in the Union ranks and did not discuss the matter in public.

Colonel Terrill did not remain long in Richmond, but returned home and followed the expedition to the Northwest. From Beverly, William recommended Doctor William J. Bland for an appointment in the medical department on June 24. He noted in his letter to Governor Letcher, "I shall remain with the army till the fight takes place."[40] Duty and business, however, called him elsewhere.

On July 5, he was in Staunton, where he settled an account for supplies purchased by Captain Archibald T. Richards for the use of the Bath Cavalry. The account amounted to nearly a thousand dollars, which he personally paid. The county reimbursed him for the expense on January 14, 1862, with interest.[41]

In early 1862, William applied to Jefferson Davis for an appointment to the Treasury Department as an auditor or controller. His law practice had fallen off to nearly nothing. His friend, John Letcher, forwarded the application to Davis, along with a number of letters of recommendation from prominent citizens. Among them were Joseph Mayo, mayor of Richmond; William's cousin Jackson Morton; Judge John W. Brockenbrough; William Smith; James L. Kemper; and a number of members of the Virginia Legislature. Letcher referred to William H. Terrill as "a gentleman of

John Letcher, of Lexington, Virginia, lawyer, congressman and governor of Virginia, 1860–1864. William H. Terrill frequently visited Letcher in Richmond (courtesy Library of Congress).

uncommonly fine talents, and business qualifications, and the leading Lawyer in his part of the State."⁴² The governor added that William was seeking a position in the government, as his practice was suffering due to nothing happening in the interior courts, concluding with, "He is a most skillful accountant & an efficient, energetic and prompt businessman."⁴³

Many of the letters of recommendation used phrases such as "distinguished member of the Bar of Virginia," "high character," "honorable gentleman," "unimpeachable integrity," and "well known throughout the State for his high character and eminent ability."

William called upon President Davis several times during March 1862, but was unsuccessful in obtaining an audience with him. Instead, he appealed to Davis by a letter, writing:

> I have been a practicing lawyer for a number of years but the present condition of the country has pretty much closed the doors of our courts and I am consequently thrown out of employment and during these stirring times I am impatient to take some active part in the service of our common country and being physically unable to undergo the hardships of an active combatant in the field I am induced to seek a service of a different character where I think I may be useful.⁴⁴

Although disowned by his father, Union Captain William R. Terrill still loved and worried about the safety of his Southern family. On March 28, 1862, he wrote Secretary of War Edwin M. Stanton, informing him that his father was in Richmond and that his brothers and an uncle were in the service of the Confederacy. Captain Terrill requested that "any kindness that can be shown them should the fortunes of war bring them into our power, will be very thankfully received by me."⁴⁵

Although his law practice had declined, William managed to hold onto a few clients. During the war years, he served as the agent and attorney for the Warm Springs Mountain Turnpike Company, collecting tolls from the Confederate government.⁴⁶ He often wrote letters asking for the exemption of various individuals from the county.

In June 1862, William took an active part in military operations, when he joined the staff of Brigadier General Arnold Elzey. It is likely that William served Elzey in the capacity of a volunteer aide-de-camp. The only reference to this service appears in a memorial sketch written after William's death.⁴⁷

Unsuccessful in his attempts to obtain a government position during the early part of 1862, William renewed his efforts that fall. This time, he applied to Secretary of War George W. Randolph for a position as a judge, or judge advocate of one of the military courts. He forwarded letters of reference, some dating from his earlier attempt to receive an appointment. Governor Letcher again wrote President Davis on his friend's behalf, stating that William "is an excellent Lawyer, a man of fine intellect, and in all respects eminently qualified for such a position."⁴⁸

William may have been somewhat more successful in this attempt. By

April 1863, he was serving as provost martial of Bath County, with the rank of Captain. After the summer of 1863, it appears that William was relieved of that position. The reason for his replacement is unknown.

News of William R. Terrill's death at Perryville reached Colonel Terrill in mid–October 1862. Despite having disowning him, he grieved over the death of his son. While in Richmond the following month, a friend handed him a copy of the *Louisville Journal* containing an article concerning General Terrill. Several days later, Colonel Terrill addressed a letter to the editor of the *Richmond Enquirer*, correcting statements made in the Kentucky newspaper. He closed his letter with the sentence:

> It is a source of some consolation to me to know, that he never stood upon the soil of Virginia in an attitude of hostility to her people and their institutions.[49]

Sometime later, the Rev. William T. Price and a friend visited the Terrill home. The Presbyterian minister wrote of the visit:

> In company with a friend he [Price] passed a pleasant evening at the home where the Federal General William Terrill was born & reared, who was killed in the Battle of Perryville, Kentucky. The visit was attended with sad & yet interesting associations. The family spoke of him freely, yet no tear was wept over the untimely fate of him who was at one time the pride and joy of this household.[50]

The first of several raids by Northern troops into Bath County took place in late August 1863. Brigadier General William Woods Averell, a classmate of William R. Terrill's at West Point, led the raid. The people of the Warm Springs area suffered heavy losses because of this raid. The *Richmond Sentinel* reported on September 15:

> On their advance they destroyed a great deal of property in Bath county, along the line of the Warm Springs and Huntersville turnpike. A scene of desiccation and ruin marked their track wherever they stopped. A number of negroes went off with them from the Warm Springs. Amongst the sufferers at Warm Springs from their thieving and destructive propensities were Geo. Mays [sic], Esq., proprietor of the hotel, Wm. H. Terrell [sic], Esq., and others. They took horses, corn, wheat, &c., literally stripping the country as they went of every thing that could sustain life or promote locomotion.[51]

The citizens of Bath County again elected William to the position of prosecuting attorney at the local elections on May 26, 1864. At the next court, held on July 23, 1864, he took the various oaths prescribed by law: the Oath of Fidelity to the Commonwealth of Virginia, the Oath to Support the Constitution of the Confederate States, the oath against dueling, and the oath of office.

During the early part of 1864, William spent a great deal of time in Richmond. After James' death at the battle of Bethesda Church on May 30, William wrote his friend John Letcher:

> My gallant Boy met his destiny most gloriously and in a glorious cause. I hovered around him for four weeks, following him up day after day until he fell. He

fell a matyr [martyr] to the cause in which he embarked as you know, as one of its earliest devotees. He fell mortally wounded at the head of the invincible *Thirteenth* but rose again as commander of his Brigade and whilst leading it upon the enemy's breastworks under a murderous fire of canister and grape shot, was shot through the head and died *instantly*. I succeeded in recovering his body after the lapse of seven days and had it interred.[52]

The war was hard on William, being unable to make a living as an attorney. He told the former governor:

> I have suffered much in various ways since the commencement of this cruel and bloody war, but this [is] the hardest blow I have ever received and in addition to that I am now a refugee from my home without being able to hear a single word as to the condition of my family or as to the extent of the injury done to my property by the infernal vandals.[53]

Union forces marching through Bath County in the spring of 1864, forced William to become a refugee.

Undoubtedly, William suffered from depression, brought on by James' death. Doctor George P. Terrill, writing his younger brother Philip, said that in the fall of 1864, William was at home and in very low spirits. By the 4th of November, it seems that William had rallied, and was in Richmond. George mentioned that their father "was looking remarkably well and was engaged in making some money out of parties desiring his advice & services in reference to exemption from service."[54]

Just when it appeared that William was coming out of his depression and grief, tragedy again struck the household. The youngest of the Terrill children, Philip Mallory, fell mortally wounded in a battle near Winchester on November 12, and died the following day. The wounds, some reports say, were the result of "reckless bravery."[55]

News of Philip's injury reached William, but word of his death did not. While in Staunton, on November 24, William wrote to Major General Thomas L. Rosser, commander of the brigade to which Philip belonged:

> I had a son, Philip M. Terrill, a private in the 12th Regiment of Virginia Cavalry, in your command who I understand was very badly wounded in an engagement with the public enemy on the 12 inst. but I have not heard from him since. I beg of you the favour to inform me at your earliest convenience what has become of my brave boy.[56]

Family lore records that William had Philip's body brought to Woodstock, in Shenandoah County, and buried there. The exact location of Philip's resting place is unknown.

A story has persisted through the years that when Colonel Terrill learned of Philip's injury, he rode all night on horseback to reach his side. Arriving at the house where his son lay about the first light of dawn, he learned that Philip had just died.

This story is only family lore and tradition. The letter to General Rosser puts the story to rest. William did not learn that Philip had died until sometime later, and in January 1865 asked his daughter to send him the particulars of his death. Besides, the distance from Warm Springs to Winchester (more than 150 miles), in addition to William's age and size, makes such a ride impossible, even for a younger man.

By the middle of January 1865, William's once peaceful home became a place of excitement. He wrote Emily about the change:

> My house is now full of soldiers of Rosser's command returning from a very successful raid in the North Western part of this State and in the course of conversation I ascertained that several of them are from Frederick County.[57]

For the first known time since the death of William R. Terrill, his father expresses grief over his death. He asks Emily if she has a copy of the sermon delivered at William's burial, and if so, he would like to have a copy of it. He stated that he had one, but it was lost soon after it arrived. The old fellow continued, speaking of his beloved son:

> He [William Rufus] was such a noble, high minded honorable gentleman. Oh how bitterly he regretted the state of things which separated him from us. Nothing but his unbending sense of duty constrained him. It was an error of the head and not the heart that mislead him. How can we have the heart to judge him harshly? We who knew him well and loved him best. Oh that I could visit his grave.... Do you ever hear from his widow? If so, where is she?[58]

He informed Emily that he had written brief memoirs of "my three sons who were slain in battle."[59] He told her that he had sent the memoirs to Salem so that George might preserve them for the family, and that he would ask him to send her copies. He also promised to have a set of the memoirs sent to James's widow. Of the three memoirs, only those of James and Philip survived. He added, "I don't intend it shall be published because the cold and uncharitable world would take but little interest in it."[60]

In addition to the war costing him three sons, raids by the Yankees during the last three years cost him at least thirty thousand dollars. He informed Emily:

> I am now in a very destitute condition. I have ... about two hundred pounds of pork, the same quantity of beef, half a barrel of flour and no grain and am puzzled to know where I am to get supplies. Confederate money don't buy anything.[61]

Among his losses during the war were "a number of my valuable papers as well as many belonging to my clients ... as well as my most valuable account books, none of which have I been able to recover."[62] This loss had a serious effect on William's practice, leaving many accounts uncollected.

William also brought up the issue of slavery in his letter:

> My exertions to keep Archy from going to the enemy were unsuccessful. I hired him to the quarter masters Department at Staunton and when the enemy came in

"My Name Is Terrill." Drawing by an unknown artist of Colonel William H. Terrill, found among the papers of former governor John Letcher (Virginia Historical Society, Richmond).

there last fall, he went off with them. I have now but one negro left except those of the old stock. What little property I may have left I intend to divide between yourself and James' little children, but I doubt very much whether our negroes will be worth having in a year or two and I, entertaining that opinion would sell all of mine now, but for the fact that Confederate money, which is our only currency is so greatly depreciated as to be almost [worthless].[63]

William and Rachel had a houseguest for the last few days of January 1865. Private Benjamin M. Haines, a member of the Confederate Signal Corps, stayed with the Terrills from January 27 to 31. He wrote:

I boarded with Mr. Wm. H. Terrill, who was the father of Lt. Col. Terrill, of the 13th Virginia Infantry, so when my day's work was done I would go down to his house and he would read the letters he got from his son, so by that I would get to hear from the old 13th every day while [I] stayed with him, he was a good questioner, but I did not tell the old man I used to tramp around under his son. I thought I would just keep that part of it to myself.[64]

Reconstruction and a New Set of Problems

At the close of the war in April 1865, the United States military occupied the entire South and enforced martial law. In little more than three months, on July 27, 1865, with civil government reinstated, William resumed his duties as prosecuting attorney. After a lapse of four years, William was somewhat concerned of his ability to try a case when he made his first court appearance in March 1866. When it was over, he noted with pride that he still knew the business.[65]

Nearly a year after the close of the war, William again commented on the family members that were absent from their midst. He wrote to Emily in January 1866:

Your old Fathers love for you so far from diminishing, increases as the tottering steps of age carries him daily, nearer and nearer to his grave. I *cannot* and *would not, if I could* forget, those loved ones of ours who are now in the cold embraces of the grave. Your sainted Mother, your sister and your brothers, who have been taken from us are scarcely ever absent from my mind ... I frequently meet with soldiers of the late Confederate army who served in the same commands to which James & Philip were attached and they invariably have something to tell me about them. One gentleman remarked to me not long since, that James' "Clarion voice heard above the din of battle always, indicated the spot where the contest was most desperate and the carnage greatest" and that he was universally regarded as one of the best and bravest officers in the army; poor fellow, like your husband, he had great injustice done him by the Government. He ought to have been a Major General long before he fell in battle. Philip, too, was regarded as one of the most gallant soldiers and accomplished gentlemen in his branch of service. What a comfort would both these boys now be to me, had they survived that *cruel* and *unnecessary* war. It has robbed me of the best of boys and almost beggared me in my old age, but it is [useless] to complain.[66]

Two months later, William described his living conditions in a letter to Jeremiah Morton:

> I am strugling [sic] very hard to make "buckle & tongue" meet. The war left me as flat as a flounder. I lost by it upwards of thirty negroes and not less than twenty five thousand dollars, in debts due to me.... Thank God, my health never was better than it has been for the last four or five months. I have as much energy as I ever had, but ... my underpining [sic] is giving way. I have not my former facility of locomotion. I am bracing myself up for a vigorous prosecution of my practice of my profession. I have put on the harness once more and the people hereabouts say, that "Richard is himself again." My practice will hereafter be confined to three counties, Bath, Alleghany & Highland. I have been *disbared* [sic] in Greenbrier & Pocahontas now in West Va., by the teste [sic] oath required of lawyers, before they are permitted to practice in those counties. Pocahontas was the most profitable county to me in the whole range of my practice but I now have to give it up for the reasons before stated. I am living in a very economical way, having but three in [my] family, my wife, myself & a white woman whom I hire as a cook and house servant generally. I have had no colored servant since last fall. I occasionally hire a man at fifty cents a day to chop fire wood. I have to feed my cows & horses myself, a very unpleasant business in cold weather. I sometimes have to shell corn to send to mill but that seldom happens as a bushel & a half of meal lasts about two months. Our cooking is done in my wife's chamber; we have kept but one fire going during the past winter. We have but two meals a day, breakfast at 9 & dinner at 4 o'clock. I have been fortunate in laying in an abundant supply of provisions, meat enough to last us two years, at the least, supply of groceries rather short but easily replenished when necessary. I used to lay in sugar & coffee by the barrel & bag but now, they being *cash* articles and cash very scarce, I purchase them by pounds not exceeding eight or ten pounds of either at any one time. We have an abundance of milk & butter. We have sold during the winter & late in the fall about a hundred & fifty pounds of butter from two cows. I have not had a hundred & fifty dollars in money since the fall of Richmond. We have very little money in circulation here.[67]

William Henry Terrill, 1868 (courtesy Evelyn Lee Moore).

In 1866, the United States Congress proposed the Fourteenth Amendment to the Constitution, severely limiting the activities of the former Confederates. Twenty-eight states had to ratify the amendment in order to make it a part of the laws of the United

States. By July 9, 1868, the amendment became law. The third section of the Fourteenth Amendment states:

> No person shall be a Senator or Representative in Congress, or elector of President or Vice President, or hold any office, civil or military, under the United States, or under any State, who, having previously taken an oath, as a member of Congress, or as an officer of the United States, or as a member of any State legislature, or as an executive or judicial officer of any State, to support the Constitution of the United States, shall have engaged in insurrection or rebellion against the same, or given aid or comfort to the enemies thereof. But Congress may by a vote of two-thirds of each House, remove such disability.[68]

Because of William's service as prosecuting attorney (judicial officer) and provost marshal in Bath County during the war, the Fourteenth Amendment barred him from practicing law. At the fall term of the Bath County Circuit Court, held on October 28, 1868, William's thirty-year career as prosecuting attorney ended.

In the spring of 1868, William wrote Emily about his health: "I am able with some difficulty to get about on Horse back. You will be surprised to learn that I have the gout in both feet, an affliction with which I never expected to be visited."[69] Evelyn Lee Moore, granddaughter of Mary Jane Pitzer Wise, wrote of her "Uncle Billy": "Disabled by age and pain, he walked the mile to his office every day, accompanied by a servant carrying a chair that was put down at intervals so he could rest."[70]

Late in 1868 or early 1869, William visited the United States Congress, asking for their assistance in being relieved from the dis-

Carte De Vista (CDV) of William H. Terrill, taken in Washington, D.C., in 1871 (author's collection).

abilities imposed by section three of the Fourteenth Amendment. His plea was successful, and by act of Congress on February 6, 1869, he was relieved of the disability imposed by the amendment.[71]

With the test oath suspended in West Virginia, and the exemption from the effects of the Fourteenth Amendment, William could resume the practice of law. In 1870, William was once again serving as prosecuting attorney for Bath County, having been appointed by the court to fill the remainder of John R. Popham's term. He remained in that office until the spring of 1874, when his partner, William M. McAllister, assumed the duties of prosecutor. In all, William served thirty-four years as prosecuting attorney for Bath County.

The combination of age and poor health began to take its toll on William. William and his wife Rachel parted company sometime after December 1875. Rachel went to live with her daughter Annie Smith Scott Wills, in Hinton, W. Va., while William moved to Charles Town, W. Va., to live with his daughter and son-in-law.

This photograph of William Henry Terrill, late in life, was donated to the Bath County Circuit Court by granddaughter Mary Porterfield Morton, of Richmond. Terrill served Bath County as prosecuting attorney for more than 30 years (courtesy Bath County Circuit Court).

By the summer of 1876, William's condition had deteriorated to the point that he could not work, ending a fifty-six year career. He could write only with great difficulty, due to the stiffness of his fingers, and required assistance in dressing or undressing. William noted in a letter to Jeremiah Morton that he had not been able to attend court for the past eighteen months.

When Rachel died of heart disease at Hinton, W. Va., on February 1, 1877, William was unable to attend her funeral because of failing health. Rachel's family buried her in the Cedar Hill Cemetery, at Covington, Virginia.[72]

William died at Charles Town, W. Va., on November 28, 1877. According to family lore, the family placed his body in a metal lined coffin, and returned to Warm Springs for the burial. They laid him to rest at the side of beloved wife Elizabeth in the Warm Springs Cemetery. Several years after his death, friends and relatives erected a four-sided monument over the graves of William and Elizabeth. It bears the following inscription:

Side 1— Elizabeth Pitzer, wife of William H. Terrill, born May 24, 1805 — died at Rose Hill, Warm Springs, Virginia, April 20, 1858, aged 53 years.

Side 2 — Yea tho I walk through the Valley of the Shadow of death I will fear no evil, for thou art with me.

Side 3 — William H. Terrill, born in Orange Co., Virginia July 16, 1800. Died in Charlestown, West Va., November 28, 1877, aged 77 years.

Side 4 — Able jurist, wise counselor, faithful public servant and loyal citizen, loving and beloved friend. For 36 consecutive years Commonwealth Attorney for the County of Bath. He died as he lived, without spot or blemish.

The marker, erected with love and respect, contains several errors. Elizabeth was only 52 years of age when she died, and William served only 34 years as prosecuting attorney for Bath County, but not consecutively.

George H. Moffett, a native of nearby Pocahontas County, wrote a most complimentary tribute to William.

With the death of Col. William H. Terrill, who recently died at the home of his son-in-law, Col. Geo. A. Porterfield, in Jefferson county, in this State, has passed away one of the most remarkable men Virginia ever produced. He was the intellectual peer of any son of the Old Dominion and possessed highest literary accomplishments, yet was without a particle of ambition. In early life he served one term in the Legislature of his State, which was the only public office he ever filled except that of prosecuting attorney for the county of Bath, a position he held for thirty-seven consecutive years. Notwithstanding his self exclusion from public life, there was no man more widely or more favorably known in the State of Virginia than Col. Terrill. At the bar and at the hustings[73] he stood pre-eminent, and as many gifted speakers as Virginia possessed in those days, there were but few cared to meet him in debate. He is said to be the only man who ever got the better of Extra Billy Smith in a political discussion.

Extra Billy was the dread of all the stump orators in his day, but on a certain occasion the friends of Col. Terrill prevailed on him to meet the distinguished stumper. Smith led off, Terrill followed, and so successful was he in destroying the argument of his antagonist that when "Extra" came to reply he broke down and threw up the sponge.

I have said that Col. Terrill was without ambition, yet if he took a pride in anything it was in the discharge of his duties as commonwealth's attorney. He was a native of Madison [Orange] county, Virginia, but soon after he was admitted to the bar removed to the Warm Springs in Bath county, where he continued to reside until a few months previous to his death. For thirty-seven consecutive years he was prosecuting attorney of Bath county, and was acknowledged the most able prosecutor in the State. He never permitted his personal relations to interfere with his duties. On the contrary it is said that his ability as a prosecutor was more fully displayed in a case where a young man, the son of an old friend, was indicted, than in any other. It had been said that Mr. Terrill would not make a vigorous prosecution against the young man, because of the intimate relations existing between himself and the father. This came to his ears, and being exceedingly sensitive about such matters, the whole force of his intellect was aroused, and the result was that the prosecution was conducted with more power and ability than any previously known in the courts of the State.

Gravestone of William H. Terrill and Elizabeth Pitzer Terrill, Warm Springs Cemetery, Warm Springs, Virginia. The family raised money for the monument by selling subscriptions (author's photograph).

It was once the fashion in Virginia for the prosecuting attorney to deliver the charge to the grand jury instead of it being done by the Judge as is now the case. The famous Mr. Pettigrew, of South Carolina, who was exceedingly fastidious in his manner and dress, was visiting the Warm Springs during the summer season, and was shocked to see Colonel Terrill charging the grand jury with a pipe in his mouth.

He possessed a

Commanding Personal Appearance.

He was six feet two inches tall, weighed about 280 pounds and very straight. He was extremely urbane and dignified in his manner, but his dignity could relax as gently and with as much facility as ice thaws beneath the warm rays of the sun, when he came in contact with a set of jolly good fellows. Visitors at the Warm Springs for the last few years will remember the peculiar staff with which he always walked. It was as tall as himself, with a handsome silver knob on top of it. When asked why he used such a peculiar walking stick, he would reply that it was all that was left him from the wreck of war. He had been possessed of a large fortune, which, together with most of his family, had been swept away in the conflict. He was possessed of a rare fund of anecdotes which he could relate in the most inimitable style, and wherever there was jolly sociability his presence was always sought. He was always ready with a joke, and could give a humorous coloring to the gravest subject. He was in Washington City immediately after the war. A number of prominent Republicans who had known and loved him in *ante bellum* days, were prompt to call on him, and were profuse in expressions of sympathy for his misfortunes during the war, and all of them offered their services to aid in an effort to remove his political disabilities. The Colonel dropped his lower lip in a way which those who have ever seen him will be sure to remember, and with a chuckling laugh peculiar to himself, replied that he didn't care anything about the removal of his *disabilities*, but he would feel obliged to them if they could suggest some plan by which his *liabilities* might be removed.

A War Episode.

I remember one little incident illustrating the convivial disposition of the great lawyer, and how he could unbend from the dignity which sat so naturally upon him, and play the boy again, although at the time he was approaching his three score and ten. It was in June, 1862, when he was serving temporarily on the staff of Gen. Elzey—Jackson's corps was making its famous march from the Valley of Virginia on its way to strike McClellan's rear in front of Richmond, a movement which took "Little Mac" wholly by surprise. The division stopped to rest for the night near "Anderson's Turnout," just above Hanover Junction, and the staff rode off to hunt around in the neighborhood for quarters at a farm house. Col. Terrill reined up at the mansion of an old gentleman of vast estate but who lived alone, except the large number of negroes who inhabited his plantation. The wife was dead and the old gentleman had no children to brighten his home and inherit his fortune. But he was a gentleman of the olden school and gave a royal welcome to the venerable and dignified looking officer who had called to crave his hospitality for the night. A magnificent supper, too tempting for a soldier, was spread, and cooked in a style as only the old Virginia negroes could cook it. After supper the cloth was removed and "Lone Jack" tobacco and real Powhatan pipes set out. The cellar, too, was invaded and bottles of Madeira brought out, and the cobwebs being brushed off, were opened and the sparkling contents pledged to the health of host and guest. As their blood grew with the wine, their hearts grew young, and to the minds of each with joyous freshness came the gay scenes and happy pastimes of youth. Tom, the old plantation fiddler, was called in. After being furnished with a couple of glasses of the cob-webbed Madeira, the frosty-headed darkey announced that he too felt forty years younger, and was willing '"to declare afore God dat he believed dat was the same wine dat the ole boss of all, Mars William's father, had put in dat dar cellar when he was a chile,"' and wiping his mouth with the back of his hand, began to tune up his violin, which, too, seemed to grow younger under the molifying [sic] influence of the occasion. In a few moments Tom had succeeded in satisfactorily establishing the telephone between the bow and his foot, and by the time he had fairly launched into that ocean of music, which flows from a violin "Money-Musk," the two old gentlemen were on the floor, and the dance went on. Here was a picture that Hogarin could not paint, and a dance that the author of "Tam O'Shanter" could not describe. On one side of the grand old hall built in real English style, was the massive Colonel, with body erect, head slightly thrown back and with all the elasticity of youth, giving to perfection the double shuffle, while on the other side of the room as his *vis a vis* was the venerable host rivaling in ability the soltaire [sic] figure danced by his guest. Then they "cross over" and each changing position in the room and again facing, simultaneously they cut the "pigeon wing." So the night was spent, and as the Colonel rode away in the morning in company with his younger comrades, and turned at the top of the hill to take a parting look at the hospitable mansion, the proprietor with his white locks gleaming in the morning sun, was seen standing at the gateway and waving his hand, while at that distance could be distinctly heard the oft repeated "farewell, gentlemen, farewell."

A Peace Episode.

I recollect another little incident illustrating the opposite side of his nature. It was a scene full of pathos and manly dignity. At the time he located in Bath county, he commenced the practice of his profession in Pocahontas, the adjoining county, and continued his practice in the courts of that county until he was excluded by the "attorney's test oath," in 1865. He was always a favorite with the people of Pocahontas county, and as he commanded their confidence, he also commanded a most lucrative practice in their courts, and the people felt the harshness of the proscriptive policy of West Virginia as severely in being deprived of the legal services of Col. Terrill as perhaps in any other particular. In 1869 the test oath was repealed, and at the April term of the Circuit Court the proscribed lawyers were admitted to the bar. Judge McWhorter, wo had succeeded the notorious Nat. Harrison, was on the bench. As soon as the Judge had disposed of the grand jury, the imposing form of Col. Terrill was seen to rise from the bar. In a voice tremulous with emotion, he announced that, as the records of the court would show, just forty years ago from that day he had was admitted to the bar of Pocahontas county; that for forty years he had gone in and out among the people, blameless; that he had seen a new generation grow up around him, yet he felt that he possessed their confidence as fully as he had done that of their fathers, he pointed with pride to a professional life of forty years as the best vindicator of the purity of his life and conduct; and yet for the sole crime of being true to his section and true to the honest convictions of his heart, he had been proscribed and denied the right to earn a living by the practice of his profession, and he felt deeply the humiliation of being compelled to ask for readmittance to a bar of which he felt that he was the father. The scene, the eloquence of the old man, the dignity and pathos with which he made his own motion for admittance to the bar, impressed all as a most scathing rebuke to that policy of proscription adopted by West Virginia Republicans at the close of the war.

"He Sleeps Well."

The war was a heavy blow to Colonel Terrill. Its close left him wrecked in fortune and robbed of his children. He lost three sons in the struggle. The oldest, Gen. Wm. R. Terrill, espoused the Federal cause. He had been educated at West Point and was serving in the regular army at the breaking out of hostilities. His sympathies were with the South, but his conviction of duty led him to prefer the old service. He wrote to his father for advice; that advice was "to follow his convictions." William commanded the old Sherman [crossed out and Bragg written in the margin] battery at the battle of Shiloh, and saved Grant's army from destruction. For his gallantry in that battle he was promoted to the rank of Major [crossed out and Brigadier written in the margin] General, and fell soon after at the head of his division at the battle of Perryville. The second son, Gen. James Barbour Terrill, fell while leading his Confederate brigade in a charge at Cold Harbor. His youngest son, Philip Mallory Terrill, who was a soldier in Rosser's Confederate Cavalry was killed in one of the battles in the Shenandoah Valley in 1864. The loss of his three gallant boys broke the spirit of the father, and it was easy to perceive that his heart was buried in the graves of his children. His vigorous constitution yielded to the accumulated troubles which weighed so heavily upon him, and at last retiring from his profession, he sought rest in the family of his only daughter, who affectionately nursed him in his dying hours, and thus peacefully he passed away in the 77th year of his age.

Those unacquainted with Col. Terrill, may think that to his virtues I have been very kind and to his follies a little blind; but I remember him as the cultivated and scholarly gentleman, whose mind was stored with historical and classical lore, and with whom I never conversed but I learned something, I remember him as the brilliant lawyer who could fascinate juries and convince judges and who say the force of his eloquence and the logic of his arguments could bear down all opposition. I remember him as the generous, warm-hearted gentleman who took me by the hand when I first came to the bar, a green strapling, and gave me words of encouragement and taught me self-confidence.

Two years ago he contemplated a visit to a brother in Rhode Island, but was dissuaded from undertaking the journey by being told that he would die there and his body be laid to rest among the bleak hills of New England. "I will not go then," he replied, "for wherever my lot may be cast in life, I want to rest in death on the bosom of my native Virginia."[74]

As Colonel Terrill died without a will, the court ordered his personal property inventoried and appraised prior to a settlement. After the inventory, it was disposed of at auction. Among the items purchased at the estate sale by son-in-law George A. Porterfield was a horsehair sofa. The sofa, appraised at $10, sold for $11. The sofa, bearing scorch marks from the tragic fire at Rose Hill, is today on display in the museum of the Bath County Historical Society.

CHAPTER II

George Parker Terrill

George Parker Terrill
1830–1884

While William H. Terrill served his state in the Virginia Legislature, Elizabeth gave birth to their second child, a son, on February 23, 1830. They named him George Parker Terrill, partly after William's brother George, a U.S. Navy surgeon.[1] A baptismal record in the Warm Springs Presbyterian Church, recorded before 1850, listed George's middle name as Pitzer.[2] This is the only reference for the use of this name.

George began his studies at the Virginia Military Institute as a Pay Cadet[3] in September 1845, taking up residence in Room Number 12. His roommates were Cadets Briscoe G. Baldwin, James W. Baldwin and Christopher V. Winfree.

His uncle and namesake, in a letter to William H. Terrill, wrote:

> Your son, George, will I hope acquit himself at the military academy in a manner that will enhance the paternal pride which, even now, you take in him. I will write to him, and set before him the importance of [aptitude] in his studies and circumspection in his conduct if he is ambitious of distinction in life. I doubt however that George requires any stimulation of the kind. He seems to be a youth possessed of qualities calculated to ensure success.[4]

Evidently, George was quite a scholar. Officials at the institute examined him, and admitted him directly into the 3rd Class on September 8, 1845. Toward the end of October, his father wrote: "You do not know how much I am gratified at George's standing at the Institute. He seems much better satisfied then he was at first and is making rapid progress in his studies."[5]

George, however, encountered some difficulty at the January 1846 examinations. The superintendent issued an order on January 10, 1846, returning him to the 4th Class, because of the deficiencies in his studies.[6] It is likely an illness in November 1845 led to his downfall.

This setback seemed to agree with George, as his marks immediately improved. By the end of his first year at the institute, he ranked second in his class, and held the position of Cadet Corporal.

By the close of his second year at VMI, George's standing had slipped to 10th. Despite his decline in standings, he received a promotion to the rank of Third Sergeant in July 1847. A few days later George returned home on a leave of absence, set to expire on August 1. The institute granted him an extension in July, allowing him to report back at school on August 5.

At the beginning of his 2nd Class year at VMI, George shared Room Number 14 with Cadets Edward T. Fristoe, Richard Pollard and George E. Roberts. This session seemed to be a difficult one for George, as his standing fell to 20th in July 1848.

Portrait of Dr. George Parker Terrill (courtesy Anne Terrill Thomas).

Despite his declining standing, he held the position of 2nd First Lieutenant and was assigned to Company B, Corps of Cadets.[7]

In December 1847, George and two fellow cadets (Richard Pollard and Benjamin Ficklin) wrote President James K. Polk, seeking appointments in the army. The young men wrote:

> Having a great desire to serve our country in this, her time of need, do hereby tender our services to act in the capacity of commissioned officers, should it please your Honour [sic] to accept of them as such.
>
> Having served three years at the Military Institute, both as *Privates* and *Officers*, we flatter ourselves that we are fully qualified to fill the stations of Captains or Lieutenants, in any one of the ten Regiments to which it might please your Honour [sic] to assign us.
>
> We are thoroughly acquainted with Battalion, Company, Light Infantry & Artillery drills. We deem it useless to trouble you with a list of recommendations, but should they be requisite, we can furnish them, from the Superintendant of our Institution, (Col. F. H. Smith) and other officers of repute. We should have tendered our services when the last call was made upon Virginia, for volunteers, but we were at that time under age, and prosecuting our studies, which we did not feel at liberty to interrupt without the consent of our Parents. Our course of studies will terminate in a few days, and we will then be at liberty to act for ourselves.[8]

The young patriots' efforts went unfulfilled, and they remained at the institute.

Early in 1848, it became apparent that George was developing another problem, causing his standing to drop once more. Colonel F. H. Smith, the superintendent, reported to George's father: "I gave it [a letter dated April 7] to George to read, and asked him for a reply to it. He says what my own observations had perceived, that he commenced the course this year without paying due attention, and he has thus suffered from this cause all the session."[9]

On June 10, Colonel Smith wrote William H. Terrill about George's poor performance: "George has not been industrious this year. I am apprehensive an *affliction of the heart*, produced by a shaft from some one of our Lexington belles has disabled him. As soon as I heard of your appt. I did not fail to admonish [him] of the mortification which you would feel, should he pass an indifferent examination."[10] Despite George's difficulties, he passed and was promoted.

George's problems at the institute continued throughout his final year. In late January 1849, William having received a report of George's standing, wrote Colonel Smith:

> I have not language to express the *deep, deep* mortification of feeling occasioned by the strange conduct of my son. I have said and done every thing in my power to encourage and stimulate him to industry and application to his studies since he has been at the Institute. I have written to him line upon line & given him precept upon precept, but he has abused all the advantages of his situation and my solicitude for his advancement in his studies has been met by disobedience and ingratitude on his part, as he makes his bed so will he have to lie. At the close of his course at the Institute he will have to sink or swim by his own unaided efforts.[11]

After the Board of Visitors examined George in the summer of 1849, he graduated on July 4 from the Virginia Military Institute. He finished 21st in a class of 24 graduates.

By late 1851, George was attending medical school at the University of Pennsylvania in Philadelphia, graduating in 1853. Returning to Virginia, he wasted no time in starting a family — he married Sarah Brent Dold in Lexington, Virginia, on April 28, 1853. Sarah Brent Dold was born in Lexington on October 16, 1831, the daughter of Samuel Miller Dold and Elizabeth McFadden. Her father and one of her brothers were merchants, while another brother was a physician.

George and Sarah established their home in the little town of Salem,

General Francis H. Smith, 1862, superintendent of the Virginia Military Institute, Lexington, Virginia. (courtesy Virginia Military Institute Archives).

in Roanoke County, Virginia. George would provide medical services to the Salem community for the remainder of his life.

The first of George and Sarah's seven children, Francis "Frank" Heath Terrill,[12] was born in Salem on February 27, 1854. Their second child, Elizabeth Dold Terrill,[13] was born at Salem on September 6, 1855. William H. Terrill,[14] their third child, was born in Salem on June 21, 1857.

In 1859, George received an early birthday present. One day before his 29th birthday, Sarah gave birth to their fourth child — George Morton Terrill.[15]

A few months later, in May, George entered the local political arena, when he served the Salem Town Council as secretary. He served as secretary for two years. Later on, in May 1864, George again took up the pen and served another two-year term as secretary of the town of Salem.[16]

Like a great number of Southerners, the Terrills were slave owners. According to the 1860 Census of the United States, George and Sarah owned nine slaves. The census also revealed that George's real estate holdings amounted to $3,350, and his personal property was valued at $2,850. A few months after the taking of the census, Sarah gave birth to their fifth child, Maria Louisa Terrill,[17] on September 28, 1860.

When the clouds of war darkened the country in 1861, the Terrill family felt its effects more than most families. George's brother, William Rufus Terrill, had been in the United States Army since 1853, and despite the urging of his family, declared he would remain loyal to the Union. As a result, most of the family severed their ties with him, and the elder Terrill told his son that he could never come home again. What George's personal feelings were on this matter is unknown. Two of George's brothers—James and Philip—joined the Southern army, as did his sister's (Emily) husband, George Porterfield. By the beginning of the war, George was serving as Colonel of the 157th Regiment of Virginia Militia, and served in this capacity until 1862. George's health was not the best and prevented him from taking a more active part in the war.[18]

A few days after the battle of Rich Mountain in July 1861, Confederate President Jefferson Davis requested Governor Letcher to call out additional militia units. The governor issued a proclamation on July 13, activating the militia units north of the James River, and east of the Blue Ridge Mountains. The Roanoke Militia was not included in the call; however, the following letter and circular arrived on July 18:

> Head Quarters Va. Forces
> Staunton, July 16th, 1861

[To] The Sheriff or Clerk of Roanoke

You will find [enclosed] a summons for the militia of your county. Use your promptest efforts to have the Colonels and Commandants notified — Haste is necessary.

> M. G. Harman,
> Major, Commanding[19]

> Head Quarters Va. Forces
> Staunton, July 16th 1861
>
> To the militia of Roanoke, Craig, Rockbridge, Alleghany, Bath, Augusta, and Botetourt, — Governor Letcher, in a dispatch sent me this day, orders that I shall notify you to rendezvous at Staunton forthwith, and to direct you to bring with you any arms you may have, Rifles, Carbines, or any other efficient gun. Also to order all volunteer companies in said bounds to come. We have met with disaster in General Garnett's command. Every man is expected to rush to the rescue, or our Country's cause is lost. Come one, Come all.[20]

George acted at once upon the letter and circular, dispatching orders for the companies of his regiment to assemble at Salem on July 20. The officers and men of the 157th Virginia Militia, in obedience of this order, assembled at Salem on that date. Colonel Terrill read the letter and circular to them, citing them as his authority for calling them to duty. He then directed that all men fit for service should meet at Salem on July 23, with their arms and equipment, ready to go to Staunton. George then dismissed the regiment.

Later in the day, George received another proclamation. His regiment, he noted, was not among those called to duty. Feeling that something was not quite right, Colonel Terrill sent the following telegram to Governor Letcher on the night of the 20th:

> Salem, Va.
>
> I am in possession of a call for the militia of this county to rendevouz [sic] at Staunton forthwith, signed M. G. Harman. Is there any mistake in the call. My command is now making every preparation to take up the line of march Tuesday the twenty-third (23). Shall we go forward without reference to your proclamation of the 19th nineteenth just to hand. Please answer immedy [sic].
>
> George P. Terrill
> Comdg. 157th Regt.
> Va. M.[21]

The governor's response arrived on the evening of the following day: "Your Militia is not ordered out."[22] All the arrangements made by George to have his baggage and provisions sent to Staunton now had to be cancelled, with some expense to the regiment. A number of the officers of the regiment and some private citizens complained to Governor Letcher about Major Harman's error, stating, "Many persons and families have been subjected to great trouble, inconvenience, and expense."[23]

The 157th Virginia Militia finally answered the call to service on March 13, 1862, joining Brigadier General Henry Heth's command at Camp Buckner, near Lewisburg, Virginia. George and his militiamen remained in service until April 24, when they returned to their homes. George, as acting colonel, certified the muster rolls of the men who served at Lewisburg.[24]

In addition to serving as colonel of the local militia unit, family tradition claims that George served as a recruiting officer for the Confederate Army. In

May 1863, he submitted paperwork to the War Department, asking for the discharge of a soldier from military duty. While this is not exactly recruiting duty, it does prove George's involvement in local military affairs.[25]

In March 1862, amid the difficulties brought on by the war, the sixth child of George and Sarah was born. Anna Carter Johnston Terrill[26] was born in Salem on March 22.

In addition to his duties as colonel of the 157th Virginia Militia and to the town of Salem, George provided medical services to the Confederacy. Several large battles occurred near Richmond in the summer of 1862, resulting in a large number of wounded soldiers. At least sixty-five of the wounded soldiers recuperated at Salem. While there, George tended their wounds between July 4 and October 8. For this service, the Confederate States Government paid him $253.33.

In February 1863, the government called upon George to care for a number of smallpox patients at the hospital in Salem. For his services between February 4 and March 18, the Confederacy paid George $215.00. He continued to supply medical services to the Confederates during June and July of 1863.

In the spring of 1863, the citizens of the second district of Roanoke County elected George to the office of justice of the peace, adding to his civil and military duties. The former justice had died, and the people elected George to fill out his term in office.[27]

The late summer and fall of 1863 was an especially busy time for George, who now commanded the Roanoke County home guard. Union General William W. Averell, along with other commands, conducted a series of raids into western and southwestern Virginia that fall. One such raid, in December 1863, targeted the Virginia and Tennessee Railroad at Salem.

By this time, Salem had become a vital post on the Virginia and Tennessee Railroad. It served as a supply base for the Department of Western Virginia, and as a collection point for supplies to be shipped to troops in Tennessee. Until December 1863, Confederate authorities considered Salem too remote to attract the attention of the Union troops.[28]

The first of Averell's raids came in late August 1863. A telegram dated August 23 reported the enemy near Warm Springs, 3,000 strong. In addition, about 1,200 Union Cavalry threatened the New River Bridge. The home guard units assembled and prepared to move at a moment's notice.[29]

George's home guard command, a hundred strong, was apparently unarmed. Giles B. Cooke, the Assistant Adjutant and Inspector General of the Department of Western Virginia, sent George fifty guns and ammunition for his command. Cooke advised in his August 24 message that he would try to get additional arms together at the New River Bridge, where George could pick them up, if needed. Several howitzers were available, advised Cooke, should George want them.[30]

After moving to the vicinity of White Sulphur Springs in Greenbrier County, Averell retraced his steps into West Virginia. The danger, for now, was over.

Two weeks later, the call came again for the home guards to assemble. A Federal force entering Virginia near Bristol on September 9 and threatening Abingdon occasioned this alert. Two days later, George received orders to hold his men in readiness to protect Dublin and the New River Bridge.

On September 14, Major General Samuel Jones issued an order relieving the home guards from duty, and directed them to return to their homes. In the order, Jones expressed his "thanks to the home guards of ... Roanoke ... for the promptitude with which they met the third call for their assistance in repelling a threatened raid."[31]

Their stay at home was a short one. Five days after Jones's order, the home guards received orders to report to Brigadier General G. C. Wharton at Glade Spring, in Washington County. Adjutant Charles S. Stringfellow instructed George to "call on your men to stand by you."[32] George's home guard at this point consisted of about 100 members. This call, like the others, proved to be a false alarm.

About a month later, on October 15, the government called out Terrill's home guards again. "Call out every man who can possibly bear arms to go to Abingdon immediately. The enemy is pressing in largely superior force."[33] Five days later, reports indicated that General Averell was advancing on Lewisburg, in Greenbrier County, with a force of 5,000 men. General Jones warned the commanders of the home guard units of Averell's movements, so they could be ready for action. He added that the units were "not to turn out until called."[34] Later that day, George received instructions to "notify your men to be ready to turn out on short notice."[35] Again, it was a false alarm.

In early November, reports again came that Averell was advancing on Lewisburg. George received orders on November 5 to "notify your men to be in readiness for any move."[36] Two days later, on the 7th, he received an order to assemble all of his men at Salem.[37] The enemy was forcing General John Echols' command back from Droop Mountain, in Pocahontas County. This too, amounted to nothing, as Averell's column turned back into West Virginia after following Echols' command to the vicinity of Lewisburg.

During this time, George was serving under a contract with the Confederate government as post surgeon at Salem, from December 15, 1863, through at least September 1864.

After repeated false alarms between August and November 1863, a new call came on December 15: "Averell, with a force of 3,000 is advancing on the railroad from Sweet Springs. You will immediately move your command to Salem."[38] This was no false alarm.

News of Averell's approach reached Salem about 11 P.M. December 15. Work commenced at once to remove the stockpiled stores from various locations in the town. Word of the danger spread quickly and the residents prepared for the worst.

There was no panic, only a determined, controlled frenzy of activity, as people everywhere hid their valuables or packed them in trunks to be carried away to safety, along with themselves, on that morning[s] train from Lynchburg.[39]

Major General Sam Jones, commanding the Department of Western Virginia, with his headquarters at Dublin, called for the home guards from Liberty to Lynchburg to respond to the emergency at Salem. None answered the call, and Averell's men destroyed the carefully collected stores.

Most of the Roanoke College Home Guard Company had already left for their homes and therefore were not available to respond to the emergency. The young men, between the ages of fourteen and eighteen, were enjoying a Christmas vacation.[40]

After the December raid on Salem, George turned command of the home guards over to Lieutenant Colonel George W. Hansbrough. The native of Taylor County, West Virginia, commanded the unit throughout 1864.[41]

In April 1864, the Terrill family celebrated the birth of their seventh and last child—Samuel Miller Dold Terrill,[42] who was born at Salem on April 20.

By the fall of 1864, the future of the Confederate States was looking very dark. The battles fought since the summer of 1863, including those in the spring and summer of 1864, had taken a terrible toll on the armies of the South. George was afraid that the government would force him into active service. In the last letter to his youngest brother, Philip, George expressed those fears:

> Congress meets next week and I look for nothing less at their hands than to be thrust into the army myself. I think the indications are that Drs. & Preachers under 45 years of age will be handed over to the tender mercies of the conscript officers. I have not decided what I shall do in the event I am made liable but will abide my time and then determine in the light of the circumstances by which I may be surrounded at that time.[43]

The scarcity of troops made itself clear in March 1865. George M. Pitzer and David E. Harris, two citizens of Roanoke County, applied to the Confederate secretary of war for permission to raise a company of Negro troops. George was among the citizens recommending Pitzer and Harris for favorable consideration in raising the company.[44] It appears that the March 27 application was filed and no action taken on it.

After the war, George continued to practice medicine, and serve in the local government. In the fall of 1866, George served as treasurer of Salem, and continued those duties until the spring of 1870.[45] By that time, it appeared that he was doing well. According to the census taken of Roanoke County in 1870, he owned real estate valued at $3,500 and personal property worth $1,000.

In the spring of 1876, George suffered a serious injury when his horse stumbled and threw him. *The Salem Register* reported:

> Painful Accident.—On Wednesday night, between 8 and 9 o'clock, as Dr. G. P. Terrill was returning home from the residence of Mr. G. H. Landon, when in front

of Mrs. Hannah's residence, his horse stumbled into the ditch in the centre of Main street, made for laying the water pipes, threw the Doctor off and struck him on the top of the head with his foot, cutting a considerable gash. The wound bled profusely, and it was thought at first to be quite dangerous. The Doctor was taken to the office of Dr. J. W. Bruffey, who dressed the wound, and rendered all other medical aid necessary. The wound is not considered dangerous, but it is till very painful. We hope the Doctor will soon be all right again.[46]

The injury proved to be more serious than was first thought, as George never fully recovered. He continued to practice medicine and participate in local political affairs, but after several years, his mind and body became impaired. After more than a year of bad health and failing strength, George Parker Terrill died at Salem, Virginia, on November 5, 1884.[47] He was 55 years old.

Death of Dr. G. P. Terrill.
Died suddenly, at his residence in Salem, on the morning of November 5th, Dr. George Parker Terrill, in the fifty-fifth year of his age. Whilst from the condition of his health and from his failing strength, such an event has been for more than a year, of almost daily expectation, yet, as in all such cases when the subject has been honored and loved, its announcement has lost none of its sadness and the community feels none the less the shock of the sudden death of one of its most valued citizens.

Dr. Terrill was born at Covington, Alleghany county, Virginia, February, 1830, moving in early youth to Warm Springs, Bath county, where his father, Col. Wm. Terrill, was one of the most prominent and best known citizens. He was graduated from the Virginia Military Institute in 1849, and took his degree as Doctor of Medicine from the University of Pennsylvania in 1853. In the same year he married Miss Sarah B., daughter of the late William Dold, or [of] Lexington, Va., and entered upon the practice of his profession in Salem, where all the subsequent years of his life were spent.

With most, excellent endowments of mind and heart, integrity, a kind and considerate disposition, careful preparation and a high and honorable bearing, he soon won the confidence and respect of the community and established before middle life an enviable reputation for skill and success in his calling. In the midst of his professional work he, moreover, found time as a public spirited citizen to discharge public trusts and to contribute by intelligence and zeal to the interests of the community. He also lectured in College for several terms on Anatomy and Physiology. Reared in the Presbyterian church, he identified himself with it here, serving for a long time as one of its elders and living in its connection a useful and exemplary life.

But in the spring of 1876 in the midst of his labors and usefulness, with the promise of a long and successful life before him, he was thrown from his horse. By this fall a concussion of the brain was produced from which he never recovered. He seemed to rally, it is true, and for several years afterwards resumed his practice and other incumbent duties, striving faithfully to take up the broken thread of his life. But from the mysterious connection between the mind and its investing body, the functions of both were disordered, becoming changed and impaired in their manifestations. On Wednesday morning the hand of death was laid upon all that was

Gravestone of Dr. George P. Terrill and Sarah Dold Terrill, East Hill Cemetery, Salem, Virginia. (author's photograph).

mortal in Dr. Terrill, but the *shadow* of that hand had been resting upon him for the eight past years. We will miss his familiar form from our streets and homes, as we *have* missed his active participation in our common interest and work. But as we commit his body to the grave, the memory of all will go back to the days when his step was stronger — when he bore an active, intelligent, faithful part in all the varied relations of husband, father, citizen, and physician that he sustained.[48]

The family buried George in the Terrill family plot in the East Hill Cemetery in Salem, Virginia.

Sometime after George's death, Sarah went to live with her daughter and son-in-law (the Spencers) in St. Louis, Missouri. There she died December 1, 1894, following a short illness, aged 63 years. Six of her seven children survived her, Frank H., having died in 1888.

Death of M. S. Terrill.

Mrs. M. S. Terrill, wife of the late Dr. Geo. P. Terrill, died Saturday at the residence of her son-in-law, the Rev. J. M. Spencer, in St. Louis, after a short illness, supposed to be affection of the heart. It is expected that the remains accompanied by Dr. Geo. M. Terrill, of San Francisco, Cal., will reach Salem to-night (Wednesday) and the funeral will take place from the Presbyterian church Thursday, the interment being in East Hill Cemetery.

Mrs. Terrill was about 65 [sic] years of age, she was born in Lexington, Va., and moved with her husband to Salem in 1852 [1853], where they ever afterward resided.

Mrs. Terrill leaves three sons and three daughters, Dr. S. M. Terrill, of Sacramento, Cal., Dr. Geo. M. Terrill, San Francisco, Cal., Wm. H. Terrill, New York city, Mrs. Wm. Duncan, Denver, Col., Mrs. J. M. Spencer, St. Louis, Mo., and Mrs. J. E. Bushnell, of Oakland, Cal.

Mr. W. H. Terrill is here now and the other sons, and probably Mrs. Spencer, are expected to be present at the funeral.[49]

Chapter III

Emily Cornelia Clay Terrill (and George Alexander Porterfield)

Emily Cornelia Clay Terrill
1832–1906

As William H. Terrill continued to build his legal practice in Covington, and the surrounding area, Elizabeth cared for their infant son and daughter. Their small family increased with the birth of another girl on July 10, 1832, which they named Emily Cornelia Clay Terrill.

Shortly before Emily turned thirteen, she became a student at the Virginia Female Institute in Staunton, Virginia, boarding with Mr. and Mrs. John B. Baldwin.[1] Among the subjects she studied were Latin and French.

William and Elizabeth had high hopes and expectations for Emily. In a June 13, 1845, letter to Emily, her father wrote: "You say in your letter to your mother that you intend to be very industrious and study hard. I hope you will fulfill that promise. You do not know how much your mother and myself will be delighted should you distinguish yourself at school. I know you can do so if you will try."[2]

Emily continued her education until at least the winter of 1847, then returned home because the school closed. She remained at home only a short while, then entered a school in Lexington, Virginia.

According to one of the Porterfield family histories, Emily met her future husband, George A. Porterfield, while he was a teacher. This same history noted that the young couple had been engaged, and because of some problem or another broke off their engagement. Elizabeth Terrill, Emily's mother, took a hand in the situation, and before long, the engagement was on again.[3]

Emily Cornelia Clay Terrill and George Alexander Porterfield were married at the family home — Rose Hill — near Bath Court House on July 10, 1849. It was her 17th birthday.

After their marriage, the Porterfields lived in Martinsburg, Berkeley County, Virginia. In 1853 or 1854, George accepted a position in the Drawing Division of the U.S. Coast Survey, and the couple moved to Washington, D.C. They lived in Washington for several years, and then sometime after 1853 Emily moved to the Leetown area of Jefferson County. Her husband owned a farm about four miles west of the Kearneysville Station on the Baltimore & Ohio Railroad. Emily took over the management of the farm, which they called Elmwood. George remained in Washington for several more years, making frequent visits to Elmwood.

The first of Emily's eight children was born on December 7, 1850. She named him William Terrill Porterfield.[4]

Elizabeth Morton Porterfield[5], the second child of the Porterfields, was born in Washington City on April 23, 1853. She was affectionately nicknamed Bettie. Emily confided to her brother John Allen, in 1856, saying, "Bettie is acknowledged by all to be a perfect beauty."[6]

One of those smitten by Bettie's appearance was her uncle, William Rufus Terrill. During one his visits to Emily's home, he watched as she gave Bettie a bath. He remarked to her, "When I return, you must give me that child." Sadly, he never returned.[7] Bettie equally smote John Allen Terrill, another uncle. In the fall of 1857, John wrote his sister, telling her that he wished he could see her and the children, "especially Bettie."[8]

Emily and George's third child, John Moler Porterfield,[9] was born in Jefferson County, on March 15, 1855. Nearly a year later, he was described as being "a great, big fat fellow, with bright laughing blue eyes, fair skin, rosy cheeks and light hair."[10]

Between 1856 and 1860, two additional children were born into the Porterfield family. A boy, named George Terrill,[11] was born on August 3, 1857, and a girl, named Mary Jane,[12] was born on March 20, 1859.

Nearly two years later, Charles Alexander Porterfield,[13] the sixth child of George and Emily, was born on January 3, 1861. Their family now consisted of four boys and two girls.

Following the election of Abraham Lincoln as president, the Southern states began to split off from the Union, and the United States became a nation divided against itself. This division not only affected the government, but also caused many families to divide as well. Emily's family was one of these.

William Rufus Terrill had been a frequent visitor to the Porterfield home before the war. Now, because of his decision to remain in the United States Army, his father considered him an outcast. Emily, however, did not share her father's strong feelings on the subject, despite later reports to the contrary. She carried on a regular correspondence with her brother and his wife, as well as her sister-in-law's mother, Arietta Henry.

When Virginia seceded from the Union, George Porterfield again volunteered for military duty at nearby Harpers Ferry. With her husband off to war,

III — Emily Cornelia Clay Terrill

Emily once again assumed management of the farm. George and Emily had discussed the question of her safety before he left Elmwood. George suggested that she and the children go her father's home in Warm Springs. "You will be more secure there for the present at least than elsewhere."[14] Whether or not Emily made the journey to Bath County is unknown.

A series of disasters befell the Virginia troops in Western Virginia during June and July 1861. On July 13, at Beverly, in Randolph County, Emily's brother Philip became a prisoner of war, remaining in the hands of the Union Army for four days. Major General George B. McClellan then paroled the prisoners, allowing Philip to return to his home in Warm Springs.

Portrait of Emily Cornelia Clay Terrill Porterfield (courtesy Mr. and Mrs. Philip T. Porterfield).

Philip came to live with Emily not long afterward, and helped manage the farm. He remained with her until the summer of 1862, when he rejoined the Confederate Army.

Near the end of March 1862, William Rufus Terrill wrote a letter to the secretary of war, Edwin M. Stanton, concerning his sister and her plight. From his camp in Tennessee, William wrote on March 28:

> My sister, the wife of Col. G. A. Porterfield lives near Leetown, Jefferson County, Virginia. My brother Captain Philip M. Terrill, (captured at Rich Mountain) a prisoner on parole is with her. About the 4th of March her stock was driven off her farm and when my brother went to Martinsburg to recover it, although he exhibited his parole he was thrown into the County Jail. He was released the next day. I beg that you will be kind enough to

Portrait of George Alexander Porterfield (courtesy Mr. and Mrs. Philip T. Porterfield).

give Mrs. Porterfield a safeguard. She has a large family of small children, and all the property she claims is her own, for I know it was given her by my father. Anyhow the forms of law should be gone through with in order to confiscate them.[15]

In July 1862, Emily received a letter from her sister-in-law, Emily Henry Terrill, then in Reading, Pennsylvania: "I can not refrain from writing to you, for I am *very anxious* to know if your Husband and Brothers escaped in safety from the recent terrible conflicts before Richmond. I suppose of course some, if not all of them, were engaged."[16]

Her husband, George, having left the army, was at home. Philip was still waiting to be exchanged by the government. James's regiment, the 13th Virginia Infantry, was engaged in the fighting about Richmond. James, however, was sick during this time and did not participate in those battles.

With August came tragedy. A playmate accidentally shot and killed twelve-year-old Willie Porterfield while he was visiting his Grandmother Tabb's family. The two boys were playing with a revolver which tragically proved to be loaded.[17] His distraught parents wished to bury him in Martinsburg, by the side of his aunt Anne Porterfield Snodgrass. However, there was a problem — Colonel Porterfield could not leave his home to attend to the burial.

Neighbor A. S. Dandrich wrote Edmond Pendleton about the Porterfields' situation:

Will you see the Provost and ascertain whether the funeral procession can pass in and out of town tomorrow without a pass and obtain him a paper to that effect ... if he is unwilling to grant this, will you collect some

Elizabeth "Bettie" Porterfield (Mrs. Henry H. Cooke), favorite of uncles William R. Terrill and John A. Terrill (courtesy Elizabeth Jackson Morton).

friends—Nan's family among others and have him buried. His remains will be taken to town by Mr. Doll, who will also have the grave dug.[18]

Pendleton's efforts were successful, and the authorities issued the following pass: "Office Provost Marshall, Martinsburg, August 3rd 1862. The guards and pickets will pass the funeral procession of Mr. Porterfield without passes in and out of town. D. M. Lane, Capt., Provost Marshall."[19]

Everything remained relatively quiet in the Porterfield household until the summer of 1863. On June 3, 1863, a number of soldiers belonging to the 12th Pennsylvania Infantry visited the Porterfield home and removed a mule. The captain commanding the detachment explained to Emily that General Robert H. Milroy had ordered the seizure of all property associated with the rebel army. The officer claimed to have proof to support his seizure of the mule. Emily wrote General Milroy on June 6 about the seizure:

> Now there is no proof whatever to the best of my knowledge that the animal had ever been so used. It was found in the road nearly a year ago by a servant boy in my employment & had no brand or mark upon it. I have concluded to call your attention to this matter, not on account of any value or claim that I placed upon the animal in question, but to ascertain whether or not it was seized by your authority (which I doubted) and to satisfy myself as to what security we have in such property.[20]

According to Emily, this was not the first time that the army confiscated her stock.

> When Gen. Banks' army first came into this part of the state, several of my horses were taken for the use of the army which his Adjt. Gen. stated should be returned or paid for if they could be found, but army movements at that time prevented & they were lost.[21]

Emily then played her hole card, writing:

> My brother Gen. W. R. Terrill who fell at the battle of Perryville, Ky., asked the Dept. at Washington to give me some protection from any depredations, which if not granted, I feel sure was prevented only by the changes this section has undergone through the fortunes of war.[22]

Whether or not Emily recovered the mule, and what reply General Milroy may have made is not on record.

With the war in full swing, the necessary staples of sugar and salt were difficult to come by. The Porterfields were fortunate enough to be able to purchase a barrel of sugar and a sack of salt, which they left at George's mother's in Martinsburg until they could be moved. Sometime in the fall of 1863, a Northern scout named Noakes discovered the sugar and salt, and removed them from the house, possibly with the blessings of the provost marshal.

Making a statement of the facts on November 24, 1863, Emily asked Secretary of War Edwin M. Stanton to order the return of the supplies, or their equivalent. Stanton referred the matter to Brigadier General Jeremiah C. Sullivan at Harpers Ferry, with instructions to return the property. A letter from Arietta L. Henry,[23] who evidentially had some influence with the government, supplemented her plea. Mrs. Henry wrote on November 30: "The faithful and distinguished services, the domestic trials & the well established loyalty & sad death of my son in law Capt. Terrill, will I trust be considered an adequate apology for my request in behalf of his only sister — a native & resident of Virginia."[24]

On December 7, the War Department responded to Mrs. Henry: "I had the pleasure to obtain an order from the Secy. of War this morning, to General Sullivan commanding at Harpers Ferry, to make restitution of the articles detained from the sister of Capt. Terrill mentioned in her letter to you."[25] The papers arrived on General Sullivan's desk on December 8, and he ordered an investigation into the matter. Colonel R. S. Rogers reported on December 24:

> I have to say that according to the testimony of loyal citizens Mr. & Mrs. Porterfield belong to the class called Southern sympathizers. Mr. Porterfield was once a Colonel in the Rebel service and has never taken the oath of allegiance — but at present is discreet and quiet. The sugar and salt were taken by Thomas Nooks [sic], lately tried for horse stealing at Harpers Ferry, upon his own authority and not that of the Pro. Marshal, but all except eighty (80) lbs. of the sugar has been returned by the commissary: no part of the salt has been returned.[26]

General Sullivan, upon receiving Rogers' report on December 29, endorsed it as follows:

> Mrs. Porterfield is a violent secessionist, [and] expressed herself openly against the Government. She openly declared while her lamented brother, General Terrill, was alive that she disowned him and would not recognize him. I do not think she should be allowed to *use him* while dead.[27]

In the meantime, not having received a response, Emily wrote directly to General Sullivan:

> I wrote you about two weeks ago relative to some sugar & salt of mine, which had been seized in Martinsburg. Having received no reply to my letter I sent to the commanding officer in Martinsburg. The person sent for the articles reported that he had been informed by the Adjt. of the comdg. officer that you had countermanded the order for their return. I write now to say that whilst the articles in question are of little value scarcely worth this correspondence, if you want them, I will make you a present of them. But, I am determined not to be robbed, even with your assistance, without making the matter public.[28]

General Sullivan endorsed the letter and forwarded it to the War Department on January 7: "Respectfully forwarded with request it may be brought to attention of Secy. of War. Ms. Porterfield is intensely disloyal and takes every occasion to show her disloyalty."[29] In forwarding Emily's letter, Sullivan commented in a separate letter:

> I enclose to you a letter I rec'd from one Mrs. Porterfield. I desire it to be forwarded to the War Department that they may see the character of the Lady they are

urged to befriend. She is a violent secessionist and denounced her brother, the gallant Genl. Terrill in the most bitter terms. I intend to make her Husband apologise [sic].[30]

Brigadier General E. M. Canby, on duty in the War Department, responded to Mrs. Henry's letter on January 9, 1864:

> The Secretary of War instructs me to inform you that your communication of November 30th asking consideration for the application of Mrs. Porterfield, to have restored a quantity of sugar & salt illegally seized, was [referred] to the Comdg. Genl. at Harper's Ferry with instructions to order restitution of the property. This, so far as possible, has been done, and that officer reports regarding the seizure, which was made by one Noakes, an unauthorized person.[31]

General Canby added that a military commission had tried Noakes for stealing a horse, and that Noakes had since escaped from custody. Enclosed in his reply, was a copy of General Sullivan's scathing comments about Emily Porterfield.

Upon learning of General Sullivan's remarks, through Mrs. Henry, Emily responded to Assistant Adjutant General Canby:

> Brig. Gen. Sullivan, Comdg. at Harpers Ferry has made a report to the War Dept. relative to myself so full of falsehood that I cannot pass it by without correction.
>
> I do not suppose that Gen. S. made intentionally a false report, nor do I know his source of information. I addressed him a very respectful business letter, which he did not think proper to reply to — otherwise he might have been far better informed....
>
> In reply to the first charge [Mrs. Porterfield is a violent secessionist] I will say that at the beginning I was opposed to secession but as the war progressed, I became satisfied that it was not prosecuted solely with a view to the restoration of the Union. My views underwent a change, but my sentiments have been exposed to very few beyond my own household. I have never committed an act disloyal to the Gov't of the United States. I have not done for the soldiers of one army what I would not have done for those of the other. I have fed soldiers of both.
>
> [In response to not recognizing her brother:] This is thoroughly false. I was in communication with my brother & his family, as far as practicable, up to the time of his death, and since that sad event have had almost constant communication with his widow. My affection for him was not abated in consequence of his remaining in the U.S. Army, nor did I ever censure him for doing so, but always said I believed he acted from a sense of duty.
>
> [In response to the use of General Terrill's name:] What can I say to this is [while] Gen. Sullivan [is] a gentleman [surely], his name is not upon the register of the regular army. He should have ordered the restitution of my property as that which had been illegitimately & unnecessarily taken from a private citizen. I would desire those who have seen Gen. Sullivan's report, to see my reply to it.[32]

The communication between Emily and the Henrys soon became the subject of conversation between other members of the Terrill family. On December 15, 1863, James wrote Philip and mentioned the correspondence: "I think

... she had better *ignore the acquaintance* of Mrs. Henry, her relations toward the latter are not at all in accord with what they were several years since."[33]

Philip received a letter a few days later from Emily, in which she spoke of the relationship between herself and Mrs. Henry.

> Mrs. Henry has been exceedingly kind to me.... A few days ago she procured for me an order from the Secretary of War, to have some sugar & salt restored which were seized in Martinsburg about the time of Imboden's raid. She certainly possesses the power of fascinating to a greater extent than any person I ever knew for prejudiced to the contrary as I once was, my heart now overflows with affection for her.[34]

The relationship between Emily Henry Terrill and Emily Porterfield seems to be a strong one. According to family tradition, Emily Henry Terrill assigned the death benefit received from William R. Terrill's death, to Emily Porterfield. This aid helped the Porterfields through the lean years following the war.[35]

In March 1864, Emily again found it necessary to write General Canby.

> A few days ago a servant boy in my employ, about 13 years of age, met a party of U.S. Cavalry & went with them to the encampment at Kearneysville, taking my riding horse with him. The horse was found in possession of a soldier of Company M, 6th Michigan Cavalry, and although identified & application made for it to Col. Woolworth, Comdg. at Kearneysville, it has not been returned to me. This is the eighth horse that has been taken from me [by] the U.S. service, without one cent's compensation. As Col. Woolworth has made no reply to my application for my property, I have to apply to you for redress.[36]

The War Department forwarded the letter to General Sullivan for comment. Sullivan, then at Webster, West Virginia, reported that the unit referred to at the time of the alleged theft was a part of Brigadier General W. W. Averell's command. Here the matter ended.

In the spring of 1864, the Porterfields welcomed a new member into their family. Emily Serena Porterfield[37] was born at Elmwood on May 3, 1864.

With the South hard pressed for men in the summer of 1864, and as General Jubal A. Early was then pressing toward Washington, D.C., there was some debate over George Porterfield's returning to the army. Philip, in a letter to Emily, dated July 31, 1864, noted: "I suppose by this time the Col. has left you to go into service."[38] Despite Philip's supposition, George did not return to the army, but remained as quietly as he could on his farm until the war was over.

Despite George's efforts to remain neutral, Northern troops frequently raided Elmwood during the war, accusing him of concealing and aiding Colonel John S. Mosby and his men. Because of the constant raids, and other hardships, Emily became so nervous, that she urged George to bring one of her cousins (the Wise children) to stay with her.[39]

In the early fall of 1864, when the Southern troops briefly controlled the area about Charles Town, George made a trip to Staunton. He hitched the last pair of farm horses to the remnants of what had once been a handsome carriage, for the journey. The top of the carriage was gone, the cushions taken, and the carpeting torn off. The harness, cut to pieces by vandals, was pieced together with leather strings. The Wise children, upon seeing the vehicle, described it as "a most remarkable looking vehicle, which we called the chariot."[40]

According to Cornelia H. Wise, George Porterfield was "a man of the greatest dignity."[41] When he drove up to Loch Willow, in Churchville, he descended from the chariot in his usual dignified manner. The Wise children, Cornelia noted, could scarcely conceal their amusement.

Cornelia accompanied the colonel on the two-day journey back to Elmwood. Upon their arrival, they learned that the cavalry division of General William Woods Averell had established their camp nearby. Because of earlier outrages committed against the Porterfields' property, someone had to go to the general and ask for protection.

Emily Terrill Porterfield (courtesy Elizabeth Jackson Morton).

The colonel, forbidden to leave his home, could not go to see the general. Emily could not go either, due to her nervous state. Cornelia Wise volunteered to go to the Union camp. One of the old horses was saddled, and accompanied by twelve-year-old John Porterfield and a big English mastiff, Cornelia made the three-mile trip.

General Averell was absent when she arrived, but a Colonel Schoonmaker[42] offered his assistance. The young woman informed the colonel that the Porterfields needed a guard to protect the farm from looters. She added that her cousin, the late General William R. Terrill, had been a classmate of Averell's at West Point. This brought swift action, and the colonel "at once ... ordered a Corporal and four men to attend me and allow no one to enter the grounds without permission of the family."[43] This seemed to put an end to the Porterfields' losses.

Sometime after the close of the war (but before 1870), the Porterfields moved to Charles Town, West Virginia. George became secretary of the Valley Fire Insurance Company in 1870. The following year, at his suggestion, the company converted into the Bank of Charles Town. George then became a cashier and worked at the bank for many years afterward.

Soon after moving to Charles Town, an eighth child was born into the Porterfield family. Katherine Seton Porterfield,[44] nicknamed Kate, was born March 18, 1870. It appears that the Porterfields named her for Kate Seton Henry, sister of Emily Henry Terrill, William Rufus Terrill's widow.

Emily died of paralysis at Charles Town, West Virginia on May 30, 1906, the last of William H. Terrill's children to die. George buried her beside her beloved Willie in the Green Hill Cemetery at Martinsburg, West Virginia.

Elizabeth Jackson Morton, a granddaughter of the Porterfields, said that George Porterfield "was a gentleman of great charm" and that Emily "was a lady of rare grace and loveliness."[45]

MRS. EMILY TERRILL
PORTERFIELD.

Died at her home in Charlestown, West Virginia, on the 30th of May, 1906.

In the passing from earth to heaven of this lovely Christian character the community in which she lived and the wider circle of her acquaintance in the two Virginias have sustained a loss that causes the profoundest sorrow. Beautiful in every relation of life, as wife, as mother, as friend, she will be deeply mourned by all who knew her. In the many vicissitudes of fortune that marked her life, she never lost faith in God and His loving providence. The heavenly Father was to her "an ever present help in time of need."

To the weary and heavy-laden, she spoke words of cheer and hope; to the wounded in spirit, she bore the balm of sympathy and consolation; and through her blessed ministrations many a storm-tossed soul has found, at last, "the peace that passeth understanding." Her very presence was as sunshine in the darkness of their lives. To all she taught the gospel of patience and faith.

Of superior mind, of thoughtful nature, of wide reading and attractive personality, she was always a charming companion to persons of mature years and a never-failing inspiration to the young, to whom it was her delight to impart all that was possible of the rich fund of her information and the ripe fruitage of her culture. To her reverent mind and heart the natural world and the moral world were a constant revelation of the wisdom and goodness of God. Her soul was alive to all the glory of nature around her, but her love of flowers, almost passionate in its intensity, was to her the source of the most joy. In her last illness she would gaze for hours from her window upon the roses in the garden below that spring had arrayed in their loveliest robes. After drinking in the solace and rapture of their beauty, she would lift her eyes to heaven, as if contem-

Emily Terrill Porterfield (courtesy Mr. and Mrs. Philip T. Porterfield).

plating the glories of the world above and repeat, in a soft undertone, the sweet old poem:

> If God has made this earth so fair
> Where sin and death abound
> How beautiful beyond compare,
> Will Paradise be found.

It seems meet that a spirit so childlike in its simple faith and love should have been transplanted to the garden of the heavenly Eden in the glad hours of the earthly springtime, when the flowers, that were almost human in their companionship to her, were in sweetest fragrance and richest bloom.

[Mrs.] W. Chase Morton.
Richmond, Va.[46]

George Alexander Porterfield
1822–1919

George Alexander Porterfield was born in Berkeley County, Virginia, on November 24, 1822, the son of George and Mary Tabb Porterfield. He and a sister grew to adulthood in Berkeley County.

Young George entered the recently formed Virginia Military Academy at Lexington, Virginia, in the fall of 1840. Twenty-six students entered the fourth class that year.

Near the close of his third year at VMI, George applied for admission to the United States Military Academy at West Point. Colonel F. H. Smith, the superintendent at VMI, wrote of George in February 1843:

> If the possession of a good mind regulated by good principles be any claim to the appointment, no one deserves it more. His standing in this institution, always good, has been steadily and rapidly improving, until his position has become second in his class. In conduct, he has been distinguished by uniform attention to every duty. I unhesitatingly recommend him for the appointment and have no doubt of the manner in which he would acquit himself.[47]

From comments added to the letter by Professor John T. L. Preston, George possessed a talent for the acquisition of languages. Preston believed that the young man would do well in the future.

Colonel Claudius Crozet also recommended George for appointment to the academy. The French immigrant and member of the Board of Visitors of VMI noted in his letter that George had no demerits against him, and that he was serving as an officer in the school.[48]

When the Engineer Department reviewed the applications in the spring of 1843, George did not make the cut. Undaunted, George renewed his application in February 1844, and again, he was passed over for admission to West Point.[49]

By the time graduation arrived in July 1844, only nine cadets remained in the class. George graduated exactly in the middle of his class—fifth. Superintendent Smith recommended that George pursue a career as a teacher.

Following the superintendent's advice, George went to Richmond where he worked as a teacher. The breaking out of the Mexican War interrupted his career in April 1846. George quickly volunteered for duty, and helped two of his comrades from VMI raise a company of infantry on May 14, 1846. The Richmond Rangers, as it was known locally, was the first company raised in Virginia for service in the Mexican War. The company elected Edward C. Carrington, Jr., captain the following day, with George as 1st lieutenant, and Carlton R. Munford as 2nd Lieutenant. The company enrolled at Camp Larkin Smith, near Richmond, on May 26, 1846.[50]

Not being accepted for duty right away, George returned to his home in Berkeley County, where he became the principal of the Martinsburg Academy. He remained there until November 1846, when the government finally called upon Virginia for volunteers.

The Richmond Rangers responded to the call, and Governor Smith issued commissions for its officers, instructing them to report to Richmond as soon as possible. George left his position in Martinsburg and went off to war, as 1st Lieutenant of Company G, 1st Virginia Volunteers. According to the muster rolls for the company, George's date of enlistment was November 16, 1846. The records describe George as being 5 feet, 11 inches tall, having a dark complexion, gray eyes, and black hair. He listed his occupation as principal of the Martinsburg Academy.[51]

To lead the 1st Virginia Volunteers, Governor Smith appointed John Francis Hamtramck[52] to the rank of colonel on December 22, 1846. Colonel Hamtramck, a West Point graduate, was then living in Shepherdstown, Virginia, where he operated a large farm. Colonel Hamtramck arrived in Richmond on December 30, greeted by large crowds and military demonstrations. He assumed command of the regiment at once, and began preparing for deployment in Mexico.

The City Council of Richmond met on January 6, 1847, and resolved to

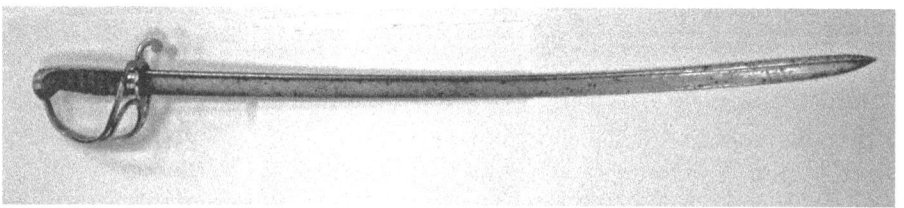

Sword presented to Lieutenant Porterfield by the Richmond City Council, 1847. The sword was manufactured by Ames and inscribed "Presented by the City of Richmond" (courtesy of Jefferson County Historical Society).

honor the officers of the two companies from that city, the Richmond Grays and Richmond Rangers. The council felt that the best way to do this was to present each of them with a sword, inscribed with the words "Presented by the City of Richmond."[53]

The council appointed a committee of three to order the swords, which they did from Ames in Massachusetts, at a cost of $30 each. The swords arrived in mid–February, but the companies had already sailed for Mexico. The council prepared a letter of presentation for each of the officers, and sent them with the swords to Mexico. George noted the receipt of the sword in a March 28 letter to his mother, stating, "It is the prettiest sword I have ever seen."[54]

George and four companies of the regiment sailed for Mexico on January 28, 1847, on board the *Mayflower*. The ship made a port of call at Havana, Cuba, on February 7, where it took on fresh water and other necessary supplies, then continued on to Brazos Harbor, near Point Isabel.

The first portion of the Virginia Volunteers arrived in Brazos Harbor on February 22, where they remained for two days. From that point, they moved to the mainland, going ashore at Port Isabel, at the mouth of the Rio Grande River. The remainder of the regiment joined them soon afterward, and the regiment boarded steamboats and moved up the river to Camargo. The garrison at Camargo expected an attack at any time, so the men of the 1st Virginia Volunteers quickly set about fortifying it.

Life in the field seemed to agree with George. In a letter to his mother, written from Camargo on March 28th, he wrote: "Mine is a soldier's life and I am fattening upon it. My weight is more now than it ever was before, and all my friends here say I am more improved than any man in the regiment."[55]

George soon found himself performing the duties of regimental adjutant, as the U.S. forces moved deeper into Mex-

First Lieutenant George A. Porterfield in his Mexican War uniform (courtesy Jefferson County Historical Society).

ico. Within weeks, George moved up to the position of Acting Adjutant General of his brigade, and soon afterward, Adjutant of General John E. Wool's division. George remained on General Wool's staff until he left Mexico the following year.

Soon after United States forces occupied Mexico City in September 1847, the officers of the regular and volunteer service formed a social club that they called the Aztec Club of 1847. Organized on October 13, 1847, the function of the club was to provide officers with good fellowship, and a place where they could pass their leisure time.[56] George joined the organization and remained a member of it for life. He served as vice president (1914 to 1915) and president (1915 to 1916) of the Aztec Club of 1847.

George left Monterey on June 21, 1848, and returned to Virginia, via New Orleans. He reached his home in Berkeley County on July 17, 1848,[57] and received his discharge three days later.

Nearly a year after returning to Virginia, George married Emily Cornelia Clay Terrill at her home in Warm Springs, Virginia, on July 10, 1849. The newlyweds made their home in a Martinsburg hotel, according to the 1850 Census of Berkeley County. While living in Martinsburg, George worked for several years as editor of the *Martinsburg Gazette*.

In late 1853 or early 1854, George accepted a position in the Drawing Division of the U.S. Coast Survey, and moved to the Georgetown section of Washington, D.C. Three years later, George was looking for a career change. Congress was then considering increasing the size of the army, and George wished to join one of the companies as captain. He wrote his father-in-law, William H. Terrill, and asked for his assistance in securing the position. Colonel Terrill wrote the superintendent of the Virginia Military Institute on December 3, 1857, asking him to support George's application. As an afterthought, Terrill added this postscript: "Mr. Porterfield has a passion for a military life and I believe will never be contented with any other. Ever since he returned from Mexico has been impatient to get back into the army."[58]

Colonel Smith complied with his friend's request, writing on December 7:

> I take great pleasure in recommending Mr. Geo. A. Porterfield ... for a Captain's Commission in the U.S.A. sh[ould] any new Regiment be organized this year. Mr. Porterfield graduated in this Institution in 1844 and served with great distinction as adjutant of the Va. Regiment of Volunteers in the Mexican war. His conduct in that post, so fully secured the approbation of Gen. Wool that he was offered an honorable post in his personal staff. This was declined by Mr. Porterfield upon the ground that he wouldn't leave his own Regiment to accept promotion. Mr. P's merits and character entitle him to the most favorable consideration of the Sec. & I hope it may be the pleasure of the Dept. to confer an appt. upon him.[59]

Once again, his efforts to gain a position in the army failed.

In the late summer of 1858, George turned his attention to a new branch of government service. During that summer, he expressed a desire to secure the appointment as U.S. Consul at Kingston, Jamaica. One of his acquaintances from the Mexican War days, Captain Henry W. Benham, wrote a letter of recommendation to the secretary of state. Captain Benham wrote on August 2:

> Mr. Porterfield was conspicuous in that responsible position [adjutant] for a most careful attention to his duties, successful management, and gentlemanly and courteous bearing to all, making his services as I considered them invaluable to the Regiment.... The impression made on me in Mexico by his course and conduct, was such that it gave me great pleasure to offer him a situation under my direction, and though the situation was a most trying and difficult one, with a combination of ill disposed persons acting against him, he bore himself with such dignity and strength of character, in his new position, as not only to be able to perform his duties most faithfully and loyally to the government, but even to disarm those opposed to him at first and to secure their full esteem and respect.... This knowledge of Mr. Porterfield has satisfied me that he would make a most faithful & efficient, as well as what is also as indispensable in my opinion — a most gentlemanly agent of our government ... and one that could be relied on in all emergencies to do his duty faithfully and to sustain the honor of our country.[60]

The following winter, in March 1859, George asked Coast Survey Superintendent Alexander D. Bache to aid him in his effort to obtain the appointment in Jamaica. Bache did so, writing that George possessed "great faithfulness & industry & punctuality in the discharge of his duties and earnestly recommend him for any employment in which these qualities are most desirable."[61]

George failed to obtain the appointment, and remained at his post in the Drawing Division of the Coast Survey for another year. He resigned his position, effective April 30, 1860, and returned to his home in Jefferson County.

The 1860 Census of Jefferson County, Virginia, indicates that the Porterfields were doing quite well. The census recorded that their real estate was valued at $14,000, and their personal property amounted to $4,700. Information collected by the census bureau in 1860 reveals that the Porterfields owned seven slaves, five females and two males.

At the beginning of the Civil War, George was living on his farm near Leetown, in Jefferson County, Virginia. When the Virginia troops occupied nearby Harpers Ferry, George joined the staff of Brigadier General Kenton Harper, as an aide, and by April 19, was serving as Assistant Adjutant General.[62] General Harper and George were acquainted with each other, both having served in the same regiment during the Mexican War. George also served as a Lieutenant Colonel in the Inspector General's Division at Harpers Ferry in April 1861.[63]

On April 25, a number of officers from the 67th Virginia Militia petitioned Governor John Letcher to assign George A. Porterfield to command the volunteer companies in Berkeley County, Virginia.

> If your Excellency shall see proper to grant the prayer of this petition, the undersigned respectfully request that you will appoint as Colonel of the Regiment, Lt. Col. George A. Porterfield now on the Staff of Major General Harper, as Inspector

General. Col. Porterfield is now a citizen of Jefferson but is a native, and was for a long time resident of Berkeley County.[64]

At Harpers Ferry, General Harper recommended the appointment be made, all the while regretting the loss of such a valuable officer. He forwarded the petition to Governor Letcher, by way of Colonel F. H. Smith, Superintendent of the Virginia Military Institute.

George, in a letter to Colonel Smith on April 29, stated:

> As I am uninformed as to the *basis* upon which the military force of the state is to be organized, I have concluded to say that if there is to be a permanent establishment, I would prefer a position in that, to one in the volunteer service, on account of the better discipline and greater efficiency it would secure.[65]

George then offered some advice to Colonel Smith, a member of the Governor's Advisory Council, about the competency of the militia officers: "I would here suggest that the officers— the field officers especially of cavalry and artillery heretofore appointed are almost all totally incompetent to the proper discharge of their duties— and that reorganization is essential to efficiency in these arms."[66]

The authorities took the advice seriously, and within a few days, all militia officers above the rank of captain were relieved of their duties. Among the officers affected was George's brother-in-law, Major James B. Terrill, then at Harpers Ferry.

On May 3, 1861, Governor Letcher commissioned George as a colonel in the active volunteer forces of Virginia, and ordered to report to Colonel Thomas J. Jackson for duty.[67] The following day, General Robert E. Lee, commanding the state forces, sent further orders to the newly appointed colonel:

> You are directed to repair to Grafton, Taylor Co., Va. & select a position for the troops called into the service of the State for the protection and defense of that part of the country. It is desired to hold both branches of the R. r. to the Ohio River to prevent its being used to the injury of the State. You must therefore choose your position with this view, that you may readily re-inforce troops on either branch.... You will also place a force on the Parkersburg branch at such points as you may select to render a suitable officer with necessary orders for his advance.[68]

General Lee, in his May 4 letter, informed Porterfield that several officers had been ordered to assist him, and that authority had been given for him to call out the volunteer companies in that section of Virginia. Once at Grafton, Porterfield was to report the number of companies mustered into service, along with their condition and how armed. To aid the colonel in forming a regiment, Lee informed Porterfield that he had sent a number of muskets to Harpers Ferry and to Major David Goff at Beverly, in Randolph County.

From his home at Elmwood, George wrote to Colonel Smith on May 9, thanking him for his assistance in obtaining his appointment. "I will enter upon my duties in a day or so & will try to sustain the honor of the State & the reputation of the Institute."[69]

Several weeks later, a modified set of instructions appeared in a letter sent to James Mason by Lee. He wrote, "Colonel Porterfield has been sent to Grafton, with instructions to concentrate there three regiments, at Parkersburg one regiment, and at Moundsville one regiment."[70] At that time, Porterfield's command consisted of only a few companies, certainly not sufficient to meet the expectations placed upon him.

General Lee's orders were slow to reach Colonel Porterfield. He reported on May 14 that he had just arrived at Grafton that morning. "The officers directed to report to me," wrote Porterfield, "are not present; nor is there any volunteer or other force here. I will at once proceed to ascertain the whereabouts of Major Goff's command, which I hope to find soon, and will then endeavor to unite with one or more companies, with which I will return and take position in or near this place."[71]

Colonel Porterfield at once asked for re-enforcements, asking the governor to send him a detachment of not less than 250 men with artillery, if the garrison at Harpers Ferry could spare them. Two days later, on the 16th, George again wrote the Richmond authorities:

> In my last report I stated that I would first get possession of the arms consigned to Major Goff, and then try to collect a force and occupy this place. I accordingly sent a messenger to Major Goff, at Beverly, about fifty miles distant, and proceeded to ascertain what force I could get, its condition, and the sentiment of the people in the counties of Taylor, Barbour, and Harrison. I also sent orders to the captains of companies, supposed to be armed, in the surrounding counties, to bring their companies immediately to a designated point, near Grafton, and there await my orders. The messenger from Beverly returned with the reply that nothing had been heard of the rifles, nor had Major Goff been informed that they were to be sent to him. This is a serious disappointment. Several companies in this vicinity are organizing and expecting to be furnished at once with arms and ammunition. I found a company organizing at Pruntytown, in this county, which will be ready to receive arms in a day or so. There is another at Philippi, in Barbour County, awaiting arms, and another in Clarksburg which will soon be ready. I have seen the officers of these companies. There are other companies forming in the surrounding counties, but all without arms and ununiformed. This force, when received, will not for some months be more effective than undisciplined militia. There are but two companies in this vicinity known to be armed. One of these, Captain Bogges,' at Weston, about forty-five miles distant, has the old flint-lock musket, in bad order, and no ammunition. The other, Captain Thompson's, at Fairmont, twenty miles from this place, has a better gun, and some ammunition. These companies are now marching towards this point; are ordered to do so, at least. This is the only force on which I have to depend, and it is very weak, compared with the strength of those in this section who, I am assured, are ready to oppose me.[72]

The colonel then proceeded to advise his superiors of the political climate in northwestern Virginia.

> I have found great diversity of opinion and much bitterness of feeling among the people of this region. They are apparently upon the verge of civil war. A few bad men have done much mischief by stirring up rebellion among the people, and representing to them the weakness of the State, and its inability or indisposition to protect them.... They and their accomplices have also threatened the property and persons of law-abiding citizens with fire and the sword. Their efforts to intimidate have had their effect, both to dishearten one party and encourage the other. Many good citizens have been dispirited, while traitors have seized the guns and ammunition of the State, to be used against its authority.[73]

General Lee responded on May 19:

> One thousand muskets and rifles and some ammunition have been sent from Staunton to Major Goff and Lieutenant Chenowith at Beverly, for the use of the troops under your command. Several hundred arms have also been sent for the use of your command to Colonel Jackson at Harper's ferry. Several companies have been directed to go with the arms from Staunton to Beverly and to gather strength as they passed along. It is hoped that a considerable force has by this means been gathered together, which will be increased by the arrangements which you have made.[74]

On May 18, from his camp near Grafton, George wrote at least two letters: one to Emily, and one to Richmond. In his letter to Emily, George explained his situation:

> For the last week [I] had anxieties & responsibilities never before experienced by me. I was ordered here to call out volunteers and take possession of this part of the State, and I can assure you there never was greater abolitionism in any part of the United States than there is here, nor has anyone had greater opposition or more difficulties to contend with than I have had in the execution of my duties.[75]

George added that he had collected a few unarmed and undisciplined companies at that point, and that he had asked for re-enforcements. If Richmond did not send additional forces, he noted, he would be in a bad way.

In his letter to Richmond, he informed the high command of his difficulties in raising troops, and asked what he must do with traitors. General Lee responded to his letter on May 24, advising Porterfield that companies from Staunton should have reached him by now, as well as one from Harpers Ferry. Lee concluded his letter:

> I hope that the true men of that region have been encouraged to come out into the service of the State. I will write to the Commanding Officer of Harper's Ferry to give you all aid in his power, and I hope you will spare no pains to preserve the integrity of the State, and to prevent the occupation of the Balt. & Ohio Railroad by its enemies. In answer to your enquiry as to the treatment of traitors. I cannot believe that any citizen of the state will betray its interests, and hope all will unite in supporting the policy she may adopt.[76]

The following day, May 25, Governor Letcher demonstrated that he had little or no understanding of the situation facing Porterfield in the Northwestern section of the state. He proposed a bold venture to supply arms for George's fledgling army.

> When you get matters in proper condition at Grafton, take the train some night, run up to Wheeling and seize and carry away the arms recently sent to that place by Cameron, the United States Secretary of War, and use them in arming such men as may rally to your camp. Recover the State arms also recently seized by the malcontents at Kingwood.
>
> It is advisable to cut off telegraphic communication between Wheeling and Washington, so that the disaffected at the former place cannot communicate with their allies at headquarters. Establish a perfect control over the telegraph, (if kept up) so that no dispatch can pass without your knowledge and inspection before it is sent.
>
> If troops from Ohio and Pennsylvania shall be attempted to be passed on the railroad, *do not hesitate to obstruct their passage by all means in your power, even to the destruction of the road and bridges.*
>
> Having confidence in your discretion, I am sure you will manage all things wisely and well.[77]

Anticipating the governor's orders, Porterfield took steps to cut the railroad. On May 25, he ordered Colonel W. J. Wiley to take the next westbound train and destroy the railroad bridges as far west as possible as quickly as he could.[78]

Colonel Porterfield also wrote to his superiors in Richmond on the 25th of May, from Grafton. He reported that with five companies he had moved to Grafton that day, and informed the Adjutant General of the Virginia Forces of the dangers faced at that place.

> The town is badly located and laid out to be occupied by a military force. It is also surrounded by eminences of such position and extent as to require several thousand men to hold it properly. Artillery on either of these hills would fully command the town. The force now here is undisciplined, and I am greatly in need of officers acquainted with their duties. I have but two or three officers at all acquainted with their duty, and these can effect but little upon a mass of militia. The quartermasters and commissaries are also inexperienced, and this is the cause of confusion and injury to the service. Having little or no assistance, I cannot correct the numerous errors constantly arising. I am not satisfied with my position here. It is weak, untenable by such a force as this against a few pieces of artillery, and yet I cannot recommend the sending of artillery here without a sufficient infantry force to protect it, for I can assure you that if they choose the enemy can bring with them from these northern counties ten to one against us. I will do the best I can, however, under all circumstances.... At the request of citizens of this county I send this by a special messenger, Lieutenant-Colonel [Jonathan McGee] Heck, who will give their views as to the state of affairs here.[79]

Quick to reply, Lee informed Porterfield on May 27:

> I have to inform you that I have ordered one thousand muskets, with a sufficient supply of powder and lead, to Beverly, escorted by Colonel Heck and Major Cowan. Any instructions you may have for Colonel Heck, address to him at Bev-

erly. Colonel Heck has been instructed to call out all the volunteers that he can along his route.[80]

This relief force did not reach Porterfield in time to be of any assistance at Grafton or at Philippi.

Receiving information on May 27 that a large force of the enemy was moving along the Baltimore & Ohio Railroad toward Grafton, Porterfield ordered several bridges destroyed. The colonel telegraphed General Joseph E. Johnston for reinforcements, but Johnston informed him that he could not send any help from Harpers Ferry—he was on his own.

Taking in account the topography of the Grafton area, as well as the number and condition of the men under his command, George decided to fall back to Philippi, in Barbour County. He reported on May 29:

> Considering our very inadequate supply of provisions and ammunition, particularly caps, and that our number of infantry was small (not more than about five hundred and fifty), and the want of any sort of training or military discipline among our men ... I concluded to remove the State arms and stores to Philippi, about fifteen miles in our rear, there establish a depot, in a friendly country.[81]

After the Virginia troops left Grafton, Northern troops belonging to General George B. McClellan's command, occupied the railroad town. Within a few days, several thousand troops poured into Grafton, and they turned their attention to Porterfield's command at Philippi.

In an attempt to rally support for the defense of Virginia, George issued the following proclamation:

> Head-Quarters Virginia Forces,
> Phillippa [sic], Va., May 30, 1861.
>
> *To the People of Northwestern Virginia:*
>
> Fellow-Citizens: I am in your section of Virginia in obedience to the legally-constituted authorities thereof, with the view of protecting this section of the State from invasion by foreign forces, and to protect the people in the full enjoyment of their rights—civil, religious and political. In the performance of my duties, I shall endeavor to exercise every charitable forbearance, as I have hitherto done. I shall not inquire whether any citizens of Virginia voted for or against the Ordinance of Secession. My only inquiry shall and will be as to who are the enemies of our mother—the Commonwealth of Virginia. My duty impels me now to say to all that the citizens of the Commonwealth will at all times be protected by me and those under my command. Those who array themselves against the State will be treated as her enemies, according to the laws thereof.
>
> Virginians! allow me to appeal to you, in the name of our common mother, to stand by the voice of your State, and to defend her against all enemies, and especially to repel invasion from any and every quarter. Those who reside within the State, who invite invasion, or who in any manner assist, aid or abet invaders, will be treated as enemies to Virginia. I trust that no Virginian, whether native born or adopted, will refuse to defend his State and his brothers against invasion or injury. Virginians! be true, and in due time your common mother will come to your relief.

Already many of you have rallied to the support of the honor of your State and the maintenance of your liberties. Will you continue to be freemen, or will you submit to be slaves? Are you capable of governing yourselves? Will you allow the people of other States to govern you? Have you forgotten the precepts of Madison and Jefferson? Remember that the price of liberty is "eternal vigilance!" Virginia has not made war! War has been made upon her and the time honored principles. Shall she be vindicated in her efforts to maintain the liberties of her people, or shall she bow her head in submission to tyranny and oppression? It seems to me that the true friend of national liberty cannot hesitate. Strike for your State! Strike for your liberties! Rally! rally at once in defence [sic] of your mother!

G. A. Porterfield,
Colonel of Volunteers Commanding.[82]

The day after issuing the proclamation, George wrote Governor Letcher, reporting his situation and responding to the governor's orders of the 25th.

Your letter directing the seizure of arms at Wheeling and Kingwood came too late. Having received reliable information of a movement by which a large force was to be thrown upon Grafton from Wheeling & Parkersburg I had just ordered the destruction of bridges on the roads leading to those places. This destruction kept back the advance of these forces. They appeared at the burnt bridges soon after they were consumed.

Finding my position in Grafton untenable by the force at my command & knowing that a repulse would be fatal to the interests of the State in this section, I concluded to withdraw to this place. Immediately after my arrival here I sent a party of picked men & instructions to destroy the Cheat river bridge & thus save Harpers Ferry which has this moment returned without accomplishing their purpose.

I had before the receipt of your letter enquired in regard to the muskets supposed to be at Kingwood, & found they had been placed in the hands of a party under the lead of a man named Kirk & that a search for them would be almost impracticable. The rifles in Wheeling had also probably been distributed. But of this I could get no reliable information.

I have done the best I could for this command. I regret that I could not have had the aid of efficient officers and men. For want of experience both are deficient.

There are now here about 800 men — the numbers having increased within the last day or so.[83]

After reaching Philippi, Colonel Porterfield was joined by a number of companies, mostly unarmed, bringing his strength to about 800 men. The colonel took steps to arm the companies and whip them into some semblance of military organizations. To properly arm and train these men would take time; however, time was against Porterfield and his Virginians.

One of the most severe obstacles facing Porterfield was the lack of ammunition and especially musket caps. The men had only a half-dozen cartridges each, sometimes fewer, and lacking cartridge boxes, they stuffed the paper cartridges into their pockets. When needed, moisture had rendered them useless.

On the afternoon of May 31, the Rev. William T. Price met with Colonel

Porterfield. Price, who had accompanied troops from Highland County as chaplain, noted the meeting in his diary:

> I met Colonel Porterfield, and was invited to take tea with him at his quarters, and I found him a very intelligent and affable gentleman. Colonel Porterfield spoke rather despondently of the unprepared condition of Virginia to meet invasion successfully. He regretted very much the lack of order, preparation and discipline among the troops now at the front, but he hoped all might come right after a while.[84]

On the afternoon of Sunday, June 2, two young women rode into Philippi and asked to see Colonel Porterfield. They explained that a large force of Northern troops planned to attack him the next day. After listening to their story, the colonel thanked them, and went about his business.

As additional information reached the colonel, he ordered the baggage and supplies packed up, ready to leave Philippi. About sundown, Porterfield called for a meeting of his officers—a council of war. Most of the officers assembled in Porterfield's quarters, but the colonel was not there. In his absence, the officers agreed that retreat was the better part of valor, and the sooner the better. When Porterfield arrived, the officers told him of their decision.

Colonel Porterfield then advised the officers that Richmond had ordered him to establish a rendezvous at Grafton, for the purpose of holding and defending the region. It was, he said, his business "to fight and not retreat."[85] Because of the dissatisfaction expressed by some after his retreat from Grafton, which many of his subordinates recommended, he was now determined to stand and fight.

When the meeting was over, the officers returned to their companies, and settled in for a long, rainy night. As the officers were leaving the colonel's quarters, Lewis A. Phillips, of Ritchie County, arrived with additional information. This information, testified Hansbrough, probably caused Porterfield to decide to retreat during the night, unless prevented by bad weather.[86]

In 1899, Colonel Porterfield related a different account of these events. After holding the council of war on the evening of June 2, he recalled that

> there was a general understanding that we would retreat, but no time was fixed at which it should begin. Infantry pickets were posted as usual on the roads leading towards Grafton, and the cavalry officers were ordered to scout the same throughout the night. A drenching rain began near midnight and continued for several hours. The guards being without cartridge boxes, and carrying their ammunition in their pockets, which, by exposure to rain, would become wet and unserviceable, left their posts and came in without being relieved. No report was made to me during the night.[87]

Major D. B. Stewart visited Porterfield that evening, and later wrote that he was "surprised" to hear Porterfield say "he believed he would stay and give them a little brush in the morning."[88] Major Stewart reminded the colonel that

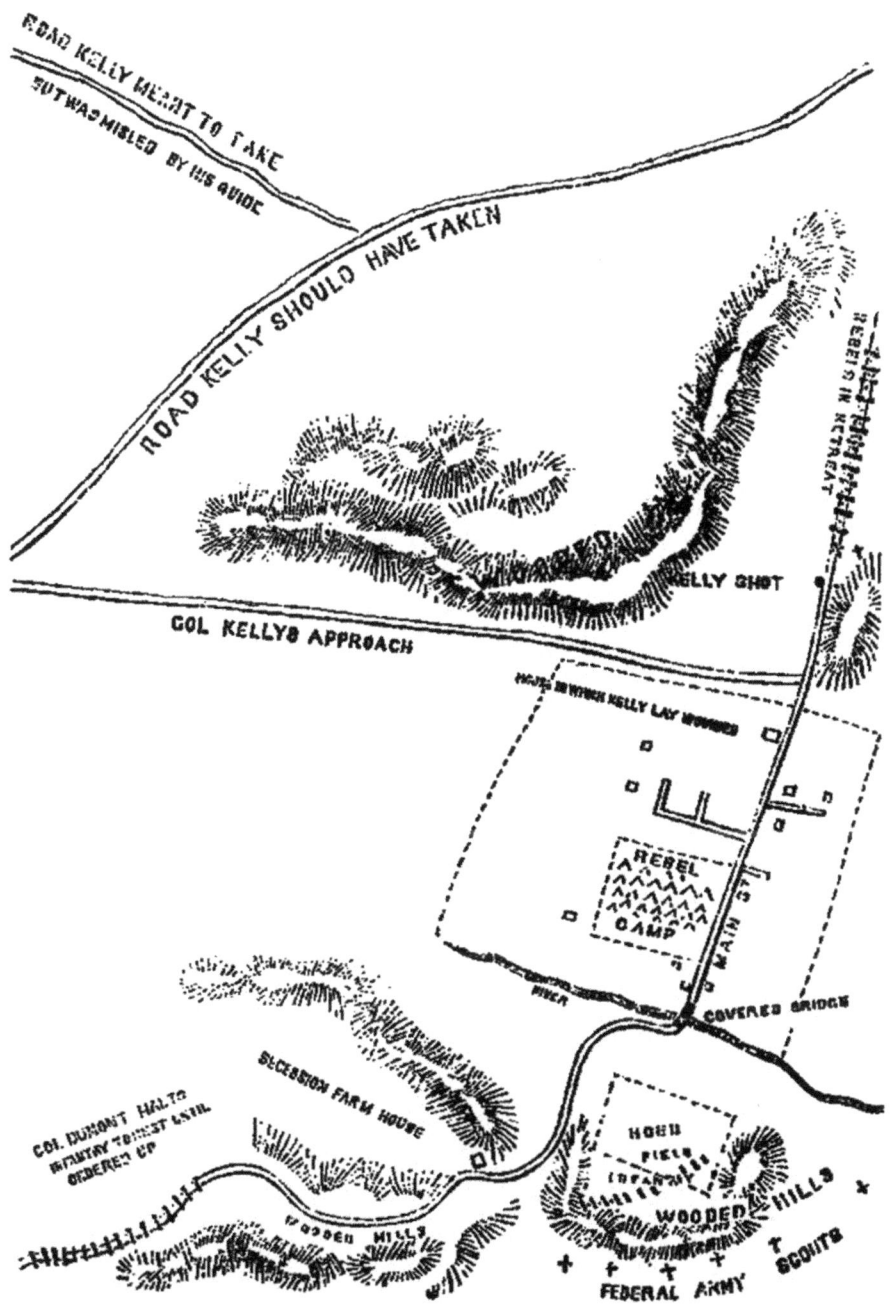

Plan of the Battle at Phillippi [*sic*], Virginia, June 3, 1861. This is considered by many to be the first land battle of the Civil War (Frank Leslie's Illustrated News, June 22, 1861).

his force was a small one and lacked sufficient ammunition to put up a fight. The colonel was determined to try it anyway.

Colonel George W. Hansbrough was correct in thinking that Phillips' information caused Porterfield's decision to retreat. Porterfield now decided to leave Philippi about midnight, unless it rained, and then the evacuation would take place at a later hour.

A hard rain began to fall about 8 or 9 P.M., and continued throughout the night. The rainfall was so hard that the Quartermaster, Captain B. J. Jordan, ordered the quartermaster and commissary stores removed from the wagons, lest they be ruined.

One officer of Porterfield's command, watching the rain beat against the window, remarked, "Hell, any army marching tonight must be made up of a set of damned fools."[89]

Through some mistake in orders, the pickets left their posts about midnight. No one in their right mind, they concluded, would be out on a night such as this. In their opinion, there would be no attack that night.

Early on the morning of June 3, about daylight (4 A.M.), the Virginians were jarred awake by the thunderous boom of cannon. Union troops, by a night march, had brought two guns into position on the heights overlooking the town. In addition, two columns of infantry were moving into position, with the intention of catching Porterfield's little army between them and annihilating it.

The rush was on. The Virginia troops left Philippi in a disorganized mass, without any order from Colonel Porterfield, moving south toward Beverly.

When the firing began, Lieutenant Chenowith reported to Colonel Porterfield that the enemy was upon them with their artillery. Colonel Porterfield continued to dress in a calm, collected manner, remarking, "Indeed, is that the case?" Porterfield then asked the lieutenant to order the companies to form in front of their quarters.[90]

Porterfield then went to the stable, saddled his horse, and rode into the main street. Meeting his quartermaster in the street, he asked, "Captain Jordan, where are the troops?"[91]

Jordan explained that the troops had passed off to the left. Glancing in that direction, Porterfield took note of a number of soldiers in the street, all dressed in blue. He then began to ride toward them.

On the morning of the attack, Stewart went out in front of the hotel, found Porterfield mounted and in the street, facing the road leading to town from the direction of Grafton.[92] He could see the enemy troops marching into the town, and started riding toward them. Stewart, believing the colonel was making a mistake, rode out to join him, asking if he was close enough to the enemy. Porterfield responded, "O, no, those are our own men." Stewart then inquired if the colonel had noticed that the troops were marching under the Stars and Stripes. Porterfield then exclaimed, "Why, yes, and the blue uniform." All the while, the two officers continued toward the enemy. When within a hundred and fifty feet of them — near enough to see the brass buttons on their uniforms — Porterfield turned his horse and rode out of town, followed by Stewart and Acting Adjutant Robert Johnston.[93] These three were the last of the command to leave the town.

An account of the events of the morning of June 3 appeared in the *Staunton Spectator* and was less than flattering to the colonel.

> They [Virginia troops] found to their utter surprise and amazement that the enemy, in overwhelming force, had "caught them napping," and were cordially bidding them "good-morning" in the strong voice of deep-mouthed cannon. The Commandant, Col. Porterfield, looked out of the window, witnessed the cordial greeting the enemy was bestowing upon our men, and with a wise appreciation of their good fortune, gave the command, "Run, boys, run!" and as they had learned the first duty of the soldier, they promptly, and with commendable alacrity, obeyed the command of their superior officer.[94]

In contrast, the description of Porterfield that morning, given by Quartermaster Captain B. J. Jordan, was most favorable.

> The conduct of Colonel Porterfield was perfectly cool, calm and collected, and from his conduct that morning, I felt increased confidence in his bravery & courage. I considered him entirely fearless, so far as his own person was concerned.[95]

Captain Jordan noted that Porterfield seemed determined to halt the men and make a fight of it.

All of the baggage and quartermaster stores fell into the hands of the enemy. Among the baggage captured at Philippi, were Colonel Porterfield's headquarters papers and personal trunks.

Several newspapers throughout Virginia reported that Porterfield was among those killed at Philippi. This was, of course, an error, but the reports certainly caused some distress to Emily and her family.

Accompanying the Northern troops at Philippi was Captain Henry W. Benham, an officer in the Engineer Department. "I had known the rebel commander (Col. Porterfield) in Mexico," wrote Benham, "as adjutant of Hamtramck's Virginia regiment, and esteemed him so much, that I had, years afterwards, given him a clerkship in Washington."[96]

Benham discovered that Colonel Porterfield's personal baggage was among the captured property. He noted, "We neither wished to pillage nor retain [the baggage], as our men had not, at this time, their appetites whetted for plunder."[97]

Captain Benham asked General Thomas A. Morris, at Grafton, for permission to return the baggage to Porterfield. Upon approval of Morris and McClellan, Benham selected a "shrewd, confident officer, with a few men and a wagon" to take it to Beverly. Benham continued:

> I regret to say that I received in answer a letter from Porterfield, which, though very civil otherwise, was not entirely ingenuous, denying, as it did that the trunk

was his own. On which I replied to him that it contained his commission as colonel, military books with his name in them, and the hat and epaulets of his rank. This commission I had retained; and subsequently, in August, I received a letter from his wife at Martinsburg, Va., on our border-lines, which requested the return of that commission; while she enclosed me the proceedings of a court of inquiry upon her husband for this flight from Philippi.[98]

Soon after this article appeared in 1873, Porterfield wrote a rebuttal, calling Benham a former friend, who had slandered him. The nature of the dispute between the two old soldiers is unknown.

Despite Benham's claim that the Union troops did not plunder Porterfield's personal trunks, there is undisputed proof to the contrary. Among the Abraham Lincoln Papers at the Library of Congress, is a letter addressed to Mrs. E. C. Porterfield, Leetown, Jefferson Co., Va. In the corner of the letter is a notation that indicates the letter was "Captured with Col. Porterfield's baggage at Phllipi [sic], Va. June 3 1861. H. W. Benham, Capt. of Eng."[99]

Lieutenant B. C. Shaw, of Company F, 7th Indiana Infantry, recalled:

> Col. Porterfield's private trunks, including a fine new uniform, with large gold bullion epaulets, and a fine sword recently presented to him, as I remember it, by the ladies of Buckhannon, Va., the value of the capture became apparent. The sword and uniform were returned to the owner, under a flag of truce, and a day or two later, with his private papers, but the official ones were sent to the General commanding at Grafton.[100]

An account of the Philippi affair, appearing in a Philadelphia newspaper, noted, "The hat and epauletts of Colonel Porterfield, the Secession commander, were picked up in the road."[101] It would seem that the Union men had indeed plundered the colonel's trunks, but Captain Benham recovered many of the articles.

Captain Chase, one of the Indiana soldiers, returned the trunks of Colonel Porterfield. Upon meeting Porterfield near Beverly, Chase reported that the colonel "complained blisterly [sic] of his luck and laid the blame entirely on his officers. These," Porterfield complained, "were drunk about 28 hours in the day." Chase concluded that the affair at Philippi had ruined Porterfield.[102]

From Beverly on the morning of June 3, a Randolph County company broke camp and started to Porterfield's assistance. They met his retreating men near Laurel Hill and learned the details of the attack. The disorganized soldiers told the Randolph men that "Col. Porterfield ... had allowed his camp to be completely surprised and routed about day-break. The men regarded this as criminal carelessness; indeed there was so much indignation, that some feared the Col's life was in danger at the hands of his own men."[103]

James N. Potts, one of the Randolph Company, recalled: "I found much bitter feeling among the boys toward Col. Porterfield for what they called criminal carelessness in allowing the enemy to surprise them. If these brave boys had been properly officered they would have put up a stiff fight, but as it was only a running skirmish."[104]

The men were correct in their belief that had they been properly officered they would have fought. The proper officers should have been those in command of the individual companies. Their inexperience, coupled with the opinion that it was all a lark and would quickly be over, led to the disaster at Philippi.

Another soldier, John H. Cammack, recalled the feelings and the events of June 3:

> The plans were very beautifully laid for our capture, and it did seem that Col. Porterfield could hardly have managed our affairs to suit the Federals better, had he been working to that end.
>
> As we went out of town, and when near the timber on the road I found myself near Col. Porterfield. I walked some distance close to his horse. He gave no orders, and seemed to be utterly unconcerned about his men or for his own personal safety.[105]

Also present at Philippi that morning was David Poe, a native of Taylor County, Virginia. Writing fifty years after the fact, Poe noted that the events at Philippi made the "Virginians believe (and we will always believe) that we were sold out. We were so strong in that belief that Col. Porterfield could not command us again."[106]

The first reports of the disaster at Philippi reached Staunton on June 6, brought by two men by the names of Spalding and Cook. Major M. G. Harman, the Quartermaster at that post, immediately telegraphed a report to Richmond, marked to the attention of Governor Letcher or General Lee. A second telegram from Harman, similarly addressed, called the affair "a disgraceful route" and called for Porterfield's replacement.[107]

In the flurry of telegrams that Major Harman sent to Richmond on June 6, he reported that Porterfield's command had but little ammunition of any kind. The major noted that a wagon train of supplies and several companies of re-enforcements would leave Staunton at 10 o'clock on June 7, picking up additional volunteers along the way.

Among the dispatches that Harman sent to Richmond that day was one addressed to General Lee personally. Harman wrote:

> From all the information that I have received I am pained to have to express my conviction that Colonel Porterfield is entirely unequal to the position which he occupies. The affair at Philippi was a disgraceful surprise, occurring about daylight, there being no picket guard or guard of any kind on duty. The only wonder is that our men were not cut to pieces. They were all asleep, and were only aroused by the firing of the enemy. The safety of the Northwest and of our inexperienced soldiers depends upon an immediate change of commanders, and giving the command to a bold and experienced leader.[108]

A number of other telegrams were sent to Richmond on June 6, all calling for the replacement of Porterfield as commander. The northwest needed an officer of experience. Lieutenant Normount worded his telegram rather strongly: "Every body wants Genl. [Thomas Turner] Fauntleroy here, can he come—there is indignation against Porterfields conduct. Sheffey, Hill, Skinner and others demand Genl. Fautleroy."[109]

Harman also informed Porterfield that a supply of ammunition was on the way, along with artillery, cavalry and infantry. Additional troops would join the column along the way. He promised reinforcements from President Davis would soon follow. He forwarded a message from General Lee, telling Porterfield "to be valiant and maintain his ground until relief reaches him."[110]

Porterfield made his first report from Huttonsville, on the 9th, reporting the strength and condition of his command. He wrote that he had at Beverly about a thousand men, of which 180 were cavalry.

> This force is not only deficient in drill, but ignorant, both officers and men, of the most ordinary duties of the soldier. With efficient drill officers they might be made effective; but I have to complain that the field officers sent to command these men are of no assistance to me, and are, for the most part, as ignorant of their duties as the company officers, and they as ignorant as the men.[111]

Porterfield added, "My own reputation has been injured by the character of my command; in fact, if it had been intended to sacrifice me, I could not have expected less support than I have had."[112]

Indeed, George's reputation had suffered serious injury. Charles B. Hopkins, a resident of Healing Springs, in Bath County, Virginia, wrote to President Jefferson Davis on June 10, 1861, concerning the general feeling in Bath and surrounding counties regarding Porterfield. Hopkins wrote:

> When I reflect upon the actions and conduct of Col. Porterfield at Phillippi [sic] and the transactions since his retreat from there, I am like many others led to fear that all is not right, and tremble for the lives of our noble hearted men, he (Porterfield) having sufficient and ample notice given him of the approach of the enemy, two Ladies having ridden some forty miles to give the alarm, he suffered his men to retire to rest, placed as the Captain of the Gard [sic] a notorious drunkard who called the Gard [sic] in before eleven o'clock the consequence was they were taken by surprise, made a most miraculous escape, in only losing their baggage, ammunition, and some of their arms, after their retreat Col. Porterfield's Trunk &c., his individual property was sent to him, we think that such actions should be examined into closely and that at once without delay, as we all believe that his appointment was through the persuasion and influence of his Farther [sic]—in—law Wm. Terrill of this County, in whom the people generally has no kind of Confidence, he being too slow in taking sides with the South, and having expressed his opinion at different times too freely in opposition to the intrusts [sic] and actions of the South, and at this time has a son an acting officer in the Northern Army, the people being generally very suspicious of his motives.[113]

Colonel Porterfield wrote General Garnett on June 11, reporting the conditions in the northwest and complaining about the lack of proper supplies.

> I have never received any other than the most limited supplies from that place [Staunton]. The percussion caps sent have nearly all been of small size for shot-

guns and not large enough for muskets. As re-enforcements are now expected, and we shall have active service in this part of the State, I desire to be continued on duty here. It was not until after repeated calls for aid, and when left with a small militia force entirely unprepared for the field, that I asked for duty elsewhere.[114]

The re-enforcements mentioned by Porterfield were then at Hevener's Store, in Highland County, Virginia. Lieutenant Colonel Heck, commanding the expedition, wrote that 300 volunteers from the militia joined the expedition, bringing the total to about 700 men. The balance of the militia assembled at that point returned to their homes.[115] One of the companies added by Heck was the Bath Grays, in which Philip M. Terrill was serving as 1st Lieutenant.

Brigadier General Robert S. Garnett was on the way to Huttonsville to take command of the Virginia troops now under Porterfield. The general reported his progress to Confederate Adjutant General Samuel Cooper on June 13 and requested that Cooper send him several experienced officers. He was, it seems, beginning to understand the obstacles faced by Porterfield.

That same day General Lee responded to Porterfield's letter of the 9th. "I regret," wrote Lee, "much the unfortunate circumstances with which you have been beset, and appreciate the difficulties you have had to encounter.... Your services will be very valuable to General Garnett, in giving him information as to the state of affairs in the country under his command, and in aiding him to achieve the object of his campaign."[116]

General Garnett arrived at Huttonsville on June 14 and assumed command. He at once set about creating order out of the chaos he found there. At that time, there were twenty-three companies of infantry reported for duty, all miserably armed and equipped. From these, Garnett formed two regiments and a battalion. Ten companies became the 25th Virginia Infantry, with Lieutenant Colonel Jonathan M. Heck in command. Rightfully, the regiment should have belonged to Colonel Porterfield. A general order dated June 1, 1861, placed Colonel Porterfield in command of that regiment upon its organization.[117]

As Garnett lacked confidence in Porterfield's abilities, he was reluctant to give him command of the regiment. Instead, the general assigned him to command the post at Beverly, where Garnett established his supply depot.

More than fifty years after the war, Porterfield commented on his being relieved of command. "I had no objection to being relieved. I filled the position I had because I had been ordered to. I would at the first have preferred it had been given to some one else." In another account, he said that Garnett assigned him to the "unimportant command of Beverly."[118]

General Garnett marched from Huttonsville on the evening of June 15 to occupy the passes at Rich Mountain and Laurel Hill. General Garnett sent the 25th Virginia Infantry to occupy the pass on Rich Mountain, while the remainder of the troops accompanied him to Laurel Hill.

Soon after Garnett's arrival at Huttonsville, George asked for a court of inquiry to examine the circumstances of his surprise at Philippi. He first requested the court of inquiry on June 13, by writing to the Adjutant General of the Virginia Forces. Two days later, June 15, he made the same request to Captain James L. Corley, Garnett's Assistant Adjutant General.[119] General Garnett agreed and ordered the court to convene at Beverly on June 20.

The court was composed of Colonel William B. Taliaferro, Lieutenant Colonel John Pegram, and Captain Julius A. DeLagnal, and met behind closed doors in Beverly. Over the course of three days, the court examined ten officers and five civilians, with George asking questions on his own behalf. A transcript of the proceedings, along with the findings of the court, was prepared and sent to General Garnett. Adding his decision to the record, Garnett forwarded the documents to General Lee in Richmond.

Porterfield sent a copy of the proceedings, minus the testimony, to Colonel F. H. Smith, on June 26. Again, Porterfield placed the fault with his officers, assuming none of the responsibility himself.

> No one acquainted with the condition of N. W. Virginia from the time of my arrival in it, can form any idea of the difficulties against which I had to contend. My surprise was the fault of my officers, not of mine.
>
> I do not know upon what grounds Gen. Garnett considers a Court Martial necessary. It may be that he is influenced by the numerous false reports which have been circulated against me. The *truth* I do not fear. Nothing but *falsehood* do I shrink from in such matters.
>
> I have been peculiarly unfortunate in being sent to this part of the State. My appointment was based upon the application of several companies from my native county, who knew me and wished me to command them. With them I would have preferred to serve. But being ordered here, I obeyed. A succession of retreats before an overpowering foe, or disaster has been inevitable, & I would have been censured alike for the one or the other. I must meet the consequences whatever they may be. I would much have preferred to die by the enemies hands at Grafton, than have been wounded as I have been by my own State.[120]

The Headquarters of the Forces, in Richmond, published the findings of the court of inquiry on July 4, 1861. The opinions expressed by the court and by General Robert E. Lee, placed the fault with the commanding officer — Colonel Porterfield. The members of the court wrote:

> 1st. That the commanding officer, having received information, deemed by him sufficient to prepare for an early retreat, erred in permitting himself to be influenced by the weather, so far as to delay the execution of his plan.
>
> 2d. That the commanding officer did order dispositions to be made to prevent surprise; but a misunderstanding as to the time at which the scouts were to be called in, and a total want of proper vigilance on the part of the infantry pickets, caused a surprise, which distinct and definite instructions, properly executed, would have avoided.
>
> 3d. That the commanding officer erred in not advancing and strengthening his picket beyond the usual limits under the circumstances.
>
> 4th. That the commanding officer exhibited upon the occasion decided coolness,

self-possession, and personal courage, and exerted himself, as far as possible, to effect a retreat in good order."[121]

General Lee, after reading the proceedings of the court of inquiry, carefully deliberated the proper course of action to take with Porterfield. He agreed with the opinions expressed by the court of inquiry, and felt they were supported by the testimony given. Lee then complimented Colonel Porterfield for his "coolness, self-possession, courage, and energy displayed" at Philippi.[122]

Not wishing to deal with Porterfield too harshly, General Lee decided to let the published opinions of the court of inquiry serve as punishment in this case. He hoped "that the sad effects produced by the want of forethought and vigilance ... [would] be a lesson to be remembered by the army throughout the war."[123]

Soon after the conclusion of the Court of Inquiry, but before its findings reached Richmond, the Virginia Convention withheld confirmation of Porterfield's appointment as Colonel. Through the efforts of Colonel Smith and Governor Letcher, the convention confirmed the nomination. The governor informed the members of the convention that he had reliable information from Beverly that the court of inquiry had honorably acquitted Colonel Porterfield.[124]

On July 11, 1861, the Southern forces suffered a disastrous defeat at Rich Mountain, near Beverly, in Randolph County. The forces there, commanded by Lieutenant Colonel John Pegram, retreated and scattered into the mountains. Colonel Pegram surrendered a large portion of his command on July 13 at Beverly, including about half of Porterfield's 25th Virginia Infantry.

At dusk on July 11, General Garnett and his army evacuated the fortifications at Laurel Hill. It is likely that Porterfield carried word of the Rich Mountain fight to Laurel Hill, and then accompanied Garnett on the retreat. In a 1904 letter, George stated: "I was with Garnett's command when he began his retreat, at dusk on the evening of July 11th, also when he turned down the St. George road, about two hours later."[125]

His movements after leaving Garnett are unknown. General Garnett was killed and his army scattered into the wilderness on July 13 at Corricks Ford in Tucker County.

The following month as the Southern forces moved westward again, the Army of the Northwest fell under the command of Brigadier General William Wing Loring. General Loring chose Colonel Porterfield to be his chief of ordnance on August 9, 1861.

From the events of the summer of 1861, one can form a mental image of Colonel Porterfield. Here was a man with a military education, who served with distinction during the Mexican War, in a clerical position (Adjutant). He also worked as a teacher, editor of a newspaper, and in the drawing division of the U.S. Coast Survey office. He desired a position of authority and command. He got his chance in May 1861 when Governor Letcher gave him a commission as colonel and sent him to Western Virginia. His occupations of Grafton and Philippi both ended in retreat, the latter causing serious damage to his career. Afterward, Garnett assigned him to command the post at Beverly, and General Loring detailed him as Ordnance Officer; both positions required huge amounts of paperwork.

Colonel Porterfield was angry and frustrated about the situation into which the Richmond authorities had thrust him. The people and press of Eastern Virginia severely censured his actions, as did the soldiers of his own command. Perhaps he took out his frustrations on those around him, as exhibited by Lieutenant Potts' encounter with him at Valley Mountain. The lieutenant wrote:

> I remember going to the ordinance officer one evening to get some cartridges for some men who had been ordered to the front. I was wearing a plain jacket, without any marks to show that I was an officer, and the officer treated me roughly, and as I thought, ungentlemanly; but I persisted and told him I was in a hurry and must be waited on without delay. Whereupon he ordered me very roughly to go back to my quarters and tell the commandant of the company to either come for the ammunition in person or send a requisition. Well sir, I said I have already taken that precaution and had him to come for it himself. He said, "who is in command of your company?" I replied I enjoy that distinction myself sir. Oh, said he, is this Lieutenant Potts? Lieutenant, I beg your pardon sir." I was provoked at the man, and told him that a private soldier who had enlisted in his Country's service was entitled to decent treatment as well as any other man, and that it was my opinion that a man who could not treat a private soldier in a gentlemanly manner was not fit for any official position in the army. I learned afterwards that this officer was Col. Porterfield, who three months ago had so ingloriously and precipitately fled before the enemy from Philippi.[126]

In early August 1861, General Robert E. Lee joined the Confederate forces on Valley Mountain. He drafted a plan to drive the Union forces back and reclaim the vital Staunton to Parkersburg and the Huttonsville to Huntersville turnpikes. The plan required the coordination of two simultaneous attacks by five separate columns of troops. Two columns would attack Cheat Summit from the Confederate position on the Greenbrier River at Camp Bartow. Once the attack commenced, three additional columns would move against Cheat Summit, Cheat Mountain Pass, and Elkwater from Lee's position at Mingo Flats. The attack was set to begin on September 12.

To put it simply, the plan failed. The enemy forced the troops from Camp Bartow to retire before they reached the fortifications on the lofty Cheat Summit. At Mingo Flats, the Confederates made a half-hearted attack on the Federal position at Elkwater, and were easily repulsed. This failure seriously damaged Lee's reputation, and earned him the nickname of "Granny" Lee.

The following day, September 13 (a Friday), a reconnoitering party was sent out to examine the enemy position near the mouth of Elkwater. Major Fitzhugh Lee, one of Lee's sons, commanded the detachment of cavalry ordered on the expedition. Lieutenant Colonel John Augustine Washington, an aide on

Lee's staff, requested permission to go along. Reluctantly, Lee consented, and Washington set out with great excitement.

The Confederates advanced cautiously to a high point overlooking the mouth of Elkwater Fork, from which Lee made his observations. Clearly visible in the distance was a lone horseman, identified as a Federal picket. His observations complete, Lee started back to camp, but Washington interrupted. He urged Lee to rush the lone soldier and take him prisoner. Lee was hesitant, but outranked and swayed by Washington's enthusiasm, finally agreed. Taking two enlisted men with them, Lee and Washington dashed off.

As the Southerners clattered along the road, the sound of their horses reached the ears of a scouting party from the 17th Indiana Infantry. Concealed by the thick underbrush along the road, the men turned toward the sound, and caught sight of the riders. Identifying them as rebels, they at once opened fire at a distance of about 20 yards. Their aim was true, and three balls struck Colonel Washington in the back, knocking him from his horse. The same volley killed Major Lee's horse, and wounded one of the men accompanying them. Major Lee quickly arose and caught Washington's horse, and escaped on it.

The men of the 17th Indiana rushed out into the road, to the side of the fallen officer, who still clung to life. The stricken Washington exclaimed, "My God, give me a drink!" The Indianans granted his request, and while they prepared to take him to their camp, he died. Washington lived about fifteen minutes after being wounded.[127]

The Northerners carried Colonel Washington's body to the quarters of Colonel Waggoner, where they examined it. From the evidence gathered from his personal possessions and some bloodstained letters, it was quickly determined that this was the body of John A. Washington. Word spread quickly throughout the camp that the traitor and relative of George Washington had been killed.

On the morning of September 14, Washington's body was placed in an ambulance, to be sent to the Confederate lines. A small guard, under a flag of truce, accompanied the ambulance. After going about a mile, they met Colonel Porterfield with a small party of men, also under a flag of truce, sent out to ascertain the fate of Washington. The escort turned over Washington's remains to them, and Porterfield took the body to General Lee's camp.

Upon learning of Washington's fate, Lee was much saddened. In a letter to Governor Letcher, Lee wrote: "His zeal for the cause to which he devoted himself carried him, I fear, too far."[128] The general made preparations to send Washington's body to his family at Charles Town, in Jefferson County.

The sad duty of conveying Washington's body to Charles Town fell to Colonel Porterfield. One must wonder whether Lee detailed him for the duty or if he volunteered for the opportunity to visit his own family. Nevertheless, the journey planted seeds of friendship, which eventually joined the two families, when Serena Porterfield married George Washington in 1886.[129]

In early November 1861, on the 3rd, Porterfield wrote General Lee from Huntersville, in Pocahontas County, Virginia. "I would like to be assigned to duty in the spring or earlier, with the army of the Valley."[130] He made this request because he was well acquainted with that part of the state. His request fell upon deaf ears.

Later in November, on the 20th, General Loring wrote the War Department, asking for the consolidation of the remnants of the 25th Virginia Infantry and Colonel George W. Hansbrough's 9th Battalion into a full regiment and that Porterfield be given command of it. The consolidation required the approval of Governor Letcher, who refused to approve it, and no action was taken on the request. "This refusal," wrote Porterfield, "of course, was mortifying to me, as I wanted the command of a regiment."[131]

When the soldiers of Hansbrough's Battalion learned of the proposed consolidation, and that Porterfield would again command them, the officers called a meeting. After some discussion, a resolution was prepared and forwarded to the secretary of war: "Resolved — That we have tried the bravery and know the generosity and kindness of some of our officers now in command and most of us having at one time been under the command of Col. G. A. Porterfield, are positively opposed to going under him again."[132]

Undaunted, Porterfield appealed directly to Governor Letcher on December 14, from Staunton:

> Gen'l Loring by letter to the War Dept dated the 20th ult. recommended the formation of a new regiment from odd battalions & companies of the North Western army & my assignment to the command of it by the Secretary of war. This has not yet been acted upon by the War Dept.
>
> Since this recommendation was made, the officers of the 31st Va. Regt (lately Reynolds & Jackson's) have petitioned for my assignment to their command — which petition I enclose. The General considers that this assignment should be made by you.
>
> As the regiment to which I was assigned the 25th was surrendered by Pegram in the Rich Mountain, I am left without one & have to request that you will either assign me to the 31st which I would prefer or have me assigned by the War Dept. to the new one proposed as recommended by Gen. Loring.[133]

The governor ignored Porterfield's plea and petition.

In the winter of 1861 and 1862, Porterfield accompanied Loring and his army to Winchester and Romney. There he met General Thomas J. "Stonewall" Jackson. After participating in an operation near Bath, Morgan County, Virginia, Jackson offered Porterfield a position on his staff. Porterfield refused, stating he liked Loring and did not wish to leave his staff.

Not long afterward, Loring and Jackson had a falling out, and the War Department assigned Loring to duty elsewhere. Before leaving the Army of the Northwest on February 9, 1862, Loring granted Porterfield a leave of absence, to expire the following month.

At Winchester, Colonel Porterfield reported for duty on March 5 by letter to Adjutant General Samuel Cooper. Making a trip to Richmond, the colonel again brought up the topic of a regiment to command. On the 26th, Porterfield asked the War Department to again consider the consolidation of the remnants of the 25th Virginia and Hansbrough's Battalion, and that he be given command of the regiment.

General Cooper wrote on April 3 that he believed the two units could not legally be consolidated. He noted that Colonel Porterfield still commanded the 25th Regiment, and by all rights, could take charge of the remnants of that regiment. If necessary, Cooper noted, he would issue an order to that effect.

Porterfield rejoined the Army of the Northwest on Shenandoah Mountain, east of McDowell, before April 15. Four days later, Colonel Edward Johnson, commanding the Army of the Northwest, left Shenandoah Mountain to meet with "Stonewall" Jackson near Harrisonburg. In his absence, the senior colonel — George A. Porterfield — was in command.

There was an order from General Robert E. Lee, in which the general gave specific instructions for Johnson to fall back to Staunton if the enemy forced Jackson to fall back to Swift Run Gap. Porterfield, of course, would have had access to this order, as well as to the many rumors coming in from Staunton. Information was at hand that Stonewall Jackson had indeed fallen back to Swift Run Gap, making it easier for Northern troops to move against the rear of the Confederates at Shenandoah Mountain. Porterfield gave the order to retreat shortly after Johnson left the camp. The soldiers destroyed a great quantity of military stores and personal property, and the Army of the Northwest fell back to Valley Mills and West View, a few miles west of Staunton.[134]

After conferring with Jackson at Swift Run Gap, Johnson started back to Shenandoah Mountain. He was greatly surprised to find his army had abandoned their camp and was now near Staunton.

Johnson reorganized his command on April 21, dividing it into two brigades. He assigned Colonel Porterfield to command the First Brigade, which was composed of the 12th Georgia Infantry, 25th Virginia Infantry, 31st Virginia Infantry, and Hansbrough's 9th Battalion. The 8th Star Artillery, from New Market, was also attached to Porterfield's brigade. Colonel John Brown Baldwin, a 42-year-old attorney from Staunton, commanded the Second Brigade.[135] The following day, Johnson reassigned the New Market Company to Baldwin's Brigade, and ordered the Lynchburg Lee Battery to join Porterfield's Brigade.[136]

Four days after George took command of the brigade, Johnson took the bold step of consolidating the 25th Virginia and the 9th Battalion. This move, later declared illegal by the War Department, was what was best for Johnson's army at the time. Finally, George had his long awaited command.

The one year term of enlistment for many of the men of Southern army had expired, or was about to. Johnson had already reorganized his command,

and ordered elections held on May 1 to select new officers at the company and regimental levels. As colonel of the 25th Virginia Infantry, George faced re-election. Many officers were not re-elected to their commands. Colonel Porterfield was one of these. Porterfield wrote later that he was not re-elected "by what remained of my regiment on account of the schemes of others for my position."[137]

Edward Johnson took it upon himself to help Porterfield. He wrote to the War Department, asking that the Secretary of War grant Porterfield a commission as Brigadier General. He referred to Porterfield as "a meritorious officer ... well deserving of promotion."[138] The War Department took no action upon Johnson's request.

Porterfield now applied for a position in the government. He commented in his application, "I have been of late in command of a Brigade in the Northwest army, in which position Gen. Johnson wishes me retained."[139] Once again, he failed.

This was the final blow to Porterfield's career. Feeling that the authorities had mistreated him since the beginning of the war, combined with his failure to be re-elected, and win promotion, Porterfield decided to retire from military service. Accordingly, he returned to his home in Jefferson County, and remained there for the remainder of the war. In June 1908, Porterfield wrote: "Having thus been left out of the service from no fault of mine, and my family being in the country and unprotected, I concluded to remain out."[140]

Major General Nathan Banks ordered George's arrest in June 1862, soon after he returned home, because of his service in the Confederate States Army. General Banks released Porterfield on parole, allowing him to return home. One of the conditions of his parole and release confined him to the house-yard of his home, which he could not leave without permission.

On August 9, George wrote to his old comrade Major General John E. Wool and explained that during his absence from home, the U.S.

Colonel George Alexander Porterfield (c. 1895) (courtesy Virginia Military Institute Archives).

Army had taken much of his property. He stated, "There are not enough horses on the farm for its cultivation several have been taken by the U.S. Army." He asked General Wool for some security for his property, to prevent further seizure. He concluded his plea for protection, telling the general of their recent loss. "I and my family are in deep distress having just buried my eldest son, a bright & promising boy of twelve years, who was accidentally shot by a playmate a few days ago."[141]

When the war ended in 1865, George was ruined and in debt. As he could no longer make a living on the farm, he moved his family to Charles Town about 1870. There, he became the secretary of the Valley Fire Insurance Company. The following year, at his suggestion, the company became the Bank of Charles Town, where George worked as a cashier until 1900. In addition to his duties at the Bank of Charles Town, George served the people of Jefferson County as general receiver of the Circuit Court for 25 years.

In April 1887, George applied to the United States Government for a pension based on his service during the Mexican War. The pension was granted, and under the act of January 29, 1887, George began received the sum of $8.00 per month in June 1887.

After the death of Emily in 1906, Porterfield lived by himself. By 1910, his widowed daughter, Serena Washington, had returned home, and lived with her father until his death on February 27, 1919. Porterfield's death was attributed to debility, due to extreme old age — he was 96 years old when he died.[142] He is buried in the Green Hill Cemetery, in Martinsburg, W. Va., beside his wife, Emily, and son William.

COL. GEORGE A. PORTERFIELD DEAD
Last W. Va. Veteran of Mexican War
Answers Last Roll [C]all.

Col. George Alexander Porterfield the last surviving veteran of the Mexican War in West Virginia, and the oldest alumnus of the Virginia Military Institute died at his home in Charles Town, Thursday morning, February 27. Debility due to extreme age caused a gradual decline in his physical powers, making his death a reasonable expectation at any time within the past two or three years.

Col. Porterfield was born in Berkeley County, Virginia, now West Virginia, November 24, 1822. On the 24th of last November he celebrated his 96th birthday anniversary.

The Mexican war coming within a few years of his graduation from the Virginia Military Institute, he in association with Capt. Corrington, organized a company of Infantry in Richmond. He was made adjutant of the regiment upon the completion of its organization. Later in the war he served as assistant adjutant under General Wool. In the War between the States he served in the Confederate army, undergoing the hardships and perils of many campaigns.

The war over, Col. Porterfield became a farmer, residing for some years near Leetown. In 1871 he with others organized the Bank of Charles Town, the first banking institution to open for business in this county after the war between the States. He became its first cashier, and continued in that position until he was 75

Gravestone of George A. Porterfield and Emily Terrill Porterfield, Green Hill Cemetery, Martinsburg, West Virginia (author's photograph).

years old, keenly alive to the bank's interest at an age when most men are in retirement.

Holding a membership in the Aztec Club, composed of veterans of the Mexican War in Washington, he found much pleasure in attending its meetings in his old age, mingling with the men who were with him in the invasion of Mexico in 1847–48. His death leaves only two members of that Club surviving.

Col. Porterfield is survived by two sons, Mr. John Porterfield, present cashier of the Bank of Charles Town, and Mr. Charles Porterfield, editor in the Thompson law book publishing company at Northport, Long Island, New York; and two daughters, Mrs. W. Chase Morton, of Richmond, Va., and Mrs. George Washington, of Charles Town. The funeral was held on Friday, with a short service at Col. Porterfield's home. The body was taken to Martinsburg for interment.[143]

Chapter IV

William Rufus Terrill

William Rufus Terrill
1834–1862

The female majority in the family changed while the Terrills still lived in Covington. Elizabeth gave birth to a new son on April 21, 1834,[1] whom they named William Rufus Terrill. He would prove to be both a source of pride and heartache to his father.

William R. Terrill received his early education from the Classical and Mathematical School, operated by Pike Powers, in Staunton, Virginia. In 1848, William's father tried to find a place for him in the mercantile business but failed. The elder Terrill then turned his attention to the United States Military Academy at West Point, New York, and called upon his powerful acquaintances to obtain an appointment for his son.

Congressman William B. Preston placed the name of William R. Terrill on the list of applicants for appointment in December 1848. General Joseph G. Totten, commanding the U.S. Army Engineer Corps, which oversees the military academy, followed up and requested additional information about young Terrill.

William H. Terrill responded:

> The name of my son is William R. [Terrill.] He will be sixteen on the 20 April next, of good size, more than five feet high, is free from any deformity, disease or impurity and in short possess all the qualifications, mental and physical, prescribed by the Secretary of War for the admission of Cadets into the Military Academy.[2]

The description of William given above leaves out two important features—the color of his hair and eyes. A better description appeared in his obituary, published in February 1863, noting that William "was of good stature and well formed. His hair was flaxen and waving; his eyes a tender blue, his complexion rich, and his whole expression kind and gentle, but downright and decided."[3]

President Zachary Taylor conferred a conditional appointment as Cadet in the service of the United States upon William Rufus Terrill in February 1849.

William accepted the appointment from the 12th Congressional District of Virginia on April 9, 1849. His father gave his consent for his son to sign the contract, which would bind him to serve the United States for a period of eight years, unless sooner discharged.[4]

The Military Academy

William began his military career on June 16, 1849, when he arrived at West Point. He reported to the Captain overseeing new cadets, and received his room assignment. William shared room 49 with fellow candidates Owen Fort Solomon, Connaly T. Litchfield, and William P. Craighill.[5]

He arrived in time to help prepare for the summer camp, which included putting up tents. On June 24, he appeared before a medical review board, another step in the process of becoming a cadet. The review board recorded the result of this examination as follows:

Born: Virginia
Residence: Virginia
Age: 16 years, 2 months

U.S. Military Academy, West Point, New York, in 1861 (courtesy U.S.M.A. Archives).

Height: 5 feet 7 inches
Axillary Measure of Chest: 32 inches
Vaccine Mark: distinct
Vision: good.[6]

In the middle of October 1849, William wrote his sister Emily, giving her an account of his life at the academy.

> I have no news worth communicating, so dull and uninteresting is everything connected with the Academy, it is always the same old routine of duty, we have guard mounting, a drill and parade every day, a day never passes without we have guard mounting and parade it makes no difference if it was to hail brickbats, the guard mounting in the morning and a parade of some sort (either dress or undress) must come off. I have seen the guard march on, in camp when the rain was pouring down in torrents. When it is raining the guard now marches on in the porticoes of [the] new barracks.... I rise in the morning go to reveille roll call, return, make up my bed, light my lamp and go to studying, and study until surgeons call and then clean my room and put things in order, and by the time I get through the breakfast drum beats. I then go to breakfast roll call, and march to breakfast, after marching back from breakfast, I go to the post office and if get a paper or letter I read it and spend the rest of the half hour (which we have after every meal) in looking over my lesson and so soon as the bugle calls "To quarters" I march to the section room and stay there one and a half hours after which time until dinner I study my Ethics, and when the dinner drum beats I march to dinner, after returning from dinner I spend my leisure half hour in the same manner as I did the one at breakfast. When the Bugle Calls to Quarters, I march to the Ethical Academy and there spend another hour and a half, and then return to quarters, and in half an hour more the Bugle blows release from quarters, and ten minutes after blows for drill. When we get marched out on the plain (with our guns and accoutrements) and drilled for an hour by the assistant instructor in tactics (at the present) in skirmish drills, after [marching] in, the drum beats in about 10 minutes for [parade] we march out on the plain if the weather admits and have a dress parade, and if the weather does not admit of it, we have an undress parade, after returning we march to supper, after supper we have another leisure half hour, and then the bugle calls to quarters again, we spend the time from that until tattoo in studying, and when tattoo beats, we shut up our books, spread our beds, and recommence our studies until taps, when we blow out our lights, jump into bed and fast asleep dreaming of home and its occupants, and perchance we sometimes dream of our sweethearts that those who are so fortunate to have one, but as for myself I do not care about them.[7]

William underwent his first examinations in January 1850, standing 15th in Mathematics, and 26th in Ethical Studies. On a list of cadets at the Military Academy, William ranked 17th out of 221 in General Merit. The superintendent recommended that he receive his cadet warrant. William reported to Emily, "I have passed my January examination, with some degree of credit."[8]

On February 2, 1850, William appeared before Judge D. W. Bate, of Orange County, New York, and signed his cadet warrant. He was now committed to serve in the army for eight years. Part of his oath read:

I will bear true faith and allegiance to the United States of America, and that I will serve them honestly and faithfully against all their enemies or opposers whomsoever; and that I will observe and obey the orders of the President of the United States, and orders of the officers appointed over me, according to the Rules and Articles of War.[9]

At the end of his second year at West Point, the superintendent granted William a leave of absence (as was customary), so he could go home. The orders directed him to return to the Academy by 2 P.M. on August 28.

A serious incident occurred in early September 1851, involving William and another cadet — Phillip H. Sheridan, of Ohio. William was at the time a Cadet Sergeant in Company C, Battalion of Cadets. His explanation of the incident, dated September 9, tells what happened:

> I being a file closer to the first platoon of "C" comp[any,] battalion of Cadets at the formation of the said company for parade, did order Cadet Sheridan to dress back; whereupon he turned partly around and said "you must not speak to me in ranks Mr. Terrill," and if I remember aright I said "stop talking in ranks." So soon as the ord'ly Sergeant brought the company to a rest he made towards me, but upon the 1 Lieut. calling the company to attention, he returned to his former posi-

Lieutenant George Crook (left), Cadet Philip H. Sheridan (center), and Lieutenant John Nugen (right). Sheridan attacked Cadet Sergeant William R. Terrill in September 1851, resulting in his suspension for a year. In October 1862, Terrill and Sheridan shook hands and settled their differences (courtesy U.S.M.A. Archives).

tion, having merely broken through the rear rank; as soon as the 1st Lieut. had inspected the company and brought it to a rest he ran towards me with his bayonet lowered, and said "God damn you sir, I will run you through" I stood still, and told him "to run ahead," after standing with gun pointed towards me for a few seconds, he resumed his place in ranks, and commenced cursing; I then told him he must stop his cursing, as I could not stand it, and if it were not for my office I would knock him down; he then said *damn you* I do curse you. I then told him that I should have to report him; he said no more, and the company was soon after marched to parade.[10]

Cadet Sheridan, who was a year ahead of William, submitted an excuse, giving his view of the incident:

> I was spoken to by the file closer in an improper tone. I was ordered by him to dress when I was accurately dressed. The file closer has been making use of his authority to oppress files in ranks, by speaking to them improperly, unnecessarily, and continually and as a confirmation of this statement I would respectfully refer the Comdt. [Commandant] to Mr. Hawkins, Wilson T., Mr. Spratt, or any other file on the right of "C" company.[11]

This should have been the end of the matter, but for Sheridan it was just the beginning. The next day, Sheridan discovered William sitting outside the barracks, and attacked him. In the ensuing fisticuff battle, Sheridan received a beating. Again, each cadet turned in a written explanation, and the commandant charged both with violation of the 134th Paragraph of the Academy Regulations, which prohibited fighting. After investigation of the incident, Superintendent Henry Brewerton dropped the charges against William.

William's explanation of the fight is as follows:

> I acted altogether in self defence, and could not do otherwise; I was seated with my head turned to the left when Mr. Sheridan came up and struck me from the right. The only alternative I had was to knock him down or run, and I course selected the former. I was not aware of his approach until I heard some one curse. I turned my head to see who it was, he struck me; I do not think I could have acted otherwise, without reflecting upon my character as a gentleman.[12]

Additional details of the incident appear in a report by the Commandant of Cadets, Captain B. R. Alden to the Adjutant of the Military Academy.

> Cdt. Sergt. Terrill, says that he was sitting in front of the barracks, at one P. M. the 10th inst. when Cdt. Sheridan approached him saying "God damn you" and struck him in the face. Cdt. Terrill in defending himself struck Cadet Sheridan several times. They were then parted by Cadets standing near.[13]

The commandant of cadets arrested Sheridan, and the incident reported to Brigadier General Totten, the Chief Engineer. For such a serious breach of military discipline, Sheridan faced dismissal from the academy. Instead, Superintendent Brewerton recommended that Sheridan leave the academy until August 28, 1852. Brewerton, when making this recommendation took Sheridan's previous record of good conduct into account.

Early November 1851 found William under arrest, charged with failing to obey the orders of his Section Marcher. The *Register of Delinquencies* recorded the November 4 incident as "insubordinate conduct, not taking his place in front ranks at 8 o'clock class parade."[14] Captain B. R. Alden, the Commandant of Cadets, placed him under arrest on the morning of November 8. Captain Alden explained that Cadet Terrill's section marcher had ordered him several times to take his place in the front rank at the 8 o'clock class parade, but Terrill failed to obey the order. His excuse for the incident was not sufficient, and Captain Alden placed him under arrest.

William appeared to be out of control. In the three months since the academic year commenced, he had accumulated 35 demerits, 17 of them in November alone. The Monthly Class Reports and Conduct Rolls for November indicate that William earned the third most demerits of any cadet at the Academy.[15] In December, he added a dozen more.

Later in December 1851, Cadet James E. B. Stuart, a cousin of the Terrills, wrote of William: "The cadet whom you saw at the Springs is named Terrill; he enjoys the reputation of being the ugliest man in the Corps; and so I hope you will not consider him as a fair specimen so far as looks are concerned. But he is a very good hearted fellow if he *is* ugly."[16]

The thing that is remarkable about Stuart's description of William comes from a letter written by William in the spring of 1856. William, writing his brother John Allen, told him, "You must try and hold yourself straight and look as manly as you can, as I have a great pride in the good looks of the family."[17]

William's last year at the Academy was a rough one for him, as he quickly earned demerits. His swift accumulation of demerits prompted his father to write Colonel Robert E. Lee, then the superintendent of the military academy. By March 1853, William was within 17 demerits of dismissal from the academy.

By April, the gravity of the situation must have impressed itself upon William. He added no new demerits, and was recognized for correct deportment, ranking 8th on that list. He repeated the performance in May, again adding no demerits and rising to 6th on the list of those distinguished for correct deportment.

William graduated from the military academy on June 17, 1853, ranking 16th in a class of 52 cadets. Having successfully completed his studies at the academy and passed his examination, the superintendent submitted William's name to the secretary of war for promotion in the army. As was the custom, William wrote Adjutant General Samuel Cooper on June 16:

> I have the honor to apply for promotion in the Ordnance, failing in that the 3rd Reg't. Artillery, failing that any regiment of Dragoons or Infantry.
> My address during my leave of absence will be West Point, Orange County, N. Y.[18]

The War Department assigned William to the 3rd U.S. Artillery, with the rank of Brevet Second Lieutenant. William accepted his appointment on July

14, 1853, and once again took an oath to "bear true allegiance to the United States of America." The new officer took these words seriously and obeyed them fully.

In December 1853, William received new orders from the War Department, assigning him to duty as a Second Lieutenant in Battery E, 4th U.S. Artillery at Fort Hamilton, New York.

In May 1855, William had the opportunity to travel to Texas. He left Fort Hamilton on May 29 to report to the superintendent of the recruiting service at Governor's Island, New York. There, the commanding officer directed him to escort a detachment of 75 recruits to Corpus Christi, Texas. The detachment left the recruiting depot on June 6, 1855. William commanded the detachment from June 16 to July 15, 1855. He then returned to Fort Hamilton, reporting for duty on July 31, 1855.[19]

Daguerreotype of Lieutenant William Rufus Terrill, U.S. Army (courtesy Bath County Historical Society).

The War Department issued orders in August 1855 assigning William to duty as an assistant professor in the Department of Mathematics at the military academy.[20] As such, he would be teaching members of the fourth class. William joined the academy Staff on September 4.

While discharging his duties in the Department of Mathematics at the academy, William took a hard look at the course. Mathematics was one of William's strong points while a cadet at the Academy a few years previous. By December 1855, William had nearly completed the revision of the mathematics course.[21]

President Franklin Pierce nominated William to the Senate for promotion to 1st Lieutenant on May 23, 1856, to be effective from March 31. A week after the president made the nomination, Horaito G. Wright, of the Engineer Department, recommended that William be relieved from duty at the academy at the expiration of the academic year. Wright gave no reason for the recommendation.

The War Department quickly complied with the request and issued orders on June 3, 1856, for William to report to General-in-Chief Winfield Scott after July 1.

William, now a first lieutenant reported to General-in-Chief Scott on July 1, 1856. Scott ordered William to join his company (Battery L, 4th U.S. Artillery) at Fort Mackinac, Michigan. After a leave of absence, William joined his company on September 10, 1856.

Up to this time, William's military career had been somewhat mundane, but that was about to change. Soon after joining his company, he learned that they were under orders for Florida, to take part in the Third Seminole War.

As preparations were underway for the journey in early October, William took an opportunity to write his brother-in-law, George A. Porterfield. William confided:

> I have quite a bleak prospect before me, but I trust in the goodness and mercy of God, and hope not to end my days in Florida. Every place and prospect I have in life has been blasted by this order, and now from necessity I must continue to be a soldier. I very much fear that I shall have very little inclination to leave the army at the expiration of a year.... I feel very happy and contented in my new position, and I trust that not many months will elapse before I prove myself a good officer. Our object in going to Florida is to remove those Indians. We will have a hard time of it, and many a poor fellow will leave his bones there. Fever will be more powerful by far than Indians.[22]

Lieutenant William R. Terrill, U.S. Army. Note use of optional white uniform trousers (courtesy Bath County Historical Society).

William and his company began the trip to Florida on October 12, 1856. The first leg of the journey commenced about 6 P.M. that evening, when they sailed for Fort Independence, Boston Harbor, on the propeller ship *Adriatic*. Captain Williams reported that the party consisted of himself, three lieutenants, thirty-two enlisted men and three camp women.[23]

William, now serving as Adjutant for the battalion, arrived at Fort Independence

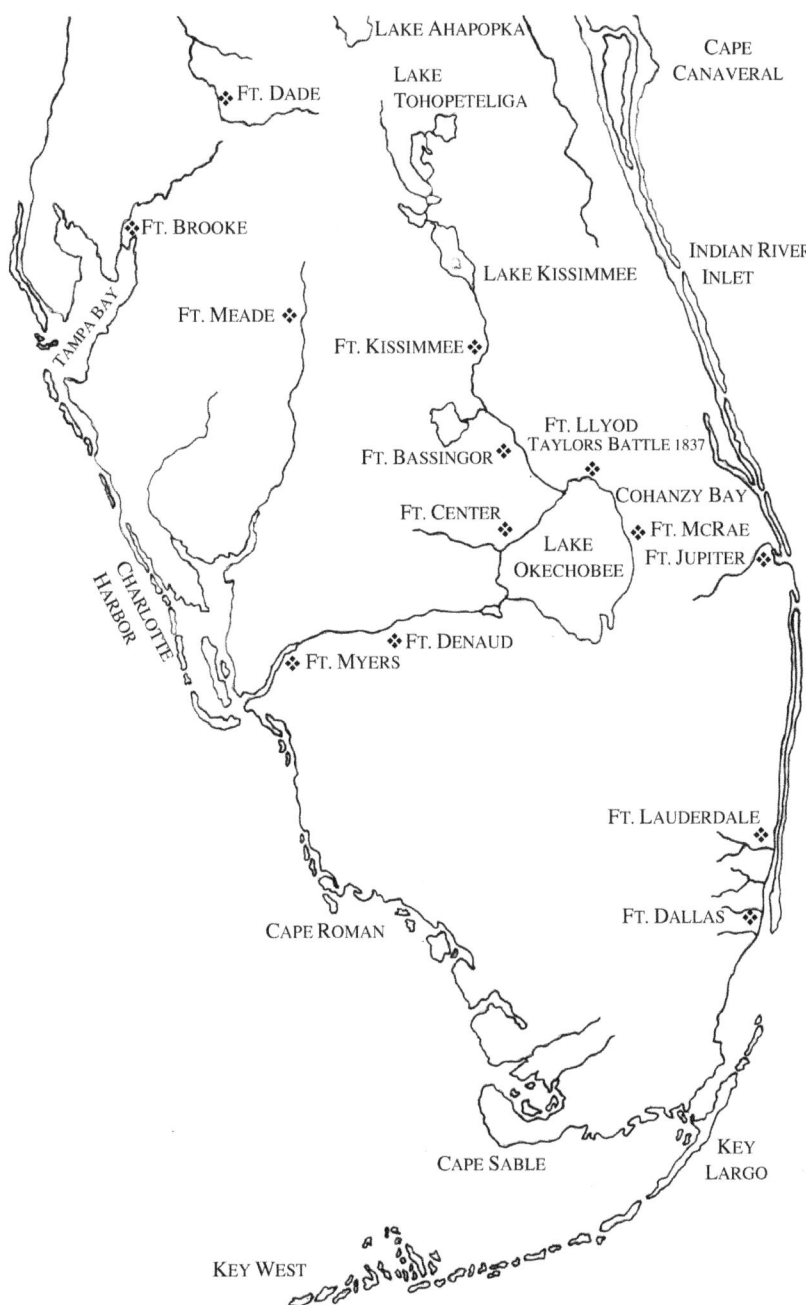

Map of military posts and forts in Florida, 1857, many of which Lieutenant Terrill served at (map by Andrew J. Neilsen).

about 1 P.M. on October 19. The company remained there until 4 P.M. on the following day, when they set sail on the ship *Arkwright* for Fort Myers, Florida.

After an uneventful voyage of twenty-one days, William and his company landed November 10 at Charlotte Harbor, on the gulf coast of Florida, at the mouth of the Caloosahatchee River. Lieutenant Orlando B. Wilcox, Company C, 4th U.S. Artillery, recalled the landing: "We ... tumbled, or threw ourselves with impetuosity overboard, leaving the best part of our baggage on the ship.... The landing was effected with as much haste as if we had been an army under full retreat before the enemy."[24]

To reach Fort Myers, the soldiers had to pile onto a smaller craft, named the *Jasper*, a steam lighter. The trip up the Caloosahatchee River, a narrow, shallow, winding stream, was a laborious one for the *Jasper*, which was poorly suited for the job at hand. William, it appears, remained behind at Charlotte Harbor with the greater part of the baggage.

At Fort Myers, which they reached that same day, they packed the baggage into six covered wagons and the detachment started the 28-mile march to Fort Denaud at 4:30 P.M. The soldiers now caught a glimpse of the country that would be their home for the ensuing months. Lieutenant Wilcox wrote: "The country was sandy but hard under foot, covered with pine & palmetto trees wide apart, & small palmetto & mangrove undergrowth, in which an Indian might hide within the toss of a jackknife."[25]

After marching eight and a half miles, the men went into camp for the night at a place called Horse Hole. Arising at 4 A.M. November 11, they continued the march for Fort Denaud. Again, Wilcox commented on the march:

> The day proved hot, the road grew heavy & rough with palmetto roots, & water lay more than ancle [sic] deep over many a road. To us on horseback it was nothing, but to the men, most of them recruits & unaccustomed to marching, were sorely put to it to keep up, although the gait required was slow & the halts frequent.... Coming to within three miles of Fort Deynaud [sic], the road plunged into deep sand, not like that already passed over.[26]

Once the command caught a glimpse of Fort Denaud late on November 11, they certainly must have wondered to which level of hell they had descended. The fort consisted of "a cluster of sheds, which in the distance looked as if the roofs were of new shingles, but which proved on coming nearer to be palmetto thatch. The place now looked like a Hottentot village, & the garrison like scarecrows. They had been long reduced by fever & diarrhea, scarcely a corporal's guard fit for duty; but their deep sunken eyes brightened at sight of us who had come to relieve them."[27]

The former commander of the post, Captain Gibson, and his men left at 3:30 A.M. November 12. Before leaving, he advised those remaining at the fort "to blow out their brains."[28]

William finally joined his comrades in arms on November 22, arriving onboard the steamer *Ranger*, along with most of the baggage for the post. Lieutenant Wilcox recorded William's arrival at Fort Denaud, noting that his fellow officers called Lieutenant Terrill "Stud."[29] Once on post, the commandant quickly assigned William to duty as adjutant, treasurer of the fort, and placed in charge of the post bake-house (bakery).

By the 3rd of December, the Florida climate had taken its toll on the men. At least forty-six of the soldiers were sick, as were several of the camp women. A couple of the soldiers and a child had already succumbed to the sickness.

After remaining at Fort Denaud for a month and a half, the two companies moved to Fort Myers on December 26, arriving there the following day. At that post, William's company boarded the steamer *Ranger* at 1:30 P.M., which carried them along the Caloosahatchee River to Fort Center, Florida. The company moved from Fort Center to Fort McRae in January 1857, leaving William at Fort Center.

On February 1, 1857, William and a detachment of men left the fort in a small boat to join the company at Fort McRae. After a difficult journey of four days, including getting lost in the Everglades, he finally reached Fort McRae on February 4.

Days later, William was once again on the move, back into the wilderness. Colonel Joseph Roberts, learning that Indian sign had been found in the neighborhood of General Taylor's battle ground, ordered William and Lieutenant Bagley to take thirty-one enlisted men and make a full examination of the area. William left on the morning of the 14th, with seven days' rations, and returned on the evening of the 17th without sighting any Indians.

In early March 1857, on the 9th, William's workload substantially increased. His commander assigned him to the additional duties of Acting Assistant Commissary and Subsistence and Acting Assistant Quartermaster.

William's company, Battery L, changed their station on March 25, 1857, moving once again to Fort Center. Four days later, the company boarded several small boats and started for Fort Kissimmee, arriving there on April 6. The conditions at this post were undoubtedly as crude as those at Fort Denaud. According to the records of the post, the soldiers christened their new home "Shitville."[30]

Soon after reaching Fort Kissimmee, the company examined Lake

Dr. Thomas A. McParlin, U.S. Army, who served with Lieutenant Terrill in Florida (courtesy National Library of Medicine).

Istokpoga, its islands, and the country about it. Returning to Fort Kissimmee on April 18, the company immediately set out for Lake Kissimmee. After examining that lake, islands and vicinity, they returned to camp on April 26. The soldiers could find no recent sign of Indians in the area.[31]

In May 1857, William again led a detachment into the wilderness, searching for Indians, but found none. The detachment left Fort Kissimmee in boats on the first of May, and proceeded down the Kissimmee River to Fort Bassinger. Turning about, they started back along the Kissimmee River, examining Lake Kissimmee, the Lower and Upper Cypress Lakes, and Lake Weohyakapka. Finding no sign of any Indians, the company returned to Fort Kissimmee on May 21.

William and his company spent the summer of 1857 at Fort Kissimmee, searching for sign of the Seminoles in the area. When Battery L, 4th U.S. Artillery left the fort on the morning of August 12 for Fort Meade, William remained behind at Fort Kissimmee, as Commissary and Quartermaster Officer. Doctor Thomas A. McParlin noted: "Lieut. Terrill is ordered to remain here to act as Qr. Ms. and Commissary. This separates him from his company and does not please him."[32]

Near the end of August 1857, William applied for duty with the U.S. Coast Survey, then a division of the Treasury Department. Addressing a letter to Professor Alexander Dallas Bache, the Superintendent of the Coast Survey, on August 29, William stated:

> I would respectfully apply to you for duty on the Coast Survey. I would prefer office duty, but would not object to the field should you think my services would be more useful there. Should you be pleased to take the matter into consideration, I would refer you to Prof. Church of the U.S. Military Academy under whom I served; to Professors Davis, Mahan, Bartlett & Agnel for any information that you may wish to obtain about me.[33]

A month later, Bache responded to William's application from Bangor, Maine. He informed William that he had taken steps to determine if it was likely that the authorities would grant such a detail. Unfortunately, Bache commented, the department would reject the application, and felt that it would be best not make the request at all.[34]

On August 29, William received orders relieving him of the Commissary and Quartermaster duties at Fort Kissimmee. The order directed him to rejoin his company, which he did on September 23 at Fort Brooke, Florida. A week later, the battery sailed on the steamship *General Rusk,* en route for Fort Leavenworth, in Kansas Territory.

The voyage took William to New Orleans, which they reached on October 3, 1857. Changing steamers, the battery sailed up the Mississippi River the following day on the *Hiawatha* for St. Louis, Missouri. The *Hiawatha* docked in St. Louis on the 11th and continued her voyage to Jefferson City the following day. At that point, the battery again changed vessels, now boarding the steamer *New Lucy*, which carried them to Fort Leavenworth, Kansas Territory. William and his comrades went into camp on October 16.[35]

A month after reaching Fort Leavenworth, William left on a sixty-day leave of absence, departing on November 16, 1857. He had the option of applying for a two month extension should the need arise.

From Fort Leavenworth, William went to Fishkill Landing in New York, where he remained for several weeks, before going to Washington, D.C., and Warm Springs. William planned to be in Washington on December 20. His sister Emily wrote: "We are expecting William to-night on his way to Charlottesville. I think his staying so long in New York is very strange, but I don't think William is deficient in filial affection."[36] William's lingering in New York would be explained the following March.

While on leave of absence from Fort Leavenworth, William married Emily Drennen Henry, daughter of Major William S. Henry and Arietta L. Thompson Henry. The ceremony took place March 9, 1858, at the residence of Emily's uncle, W. Smith Thompson, in Montgomery County, Maryland.[37]

Emily Drennen Henry was born at Fort Smith, Indian Territory, on September 4, 1840. Her father, an 1835 graduate of the military academy, served with distinction in the Mexican War. When he died in New York in 1851 at the age of 34, he was a Major in the 3rd U.S. Infantry. Emily's mother, Arietta Livingston Thompson, was a granddaughter of Daniel D. Tompkins. Tompkins had served as governor of New York (1807–1817) and as vice-president in the administration of James Monroe (1817 to 1825). Needless to say, Mrs. Henry was well connected in many influential circles. This influence would become apparent in a few years, benefiting both William and his sister Emily T. Porterfield.

The day after the wedding, Professor A. D. Bache sent a request to Secretary of the Treasury Howell Cobb, asking him to detail William for duty with the Coast Survey. Bache, a graduate of the U.S. Military Academy, closed his letter of request by asking an additional favor: "If he is detailed it is not desired to interfere with his present leave of

Emily Drennen Henry, wife of William R. Terrill (courtesy Evelyn Lee Moore).

absence."[38] It seems rather ironic that the day after he married the daughter of Arietta Thompson Henry, Professor Bache requested his detail to the Coast Survey. Mrs. Henry corresponded with the Secretary of War about that time, and performed copy work for the Coast Survey office.[39]

A week later, on the 17th, the War Department issued an order directing William to report by letter to the Secretary of the Treasury for instructions. The same day, William complied with the order and reported to Howell Cobb for instructions for duty on the Coast Survey.[40] Secretary Cobb forwarded William's letter to Professor Bache, requesting Bache to give William the necessary instructions. Bache complied on March 19, directing William to report in person to the Coast Survey Office when his leave expired.[41]

President Thomas Jefferson created the Survey of the Coast office in 1807, later known as the U.S. Coast Survey. Its purpose was to make a survey "of the coasts of the United States, in which shall be designated the islands and shoals, with roads or places of anchorage, within twenty leagues of any part of the shores of the United States."[42] The name changed to the U.S. Coast Survey in 1836, and the Department of the Treasury oversaw its operation. Today, it is known as the United States Coast & Geodetic Survey, a part of the National Oceanic and Atmospheric Administration (NOAA), U.S. Department of Commerce.

William Rufus Terrill, U.S. Army (courtesy Massachusetts Commandery Military Order of the Loyal Legion and the U.S. Army Military History Institute).

William and his new wife took up residence in the Georgetown section of Washington, D.C., and he settled into his new duties with the Coast Survey. Professor Bache first assigned him to office duty, as he had requested, where he made computations and drew charts. It is interesting that William worked in the drawing division, as that subject had been one of his lesser talents at the military academy. He, however, must have overcome whatever it was that inhibited his drawing ability. His ability as a drafter is apparent when you examine his field books for the Florida surveys.

In August 1858, William commenced working with a survey party on the Hudson River in New York. Two months later, William prepared to lead his own survey party at Charlotte Harbor, Florida. This was very close to the same area where he had served in the previous year against the Seminole Indians.

An assistant with the Coast Survey has many responsibilities. He must organize a party of competent men, oversee the outfitting of a ship for sea, and lay in provisions, supplies and equipment for the planned work. The Coast Survey hired a sailing master to take charge of the ship. The workers performed double duty, serving as sailors, construction workers and as members of field parties.

William spent the next three years working with survey parties. During the summer months, he worked in New York, and spent the winter months in Florida. In December 1859, the Department of the Army transferred William to Battery C, 4th U.S. Artillery, allowing him to continue his duties with the coast survey.

Alexander Dallas Bache, superintendent of the U.S. Coast Survey and close friend of W. R. Terrill (courtesy Library of Congress, Prints and Photograph Division).

In the spring of 1860, William received orders to join his company in Utah, the company being in need of an officer. The following week, political figures wrote to the secretary of war requesting him to reconsider William's reassignment. In the course of two weeks, many pleas and appeals arrived asking that William remain on Coast Survey duty. James M. Mason, the Virginia congressman, and Virginia governor John Letcher sent letters to Secretary Floyd.

William's term of duty with the Coast Survey was due to expire in March 1862. The delegation of Virginia congressmen asked Floyd to allow him to remain until that time. Besides, Professor Bache wished to retain William "on account of his experience, and aptitude for the work."[43]

On April 20, the secretary of war concluded that the War Department could not do without the services of William, and denied the appeals set before him. Despite Floyd's ruling, appeals continued to arrive at the War Department in Washington. Within a week, Floyd again denied an appeal to keep William on the Coast Survey duty, stating that General Scott had requested the reassignment as there were no commissioned officers with the company in Utah at present.

The next week, Professor Bache advised William that the War Department had rejected all appeals. He wrote:

> I had hoped that you would have been allowed to remain the full term of four years on the Coast Survey & that adding experience to your natural adaptiness to the work you would have been ever increasingly useful to it. Your service in the field on the Coast of Florida and also as associated with Assistant Blunt on the Hudson River were highly acceptable, giving in the short period of your service, decided evidence of your zeal, industry and ability in the discharge of some of the most critical duties devolving on an officer of the Coast Survey. Having no choice left, I can but give with regret the direction requested, namely that you report in person at the War Dept. for further orders.[44]

Upon receiving Bache's letter, William immediately wrote to Adjutant General Samuel Cooper, requesting the secretary of war to reconsider the matter. This last appeal succeeded, and the War Department allowed William to remain on duty with the coast survey.

With the election of Abraham Lincoln as president of the United States on November 6, 1860, the internal bindings of the country commenced to come undone. South Carolina broke away from the Union on December 20, 1860, the first of the Southern states to take such a drastic measure. The State of Florida joined in the secession movement, leaving the Union on January 10, 1861.

Given the state of affairs in Florida, Professor Bache wrote William on January 9:

> Should the signs of the times in Section VI indicate that your operations will be interfered with, or the public property in your charge be exposed to seizure, you are authorized to close your work, returning your vessel to the Coast Survey depot at the New York Navy Yard, and reporting in person to this office in Washington.[45]

William left Charlotte Harbor on January 17 for Tampa, where he picked up lumber, water and the mail. Upon his arrival at Tampa, he noted, "I received the first intelligence of the misfortune that had befallen our country."[46] William acknowledged the receipt of several letters from Bache on the 20th, both dated in December 1860. He then wrote:

> I regret exceedingly that there are no instructions from you in regard to my continuing or stopping work. I shall therefore presume that you intend me to continue my operations until such a time as I shall hear from you or circumstances warrant the responsibility I may take of sending my schooner to New York City whence she came. Rest assured I shall not surrender the government vessel and property in my charge to any state authorities unless ordered by you.[47]

Writing again a week later from Tampa, William reported to Bache: "There seems to be no feeling of hostility to the Coast Survey, but any government ves-

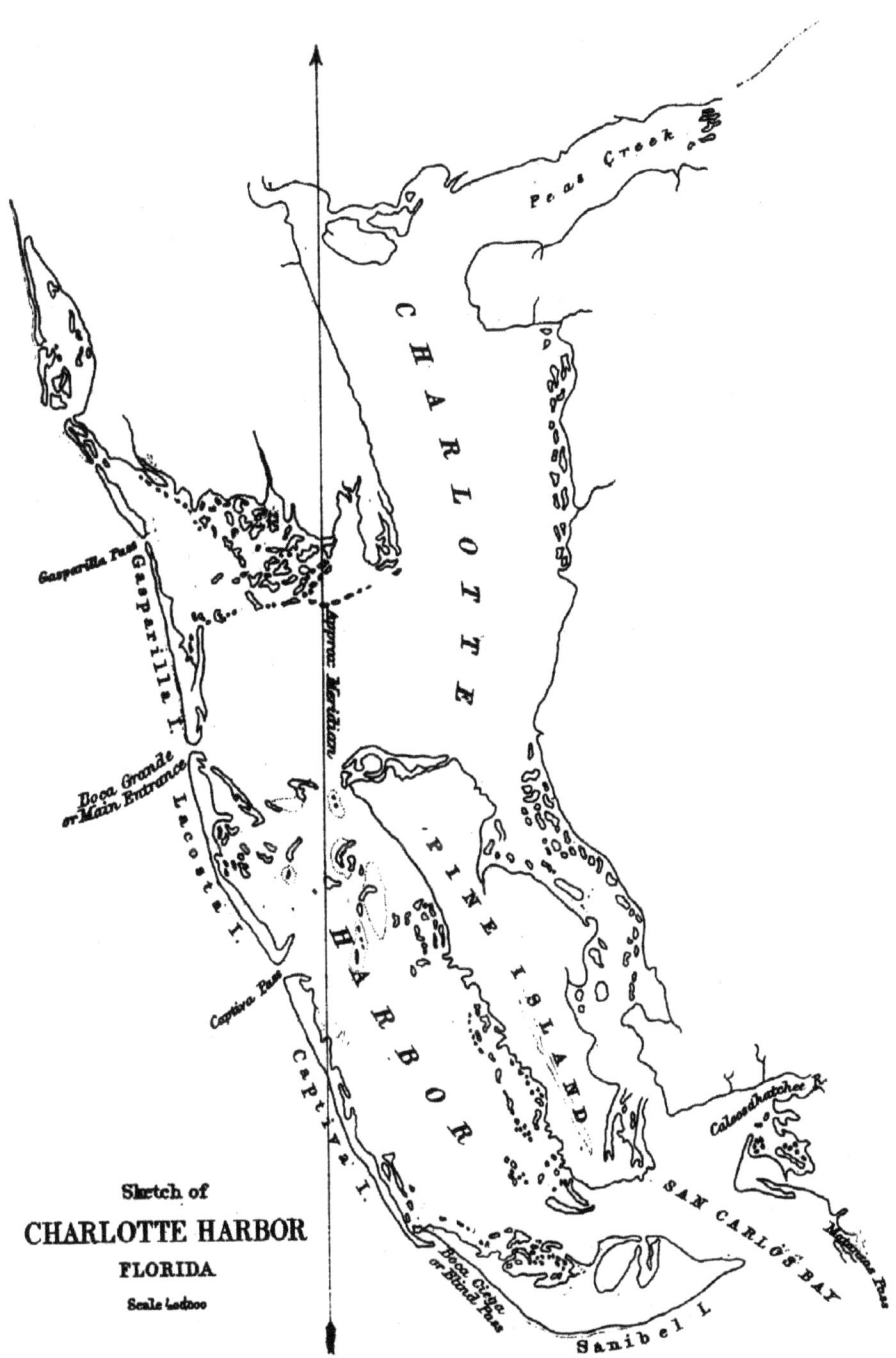

Drawing of Charlotte Harbor, Florida, 1863, much of the work completed by Lieutenant W. R. Terrill between 1858 and 1861 (courtesy Library of Congress, Geography and Maps Division).

sel carrying a *gun* or any gov. [government] uniforms are not considered as desirable visitors."[48]

William returned to Charlotte Harbor aboard the schooner *Bailey* the following day (29th), where he continued his work.

Professor Bache responded to William's January 20 letter on the 31st:

> Referring to the last paragraph of your letter of Jany. 20 I would say that the mission of the Coast Survey is strictly scientific, civil and pacific, that the vessels are unarmed and that resistance to lawless violence is not one of the contingencies of their construction or use. I wish you to leave the section if you judge any seizure will be attempted and in full time and I doubt not your discretion in the matter.[49]

Professor Bache officially ordered William to close his operations in Florida on February 5, 1861. The superintendent directed William to send his schooner and all government property and funds to the depot in New York. Bache asked William to report to the Coast Survey office at Washington in person.[50] William received Bache's letter, sent by special messenger, on February 22.

A few days after receiving the order to cease work, William wrote Bache from Charlotte Harbor, reporting that he intended to go to Tortugas, and there send the schooner on to New York. He added that he would return to Washington, via Havana, the "soonest and speediest route." He closed his letter, adding, "I have no doubt that our schooners would be taken by unresponsible persons if they got a chance to take them."[51] William finally left Charlotte Harbor on March 2, sailing to the island of Tortugas, off the southwestern coast of Florida, nearly seventy miles from Key West.[52] The schooner reached Tortugas two days later.

While at Tortugas on March 9, 1861, William wrote a letter to his father. The letter was comparatively short, comprising only three small pages, but conveyed a powerful message:

> I am here anchored under the flag of *my country* getting my schooner ready to send North to New York whence she came. I had to suspend my work on account of the distressing state of affairs in the country. I hope to reach N. Y. about the last of this month—and hope you can arrange it to meet me there or in Washington. I will telegraph to you upon my arrival. I am as I ever have been *true* to *my oath*, *true to my country—and true to* the *flag* that floats over [it.] Whose folds I should prefer to be my winding sheet rather than see the dissolution of this once glorious country. I see you are a member of the convention and called a *Union* member. My great wish is that you and I may never differ upon that great *question*. As long as I have a country and a government to serve I wish to be true to it. Were I to be false to one I could hardly be a valuable acquisition to another. My love to your wife, my brothers and sister. Kind remembrances to all enquiring friends. Very truly your son, W. R. Terrill. Any letter addressed to the care of the Quartermaster U.S. Army, New York will reach me upon my arrival there.[53]

William remained at Tortugas until March 19, when he took his schooner to Havana, Cuba. There, on the 25th, he ordered the *Bailey* to sail for New York, while he boarded the U.S. Mail Steamer *Quaker City*, also bound for New York.

While in transit, William wrote Professor Bache on March 29. He informed the head of the Coast Survey that he would remain in New York until the schooner arrived and was properly laid up. That accomplished, William said that he would report to the Coast Survey Office in person. Enclosed in his letter, was a brief statement to Bache, reporting the sighting of three foreign warships, loaded with troops. William noted that rumor named Mexico as their eventual destination. William concluded his statement by saying, "The distracted condition of our own country renders it a fitting moment for carrying out the long cherished plans of the Spaniards. I trust our country may soon be reunited upon a firmer basis and be able to frustrate the plans of absolutism on this continent at least."[54]

William arrived in New York well in advance of his schooner, which did not reach port until mid–April. After storing the equipment in his trust, William went to Poughkeepsie, New York, where he awaited further orders from Bache.

By this time, however, Secretary of War Simon Cameron had already requested William be detached from the Coast Survey and returned to regular duty. Chase directed on April 18, 1861, that William report to General Winfield Scott, in the Department of Washington, for duty. S. P. Chase, the secretary of the treasury, forwarded Cameron's request to Professor Bache the following day. Bache officially notified William of his recall by letter on April 24 and again on April 26. Writing again on the following day, Professor Bache told William that he wished to see him when he arrived in Washington and congratulated him on his decision to remain by the Stars and Stripes.[55]

The War Begins

William reported to General Winfield Scott for duty on May 4, 1861, at which time Scott assigned him to the command of Company F, 4th U.S. Artillery, stationed at Washington Arsenal. He assumed his duties the following day, and quickly commenced to recruit and train the company.

A few days after his assignment to duty at Washington Arsenal, Professor Bache wrote Secretary Chase, asking him to make a favorable endorsement to the secretary of war on William's behalf. Bache wrote:

Captain William R. Terrill, U.S. Army (courtesy Evelyn Lee Moore).

> Lieut. W. R. Terrill, USA has served five [three] years upon the Coast Survey most faithfully, he is one of the best officers who has been detailed upon the work being zealous, intelligent, laborious, and discreet. It is a great merit in these times that he is loyal and true to the government which has educated and made him the man he is. I should esteem it a privilege to serve him in his professional advancement, and would respectfully request that you will upon this testimonial in behalf of Lieut. Terrill, with your endorsement to the Secretary of War. Lieut. Terrill desires to obtain one of the vacancies in the Department of Instruction of the Army & I have great pleasure in saying that his business qualities fit him well for such a position.[56]

The War Department rejected the recommendations to assign William to specific duty, having other plans for William and his talent.

On the 4th of May 1861, President Abraham Lincoln ordered the creation of a light artillery regiment, to be designated the 5th U.S. Artillery. William received an appointment as Captain of one of the twelve companies, effective May 14, 1861.

According to family history, William visited his Aunt Mary Jane Wise during the early days of the war, trying to decide what to do. Evelyn Lee Moore, a second cousin, later wrote of the visit.

> When war threatened in 1861, he was torn between two loyalties—to his home and state and to his country. He came to my grandmother, his favorite aunt, to talk over his tragic decision, his own mother having died in 1858. Grandma was always wise. There was no urging, no recriminations, only the advice to follow his conscience. He remained in the Federal Army after requesting that he would not be stationed in Virginia.[57]

From other correspondence, it appears that William had already made his decision as to where he would remain. The letter to his father on March 9, along with correspondence to Professor Bache, made his intentions very clear. If William visited his aunt in Culpepper, it must have been just before his reporting to General Scott in Washington.

In explanation of his decision to remain loyal to the United States, William reminded his father of the gift received in 1853 when he graduated from the military academy. His father had then given him a copy of the United States Constitution, and exacted an oath from him "to remember forever his oath taken to support it."[58]

A similar story suggests that upon his graduation from the military academy, the proud father presented his son with a Bible and a copy of the Constitution and swore him to be loyal and true to both.

A sketch of William, written a few days after his death, noted:

> He was a most accomplished ordnance officer, and stood alone, of all his Virginia family, in loyalty to the Union. The greatest efforts were made to swerve him from his allegiance; letters were addressed to him from his father and brother, endorsed by Jeff Davis, proffering him any military position in the Confederate

service, but he rejected all the temptations with a noble scorn; and returned this reply in substance: "The Union cause, to which I have devoted my life, has nothing but honor to endear it, and it has no terror but that of death, which a soldier must always expect. The rebellion however offers nothing but dishonor and disgrace, and I shall adhere to the flag of the Union, and give my life if necessary in support of the legally constituted Government of the United States."[59]

According to Colonel William H. Terrill, this story is mostly fiction. While in Richmond in mid–November 1862, one of his friends handed the elder Terrill a copy of the *Louisville Journal* in which this article appeared. On November 19, Colonel Terrill wrote a letter to the editor of the *Richmond Enquirer*, requesting them to publish the article, along with his letter. He wrote:

> Whiht [While] it is true that the younger brother of Gen. Terrill and myself addressed letters to him early in 1861, urging him to abandon his position in the Federal service, and return to his native State, where he would find a more congenial and patriotic employment in defence of the homes and firesides of his father, and brothers, and sister, but it is *not true* that those letters were endorsed by President Davis in *any manner* nor is it true that we received the reply put into the mouth of my son by the Louisville "Journal." The unfortunate course pursued by my *deluded* boy, was the severest blow I have ever received, and has made my heart bleed ever since.[60]

Thirty years after William's death, Francis Darr wrote to Emily Porterfield about her brother: "He often spoke to me of two letters from his father. One when he graduated at the Academy, and one received after your father knew of his (Wm's) decision to stay on the Union side. He never expressed any bitterness about the latter letter, but spoke of his father as 'the dear old man.'"[61]

William's father responded to his son's letters, writing on May 15, 1861, using the formal salutation "Sir," followed by:

> Your two letters of the 29th ultimo & 7th inst. [were received]. I am *overwhelmed* by the position you have taken. It is the bitterest cup that has ever been commended to my lips. You are truly *demented*. Your talk about loyally to your oath is all *stuff*. Oh! how it makes my heart bleed to think that while Virginia's son's are rallying to the defence of her firesides & her homes, that my son is found playing the part of Benedict Arnold. If you persist in your present course, your name & memory will be execrated not only by those who were once your friends in the south, but even by the very *devils* with whom you are now waving against your native land. Sir, If you carry out the purpose you have avowed — no matter what may be the result, you will never be permitted to visit your native state *but to die*. You would be hung before you could get twenty miles within the limits of Virginia. You are *strangely deluded*. Our people except a small portion of the N. West are united as one man, and are all enthusiastic, our soldiers & they are legion, are clamorous to be led on to battle, all your brothers and even your Father whose years would exempt him will be in the fight, and can you be so recreant & so unnatural as to aid in the made attempt to impose the yoke of tyranny upon your kith & kin. Do so, and your name shall be stricken from the family record, and only remembered in connection with your treachery to this country that gave you

birth. This letter may not reach you because of the strict surveillance established by the Post Office Dept., but should it reach you, I beg you to be assured that every word I have written is as true as Gospel & that should you disregard this last appeal, I shall never again subscribe myself

Your Father.

P. S. — The Gov. of Virginia has frequently inquired for you and has been ready to give you a commission fully equal to that you how hold, if you conclude to retrace your steps and return to Virginia you will be taken care of.[62]

A few days after the letter from his father arrived, unknown to William, his mother-in-law Arietta L. Henry sent a copy of the letter to Professor Bache, with the request that he intercede for William. The professor, writing from Capitol Hill on May 20, brought the letter to the attention of Colonel George W. Cullum, an aide-de-camp to General Winfield Scott:

> Lieut. W. R. Terrill, U.S.A. has served on the Coast Survey for nearly four years, & has shown himself a true man of action, industrious, reliable, of good judgement [sic] & temper, [and] of capacity.
>
> His family are secessionists & the strongest inducements have been held out to him to abandon the flag which he has with manly conscious, resolution, determined [not] to do under any circumstances.
>
> That you may see what kind of arguments have been used, I enclose a copy of a letter, parts of which if opportunity offers I should be glad that our good & great General should hear; it comes to me from Lt. T's mother in law & he has no knowledge that I have it, or that I am writing about him at all.
>
> A man who [is] a dutiful son & affectionate brother should resist such appeals ought to be encouraged — should he not?
>
> Instead of being ordered to the fight against his father & brothers he should have some duty elsewhere — should he not?
>
> I recommended him for a place in the Commissary's department, but it was filled.
>
> Will you not help me to have him assigned to some duty which will show the appreciation of his course, give him promotions, & turn his face away from the Virginia forces?
>
> Do not forget that this is not what Lieut. Terrill asks, he is ready for any sacrifice.[63]

General Scott granted the appeal and assigned William to duty elsewhere. Later in the summer of 1861, William received orders to go to Newport Barracks, in Kentucky.

Later correspondence between William and Professor Bache reveals an attempt to conceal a letter from William's father. Professor Bache urged Mrs. Henry to keep the letter from her son-in-law — probably the letter disowning him. William, however, learned of the letter and the cover-up in July 1861.

William retained command of Battery F, 4th U.S. Artillery until June 7, when he was relieved. Four days later, Brigadier General Joseph K. Mansfield appointed William to the position of Assistant Inspector General, Department of Washington.[64] Hoping to obtain a better position in the service, William asked General Mansfield to help obtain an appointment to the rank of major. William believed he could be of better service to the army in a higher position, than serving in the field. The attempt was not successful because General Mansfield felt that William would stand a better chance of promotion if he were in the field.

Soon afterward, William received his appointment as Captain in the 5th U.S. Artillery. Although he was disappointed at not receiving a higher position, he nevertheless accepted the appointment.

William reported to his new commanding officer, Lieutenant Colonel T. W. Sherman, by letter on June 21. His was the first letter registered by the regimental headquarters. A week later, he received orders to report to Colonel Sherman at Harrisburg, Pennsylvania, and by July 3 was in that city.

While in Harrisburg, William wrote a fellow Southerner who also remained loyal to the United States government. On July 3, William wrote Senator Andrew Johnson, of Tennessee:

> Tomorrow you will take your seat in the United States Senate, and though I am but an humble individual I cannot refrain from telling you that my prayers and wishes are for your safety, honor and welfare which has become so identified with that of the whole country. I am a southerner, a Virginian — such in every sense of the word *save the secession*. I have a Father, two brothers, a brother-in-law and an uncle[65] on the other side (with many other relatives). They in common with many other good men left the Union when their states were rushed out by an unscrupulous minority. I am here and [an] officer of the army, engaged in Recruiting service. For the past two months I have been on duty in Washington. Gen'l. Scott, Gen'l. Mansfield and Prof. Bache, the superintendent of the Coast Survey know me well and have been my kind friends.
>
> I hope that reason may resume her sway and our misguided brethren return to their allegiance, and that the day is not far distant when we will be more fully though not more ably represented in our National Councils, than we now are.[66]

The following day, William assumed command of his company, Battery H, 5th U.S. Artillery. His subordinates were 1st Lieutenants Francis L. Guenther and Jacob H. Smyser, with Frank Rittenhouse and Israel Ludlow as 2nd Lieutenants.

As the 5th Artillery was a new regiment, William and his fellow captains were required to recruit the men for their companies. The colonel, in Harrisburg, assigned each officer a certain area to work from, and directed William to raise his company in the counties of Burks and Lebanon in Pennsylvania. He made his headquarters and recruiting rendezvous at Reading, Pennsylvania, where he recruited a large number of Irishmen.

William and his lieutenants established a recruiting station at Number 18, East Market Square. The July 13 issue of the *Berks & Schuylkill Journal* reported that Captain Terrill hoped to enlist 200 men for the regiment, and then added:

"Captain Terrill, of Virginia birth, is a loyal and gallant officer, and enjoys to a huge degree the respect and confidence of his superior officers. We hope his sojourn in Reading will be pleasant and agreeable."[67]

On the 9th, William reported his progress to Colonel Sherman: "I have rented a building conveniently situated on the principal street and in every way suitable for a Recruiting rendezvous for $25 per month. I am now all ready for Recruits but there seems to be none here, all having volunteered. On the 18th when the 25th Penn. Vols. are mustered out I hope to get some [recruits]."[68]

William found that recruiting for the regular service was not as easy as it should have been. Many of the men of military age had already volunteered for service, drawing an enlistment bounty of $30 and a three-year enlistment period. A number of men enlisted during the early days of the war for a ninety-day term, which would soon expire.

William reported this problem to regimental headquarters: "I find great difficulty in enlisting men for five years, all seem to prefer the Volunteer service which Congress has lately rendered peculiarly attractive by bounties for re-enlistment in Volunteer companies." In closing, he added: "I shall spare myself no trouble to accomplish the object for which I am here."[69]

To make the situation worse, other regimental recruiting stations opened in Reading before the end of July. William, in reporting this to Colonel Sherman, noted that they "will *materially* interfere with my operations. We are very particular to confine ourselves to the limits prescribed for us, and though desirous to promote the general good of the service I am not particularly anxious to have another take away from my arm of the service what little fruit may arise from my exertions."[70]

William later asked permission to send one of his lieutenants to nearby Mifflin County, as no regiments were recruiting in that area. The regimental headquarters granted him permission to recruit in Mifflin County on August 3.

William faced a variety of duties as captain of a company. In addition to actively recruiting men for his company and regiment, he had to feed, clothe and house the soldiers as they enlisted. In addition, military authorities periodically called upon him to muster other troops into service in the surrounding area, or to appear on a board of inspection.

Taking time from his busy schedule on August 6, William wrote his friend Professor Bache at the Coast Survey Office in Washington.

My dear friend,

Such I beg that I may be permitted to call you, for such you have indeed been to me.

It was not until about a month since that I learned accidentally of your kindness to *me* in writing to Mrs. Henry advising her not to forward one of my Fathers [sic] letters to me. The receipt of it would have made no difference in my decision.

I am only pained to see that my father can permit his prejudice in favor of his state to make him think for one moment of casting off a son who has ever endeavored to love, honor, and obey him.[71]

William then spoke about the recent battle of Bull Run, stating that he had anticipated the disaster because of the want of discipline among the raw troops. He then continued:

> I am not dismayed or discouraged, the cause for which I was educated, and whose sworn defender I am is mine in adversity as well as in prosperity. I am no[t] sympathizing with abolitionism nor secessionism, both are alike heresies which we must root out. The Constitution as written by our fathers is a very plain *Chart* to sail by and when we use any other we soon lose our reckoning and it will not be long before we are as now — "in the breakers."[72]

He told his friend of his present situation, writing:

> I have been here on Recruiting service a month — it is dull business, as the men come in very slowly.... I had hoped to be able to recruit my battery and get it into some kind of order before three months, but the men do not come in fast enough.[73]

The captain reported the results and problems facing his recruiting detail to regimental adjutant Lieutenant H. A. DuPont, on August 8:

> I have now nineteen recruits and as yet have received no clothing. The majority of the men are sadly in need of it, and it is really an injury to the recruiting service to have my men look so shabby. Again I have to have my men boarded and lodged, whereas if I had received my blankets and bed-sacks I could have them lodge in the rendezvous and cook for themselves, thus reducing the cost of subsistence per man per day about 15 cts. Of course I know the Quartermasters Department are very much pressed to furnish the troops in the field with the necessary clothing, but it is my duty to do all in my power to see that the men under my command are supplied, and at the risk of being considered impertinent I beg that the Col. comdg. will give the subject of our wants his favorable consideration.[74]

The next day, William submitted requisitions to the government for horses, ordnance (guns, limbers and caissons) and ordnance stores (ammunition, etc.) for his company. Later in the month, the quartermaster department advised William that he could expect to receive 136 horses for his company at Newport Barracks, Kentucky.

On the 17th of August, apparently in response to an inquiry by Major General George B. McClellan, William reported by telegraph that he had enlisted 31 men.[75] One of the local newspapers reported on the same day, "Captain Terrill is taking great pains to form a first class corps of men and is succeeding admirably."[76]

Near the end of August, William again made a plea for clothing for his men. Writing the Adjutant General on the 26th, William noted, "I have yet received no clothing. Requisitions have been made for clothing. The shabby appearance of my recruits does not invite enlistment."[77]

The War Department issued orders assigning William to duty in Kentucky on August 29, 1861. The order went first to the regimental headquarters in Harrisburg, which issued its own order on September 2. Another officer relieved William from duty at Reading, and directed him to take the public property and funds in his charge to Newport Barracks, Kentucky. Once there, he would continue to recruit and organize his company as a battery of light artillery.[78]

On September 7, the *Berks & Schuylkill Journal* reported that Captain Terrill with "his Lt., Orderly Sgt., & 15 recruits" left on the 5th "for Newport, Ky., where he is to join Gen. Anderson's Div."[79]

The *Reading Daily Times* reported the departure of William: "The Captain has about him all the marks of a true soldier. There is no bluster, no boasting, no display; but in place of those we find a quiet confidence, a modest, and a gentlemanly bearing, ever found in the true soldier."[80]

William reported for duty at Newport Barracks, Kentucky, near Cincinnati, Ohio, on September 7. His commanding officer was Brigadier General Robert Anderson, of Fort Sumter fame, now commanding the Department of the Cumberland.

At his new post, William got his battery organized, equipped and ready for the field. He sent Lieutenant B. F. Rittenhouse to Louisville, where he opened a recruiting office. Soon afterward, the following notices appeared in the *Louisville Journal*:

FLYING ARTILLERY.
100 RECRUITS WANTED, for three years, for Battery H, 5th Artillery, U.S.A., to be under the command of General Anderson. None but able bodied unmarried men, between the ages of 18 and 35, need apply. All men will receive their boarding and clothing as soon as they are enlisted.

Lieut. B. F. RITTENHOUSE,
Recruiting Officer,
Corner of Eighth and Main Sts.[81]

---

100 Recruits Wanted for Battery H, 5th Artillery U.S. Army. To serve three years. This battery will be commanded by Capt. W. R. Terrill, 5th Artillery (a Virginian), and be attached to the command of Gen. Anderson. None but able bodied unmarried men, between the ages of 18 and 35, need apply. All men will be fed and clothed as soon as enlisted. Rendezvous corner of Eighth and Main Streets.

B. F. RITTENHOUSE,
2d Lieut., 5th Artillery U.S.A.
Recruiting Officer.[82]

Private Daniel C. Bickel, of Stouchsburg, Berks County, Pennsylvania, reported to the *Berks & Schuylkill Journal* on the 11th from Newport Barracks:

Having a few leisure moments, I devote them to writing a few lines to you, to let you know that we arrived safe, in good health and spirits, at these Barracks, on the 7th instant, and pitched our tents and arranged our things. Our tent is a very pleasant one, capable of lodging fifteen men comfortably, though we have but eleven in it — all from Old Berks, as we are not ashamed to own [up to]. There are three hundred or more in the Barracks at present — all first-rate men. A number of them have volunteered to join our company. They like the appearance of our Captain. We will have our company full in a short time. We have two recruiting officers in Cincinnati, though recruits there are scarce. Our Barracks are located very pleasantly on the banks of the Ohio river, opposite Cincinnati, with Covington on our left and Newport in the rear, all in full view from the camp. We expect to leave here for Carthage in the course of ten or twelve days. We have no place for horses here, but have been furnished with splendid uniforms, excelling anything of the kind I have yet seen. We begin to feel like soldiers, and like doing a soldier's duty. Our rations are good and we have plenty to eat, and Captain Terrill sees that his men are well provided for in every respect, and we are all determined to stand by him, as he does by us. He has selected six of our squad to fill non-commissioned offices, and two for buglers, who are taking instructions.[83]

By the middle of September, William obtained permission to buy horses in Cincinnati for one section (two guns) of the battery. About the same time, he wrote the Chief of the Ordnance Department, General Ripley, requesting that he be supplied with fifty fuses, "driven as to burn for 25" & 30". There may arise cases as did in the Battle of Bull Run where such a fuse would enable me with the Parrott Gun to burst spherical case among the enemy whilst at a great distance. *I beg that my Ordnance stores may be hurried up as we expect warm work soon.*"[84]

Two weeks later, William again addressed General Ripley concerning the difficulty in obtaining sabers and Colt revolvers for his men. He acknowledged that Ripley had ordered the weapons, but they had not arrived yet. William asked the general to hurry up at least a part of them, as the "absence of them may cause me to lose my battery."[85]

About ten days later, the issue of the revolvers came up again in another letter to Ripley:

I have the honor to request that you will reconsider your decision in regard to supplying me with Colt pistols called for in my requisition so far at least as to give me a portion of them at present, and I can then wait for the remainder until such a time as you may see fit to direct. I would not presume to press this matter did I not deem it my duty as a soldier to provide my non commissioned officers &c. with the weapons wherewith properly to discharge their duties. And in case of my battery being stormed to make some decent sort of resistance. And last [but] not least to prevent panic stricken volunteers (as they did with other batteries in the battle of Bull Run) from cutting my horses out of the traces and running away with them. My requisition called for 66 Colt revolvers. I have already received the holsters for them. I therefore respectfully request that you will be kind enough to direct me to be furnished with 20 Colts Revolvers and 2000 rounds of ammunition for them. I have now no ammunition for my own pistols.[86]

Meanwhile, back in Virginia, the local newspapers had been completely silent on the subject of Captain Terrill's loyalty. That changed with the

September 24 issue of the *Staunton Spectator*, published in nearby Augusta County:

> **Loyalty of Slaves.**—The slaves belonging to Messrs. Geo. Mayse and Wm. H. Terrill, of Bath county, who were hired at the Salines [salt works] in Kanawha county, as soon as the Yankees approached the place, they were at work, struck a bee line for the homes of their masters at Bath Court House. The slaves of Mr. Terrill have shown a degree of loyalty to the South, which their young master, William Terrill, now in the service of the Lincoln Government, would do well to emulate.[87]

The beginning of October found William still needing recruits to fill out his battery. He reported his strength as forty-four men on October 4. In a letter to Adjutant General Lorenzo Thomas, William noted that several companies of the regiment were at full strength. "I contributed 35 recruits to the filling up of those batteries. Those 35 men would enable me now to take the field. I have now one section organized, and I am using every earthly endeavor to raise another."[88] William then asked the Adjutant General to order Colonel Sherman to send him as many recruits as Thomas saw fit to allow.

His plea for additional recruits brought swift results from the Adjutant General's Office, which issued an order on October 12 to send 60 picked men to Captain Terrill "with all possible dispatch."[89] Lieut. V. H. Stone commanded the detachment of fifty-four men, with instructions to deliver them to Captain Terrill. Lieut. Stone reported on October 19 from Newport Barracks: "I arrived at Pittsburg at 1 P.M. twenty minutes to late to make the connection west. I was therefore compelled to lay over in Pittsburg until 12½ A.M. Although I took every possible precaution to prevent the escape of any of the men, one man Wm. Lopper by name, made good his escape. I arrived at Newport Barracks on Wednesday evening with fifty-three in charge. Capt. Terrill was absent from the Barracks at that time."[90] Lieut. Stone turned the recruits over to Lieutenant Rittenhouse the following day.

William Rufus Terrill, U.S. Army (courtesy Library of Congress, Prints and Photograph Division).

William and his men received a complimentary report in the October 2, 1861, edition of the *Cincinnati Enquirer*.

> "Newport News.
> ARTILLERY DRILL.—Captain Terrell [sic], who has been recruiting an artillery company at the Barracks during the past month, has met with considerable success. We saw him exercising his men and horses, with their gun equipage, yesterday afternoon, on York street. One of their evolutions, "Left, about face," in the march, was admirably well done, giving evidence that they have a good instructor.[91]

A few days after this notice appeared, Terrill's battery moved their camp from Newport Barracks to the fairgrounds at Carthage, Ohio. In this new location, William continued to organize and drill his battery.

A letter to Professor Bache, written from Middletown, Ohio, on October 13 explained William's actions.

> I have now one section of my battery organized—ready for *the work*. I am engaged now in moving with it around the county in hopes of picking up recruits. It has been a *week* since I left New Port [sic] Bks. on the tour, and have gotten only three recruits, so you can imagine my success; but I still have *faith*. Had I been able to recruit in this manner whilst in Pennsylvania I could soon have filled up my battery. The country is now too well drained, nearly all of the available men having volunteered.[92]

William now informed Bache of his family in Virginia, and made a request of him:

> My wife met in Reading Pa. about ten days since a gentleman whom my father had released from prison in Richmond, Va. My father told him to say to me that if I could even now conscientiously resign to *come*, and I would find a welcome. This gentleman said that he had very often heard my name the subject of discussion with Governor Letcher and that my remaining in the "Federal Army" at first caused some suspicion to rest upon my Father [sic], but he soon convinced the authorities that it was not his wish. My father and *Uncle* [George Terrill] (whom you know) are in Richmond with Governor Letcher. I know it will interest you to learn something about my family. My next younger brother [James] was distinguished for gallantry at Manassas & in several other skirmishes since. General Johnson having published his name to the Confederate Army. He is a *Major*. My youngest brother *Philip* a Captain was captured at Rich Mountain and is now on parole. My brother in law, George A. Porterfield a Col. in the C. S. (he was in your employment on the Coast Survey) was dangerously wounded at Phillippi [sic] but is now nearly well. His family are on their farm near Leetown Jefferson Co., Va. My eldest brother—Dr. George Terrill is now at Salem, Va.—not in any public employment. I have a double object in telling you all this. Should the fortunes of war bring any of them wounded or captives to Washington there is no one whose kind offices I would implore so readily as yours shoud such be their fate I beg that you will let me know—and *perhaps* then my *loyalty* may be of service to them.[93]

By the close of October, William's company consisted of 5 officers and 142 enlisted men. The muster roll for Battery H for September and October 1861, carried the comment: "The fact there are no prisoners [from this company] in the guard house on Oct. 31 speaks well of discipline."⁹⁴

Private James F. Mohr, one of William's men, commented on the discipline in the battery:

> We have a good lot of Officers but if you dont [sic] mind you will be tied up there was two tied up already you must not miss roll call or they will put you on double duty the Captain is giveing [sic] some of them hell they are out drilling and they dont mind we catch hell once in a while too I tell you rules are strict here and all we have to do to mind them there was a green horn on gaurd [sic] one night and the Captain of the day came around the gaurd ask him who was there and he said the Captain of the day and the gaurd said if the Captain of the night would meet him he would cetch [sic] hell.⁹⁵

October brought several changes to the Army of the Cumberland. The secretary of war relieved General Robert Anderson from command on October 7 due to bad health. In his place, he assigned Brigadier General William T. Sherman to take command of the army. A week later, Brigadier General Alexander McDonald McCook assumed command the 2nd Division of the Army of the Cumberland. This entire command was under the charge of General Don Carlos Buell, who now commanded the Department of the Ohio.

A letter written by Private James F. Mohr gives a glimpse of the life of a solder in Terrill's battery:

> Revelee [sic] is at six Oclock [sic] morning and grooming right after it forty minutes stable call breakfast after it watering call at eight Oclock Cannon'eer drill between nine and ten purade [sic] till four then roll call right after it then grooming horses forty minutes then roll call and guard mounted then supper at eight Oclock roll call and at 15 minutes past tattoo.⁹⁶

William reported his battery ready for service on November 10, from his camp near Carthage, Ohio.⁹⁷ On the same date, he wrote the Adjutant General in Washington, with the following request:

> I have the honor to request that 1st Lieut. Guy V. Henry, 1st Artillery, may be temporarily attached to my Battery H, 5th Arty. Lieut. Henry belongs to a company stationed at Key West, he is now serving with one of the Light Batteries on the Potomac.
>
> The two Lieuts. belonging to my battery are on detached service — Lieut. Guenther commands a battery in Western Virginia, and Lieut. Smyser is Ordnance Officer of the Department of the Cumberland. The two 2 Lieuts. are recent appointments, and in case of any accident befalling me there is no one with the battery competent to command.⁹⁸

Between November 10 and the 19, William presented numerous requisitions for supplies and equipment for his battery. Private Mohr reported on November 18, "We will get our revolvers and cutlasses before we go. our Captain has gone after them. he started yesterday."⁹⁹

On November 19, General Buell ordered William to take his battery to Louisville, Kentucky. William complied with Buell's order on the 21st of November. Reporting at that city, Buell assigned William to duty at Camp Jenkins, located about four miles southwest of the city. A few days later, the general ordered him to Camp Gilbert, the Camp of Instruction, located about four miles east of Louisville. Here he remained for sometime, in command of the camp.

Captain Charles C. Gilbert inspected William's light battery on November 24, soon after he arrived at Camp Jenkins, and reported:

Discipline — Good

Instruction — Drill of the piece finished that of the battery commenced and in progress about two weeks.

Military appearance — Good

Arms — Four Napoleon Guns, Light 12 pr. [pounder]; Two 10 pr. [pounder] Parrot[t] Guns, rifled; Thirty Sabres (inferior); Twenty Colts Pistols; Ammunition in abundance.

Accoutrements — New, Good & Complete

Forge — complete & in working order

Battery Wagon — not yet arrived

Horses — have had the distemper; have been trained with blank cartridges & have been shod all around.

Clothing — new, good, & plenty

Camp & Gar. Equipage — Tents of the Sibley pattern new & good

Camp Equipage — complete & good

Company Books — on hand and opened

The camp of this battery is in a grove & well situated.[100]

As various batteries reported for duty at the Camp of Instruction, the military authorities placed them under the sharp eye of

Captain William R. Terrill, U.S. Army (courtesy Mr. and Mrs. Philip T. Porterfield).

Captain Terrill for training. This duty required much of William's time and attention, leaving his own battery in need of officers. With that in mind, on November 30, William again requested the return of Lieutenant Guenther from duty in Western Virginia.

One of the batteries assigned to William for training was Captain A. J. Konkle's Battery D, 1st Ohio Light Artillery. This battery was in bad condition when it reached Camp Jenkins, with more than 40 percent of the men on the sick list and the horses unfit for service. Within a month, the battery was in good condition.

The Ohio soldiers were quite complimentary of their instructor:

> Capt. Terrill was an ideal soldier of great experience and was the finest instructor in artillery tactics our battery came in contact with. It was a delight to him to take the sponge staff from an awkward No. 1, and go through the motions himself in detail, saying "you will never forget after I have shown you how once."[101]

The committee that preserved the history of the battery added the following comment about William:

> Captain Terrill had seen many years of active service on the frontier and had been in the active performance of such other duties as he was from time to time assigned to perform. He was a thorough artillerist, a good soldier, and withal a gentleman.
> Battery D owes much of its technical knowledge of the manual of the piece and the drilling of the men by detail, to Capt. Terrill. He was a natural instructor, and often remarked, "Let me show you once and you will never afterwards forget."[102]

After spending some time under William's stern direction, the Ohioans had the following to say about him:

> Capt. Terrill preceded us to this camp [Munfordville] from Camp Gilbert by about ten days. His care and thought for the batteries under his command was supreme and wonderful. We became much attached to him for his soldierly ways and bearing.... Capt. Terrill was most proficient in the drill at the manual of the piece by detail.[103]

In early November, Private Mohr reported their proficiency in the art of being an artilleryman, writing:

> We are packing our Casons wagon every day with cartridges as far as we know we expect to leave before long, from here where to we do not know, very likely to battle, we was a target shooting yesterday we shot ten loads five out of our rifle cannon and five out of our brass cannon we shot a tree down with a twelve pound ball one foot thrue and the shells of our rifle cannon would burst at the target the pieces would stick all around the target to day we don't do any thing but clean our harness and our clothes for inspection.[104]

Lieutenant Colonel J. H. Gilman inspected the artillery of the Department of the Ohio on December 2, 1861. He reported finding William's battery at Camp Jenkins, near Louisville, Kentucky, and that it consisted of two 10-

pounder Parrott guns, and four light 12-pounders. Colonel Gilman noted that he had not "seen the battery drilled" and that "it is fully equipped & in excellent condition so far as guns, horses and equipments are concerned." The colonel added that the battery had more than two hundred rounds of ammunition for each gun and was therefore well supplied.[105]

Another inspection, conducted on the 9th by Major John Buford, gives a more complete picture of Terrill's Battery. Major Buford wrote:

> Capt. Terrill was in command of a camp containing six Vol. Batteries besides his own. These occupied nearly all of his time, preventing him from giving sufficient attention to his own. He was untiring in his exertions to set them right, and to maintain discipline in his command. The police was shockingly bad, the men was very hard to control, and were committing many depredations upon the residents in their vicinity. Capt. Terrill used strong efforts to keep the men in camp, but received so little support from the other Captains, that constant complaint was made against the pilfering carried on at night. *Discipline*, good compared with that of the Vol. Batteries, but nothing to be proud of. *Military Appearance*, bad. Clothing, good material, is not fitted, unaltered, unbrushed, and presents a slovenly appearance. *Equipments*, new, not properly fitted, nor cared for. *Books*, not properly kept nor posted. *Drill*, improving, drills about four hours daily. *Messes*, one in the camp, received but little attention. *Company Fund*, none, has been neglected. *Guard Duty*, too loose. *Guns and Ammunition*, four light 12 pdr. Napoleon and two 10 pdr. Parrott, 350 rounds of assorted ammunition. *C. G. Equipage [Camp & Garrison Equipage]*, good, all Sibley tents, req. attention. *Horses and Equipments*, 137 in number. First class arty. horses, well cared for. Harness new, not properly fitted, nor cared for. *Comp. Offs.*, Studious and industrious. *N. C. Offs.*, zealous.[106]

Among other members of his family, William was the subject of rumor during early December 1861. William's brother, Philip, now a paroled prisoner, was traveling to Richmond to attend the wedding of their brother James. Along the way, he stopped to visit with the Wise family in Culpepper County, Virginia. There, Philip wrote their sister Emily, and reported the rumor:

> I learn through Mrs. Col. [A. P.] Hill, that Wm. Terrill is now on duty in Gen'l. Rosecrans division in Western Virginia. He is said to have left Washington to invade his native state, with *the greatest reluctance,* and it affords me a sad pleasure to know that his willing service, among the Northern rabble has not yet eradicated all those noble and gracious feelings & qualities of heart, which once made him the darling of his family. But this last crowning act of ignominy has severed forever the tie, that bound him to us, and I can but feel, that I had rather hear of his death than hear him branded (as he must inevitably be) as [a] traitor to his country — and that too by personal enemies of him, and his family, who rejoice in this blot up on the name. Hitherto I had entertained some hope that when he became aware of the unanimity of feeling in his State & the utter impossibility of staying a movement so general and enthusiastic, he would have drawn his sword for the South, instead of siding with her enemies. But now he has "crossed the Rubicon" and can never retrieve the steps he has taken. For having once born arms against our Government, he can only change his position by desertion: a step which pride would

"God Alone Knows Which Was Right"

forbid his taking. But enough! for it is sufficiently painful to know of this without aggravating it by comment.[107]

William wrote Professor Bache from Camp Gilbert, near Louisville, on December 16. He informed the professor of his present occupation: "I am now in command of seven batteries of Light Artillery, all volunteer except my own. I am nearly worked to death, but by perseverance am bringing order out of chaos."[108]

On December 20, 1861, William's battery joined General McCook's 2nd Division, Army of the Cumberland, Department of the Ohio. William received orders to report to the general at Munfordville, Kentucky. William complied with the order, and was at Camp Wood, near Munfordville, by December 23.

Soon after reporting to McCook, the general appointed William to the position of Chief of Artillery of the 2nd Division, which he held until June 1862. As Chief of Artillery, William had charge of all the artillery batteries in McCook's Division. The commanding officer of each battery received orders to report in person to William. The former Chief of Artillery, Captain Charles S. Cotter, would soon challenge William's authority.[109]

At the beginning of January 1862, Confederate forces under General Albert Sidney Johnston occupied Fort Henry on the Tennessee River and Fort Donelson on the Cumberland River. Confederate troops moving as far north as Bowling Green, Kentucky, prepared to defend the town.

William spent the latter part of January 1862 in camp at Camp Wood attending to the duties of Chief of Artillery, overseeing six or eight batteries. After reaching Munfordville on the 21st, McCook assigned William's battery to General L. H. Rousseau's brigade. Private Alpheus Bloomfield, Battery A, 1st Ohio Light Artillery [Cotter's Battery], wrote of William:

Drawing of William R. Terrill, prepared from the previous photograph. Note addition of brigadier general stars on his epaulettes (courtesy U.S.M.A. Archives).

The man appointed [Chief of Artillery] was the Captain

of the battery of regulars. His men were all dutch [sic], Irish, and French, and as hard a lot of men as ever were together.... This Captain's name is Terrill. He was in the fight at Bull's Run and lost every gun and all of his men but two. One a Lieut. and the other a private. He came up to our quarters and gave [the] Captain a lot of orders that were of no use to an intelligent company. It made [the] Captain mad and he turned his back and said he would not do any such a thing, that he knew how to take care of his property placed in his hands and that his battery was made up of intelligent men, and more, that he would never make slaves of them. Terrill arrested him, had him court martialed [sic], but has not gotten a decision on it yet."[110]

Private Bloomfield noted that a number of officers in the artillery resigned, placing the blame on William, and stated, "It is all owing to the rigid discipline they have been placed under."[111]

The difficulty between Terrill and Cotter arose in late December 1861. About the 23rd of December, General McCook ordered the battery commanders in the second division to report to Captain Terrill. Cotter failed to do so. About the same time, Terrill issued an order through the Battalion Adjutant, Lieutenant Israel Ludlow, for Cotter to have the harness of his battery put on poles to keep it out of the mud. Cotter responded, "I have receipted for the public property in my charge, and I am competent to take care of it, tell Mr. Terrill if he will ride through my battery, he will see that every thing is in order."[112]

The Chief of Artillery approached Cotter about his manner of responding to Lieutenant Ludlow, and Cotter spoke in an equally insubordinate manner to Terrill: "I command this Battery, I will only obey your orders as chief of Artillery, and Captain, have you anything more to say?"[113]

William did, and pro-

Major General Alexander McD. McCook, commander of the 2nd Division, Army of the Cumberland, under whom William R. Terrill served as Chief of Artillery (courtesy Library of Congress, Prints and Photograph Division).

ceeded to order the Ohio Captain to go to his tent, under arrest. Cotter refused, saying, "I will not go to my tent in arrest."[114] Cotter, however, did return to his tent. On Christmas Day, he visited some friends in the camp of the 1st Ohio Infantry, resulting in additional charges against him.

The charges against Cotter included two counts of disobedience of orders, violation of the 45th Article of War (drunkenness), and two counts of breach of arrest.

In early January, on the 8th, William asked his superiors to drop the charges against Captain Charles S. Cotter. They did not, and on the 16th of January, Cotter appeared before a court-martial. He pled guilty to all the charges against him, except that of drunkenness. After hearing the evidence against him, the court found him guilty of all the charges except one. As punishment, the court recommended that Cotter be cashiered and leave the service at once. The court also stated that "it does not believe that Captain Cotter disobeyed the order of his superior officer intentionally and knowingly or wilfully [sic] broke his arrest. The court is convinced that Capt. Cotter, being comparatively new to the service, was not aware of the peculiar duties of an officer under arrest, and from his former services and general good conduct, the court does not believe him wilfully [sic] though technically guilty of the charges preferred against him."[115]

Major Charles S. Cotter, 1st Ohio Light Artillery, relieved by Terrill as Chief of Artillery, and who defied Terrill's authority, resulting in Cotter being cashiered. President Lincoln later reinstated Cotter (courtesy Library of Congress, Prints and Photograph Division).

Captain Cotter went to Washington to lay his case before President Lincoln and the secretary of war, claiming that the charges were the result of jealousy and hate that regulars have towards volunteers. The Captain's appeal succeeded, and on April 19, 1862, the War Department issued an order announcing his reinstatement, by order of President Lincoln.[116]

Unlike the members of Konkle's Battery, the men of Cotter's Battery were not very complimentary of William and the officers of the regular army. In a letter to the *Portage Democrat*, the correspondent called the regular army officers machines, adding, "It is to be hoped that this nation will never again breed such a crop of autocrats and tyrants as now compose the regular army."[117]

While William was less than popular with the men in the volunteer batteries, his own men seemed well pleased with their captain. Private D. C. Bickel wrote on February 2: "Capt. Terrill is very popular with the men. He sees that they have plenty of everything. There is not another company in this Division as well cared for as ours."[118]

On January 31, the monotony of camp-life was broken for William. Upon his return to camp that evening, he made the following report:

> Captain: In compliance with telegraphic instructions from Head Qrs. of the Dept. through the Gen'l. Comdg. the Division, I have the honor to make the following report (viz):
>
> Gen'l. R. W. Johnson's staff and escort with the remains of [General Felix K.] Zollicoffer[119] & [Lieutenant] Balie [Bailie] Peyton crossed the pontoon bridge at 8:30 AM to-day. I accompanied them. After reaching *Rowlets* Station we turned to the left (SE) and took the Glasgow (mud) road.
>
> A range of high wooded hills approaching us from Green river, their course S.W. About three miles from the Green River bridge this road and railroad passes through a gap in these hills, the valley being less than ¼ of a mile wide: A high rocky and wooded bent to the right as you pass through. The road and railroad turn square to the right (SW) and run parallel to this range of hills till you reach Horse Cave, distant from this point [3] miles more or less. This defile is a strong position for the enemy. If they are once in position with the "*turnpike*" well obstructed it will be a difficult matter to dislodge them, as the hills on each flank are steep and rugged rendering it difficult for us to turn their flanks. Here where the railroad curves to the right they have thrown "cord wood" on the track, this can be easily removed by 20 men in ten minutes.
>
> After passing this point the valley widens. The country is cultivated, with here and there wooded hills. The valley being about one mile wide, increasing in width as you progress towards Bowling Green. Our artillery could here be used with great advantage.
>
> At Horse (cave) the turnpike from Munfordville passes through a gorge in this same range of hills. Here is a position of great strength for them or for us. Whoever secures it first in any force can make a pretty obstinate defence. Approaching Horse Cave you leave the Glasgow road at the school House and pass down a lane ¼ of a mile to the village. This lane comes into the turnpike just beyond the village. A growth of white oak bushes on the hill side thickly leaved here furnish and excellent position for ambuscades of small parties. The Glasgow road as far as Horse Cave has on either side small ponds of water into which cattle have been driven and

then shot by the rebels, their bloated bodies floating on the surface are the best evidence required of the protection to property furnished by a lawless soldiery. These can be readily removed and the water will be fit to drink in 48 hours thereafter.

About one mile below Horse Cave we came in sight of the enemies picket. They galloped back to *Woodland House*. At which place we were met by the officer in command who gave his name as Captain Turner of the "Texas Rangers." This place is nine miles from Green River bridge. Gen'l. Johnson was informed that we could go no farther. He sent a letter to Hindman requesting him to come up and receive the bodies. This was at *12 M*. Hindman came up at 3 PM accompanied by certain of his officers whom he introduced as follows: Col. Hawthorne of the Arkansas Infantry; Capt. Newton, Asst. Adjt. General &c. Also a Brigade surgeon an Adjutant, four Captains of Texas Rangers and an escort of a company of these troops. The Rangers were mounted and dressed each in his own peculiar style; were armed with two, three, and in some cases five revolvers of various sizes, and in addition nearly every one had a double barreled shot gun for which they seemed to have no cartridges, as they carried powder flasks for them. I endeavored to get all the information I could from them, and the country people. There was a rumor that Hardee had gone to Missouri & Buckner to reinforce Crittenden. I was told by country people that an order had been given to all people living on the roads to and connecting with Glasgow to fell trees across them during the next three days. And that the roads leading to Munfordville were to be obstructed in a similar manner so as to impede our advance.

We were very hospitably entertained by Mr. Ritter the proprietor of "Woodland House" who has been a sufferer for our cause.

At 3:30 PM we started on the return. I obtained permission to move in advance and on the "Turnpike." Leaving Horse Cave to the right I passed through the gorge in the hills. The road is here obstructed by trees felled across it at various points for ¼ of a mile, with the exception of about one mile from Horse Cave, this road is paved to the river. The obstructions can be removed by a pioneer party of 100 men in two hours. I moved rapidly so as to see all the road before dark. From this gorge back to Green River there is but one position which would be against us—and that no great advantage—that is at Sterret or Cave Spring. The strong positions are 1 one the Glasgow road, and 2 on the turnpike in the gorge near Horse Cave. The position marked 3 would be a favorable one for us to threaten Hindman in front while would make a night movement and get in rear of him by a column of light troops *well commanded* getting into his rear by the way of the Mammoth Cave and Dripping Springs. If we had a Brigade or more at Horse Cave the railroad in our rear could be repaired *certainly* in 24 hours.

The sketch which accompanies this memoir is rather a rough one, as I have no drawing paper or instruments.[120]

Taking advantage of the flag of truce, William forwarded three letters through the lines. The first letter, he addressed to Virginia governor John Letcher. He asked the governor to forward one of the letters to his brother Philip, and the other to his boyhood friend Alexander H. H. Stuart. In his January 30 letter to Governor Letcher, William wrote:

> I take this opportunity of letting you, and through you my father and other relatives and friends know that I am loyal and true to the Government and *Constitution*

of our fathers. I trust the day is not far distant when we shall be as one once more a united and happy people — save only the memories of this unhappy war.

Hoping soon to see you under the olive branch of peace.[121]

During late January and early February, United States troops under the command of Generals U.S. Grant and Henry W. Halleck moved against Fort Henry. The Confederates abandoned the fort on February 6, many of them fleeing to Fort Donelson.

General Halleck now proposed a bold movement. His forces would move up the Tennessee and Cumberland Rivers, while Buell moved against Bowling Green. Caught between two columns, the Confederates would be forced to abandon Bowling Green.

General Buell, however, had a plan of his own. He planned either to assist Grant in taking Fort Donelson, or to move against Bowling Green. On February 10, Buell started a part of his Army of the Ohio south toward Bowling Green.

McCook's Second Division received their orders to march on February 13. William's battery now formed a part of the 4th Brigade, under the command of General L. H. Rousseau. The 4th Brigade marched at 4 A.M. on the morning of the 14th, and was in the advance of the division. That night, the division established camp on Bacon Creek, and the following morning they resumed their march toward Nolin, Kentucky.

Meanwhile, General Buell learned that the Confederates forces had evacuated Bowling Green; there would be no battle there. At one o'clock on the morning of February 15, orders arrived directing the division to retrace their steps to the Green River. By the time William and his comrades returned to the camp on the Green River, Fort Donelson had fallen into the hands of the Union forces. The city of Nashville was the next target of the Federals.

The Second Division of the Army of the Ohio marched toward Bowling Green on the 19th of February. William commanded the advance guard of McCook's column as it moved on Bowling Green. The force consisted of Battery H, 5th U.S. Artillery, a company of infantry, and a company of cavalry. The following incident occurred on that march:

> Toward dusk on the first day of the march, the advanced guard's cavalry noticed some enemy horsemen in an open field and gave chase. The Confederate troopers spurred their mounts to the rear, making a fast escape. About an hour later, as darkness closed in, Terrill's column came upon a dense wood. The captain could see lights emanating from a point about fifty rods into the trees. He deployed his infantry company as skirmishers and sent [Gunner Peter] Fitzpatrick forward to poke around. The Irishman and his trusty mount Napoleon picked their way through the forest, passing close to a large mansion. He came upon the Federal skirmish line to the rear of the structure. The infantry's captain asked Fitzpatrick where he was going, and offered to come along upon learning that the gunner was going to find out where the lights were coming from. "You better believe I was glad of his company," Fitzpatrick later remarked. The infantryman walked beside Fitz-

patrick's horse. A little deeper into the forest they finally saw some campfires and what appeared to be an enemy camp. Fitzpatrick wanted to get a closer look but the captain's curiosity seems to have been satisfied. He ordered Fitzpatrick to report back to Captain Terrill. The artilleryman replied that he wanted to move closer, at which time the captain grabbed Fitzpatrick's reigns [sic], gave him a quick lecture on the proper relationship between officers and enlisted men, and ordered him to retire.

Fitzpatrick rode back to the main road and reported what he had seen to Captain Terrill. The battery commander sent Fitzpatrick into the woods again with orders to do a proper reconnaissance instead of turning tail at the first sign of trouble. Back the Irishman went determined to not let anyone get in his way. He moved through the skirmish line toward the enemy position. Alone this time, Fitzpatrick took a much closer look:

> "I rode in through the thickest of the woods and took a good look at the camp. There were about a dozen fires and men were lying around them in a circle. I saw a solitary sentinel on the extreme right, sitting on a log, close to a large fire. I advanced towards him shaded by the trees from his view, I asked him who commanded the post. He told me that it was Captain Walker of the Texas Rangers. He drew his revolver and ordered me to dismount and consider myself his prisoner. I didn't believe in that logic, for I had my pistol ready primed. I aimed at his right shoulder, the shot told and I trusted to Napoleon to carry me safe back to the Battery. I think I must have been about a half a mile off when I heard shots whizzing through the trees. I had two railfences to cross before I came to the road but Napoleon crossed them like a brick. Both me and my horse was received with a shout of joy, when we came up."[122]

William was so impressed with Fitzpatrick's actions, that he chose him as his orderly and personal bodyguard.[123]

Arriving at Bowling Green on the 23rd, the division rested two days, then commenced their move to Nashville.

The first United States troops entered Nashville on February 25, meeting with no resistance, as the Confederates were gone. William and the Second Division arrived there on the night of the 28th, covering sixty-five miles in 48 hours. The following day, they went into camp three or four miles south of Nashville, establishing Camp Andy Johnson.

Some excitement occurred while in Camp Andy Johnson, on March 9:

> This morning we were preparing for mounted inspection when the long roll was beat, and in double quick time Capt. Miller's, Capt. Colter's [Cotter's], Capt. Stone's, Capt. Bushe's and Capt. Terrill's Batteries were ready, every man at his post, and waiting for the word "forward," but after waiting twelve hours we were ordered to "un-hitch." I never saw men turn out in as high spirits as they did this morning. They were all certain of having a fight with the Rebels, and every man was ready and anxious to do his duty. Capt. Terrill has five batteries under his command. He is Chief of Artillery, and is considered the most able Artillery officer in the Division, and is very popular with the officers and men under his command.[124]

About the middle of March, an inspection report reached the desk of Brigadier General Don Carlos Buell. The report was less than complimentary to Terrill's Battery, but Buell considered William's past performance. This was most likely the inspection performed by Major Buford in December 1861. Buell wrote:

> It is due to Capt. Terrill to make some explanation of this report. His company was new composed mostly of recruits and young officers. On arriving at Louisville, it became necessary for him to divide his time between his own battery & many others. Capt. Terrill has all the zeal, knowledge of his duties & unwaving application of a first rate officer; and his services with the large amount of raw material (Artillery) that I have had, has been invaluable.[125]

William seemed to have an ongoing problem keeping the ranks of his battery filled. From his camp near Nashville, William requested nine men to fill up his company, noting that he now had sixteen men absent sick. He felt that should his superiors call the battery into action, he would not have enough cannoneers. He added, "I should like to have the nine men picked — not such as I received the last time."[126] General Buell forwarded his request to the War Department.

The Union Army moved further south in mid–March and established a new camp on the north bank of Duck River, opposite Columbia, Tennessee, which they christened Camp Stanton. In the movement to Columbia, Battery H again formed part of the McCook's advance force, and had frequent encounters with 1st Louisiana Cavalry. On one occasion, the battery became involved in a sharp skirmish with the Louisianans. William's bodyguard, Private Peter Fitzpatrick, received a wound in the left arm while defending his captain. Fitzpatrick later noted: "I suffice it to say that four dead lay at our feet."[127]

From Camp Stanton, William wrote the secretary of war about his family, asking consideration for them. He wrote:

> The time has come when our army marches in triumph through my native state Virginia. Though every relative I have in the world is on the other side, and though my father regrets he ever knew me, and they tell me that my name has become a reproach to the family, that its utterance causes their checks to mantle with shame, yet my feelings as a son and a brother are unchanged. And I ask for my own loyalty only that kindness may be shown to them. My sister, the wife of Col. G. A. Porterfield lives near Leetown, Jefferson County, Virginia. My brother Captain Philip M. Terrill, (captured at Rich Mountain) a prisoner on parole is with her. About the 4th of March her stock was driven off her farm and when my brother went to Martinsburg to recover it, although he exhibited his parole he was thrown into the County Jail. He was released the next day. I beg that you will be kind enough to give Mrs. Porterfield a safeguard. She has a large family of small children, and all the property she claims is her own, for I know it was given her by my father. Anyhow the forms of law should be gone through within order to confiscate them.
>
> My father Wm. H. Terrill, Esq., is in Richmond, Virginia. My brother James B. Terrill is a Major in the 13 Regiment Va. Vols. Any kindness that can be shown them should the fortunes of War bring them into our power, will be very thank-

fully received by me. Prof. A. D. Bache *Supdt* of the Coast Survey, who knows me well, can tell you that I have ever been as I now am loyal to the government that educated and made me what I am. And I am now to day as I have been since I received my Cadet Warrant (thirteen years ago) "ready to defend it against all its enemies and opposers whatever."

Trusting you will pardon the liberty I have taken.[128]

The secretary of war filed William's request, and it seems that he took no action upon it at that time. Later in the war, Emily Porterfield would call Stanton's attention to this request.

Following the loss of Forts Henry and Donelson, the Confederates fell back, giving up positions in Kentucky and Western Tennessee. General Johnston concentrated his forces at Corinth, Mississippi, a major transportation center near the Tennessee state line. Here, Johnston prepared to attack Grant's Army of Tennessee before Buell's Army of the Ohio could reinforce it.

At the beginning of April, Grant's army was encamped at Savannah, Tennessee, near Pittsburg Landing. Instead of erecting fortifications, Grant chose to drill his inexperienced troops, as he waited for Buell's army to arrive.

Shiloh — Field of Honor

On the last day of March 1862, William and the Army of the Ohio marched southward, headed for Savannah, Tennessee, on the Tennessee River. The advance of Buell's army began arriving at that location on the evening of April 6, 1862, finding the battle already in progress.

The Confederates made their attack on Grant's position on the morning of April 6. The attack was a complete surprise to Grant's men, many of which fled before the Confederate onslaught. As the day progressed, the Federals rallied and established a line at the sunken road that would become known as the Hornets Nest. Grant established a second line near Pittsburg Landing, supported by artillery and the advance elements of Buell's army.

General P. G. T. Beauregard assumed command of the Confederate forces after General Johnston received his mortal wounded in the day's fighting. General Beauregard was unaware that Buell's army was now arriving, bolstering Grant's hard-pressed troops.

William and his battery were at Savannah, Tennessee, waiting to go into battle. Late on the night of April 6, William wrote Professor Bache:

> While lying on the ground in front of Genl Grant's Hd. Qrs. waiting for the boat to take me up to Pittsburg Landing — to open on the enemy at daylight I thought I would ask the loan of a pen and ink to write to you at the last moment. Tomorrow my country may demand the sacrifice of my life to my principles — and there is I know no man living who would be more pleased than you to learn that I am *firmer* than ever — My battery is looked upon as one of our mainstays. I am also in command of two volunteer batteries which I hope will tell. Thus far the enemy have had the advantage — tomorrow we hope to turn the tide.
>
> Dr. [Dallas] Bache is my surgeon. I bid you goodbye.[129]

On the morning of April 7, Brigadier General William "Bull" Nelson made a two-mile advance against the Confederates. General Beauregard ordered a counterattack, which halted Nelson's progress but did not break his line. It was during the fighting on the morning of the 7th that William and his battery won the praises of General Nelson.

Terrill's battery of six guns was laboriously loaded aboard a small steamer for the trip to Pittsburg Landing on the night of April 6. Major J. Montgomery Wright recalled the trip: "I remembered how I had gone up to Shiloh with Terrill's Battery in a small steamer, and how, at the first break of daylight came, Terrill, sitting on the deck near me, had recited a line about the beauty of the dawn, and wondered how the day would close upon us all."[130]

Upon reaching Pittsburg Landing about 9 A.M., Terrill and his men began unloading the battery, "manhandling caissons, guns, and teams up the bluff."[131] Their presence added to the confusion and crowd gathered on the riverbank.

Scanning the crowd, McCook's aide, Lieutenant W. T. Hoblitzell, strained to catch sight of a familiar face. He soon caught sight of the tall, stern-faced, and bearded Terrill, and made his way to him. He advised the captain that General McCook needed him as soon as possible, and that he would guide the battery to his position.

Everything ready, Hoblitzell and Terrill set out on the Corinth Road, but soon became lost. Taking a wrong turn, Hoblitzell led the battery to a position near the Bloody Pond on the Federal left. This was a fortunate error for General Nelson, now hard pressed by General Hardee's Confederates. General Buell, who happened to be nearby, ordered William to Nelson's support, near the Sarah Bell Field.

The arrival of William's battery was a welcome sight, and a soldier of the 6th Ohio Infantry recalled its arrival:

> Looking over my right shoulder, with what joy I saw artillery coming through the woods at a gallop! It was Captain Terrill's battery of regulars, just up from Savannah by boat, with Terrill himself—splendid officer and kind soul of knightliest honor—riding ahead of it. He dashed out to the edge of the wood, and, with a single sweep of the eye taking in the whole situation, waved his hand for the battery to wheel into position.[132]

Within two minutes, William's six-gun battery was in position and firing on the enemy. The second round exploded a limber-chest of Captain Felix Robertson's Florida Battery. The Confederate artillerist then withdrew his guns as the gray line began to waver. General Nelson and his division resumed their advance on the Confederates, Terrill's Battery trailing along. Twenty minutes after the arrival of Terrill's battery, "the whole aspect of the battle changed."[133]

Confederate General P. G. T. Beauregard later noted that "Ammen's brigade was also seriously pressed and must have been turned but for the opportune arrival and effective use of Terrill's regular battery of McCook's division."[134]

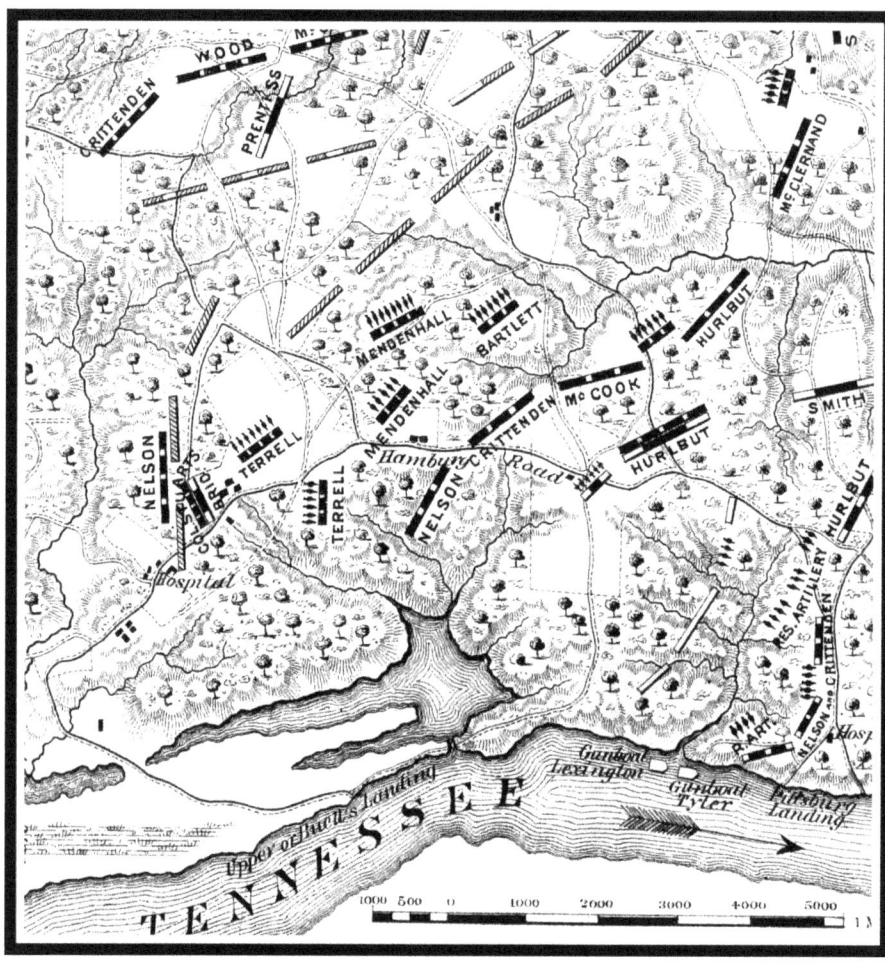

Map of Shiloh, Tennessee. Map showing positions occupied by Terrill's Battery, April 7, 1862 (detail of the Battle of Shiloh map, *The Medical and Surgical History of the War of the Rebellion* [1861–65]).

A correspondent from the *New York Tribune* witnessed the operation of Terrill's Battery on April 7:

> Captain Terril's [sic] regular battery came dashing up. Scarcely taking time to unlimber he was loading and sighting his pieces before the caissons had turned, and in an, instant was tossing in shell from 24-pound howitzers to the compact and advancing rebel ranks.
> Here was the turning point of the battle on the left. The rebels were only checked, not halted. On they came, Horse after horse from the batteries was picked off. Every private at one of the howitzers fell, and the gun was worked by Capt. Terril [sic] himself and a corporal.[135]

William now split his command, sending two guns to the right of Nelson's line to support Colonel William B. Hazen's brigade. He then advanced his remaining guns to the other side of the Peach Orchard, joining the Federal skirmish line. Battery H opened fire on the opposing artillery and quickly silenced it.

The Confederates charged in strong force on the Union skirmishers, firing a "storm of musket balls, canister shot, and shell" against the infantry and artillery. Private Fitzpatrick described the intensity of the fire, comparing it to "a handful of sand thrown against a window."[136]

The line of Union infantry near Terrill's Battery gave way before the terrible onslaught, leaving his gunners without support. William had no choice but to fall back. As he did so, he continued to fire one section at a time, covering the retreat of the other. It was during this part of the battle that William served one gun while Lieutenant Ludlow served the other, each doing the work of seven men.

An officer of the nearby 6th Ohio Infantry, who reported the event to the *Cincinnati Daily Commercial*, witnessed this scene:

> I cannot refrain here from paying a tribute to this heroic officer — the bravest of the brave. Captain Terrill's relatives are Secessionists. His father and three brothers hold high positions in the rebel army and he has been disinherited and disowned by them for his loyalty for the Union. The rebels will long remember the "Napoleons" he handled so effectively on the 7th of April, 1862. At one time during the day they approached within fifty yards of a gun that he was commanding and killed or wounded every man but one, and yet he loaded and fired it with his own hands, until the foe fell back terror stricken. The piles of mangled bodies on this side of the field speak for the efficiency of his battery. I saw him with one shell kill five horses, dismount a gun, and scatter the rebel gunners in all directions. The brilliant results of the fight on the left wing was attributable mainly to his skill and heroism.[137]

William was not the only one to exhibit great bravery that April morning. Sergeant Richard Metcalf, shot in the head, remained at his post despite the loss of blood and pain. Receiving a second wound in the left leg, he finally crawled to the rear. Private James F. Mohr commented on the bravery of his comrades: "One gunner was left at one gun when he saw the last boy fall at his gun he commenced a crying and run for ammunition again and loaded and fought till they retreated ... such boys are worth having in the field."[138]

William rejoined the main battle line, pursued by the Confederate forces. About 11 A.M., Nelson saw the danger in which the battery was now in, and approached Lieutenant Colonel Nicholas Anderson, commanding the 6th Ohio Infantry. "Colonel Anderson," said he, "I have conferred upon your regiment the honor of defending this battery, the best in the service. *It must not be taken!*"[139]

The colonel responded at once, advancing the 6th Ohio Regiment to meet the enemy. William was glad to see his friend moving to his defense, and continued to watch over his battery. Within an hour, the battery had lost so heavily, that William could not operate all of his guns, and the Confederates were getting closer. Again, Nelson came to his rescue, calling for volunteers among the ranks of the infantry. Ten men from the ranks of Company A, 6th Ohio Infantry dashed forward and quickly took their positions in the battery. Their timely arrival helped drive back the Confederate threat.

Private D. C. Bickel of Terrill's Battery recalled the fighting at this point:

> They [the Confederates] fought like tigers and made several charges on our Battery, but we played out the canister so hard that they couldn't keep up their line. Their flag was once inside of two hundred yards of my piece. They shot down six of my horses; one ball singed the hair on my head and my haversack, strung around my neck, was knocked into a cocked hat, and my cup and plate were riddled. One ball glanced and struck me on the breast, nearly stunning me, but the skin was not cut.[140]

An unidentified staff officer of the Second Division later wrote of the fight for *Harper's New Monthly Magazine*:

> Like a whirlwind Terrill followed [the arrival of Mendenhal's Battery]. His Virginia blood was up. "Nearer, nearer; give them double canister into their very faces!" he shouted to his drivers. The rebels did not take this tamely, but turned with fierce rage upon the batteries. A Missouri regiment came down on Terrill. Pitilessly he hurled a storm of fire and iron into their faces. But steadily and with even tread they still advanced. All the cannoneers were killed at one piece. Terrill and a corporal worked the gun alone, until an unknown but gallant infantry sergeant volunteered to help. Terrill grimly standing at the vent, shouted, "Canister! Canister!" Quick as light the sergeant flew to the caisson. Loaded with three charges he came back to the gun, when, struck full in the forehead, he fell dead, his body rolling to the feet of the corporal. He, brave fellow, faltered not, but drove the three charges home. Terrill's quick eye for a moment swept along the smoke-grimed piece. Then came a blinding flash, a stunning crack. Prone in their breasts the iron tempest struck the advancing regiment, blowing some from the very muzzle of the gun. They staggered, reeled; then Missouri's pride and chivalry broke, and like a shattered wave ebbed back, sweeping the supporting regiments with them.[141]

William's orderly and bodyguard, Peter Fitzpatrick, later learned from a captured rebel that "Bureguard [sic] brought a brigade of Mississippians and offered every man $100, if they could take Turrells [sic] Battery, But they found the Irishmen of our Battery to tough for them, for I must tell you that the Battery is composed of nearly all Irishmen."[142]

Private Mohr, in a letter home the following month, noted that "we have won a name upon our Battery in the Battle at shiloh that will be known for many years, every General farely [sic] worships him — that is our captain."[143]

William's report of his first battle is as follows:

BATTLE-GROUND OF PITTSBURG LANDING,
April 8, 1862.

CAPTAIN: I have the honor to make the following report:

On Sunday, April 6, by a forced march General McCook's division, to which my battery was attached, reached Savannah, Tenn., at 8 o'clock P.M. We waited in a drenching rain until 3 o'clock on Monday morning, April 7, for a steamer to take us to Pittsburg Landing. The battery was embarked by daylight, and immediately after reaching Pittsburg Landing was disembarked and hurried into action. By Lieutenant Hoblitzell, General McCook's aide-de-camp, the battery was conducted to the ground occupied by General Nelson's division, which at that time was sorely pressed by the enemy. The battery fought until about 4 o'clock P.M., when the fire of the enemy was silenced. General Nelson then moved his division forward, and we encamped on the ground the enemy had occupied the night before. In the early part of the action the right section of my battery was assigned a position near the right of the division, and was of great service in silencing one of the enemy's, which was playing on the left and center of the division. After the firing on the left became very severe the section was moved, by permission of General Nelson, to the support of the remainder of the battery, and was of great assistance in repelling the advance of the enemy. This section was commanded by First Lieut. Francis L. Guenther, who behaved with that coolness and bravery which he displayed on a former occasion in Western Virginia, and I especially commend him to the favorable consideration of the highest authorities. Sergeants Davis, Egan, and Maubeck, and Corporals Ervin and Lynch, are especially commendable, though the conduct of all the men attached to the section gave much satisfaction to their chief.

Soon after the commencement of the action I advanced the left and center sections, commanded respectively by First Lieut. J. H. Smyser and Second Lieut. Israel Ludlow, along the line of skirmishers, where the fire was most galling. I was compelled to this to gain the crest of the ridge to fire upon the enemy's batteries, which were playing upon our skirmishers. After silencing their fire they seemed to be reenforced with fresh troops, and with vociferous cheers charged along the whole line. The infantry with us gave way before the storm of musket balls, canister shot, and shell, which was truly awful. Lieutenant Ludlow's section was immediately sent to the rear to protect the retreat of Lieutenant Smyser's, which was well done. One of Lieutenant Ludlow's caissons was left here, all the horses having been killed or wounded, but we recovered it later in the day. I served one of Lieutenant Smyser's pieces (the fifth, a Napoleon) and he the other. We fixed prolonges and fired retiring. The enemy charged us, but were staggered by our discharges of canister, whilst Lieutenants Guenther and Ludlow, on our left, poured spherical case shot into them. We checked their advance three times, retiring as they charged upon us. From the vigor of their fire, their cheering, and the impetuosity of their advance I judged they were re-enforced each time. For a time Lieutenant Smyser and Corporal Roberson served the fifth piece (a Napoleon) alone. Sergeant Metcalf, chief of the sixth piece, behaved with great gallantry and devotion. Though wounded in the head by a musket-ball, he gallantly stood by his captain till wounded in the leg and compelled to crawl off. Corporal Brodie and Private John T. Carroll served at this piece until we silenced the enemy's fire. A sergeant of infantry, seeing us sorely pressed, brought up ammunition at my request. He served but a few moments, when he was shot down. I do not know his name nor the regiment to which he belonged, and was not able to find his body after the battle. Private John Marshall, of Company E, Twenty-fourth Ohio Volunteers, having expended his cartridges, threw down his musket and served as a cannoneer during the remainder of the action. He was of great service.

After checking the advance of the enemy we shelled the woods where they were, and at 3.30 P.M. all was quiet in front of General Nelson's division, when he ordered a change to the position last occupied by the enemy. The Sixth Regiment Ohio Volunteers were then reserved as a support to my battery. The skirmishers thrown to our front discovered that the enemy had abandoned that position. Seeing General McCook sorely pressed and a battery in the woods about half a mile to our right playing upon his division, I opened fire upon the battery with two Napoleon guns. In an instant that battery and one to its rear, and nearer us, opened.[144] Having but few cannoneers, I called upon Lieutenant-Colonel Anderson for a detail of men from his regiment to man the guns. The men soon came forward, and the Napoleons began to tell. Lieutenant Smyser's piece was disabled by a shot tearing off the center axle-strap, when the next recoil of the piece tore off the other two. Lieutenant Guenther, in the mean time, with his section had advanced with General Nelson's skirmishers, and he took these batteries in reverse. They were soon silenced, and I enfiladed the enemy's line with shells and spherical case-shot. My center section was posted so as to prevent our left flank being turned. Our fire must have told fearfully, for very soon General McCook's whole line rapidly advanced and drove the enemy before them, and the day was ours. After ascertaining that the enemy had retreated, Captain Fry, chief of staff, ordered me out on the road leading to Corinth, to camp for the night with General Nelson's division. We remained all night in the camp occupied by the enemy the previous night, and the next morning at daylight returned to the battle-ground.

I have already spoken of Lieutenant Guenther's gallant conduct, but I cannot close my report without doing justice to my other gallant officers. Asst. Surg. Dallas Bache, U.S. Army, who has been with my battery, and the chief medical officer of the artillery of the Second Division, was on the field of battle, attending the wounded, not only of the artillery, but of all arms, friends and foes. Words can hardly express my appreciation of his services and great devotion to duty. For five long, weary months in camp, during the most trying weather, he has been unremitting in his devotion to the sick, and yesterday his conduct on the battle-field crowned it all. First Lieut. Jacob H. Smyser, Fifth Artillery, behaved with great gallantry, and fought his piece with desperation amid the hail of missiles of every description. With but one man left at his piece he brought it safely off. Second Lieut. Israel Ludlow, Fifth Artillery, behaved with great gallantry, and for so young a man acquitted himself with great credit. I commend him and Lieutenant Smyser to the favorable consideration of my superiors. Second Lieut. B. F. Rittenhouse, Fifth Artillery, had been left on the road to Savannah with our baggage train, and did not participate in the action. I regret his absence, inasmuch as it deprives me of the pleasure of adding his name to those of his gallant brother subalterns.

The Sixth Regiment Ohio Volunteers, when selected to support my battery, came forward with alacrity. They stood by me to the last, and when the fire of two of the enemy's batteries was concentrated upon us, the shot and shell falling around us, not a man moved. Their gallant commander, Lieutenant-Colonel Anderson, proved himself a true soldier, and had the enemy charged us again, my Napoleons would have been protected by a support in which I have the utmost confidence.

I am, sir, very respectfully, your obedient servant,

WM. R. TERRILL,
Capt. Fifth Arty., Comdg. Bat. H, Chief of Arty., Second Div.

Capt. DANIEL. McCook,
Assistant Adjutant-General, Second Division.[145]

When the government published the official records, they omitted a portion of William's report. The missing text is as follows:

Annexed is a list of the Killed and Wounded.

Killed
1. Private James Carroll

Wounded
1. Sergeant Richard Metcalf
2. Sergeant James H. Reed
3. Corporal Robert Dunn
4. Private Alexander Allen
5. Private Frederick Castle
6. Private Daniel Cunningham
7. Private James Duffy
8. Private John Ebersole
9. Private Patrick Kelly
10. Private John H. Long
11. Private George Metzgar
12. Private John Mulhall[146]
13. Private Martin McFarden
14. Private Bernard Devine

Recapulation
- 1 Killed
- 14 Wounded
- 12 Horses Killed
- 7 Horses Wounded

Ammunition Expended

Light 12 Pdr. or Napoleon Gun
- 53 Solid Shot
- 19 Shell
- 65 Spherical Case
- 29 Canister

10 Pdr. Parrott Gun
- 26 Shells, time fuze
- 11 Percussion
- 11 Spherical Case
- 23 Cannister[147]

The loss to Terrill's battery during the seven hours fighting on April 7 along the Hamburg Road and at the Peach Orchard was light when compared with the losses in other units. Terrill's battery went into battle that morning with 130 men on the rolls of his battery. Of that number, only 116 were engaged in the fighting. His loss in horses was much heavier, having twelve killed and seven wounded.[148] Terrill's battery sustained most of its loss during the retreat from the Confederate onslaught at the Peach Orchard.

General Nelson, in his report of the battle, was most complimentary of William and his battery, writing:

> The powerful re-enforcements which the enemy again had received, which made the woodland in front of us at times a sheet of flame, compelled me at 9 A.M. again to ask for support. The general sent to my aid Battery H, Fifth Artillery, Regular Army, commanded by Captain Terrill. This battery was a host in itself. It consists of four 12-pounder brass guns and two 10-pounder Parrott guns. Its fire was terrific. It was handled superbly. Wherever Captain Terrill turned his battery silence followed on the part of the enemy.[149]

In addition to praising the service of Terrill's battery in his report, Nelson forwarded a copy of the above paragraph to the commanding officer of the 5th U.S. Artillery, in Harrisburg, Pennsylvania. The general explained his reason for sending the extract from his report:

> Which paragraph I copy and send to you in order that the testimony which I have borne to the distinguished conduct of Captain Terrill may be recorded in the archives of his regiment. Captain Terrill, his officers and soldiers won for themselves on the 7th April both the admiration and the thanks of the 4th Division.[150]

General Buell, commander of the Army of Ohio, praised William's service at Shiloh. In his official report, Buell wrote, "I specially commend to the favor of the Government, for ... distinguished gallantry and good conduct ... Capt. W. R. Terrill, Fifth Artillery."[151] Brigadier General Alexander McD. McCook, commanding the 2nd Division, recommended William for promotion, writing:

> The verbal acknowledgment to me of General Nelson, he [Terrill] fought his battery gallantly and judiciously, and I commend him and his officers to my superiors. Captain Terrill, on account of his strict attention to duty in the past and conspicuous gallantry in this terrible conflict, is worthy of any promotion that can be bestowed upon him.[152]

In the *History of the Old Second Division*, the writer noted that "the battery, after constant action and serious loss, had the honor of assisting in the last and most fearful repulse of the foe. Indeed it did much to cause it."[153]

Private Alpheus Bloomfield, of Battery A, 1st Ohio Light Artillery, who had spoken so critically of William only a short time before, now wrote: "Captain Terrill that we hated so fought bravely. He silenced two of the best batteries the rebels [had] after having some of his men killed. He and his Lieut. took a post of their guns."[154] A few days afterward, Bloomfield again passed on compliments for his former enemy:

I do not suppose that there ever was better fighting done than that by Terrill's men. They went into it early on Monday and stuck to it all day. He lost two men, fifteen wounded and twenty horses. The captain and his first lieutenant ascted [sic] as No. 1 on one of the guns. His guns were four smooth bore, two twelve pounders and two six pounder, parret [sic] rifle. He silenced two of the best batteries the rebels had and they tried several times to charge on two of his batteries and were defeated every time. At one time he saw the rebels crawling up on their hands and knees in a thicket to make a charge, so he attached a prolong to his piece and fired canister and grape. It did not leave a bush standing. It completely mowed them down to about two feet high. I do not see how a man could have escaped alive, and by the way the bodies lay on the ground I do not think many did escape.... We are all better pleased with old Terrill than we ever were. In fact we think he is about right in the fighting line. We thought the report was true that he had lost his battery and all of his men in the Bull Run fight but we learn that he was not there. Terrill says he has two brothers and his Father in the rebel army. All of the prisoners the rebels take had to go through his hands. Both of his brothers are officers. I have but little doubt Terrill killed more than one hundred to each one that he lost.[155]

Captain J. H. Gilman, inspector of artillery in the Army of the Ohio, noted in his official report the condition of Terrill's battery following the battle:

No injury was sustained by his guns, carriages, or equipments except that the axle-straps were torn off one of the axles by a ball, which have been replaced, and injuries to harness, which can be repaired from captured pieces. He expended with his two Parrott guns 26 shell (time fuse), 11 percussion shell, 11 case shot, and 28 canister; with his light 12 pounders 53 solid shot, 19 shell, 65 spherical case and 29 canister, in all, 242 rounds.[156]

The inspector also noted that William would require twenty horses for his battery, and a fresh supply of ammunition. The ammunition, he wrote, was already on the way.

A few days after the battle, someone asked William to tell them about his part in the big fight. William simply replied, "All I know about it is that I was in a mighty warm spot all the time, and did the best I knew how."[157]

William was not the only one receiving praise for the conduct of his battery in the battle. Private Mohr noted several days after the battle that "[the] Captain is proud of his boy's they fought nobly."[158]

William did not forget the service of the men of the 6th Ohio Infantry. On April 10, he wrote to the Adjutant of the 4th Division, commending the actions of the men who "came forward first to man my guns, when called upon."[159]

On April 17, Confederate Lieutenant Sam Harris delivered some dispatches to General Buell, under a flag of truce. Harris, in his report of the exchange, said that upon entering the Union lines, General McCook and a number of officers met him. The lieutenant turned over the dispatches for General Buell, and then McCook engaged him in conversation about the recent battle. Lieutenant Harris wrote:

During the whole conversation I was treated pleasantly and courteously. A Virginian, captain of artillery (Federal), Terrill by name, expressed a desire to see General Bragg to get his opinion as to how his battery was served during the recent fight. He also wished to send two bottles of brandy by me to General Hardee whom he knew at West Point, but which I refused to take.[160]

On April 24, 1862, the U.S. forces made a reconnaissance on the road to Corinth. The roads being dry enough to allow the passage of artillery, William and his battery went along. About 9 miles from Pittsburg Landing, they surprised a force of Confederates at Pea Ridge, near Monterey, Tennessee. Following a brief skirmish, the Confederates fled, and the Union forces returned to camp at Pittsburg Landing.[161]

William and his battery remained in camp on the field of Shiloh until early May 1862. From that position, the army moved on May 3 in the direction of Corinth, Mississippi, twenty-two miles to the south. The battery went into camp on the 12th, four miles from Corinth. Having earned a good reputation in the recent fighting at Shiloh, General McCook's Second Division remained in reserve. William's battery, referred to "as good a one as is in the service," formed a part of this force.

On May 27, McCook's Division moved forward to engage the enemy. Without firing a shot, the battery took a position within a thousand yards of the enemy entrenchments, where it remained for two days, expecting the Confederates to fire on them at any time. William's Battery H was the closest artillery to the city of Corinth.

About the 29th of May, Terrill's battery camped in the center of the 1st Battalion of the 19th U.S. Infantry. One night there were several false alarms and at least one of the teams stampeded. Captain Terrill's loud voice rang out from the right: "Be quiet men! It is only a stampede of the teams!"[162] The team continued on and caused chaos in Corinth.

On the morning of the 30th, the Northern troops made a reconnaissance, revealing the fact that the Confederates had evacuated Corinth. They then learned that Terrill's battery enfiladed a great portion of the enemy's fortifications.[163]

The battery left Corinth on June 10, 1862, and marched to Jackson's Ford, beyond Tuscumbia, Alabama. They finally went into camp about seven miles from Huntsville, Alabama. Soon after going into camp near Huntsville, the army granted William a leave of absence for 30 days, for health reasons.[164] He left the battery on June 19 and went to Louisville, Kentucky, and Cincinnati, Ohio. He never returned to his beloved company.

On June 30, 1862, General Louvall H. Rousseau wrote Secretary of War Stanton about William: "Permit me to recommend to you for promotion by brevet for good conduct and gallant service in the battle of Shiloh on the 7th of April 1862, the following persons: Wm. R. Terrill, Capt., 5th U.S. Artillery."[165]

After tending to his business in Louisville, William went to Cincinnati to visit his friend, Larz Anderson. Anderson, an attorney, was the father of the lieutenant colonel of the 6th Ohio Infantry that had rushed to his aid at Shiloh. William P. Anderson, another of his sons, became William's assistant adjutant general in September. While climbing the steps to the front door, the Andersons saw him stagger and nearly fall. Rushing to his side, they helped William into the house, placed him on a sofa, and sent for a physician. The physician quickly diagnosed William's illness as typhoid fever. Mrs. Anderson tenderly nursed him through the violent fever, and the long convalescence afterward.[166]

When his leave of absence was about to expire, William requested a forty day extension on July 14. William reported that his physician in Cincinnati said he would be unfit for duty for that length of time. He also informed the army that he would be going to Reading, Pennsylvania.[167] General Buell forwarded the request to the Adjutant General's office, with the recommendation that it be granted.

Two weeks later, Army Surgeon John Moore provided a certificate of examination.

> This is to certify that I have examined Capt. Terrill of Co. "H" 4th [5th] Reg. U.S. Artillery, and that I find him suffering from the debility consequent on a severe attack of Typhoid fever after the subsidence of the fever, he was still further reduced and his recovery protracted by an abscess of the left Parotia Glana.[168] This has just healed up. He will not, in my opinion, be able to resume his military duties, in a less period than thirty days from this date.[169]

William's wife, Emily, wrote to his sister from Reading, Pennsylvania, on July 17, reporting his sickness:

> Willie has been very ill with typhoid fever and a large abscess on his neck, greatly aggravated his sufferings. He was absent from his command on public business, and went to Cincinnati to spend Sunday with some friends and arrived at his destination just in time to be put to bed. How Providential that he was not taken sick on the road! He has had the tenderest care, and is now rapidly convalescing. He will come here as soon as he is able to travel. I expect him in a week or ten days, he will remain here until strong enough to return to duty.[170]

William was in Reading by August 4, 1862, where he reported to the Adjutant General, forwarding Dr. Moore's certificate to that office. William reported:

> I was on my way to Louisville under *orders* from the *Hd. Qrs.* Army of the Ohio, and "to return after the completion of certain duties." I was taken sick with typhoid fever, from the effects of which I am now recovering. I would respectfully request that I may be authorized to delay joining my command until the date mentioned in the Certificate. I shall not remain absent if I am able to do duty before that time as I am fully aware of the fact that every soldier is needed at his post, and none can be more anxious than I to be there.[171]

The citizens of Reading honored William on the evening of August 4. The *Reading Daily Times* reported:

> On Monday evening, Capt. Terrill, of the 5th U.S. Artillery, who done such gallant service at the battle of Shiloh, was serenaded at the Mansion House by the Reading Cornet Band. After the discoursing of some excellent music, the Captain was called for, and on whose appearance the crowd cheered vociferously. After a few remarks by the Captain, and more music, the crowd departed, well pleased with doing honor to a gallant soldier.[172]

Although absent from his beloved battery, William was in close contact with Lieut. Guenther, who commanded the battery in his absence. In addition, he handled some administrative matters while in Reading, Pennsylvania. Near the end of August, he assisted Sergeant James H. Reed in obtaining a pension from the government. Sergeant Reed was one of his men, and received a serious wound at the Battle of Shiloh in April.[173]

Near the end of August 1862, Confederate troops under the command of Major General Edmund Kirby Smith were making their way into central Kentucky. Other troops under the command of General Braxton Bragg were moving through Tennessee, hoping to draw Major General Buell away from Chattanooga. During the same period, Union troops belonging to General William Nelson held positions near Richmond and Lexington, Kentucky.

On August 29, advance units of Smith's command encountered a Union brigade just south of the Kentucky town of Richmond. The Confederates forced Brigadier General Mahlon D. Manson, the Union commander, to fall back to a defensive position near the town. General Manson sent word to Nelson that he was under attack.

About this time, Nelson asked General Wright to send William to join him. The general responded on the 29th, "Have sent for Terrill, and you shall have him if his health permits."[174] William, then at Reading, Pennsylvania, must have left for Lexington, Kentucky, as soon as he received Wright's message.

General Smith's Confederates attacked Manson in force on the 30th, breaking his brigade and forcing them to run. Late in the battle, General Nelson arrived and succeeded in rallying about 2,000 men, but it was too little, too late. To complicate matters, a wound disabled Nelson and they thought Manson was a prisoner. General Nelson and the remnants of Manson's brigade fell back to Lexington, Kentucky.

A New General

Major General Horatio G. Wright, commander of the Department of the Ohio, left Cincinnati on August 31 for Lexington, Kentucky. Upon his arrival at Lexington, he could find only about 900 of General Manson's troops. In addition to this handful of men, there were only eight other regiments there, mostly new troops. With Nelson out of service, that left only two general officers available to command of the troops. Both Brigadier General Charles Cruft and Brigadier General James S. Jackson declined the chance to take charge of the troops at Lexington. Instead, the two officers presented the names of two of their fellow officers to General Wright on September 1, 1862. They wrote:

> [We] earnestly recommend the appointment of Capt. Charles C. Gilbert, of the First Infantry, U.S. Army, to be major-general in command of all the forces here, and of Capt. W. R. Terrill, of Fifth Artillery, U.S. Army, to be brigadier-general in command of a brigade. Both of these officers are now here, rendering efficient service in many capacities, and we believe that their efficiency would be greater, and the interest of the command promoted, by conferring on them the ranks herewith respectfully suggested and recommended.[175]

General Wright then issued the following order:

> GENERAL ORDERS No. __.
> HDQRS. DEPARTMENT OF THE OHIO,
> *Louisville, Ky., September* 1, 1862.
>
> I. Capt. C. C. Gilbert, First Infantry, U.S. Army, is hereby appointed a major-general of volunteers, subject to the approval of the President of the United States, and is assigned to the command of the Army of Kentucky during the temporary absence of Major-General Nelson.
>
> II. Capt. William R. Terrill, Fifth Artillery, U.S. Army, is hereby appointed a brigadier-general of volunteers, subject to the approval of the President of the United States, and will report to Major-General Gilbert for instructions.
>
> * * * * * * * * *
>
> By command of Major-General Wright:
>
> C. W. FOSTER,
> *Assistant Adjutant-General.*[176]

With such an inadequate force to meet the seasoned troops of General Smith, Wright felt he had no other choice but to order the evacuation of Lexington. He gave the order and left for Louisville on the evening of September 1, 1862, and arrived there about 4:30 A.M. the next day.

At Louisville, Wright defended his decision to appoint William, stating: "I believe in making these appointments I have acted for the best interest of the service.... General Terrill is also favorably known to the service, has served gallantly through the war, and is, I am sure, entitled to some such mark of recognition of his services, zeal, and intelligence."[177]

General Wright concluded his report with the comment, "If the force at Lexington is brought off safely it will be due mainly to the good management of those officers."[178]

Meanwhile, back in Lexington, the troops prepared to leave for Louisville. Wagons were loaded to capacity with military stores, and the remainder burned. Late in the evening of September 1, the United States forces marched out of Lexington. William was given the task of bringing out the remaining artillery (three batteries), and moved in the rear of the infantry.

Captain F. B. James, 52nd Ohio Infantry, later recalled the march:

> Captain W. R. Terrill, of the regular artillery, who had distinguished himself at Shiloh, had been appointed by General Wright, a Brigadier General under Gilbert,

and the latter gave him the post of honor, the rear. Under Terrill's directions, a gun squad, improvised from the infantry rear guard, by a liberal application of turnpike dust and elbow grease, made one of these brass guns shine like a mirror. Many times, when the enemy's cavalry appeared in the distance, the gun was unlimbered upon some elevation, the squad stood to their places, and the fierce rays of the sun did the rest. Scott's cavalry must often have wondered why an occasional shell was not let loose at them.[179]

After a difficult march of more than ninety miles, General Gilbert and the troops from Lexington reached Louisville on the afternoon of September 5. Reporting his arrival to General Wright at Cincinnati, Gilbert was very complimentary of William and his services: "I have reached this place with my command, and it is now posted for the defense of the city. I had the most cordial and efficient support of Brigadier-Generals Jackson, Cruft, and Terrill. The reputation of the latter as an artillerist gave confidence and steadiness to the rear of the column."[180]

The march from Richmond, Kentucky, to Louisville was a difficult one for the inexperienced soldiers. First Lieutenant John Calvin Hartzell, a member of the 105th Ohio Infantry, noted in his recollections: "General Terrell [sic], a regular army officer, managed the retreat, and, though we all thought him hard and cruel, he no doubt did what he deemed the best."[181]

On the day that William reached Louisville with Gilbert's column, the *Reading Daily Times* announced his promotion: "A Merited Promotion.— Our citizens will be pleased to learn that Captain Wm. R. Terrill, of the Fifth U.S. Artillery, has been promoted a Brigadier-General of Volunteers.' He has been ordered to Kentucky."[182]

Following his arrival at Louisville, William commanded a brigade of light infantry in General Nelson's Army of Kentucky. The newly appointed general assumed command on September 6.

The first order issued by William announced that he had assumed command of the brigade, and outlined what he expected from his troops.

> It is his desire to make it as serviceable as possible and every officer and man will be required to acquaint himself with his duties as speedily as possible. After reasonable time for instructions has elapsed, those officers who are deemed incompetent will be brought before an "Examining Board" and if not found proficient will be discharged from the service.[183]

He announced his staff the same day in his second order. The members of his staff were as follows:

> Brigade Inspector — Lieutenant Colonel Wm. R. Tolles, 105th Ohio Infantry; Acting Assistant Adjutant General — 1st Lieutenant Wm. P. Anderson, 6th Ohio Infantry; Aide-de-Camp — 1st Lieutenant Charles C. Parsons, 4th U.S. Artillery; and 1st Lieutenant G. G. Hunt, 4th U.S. Cavalry; Volunteer Aide-de-Camp — Mr. T. J. Nichols; Acting Brigade Quartermaster — 1st Lieutenant M. W. Wright, 105th Ohio Infantry.[184]

In addition to assuming command and announcing his staff, William set forth the schedule he wished his troops to observe. Some activity filled every moment of the day:

Reveille at	4:30	A.M.
Company Drill from	5 to 7	A.M.
Breakfast at	7:00	A.M.
Police call at	7:30	A.M.
Guard mounting at	8:00	A.M.
Surgeons call at	8:30	A.M.
Skirmish Drill from	9 to 11	A.M.
Adjutants call	11:30	A.M.
Dinner at	12:00	M [NOON]
Field officers recitation from	2 to 3	P.M.
Company officers recitation from	3 to 4	P.M.
Battalion Drill from	4 to 6	P.M.
Dress parade at	6:00	P.M.
Tattoo at	8:00	P.M.
Taps	8:30	P.M.[185]

William had one final bit of business to attend to on September 6. Writing Adjutant General Lorenzo Thomas, William requested him to appoint Lieutenant William P. Anderson as his Assistant Adjutant General.

> He has been in the service as a private, Sergt. Major and Lieutenant since the day after the President's first proclamation calling for volunteers. He has served on the staffs of Brig. General Reynolds, Major General Nelson, 1st as Aide de camp, and then as Division Engineer. Was distinguished, for gallantry and good conduct at the battles in Western Va., Viz: Greenbrier & Carricks Ford and again at the battle of Shiloh. I know of no officer more worthy of promotion.[186]

The following day, General-in-Chief Henry W. Halleck contacted Secretary of War Stanton concerning William. His message consisted of a single sentence: "I respectfully recommend that Capt. Wm. R. Terrill be appointed a Brig. Genl. of Volunteers for gallant conduct at Pittsburg Landing, Tenn."[187]

William was quick to accept the promotion, and on September 7 sent his letter of acceptance to the Adjutant General's Office. The Adjutant General's Office returned the letter on September 22, stating that the acceptance was invalid. William had dated the letter September 7, two days before the War Department issued the actual letter of appointment.[188]

On September 8, General Wright called for William to come to Cincinnati. The general, in a message to General Gilbert, wrote, "If Terrill can possibly be spared temporarily send him here; I need him much."[189] Evidently, Gilbert could not spare William, as there is no record that he made the trip to Cincinnati. He was too busy getting his brigade into shape.

The government took swift action on General Halleck's recommendation regarding William's promotion. On September 9, President Lincoln appointed him to the rank of Brigadier General, U.S. Volunteers, for gallant conduct at

Pittsburg Landing, Tennessee. The secretary of war directed William to report to the General-in-Chief by letter.[190]

William, upon learning of Lincoln's appointing him to the rank of Brigadier General, acknowledged the receipt of the notification to the Adjutant General on September 9. He added that he accepted the appointment, and had sent a telegram to Major General H. G. Wright to that effect.[191]

Later in September, on the 21st, William again contacted the Adjutant General's Office. He requested the adjutant general date his appointment to be effective from April 7, 1862, the day he fought at Pittsburg Landing. The letter reached General-in-Chief Halleck on the 27th, who referred it to Brigadier General James S. Jackson, William's commanding officer. The Adjutant General's Office, responding to it on the 30th, told him that they could not change the date of the appointment.

Within a week of assuming command, William began applying for more experienced officers for his staff. He asked that Captain John Lewis to be assigned as his Quartermaster, and Henry C. Hodegon as his Commissary and Subsistence Officer. He had met and worked with Hodegon while assigned to the Coast Survey. Later in September, William announced his new staff to the brigade. Those now assigned were:

> Assistant Adjutant General — Captain William P. Anderson; Aide-de-Camp — 1st Lieutenant Charles C. Parsons, 4th U.S. Artillery, and 2nd Lieutenant T. J. Nichols, 10th Kentucky Cavalry; Brigade Inspector — Lieutenant Colonel William R. Tolles; Brigade Quartermaster — Captain John V. Lewis; Brigade Commissary — Captain H. C. Hodegon; Brigade Medical Inspector — Assistant Surgeon Harvey S. Taft, 105th Ohio Infantry; Ordnance Officer — 2nd Lieutenant Huntington, 4th U.S. Artillery; Acting Aide-de-Camp — Captain John Cochran, Jr., 14th Kentucky Infantry; Brigade Provost Marshal — 1st Lieutenant William R. Tuttle, 105th Ohio Infantry.[192]

Still not satisfied with his staff, William again turned to his acquaintances in the Coast Survey for suitable men. From his headquarters at Louisville on September 21, William sent a telegram to his old friend Professor Bache, superintendent of the Coast Survey, requesting Bache to send William S. Edwards him for duty on his staff. The professor responded by telegraph the following day, "Edwards shall be sent."[193]

The same day, Bache inquired of Edwards if he wanted the volunteer position on General Terrill's staff. The head of the Coast Survey sent a letter of the same date to Edwards, stating that if he wished to take the position, a leave of absence would be given him. Two days later, Bache again wrote Edwards:

> It may be that Gen. Terrill intends you for top'l [topographical] eng'r & that you will be assigned as such fr. [from] the Coast Survey, or that he wants you for aid for mil'y [military] service in which case you will have leave of absence.... If you are to be detailed as top'l engineer we should have the results of the work in duplicate as we would pay the salary.[194]

Edwards did not receive Bache's telegram until the evening of September 27, and responded the following day: "*If you advise it*, I would accept the position with much pleasure and it would be very agreeable to me to be associated again with Gen'l. Terrill."[195]

Professor Bache wrote Edwards again about the staff position on September 28:

> If Gen. Terrill wishes you as an aid I will cheerfully give you leave of absence without pay. If he wishes you to be assigned to him to execute topography I will assign you with the understanding that you are at liberty to communicate the results to the Coast Survey. I am truly happy that Gen. Terrill has met with this early reward of his bearing & mil'y [military] skill & that Providence will guide & guard him in his career.... I wrote to you last that you might at once turn over your work & proceed to join Gen. Terrill.[196]

Edwards advised Bache on September 30 that he would leave that night for Louisville, and join the general there. He would, however, arrive too late to be of much service to the general.

William, now promoted, had not forgotten about his former command, Battery H, 5th U.S. Artillery. Peter Fitzpatrick, the Irishman William chose as his bodyguard earlier that year, accompanied him as an orderly. Fitzpatrick wrote: "Our captain was made Brigadier General in Louisville and got the command of a Brigade of Green Troops in Jackson's Division. I, of course, was an old orderly of the captains and he took me with him to do the same duty now that he was General."[197]

Meanwhile, William was working hard to train and prepare his brigade for military action. Many, if not all, of his troops were inexperienced, and had not been engaged on the field of battle. William tried to apply the same professional methods he had used the previous year in whipping his battery into shape. The volunteers responded with only minimal enthusiasm.[198]

Albion W. Tourgée, a member of the 105th Ohio Infantry and author of *The Story of a Thousand*, wrote of William:

> He did not understand how to endear himself to the volunteer — especially, perhaps one might say, the Northern volunteer. His idea of command was somewhat too highly colored with compulsion to at once call forth the best efforts of an undisciplined soldiery, and he had little of that dash which made Sheridan instantly and always a leader of men. He commanded respect by scrupulous attention to duty, but awakened no enthusiasm in those under his command.[199]

By the end of September, General Terrill's light brigade consisted of the following units:

80th Illinois Infantry
123rd Illinois Infantry
101st Indiana Infantry
105th Ohio Infantry
Parson's Battery of Artillery

Garrard's Detachment (Consisting of parts of:)
7th Kentucky Infantry
23rd Kentucky Infantry
3rd Tennessee (Union) Infantry.

A soldier of the 123rd Illinois commented on the Light Brigade, writing that "the Light Brigade, will march without baggage — the Brigadier General not even taking a trunk — leaving tents and everything else which might in any way impede our rapid traveling."[200]

Tourgée, the regimental historian, wrote:

> Everybody seemed to wonder at Terrill's being in the Federal army. A story in explanation was afloat at that time. His father was said to have been a zealous divine of the Old Dominion, who, when his son left home for West Point, presented him with a Bible and made him promise to read it every day and never fail in his duty to the Stars and Stripes. When Virginia seceded the good parson would have had his son consecrate his sword to the cause of disunion; but the young officer answered him that he could not break the oath he had sworn at his father's request on the Bible he had given him.[201]

Soon after reaching Louisville and assuming command of a brigade, William took it upon himself to organize a battery of artillery for his command. He chose First Lieutenant Charles C. Parsons, an 1861 graduate of the U.S. Military Academy, to command the battery. There existed between the two men a most tender friendship.[202] The general called upon the regiments of his brigade to provide volunteers to serve the battery on September 6, and they responded handsomely. The 105th Ohio provided more than a hundred men to the battery, while the remainder of the detail came from the 80th Illinois.

Colonel J. H. Gilman inspected Lieutenant Parsons' new battery on September 29 and gave it a good report. The battery consisted of six guns — 5 light 12-pounders and a 10-pound Parrott. The inspector noted that 138 men were present for duty, and that the harness, equipment, and clothing were in good condition. Gilman noted that the battery lacked some equipment at the time of his inspection.[203]

Lieutenant Henry Harrison Cumings commanded one section (two guns) of Parsons' Battery. He later wrote of his experiences:

> We worked and drilled untiringly to get our battery into shape and learn to handle it. Our General spent his leisure time among us instructing us and inspiring us with his enthusiasm. We began to feel confidence in our skill and powers and long for the day when we could show the enemy what we could do with our guns.[204]

In addition to creating a battery of artillery for his brigade, William created a company of guards and scouts. The company, commanded by Captain Louis Chrisman, consisted of a mixture of civilians and soldiers. Terrill's Guards and Scouts received their arms and equipment on September 10, 1862.

Between that time and October 8, 1862, the company served the new general well, performing reconnoitering missions and as his personal bodyguard.[205]

In an effort to improve the morale of the citizens of Louisville, the military leaders ordered a grand review of the 10th Division. In preparation, Generals Nelson, Jackson and Terrill inspected the division and marched for Louisville. In the city, the troops passed before Major General Charles C. Gilbert and staff, where they "made a fine display."[206]

While the spectacle of so many troops in Louisville might have lifted the spirits of the citizens, the review did nothing but anger the soldiers who made the march.

The day was extremely hot and sultry, and required a march of at least two miles for the men of the 33rd Brigade to reach the city. William ordered his men to strike their tents and load the wagons in preparation for an inspection. In addition, the men were required to strap on their knapsacks, fully loaded with equipment.

James G. Crawford, a member of the 80th Illinois Infantry wrote that many of his regiment thought they were going to Louisville to board a railroad car for some part of the U.S. He recalled the march:

> To our surprise we were marched into Louisville. Then up and down the principal streets till wearied and exhausted. The men were ready to fall down and die. He (the General) then turned us about and made us start out for camp again. This was trying on our men. Some fainting fell in the streets and we had to pass on and leave them to the mercy of some citizen. Others were sun struck and fell dead in there tracks. The loss out of this Reg. is 6 dead and about fifteen that the doctor says will not get better and then for what purpose was all that done. That is one thing that I do not know unless it was to gratify the passion of our General. I think if ever any man was accountable for the lifes [sic] of his fellow men he will be accountable for those that died yesterday.[207]

A number of the soldiers from the 80th Illinois and 105th Ohio swore vengeance on the generals for subjecting them to something that "did not amount to a row of pins."[208] The men of the 80th Illinois seem to have singled out William. Private Crawford noted: "The men are highly displeased at the General[s] and threaten to shoot them the first fight they have. I think my self that he [Terrill] will never see more than one engagement unless he changes his ways some little."[209]

John C. Hathaway, a sergeant in Company E, 105th Ohio, wrote that the review "killed more than the retreat [from Richmond, Kentucky]. The boys swear that Generals Terrell [sic], Jackson & Nelson shall not live through a battle."[210] Private Josiah Ayre, also of the 105th Ohio, noted in his diary, "Our men are all down on General Terrill for putting us through as he did."[211]

Stanley Lockwood, another member of the 105th Ohio Infantry, noted the cause of the regiment's dislike for their commanding officer in a letter home. He wrote that General Terrill "had struck a soldier over the head with a saber because the man had left the ranks on an extremely hot day."²¹² Private Lockwood continued, stating that "many a soldier had loaded his weapon for self-protection against the general."²¹³

The Ohio soldier went even further, stating that Terrill "is a drunken old tyrant and deserves to be shot by his own men and if he don't come to that fate it will be because the oaths of hundreds of men in the 105th Regiment is good for nothing."²¹⁴

A year after the fierce battle at Perryville, some of the soldiers still referred to their dislike of William. James G. Crawford, of the 80th Illinois Infantry, compared William to another general in a letter home on October 8, 1863: "Gen. [Joseph] Hooker is a man apparently about 45 yrs. of age rather tinged with gray, stout, strong & healthy and altogether a very gruff looking Customer. He may be a good Gen. but I dont [sic] like his looks as a man and would term him 'Terrill' No. 2."²¹⁵

After the review, William reprimanded Colonel Albert S. Hall, of the 105th Ohio Infantry, for failing to obtain an essential implement of war — a regimental flag. On the march back to camp, they came upon the color bearer of one of the Indiana regiments along the road. Overcome by the intense heat, the soldier fell to the ground, firmly clutching his regimental flag in his hand. A part of the flag spread across the dust of the road. When William saw this spectacle, he leaped from his horse and seized the flag. As the advance of Colonel Hall's regiment came up, William handed it to the colonel, remarking, "Here is a stand of colors for you; see if your regiment can keep them off the ground!"²¹⁶

Colonel Hall summoned a nearby Sergeant and gave him the flag. As he handed it to the soldier, Hall noticed that it was an Indiana state flag. He commented to the general: "But this is a State flag, general, we are Ohio troops, not Indianans." William replied curtly, "No matter; keep the flag until I order it returned."²¹⁷

As it turned out, the order never came. Several weeks afterward, the 105th Ohio carried the flag into battle. The flag, furled upon its staff and covered with a black case, showed only the edges of its colorful tassel. Several months later, Hall returned the flag to its rightful owner. The flag bore some "honorable scars, received in a battle in which the regiment it belonged to was not engaged."²¹⁸

About a week after the review at Louisville, William issued orders detailing the musicians to carry the wounded from the battlefield during a battle. To keep the men in the ranks, William ordered, "During a battle, guards will be placed in the rear of each Division with orders to arrest all skulkers and to shoot down all who desert the ranks from cowardice. Let this order be rigorously enforced."²¹⁹

Late in September, General Terrill received a report that Bragg's army was advancing on Louisville. William was then in camp about two miles east of the city and upon learning of the rumored threat took action to defend the city. The men named their camp Camp Terrill, in William's honor.²²⁰ A member of the 123rd Illinois Infantry wrote:

The whole brigade were ordered out for fatigue duty, and put to work digging trenches and chopping timber, and otherwise preparing to resist th[e] attack expected.... Our entrenchments, which are sufficient to afford ample protection to the whole regiment, are now completed, and are pronounced superior to any similar work in this vicinity. The trenches are finished up with the greatest neatness, and ranging in such away [sic] as to command every ravine and other avenue of approach. The earthworks are surmounted by huge logs nicely hewn, with port holes for each musket, the whole presenting an appearance decidedly secure.[221]

John Holbrook Morse, a member of the 105th Ohio Infantry, described the trenches and the readiness of the troops for battle:

Our men have most of them been at work on the trenches for the last two days. They dig three feet wide, three feet deep and throw the dirt up in front so that it makes about five feet depth. They are so that if we should get whipped we could fall back here and defend the city. But we are not much scared yet; but still I for one would like it if we were better drilled before we went into an engagement.[222]

Late in September, William turned his attention to his old company. He recommended 1st Lieutenant Francis L. Guenther for promotion, to command the company or as Chief of Artillery. He signed the letter in a most peculiar way — as Captain, Battery H, 5th U.S. Artillery and as Brigadier General.[223]

In the letters and diaries of Private Bliss Morse of the 105th Ohio Infantry, we find a glimpse of William as a general officer. Morse wrote on September 28: "Our Brig. Gen. Terrill is a tall light haired man with a coarse voice which makes him quite a target for the boys to mock at. He loves good liquors and beef for his table was well supplied with them while I was on guard before his quarters."[224]

Another source describes William as "a tall, stern-faced officer with an exceptionally loud voice."[225]

Confederate General Bragg's supplies were running low, so he moved his army to Bardstown, 40 miles from Louisville. At the same time, Major General Smith's army was scattered between Lexington and Frankfort, some 50 miles from Louisville. Union Major General Buell, fearing that Bragg planned to move against that city, rushed from Cave City, Kentucky, to Louisville, arriving there on the 25th.

On the morning of September 29, an event occurred at Louisville that some viewed as a disaster and others as justice. A few days before, General Nelson had an altercation with a subordinate, resulting in the arrest of Brigadier General Jefferson C. Davis. On the morning of the 29th the two officers met in the lobby of the Galt House; tempers flared and Davis flicked a crumpled calling card into Nelson's face. "Bull" Nelson responded by slapping Davis in the face, then turned and walked away. Davis was enraged and out of control. He grabbed a pistol from a bystander, followed Nelson, and shot him in the chest. Nelson died an hour later.

The shooting of Nelson received mixed reaction. William was outraged at the death of his friend, and "demanded that Davis be hanged on the spot for 'this inexcusably despicable act.'"[226] Cooler heads, however, prevailed, and Davis was placed under arrest. Generals James S. Jackson and William R. Terrill pledged that they would not rest until Davis received his due punishment. Before they could carry out their pledge, both were killed.

The officers were not the only ones thrown into turmoil by Nelson's murder. Many of the enlisted troops that had served under Nelson were angered, while others felt that Nelson got what he deserved.

Later that day, General Buell proceeded with the planned reorganization of his army, absorbing into it a large number of new recruits. Buell divided his twenty-five brigades into three corps, commanded by Major General Alexander McCook, Major General Charles C. Gilbert, and Major General Thomas L. Crittenden. The First Corps (McCook's) consisted of three divisions, commanded by Brigadier Generals James S. Jackson, Louvell H. Rousseau and Joshua W. Sill. The latter was a classmate of William's from West Point.

In the reorganization, William's light brigade became the 33rd Brigade, part of the 10th Division in McCook's Corps, Army of the Ohio. Brigadier General James S. Jackson, a former congressman, commanded the 10th Division. The two brigades in his division were composed of new recruits, all of whom it seemed hated Jackson. The source of this hatred was the punishing march from Lexington to Louisville, and the grand review held a few weeks prior. Unfortunately, William's association with the review caused the men to hold a grudge against him as well.

Most of the troops in these three corps would move with Buell to meet Bragg. Meanwhile, Sill's Division of McCook's Corps moved to occupy Smith's attention at Frankfort, hopefully to prevent his joining Bragg's forces. By October 7, Bragg's forces were at Perryville, a small town along the Chaplin River.

The Last Days

William and his brigade left Louisville at daylight on October 1, 1862, and marched eastward toward Fishersville, Kentucky, to meet Bragg. They left their tents and heavy baggage behind, guarded by men unable to march. Albion W. Tourgée, 105th Ohio, recalled: "The roads were dry and hard; the weather was delightful; the men in the best of spirits."[227] Another soldier of the 105th Ohio reported on this bright October morning, the men were "jubilant, and anxious to meet the foe."[228] The two other corps of Buell's army marched toward Bardstown, Kentucky.

A member of Colonel Garrard's detachment went out foraging on the road between Louisville and Taylorsville, Kentucky. General Terrill caught him as he returned. Captain Robert B. Taylor wrote of the incident:

> John Coleman was missing tonight, and did not turn up until early next morning, he was a wonderous [sic] eater, and had gone out during the march today, on a foraging expedition, on his own account, he was detected upon his return as he

was getting over the fence into the main road, by General Terrill himself and made to march into Headquarters and cook his captured (2 ducks and 1 turkey) for the General's supper that night.[229]

The search for rations and water brought punishment to many of the soldiers of the 33rd Brigade. A soldier in the 101st Indiana Infantry, wrote:

> Many of the boys will remember this place [Bloomfield] on account of the number of fat hogs that evaporated from a pen near our camp, and the boys that were arrested by Terills [sic] orderlies, as they wandered down that dry rocky branch in search of good water, taken to headquarters and assigned the pleasant duty of carrying a rail several hours on the side of a hill as a punishment for being caught out of camp.[230]

While William and his men were marching from Louisville to Perryville, his friend W. S. Edwards was traveling to join him. On October 8, Edwards reported to Bache from Louisville: "I arrived here this A.M., being detained only one day, by missing the connection at Pittsburg. I find that Gen'l. Terrill is in the advance at Springfield and has been fighting all day to day. I proceed to join him tomorrow via foot."[231]

By the afternoon of October 4, McCook's column was in camp at Taylorsville, where they rested until the 6th. On Monday morning, they marched to Bloomfield, and on Tuesday to Mackville. The troops reached Mackville about 8:00 P.M. on the 7th. They were about ten miles from Perryville.

While in camp at Taylorsville, their rations gave out, forcing the soldiers to subsist on parched corn, supplemented with a few bits of bacon. Water was scarce and often bad. On the eve of the battle, very few canteens contained any water at all.

On October 7, while marching to Mackville, Captain Taylor had an occasion to talk to William. Having taken two canteens and filled them with water at a nearby residence, Taylor hesitated for a brief moment to talk with the ladies of the house. A few minutes after mounting his horse, he saw the general approaching at the head of the brigade.

> He saw me at the side of the road talking to the ladies and as I bid them good by [sic] and moved out into the road, he said something about my gallantry. I told him as I rode along about what the old lady had imparted to me and the circumstances that caused my being with them, and upon learning I had gone for fresh water, asked me if I had drunk it all. I told him I had drunk as much at the well as I possibly could and come off with both canteens full. I offered him a drink, and he pulling a small flask out of the side pocket of his coat replied "Won't you take a little of something stronger first?" I replied, "after you General." He said No! He never drank anything strong upon a march when it was so warm, and dusty, that it only increased his thirst. The flask was full, and I really was ashamed of acknowledging to him that I thought a little of the ardent would do me good as I had walked hard that day—He thought so too, and I took a pretty good "swig" and returned him the flask. He took a long drink out of one of my canteens and as I

had the other one full, told him to take one of them as I had enough water in the other to do me that day—He thanked me, took the canteen.[232]

General Buell, with the 2nd and 3rd Corps, arrived near Perryville on the evening of October 7. The general ordered his men not to attack until all three corps had arrived.

A few days before the battle of Perryville, an old antagonist from William's past made his appearance. As Brigadier General Philip Sheridan strode through the camps, a familiar voice reached his ears. It was a soft Virginia drawl, one that belonged to his old enemy from West Point—William R. Terrill. Pausing only briefly, Sheridan stepped into the firelight opposite Terrill. The two men stared at each other for a moment, then, Sheridan extended his hand in friendship and reconciliation. William accepted Sheridan's hand and invited him to join them for a cup of coffee. Sheridan accepted, and took a seat. The two men exchanged small talk as they savored the coffee. Finishing his coffee, Sheridan arose, shook hands with William, wished him well, and departed. Later, Sheridan remarked that he was always glad that he and William had met and settled their grievances.[233]

On the night of October 7, gathered about a campfire were Brigadier General James S. Jackson, Colonel George Webster, and General Terrill. The topic of discussion among the officers was the odds of an individual being killed or wounded in battle. William, being the mathematician in the group, theorized that given the large number of men engaged that their chances of either were relatively slight. Twenty-four hours later, all three would be dead.

Another matter that certainly weighed heavily on William's mind that October night was the inadequacy of his troops. Having done what he could to prepare them for battle, he still felt that their faults would result in the sacrifice of his life. Learning of his feelings, a chaplain suggested that he prepare for death. William replied simply, "I have been prepared to die for a long time."[234]

The Battle of Perryville began during the early morning hours of October 8. As the day progressed, more and more troops confronted each other. By early afternoon, most of Buell's troops had arrived at Perryville. General McCook's Corps assumed a position north of Perryville, on the Union left. His line of battle ran from north to south, facing eastward, with his left flank near the Benton Road and his right across the Mackville Road. General Jackson's 10th Division was still on the road, marching to form on the left flank.[235]

Here a disastrous mistake occurred. An immense cloud of dust arose along the Harrodsburg Pike, causing the Union troops on the north side of the town to believe that the Confederates were retreating. Nothing could have been farther from the truth. The Confederates were moving into position to strike the Union left—McCook's position. When the attack came, it was a complete surprise to the troops on the left.

At 2:30 A.M. on October 8, the order to march at 3:00 A.M. reached the 33rd

Brigade. By daylight (6 A.M.), the soldiers were marching along the Mackville Road, toward Perryville, about ten miles away. William detailed the 101st Indiana Infantry to guard the division train, and they remained behind with it. William's brigade marched in the rear of the column, following Colonel George Webster's brigade. A member of the 105th Ohio described the conditions: "[We are marching through] an uneven country where water seemed a rarety [sic] and running streams unknown. The day was quite warm, and we suffered much from thirst, which our rations of parched corn by no means served to allay."[236]

The men marched slowly, making frequent halts, and finally stopped at the Dixville Crossroads (at the intersection of the Mackville Road and the Benton Road) about 11 A.M. The men fell out on the right side of the road, a half-mile behind the Russell House, stacked their arms and either prepared a meal of parched corn or napped on the ground. Lieutenant Parsons, commanding the artillery, arrived and halted on the left of the road.

That morning, General Terrill sent his guards and scouts out to reconnoiter the country on the left of the Union position. While doing so, Captain Chrisman and his men encountered a body of Confederate cavalry. The rebels demanded Chrisman's surrender. Captain Chrisman countered by ordering his men to open fire. As the men fired, they began to fall back to the main Union position.

Receiving orders to take a position on the extreme left of the Union line, General McCook began placing his men in line of battle. General Rousseau's

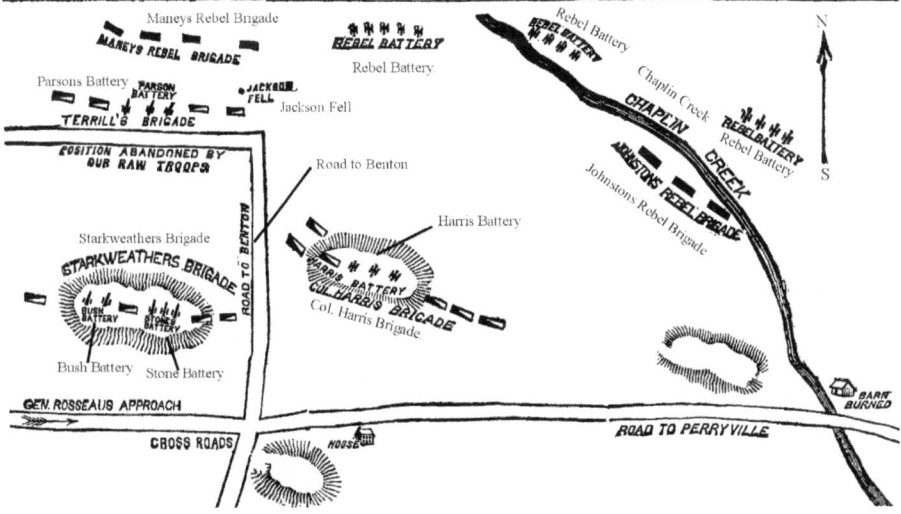

Map of the Perryville Battlefield, October 8, 1862, adapted from the *New York Tribune*, October 15, 1862, which had numerous misspellings.

Division, having come up first, had already formed a line on and to the left of the Mackville road. Colonel Leonard Harris' 9th Brigade formed the left of Rousseau's line. Colonel George Webster's brigade, of the 10th Division, was the next to come into line, forming on the right of the Mackville road, in the rear of Rousseau's line.

General McCook now pondered where to assign Terrill's brigade. Should he place him in reserve behind Rousseau's veterans, or should he use Terrill to extend Webster's line to the left? Colonel Harris and Captain Beverly D. Williams, McCook's guide, suggested another option. They proposed that Terrill's men be placed on a high ridge about four hundred yards northeast of Harris' left. The high ground overlooked Walker's Bend, on the Chaplin River, to the east, and a deep valley to the north. General McCook decided to examine the ground for himself, and was delighted at what he found. The general agreed to assign Terrill's men where they could command the Chaplin River. Most prized of all were the pools of water glistening in the river some six hundred yards below. McCook, however, had one concern: the position would throw the troops well in advance of the others in the line of battle. The general decided to go ahead and assign Terrill's inexperienced men to this advanced and isolated position, and sent for Generals Jackson and Terrill.

General Jackson likely joined McCook first, and received his instructions. Captain Samuel M. Starling, a staff officer, was sent back to bring up Terrill's brigade. Starling wrote: "That was my first order received, I repeated it to Jackson to be sure I was right, and then such a clattering over the rocks at full gallop you never saw. I dashed up to Genl. Terrill.... Told him what was wanted, and acted as guide to bring up his men."[237]

William and Starling had become friends during their brief time together in the fall of 1862. The general, according to Starling, frequently told him that "when this cussed war is over I am coming down to your little town to see you."[238]

Joining McCook and Jackson, William received instructions as to where his men were to form. Jackson directed him to occupy a ridge running from Open Knob southward to Widow Gibson's house. In addition, he was to plant his artillery on the knob, facing northward, and to support it with a strong infantry force. After establishing his line, the general told William to advance a line of skirmishers down the river, and showed him the water. William assured his superior that his men were coming up and would soon be in position, adding, "I'll do it, and that's my water."[239]

General Terrill sent for Lieutenant Parsons' guns and moved them into position on the left front of the line. Albion W. Tourgée noted in his regimental history: "How we envied the eager comrades as they swung themselves into their saddles and dashed for at a sharp trot!"[240]

It was now about 1:00 P.M. To support the artillery, William brought up the 123rd Illinois and Colonel Garrard's Detachment. He placed these units on the left of Rousseau's line, angling back in rear of the battery. The 123rd Illinois formed the primary support for Parsons, and Garrard's men fell in behind them. Captain Taylor, of Garrard's detachment, noted that as William led the men to their position, he looked "every inch a soldier."[241]

A newspaper correspondent who accompanied the army that afternoon, recalled:

> Down the road to Benton Terrill advanced in gallant style, forming north of the road at the angle to the west. Parsons' battery was in his center, and the One Hundred and Twenty-third Illinois formed his right. This brigade was three hundred yards in the front of Colonel Harris and to his left.[242]

As soon as Parsons' guns reached their assigned position, they opened fire on a body of Confederate cavalry, clearly visible to the north, across the Chaplin River. Within minutes, the veteran troops of George Maney's brigade approached the battery from the east. Captain Starling recalled the scene:

> The enemy came creeping along through the weeds[,] their dress so of the color of grass that you could hardly see them, and got behind a rail fence 130 yards from the cannons. The cannons opened on them with grape shot and while this firing of grape was going on, the Ohio [Illinois] regiment was lying on their faces 20 yards in the rear of the cannon.[243]

It was now about 2:10 P.M. Both James S. Jackson and Terrill had accompanied the guns of Parsons' battery into their position on Open Knob, and were watching its operation. Lieutenant H. H. Cumings, commanding a two gun section of the battery, wrote:

> Our battery was thrown forward to the extreme left of the line. No reconnaissance was made in our front. A short distance in front of us and extending far to our left was a dense woods which, as the event proved, was full of the enemy. They charged us at once. Their line extending far beyond and wrapping around our left pouring down our line an enfilading fire.[244]

In order to meet this new threat, the guns of Parsons' battery had to be turned to the right; a task that the inexperienced artillerymen found difficult. Nevertheless, the guns were turned and opened on Maney's Confederates.

Absorbed with the operation of the artillery, William's staff officers posted the infantry. "He was by training, almost by instinct, an artilleryman," wrote Albion W. Tourgée, "and his battery's action eclipsed in interest the maneuvering of his brigade."[245]

Meanwhile, the 105th Ohio Infantry rested near the crossroads, about a half of a mile away. Suddenly, the loud boom of the artillery startled them. The officers quickly called out, "Attention, Battalion!" and the men hastened to form ranks. One of the soldiers recalled:

> With quickened steps, the men resumed the march, unmindful now of the heat and thirst. Louder, more continuous, grew the cannonade, and soon blue wreaths of smoke, just discernable above the tops of the trees away to the left, told where

the conflict had begun. Parson's battery of our brigade had opened the battle, and the regiments of infantry now prepared to act their parts in the bloody drama.[246]

Colonel Hall ordered two companies of the 105th thrown out as skirmishers. The same Ohio soldier wrote of the advance: "Over hills and through cornfields, now lying down, and now advancing, we moved until ordered to rejoin the regiment then lying under a ridge partially wooded, on which, farther to the left, where there was no timber, was planted Parsons' battery."[247]

As the men of the 105th were suffering from thirst, three men from each company went out in search of water. The remaining men of the regiment, about 500 strong, began their advance. An officer soon met them, and urged them to hurry forward. The order "Double-quick!" rang out, and the soldiers surged forward.

The *New York Herald* correspondent wrote of the attack:

> The rebel right advanced a mass of human beings. Your correspondent, standing in the rear of the One Hundred and Twenty-third Illinois, saw from behind his tree the several lines of the enemy as they advanced to the attack. The sight was most magnificent. He felt as if the single brigade of Terrill would be swept away. The fire opened from the rebels and was replied to all along the line. The One Hundred and Twenty-third Illinois suffered terribly. The rebels advanced rapidly discharging a terrible fire, under which the raw troops of General Terrill wavered. The horses of the battery (Parsons') fell at every volley, and the men this morning lie still about the single caisson left of the battery.[248]

Lieutenant Cumings, the infantryman-turned-artilleryman, noted: "Our infantry supports gave way; we did not know enough to leave. We gave the enemy canister as fast as we could fire, but they soon routed us and took all our guns except one which did not get into action."[249]

As the troops of Maney's Brigade came within a hundred and fifty yards of Terrill's beloved battery, the fear of losing the guns overwhelmed William and he panicked. This panic caused William to make a disastrous decision. He ordered Colonel Monroe, commander of the 123rd Illinois, to make a bayonet charge on the approaching enemy. William then turned his attention to the battery, encouraging the men in its operation.[250] It was now about 2:50 P.M.

The 123rd responded gallantly and raced down the hillside. Then, just as quickly, they returned, leaving behind nearly two hundred of their comrades. Colonel Garrard's Detachment, numbering only 194 men, took part in the charge. They, too, lost heavily.

R. W. Houghton, a member of the 123rd Illinois, wrote:

> Gen. Terrill, who commanded our brigade, was promoted from Captain of Artillery to Brigadier General, and although a brave man and thorough artillerist, was inexperienced in the handling of troops. When called into the fight, we occupied the extreme left, and were ordered to charge by the General, the two left companies, Captain Talbutt's and Captain Hart's and part of Captain York's and Van Buskirk's, (the incessant roar of artillery and musketry being so great that the order

was not heard any further to the right) went in with great gallantry, with an exultant yell, charging in fine style two hundred yards to a fence, over that and thirty yards beyond, into the very lines of a rebel regiment, dealing death and consternation to their antagonists, whom they could not really see until within twenty yards, and keeping up the fire until from the tremendous flank fire coming from both right and left they were ordered to retreat, which they did calmly, and considering the rawness and undisciplined state of the regiment was conceded to have been well done. This charge was a fatal error, and one in which the 123d Illinois was sacrificed.[251]

Another account, also by Houghton, noted:

We had hardly formed a line of battle until Gen. Terrell [sic], of our brigade, ordered a charge by the 123d. Col. Monroe, seeing the rashness of the movement at a glance, quickly countermanded the order, but it did not get to the left wing, and they made the charge gallantly by the four left companies, upon an unseen foe, dashing fairly into their midst, as they were stationed in a narrow ravine.[252]

Houghton wrote, "The General gave us the most prominent position, and frequently remarked before dying that we fought splendidly with the valor of veterans."[253] One thing for certain, those that survived the battle of Perryville were certainly entitled to the title of veteran.

As the 123rd Illinois returned from the useless bayonet charge, General Jackson received a bullet in the breast, and fell dead. A newspaper account reported that when the bullet struck him, he exclaimed, "Oh, God!" and fell dead without a struggle.[254] The command of the division now fell upon William's already burdened shoulders.

The scene personified the word chaos. An Ohio soldier described it:

Clouds of smoke envelope and obscure the field, from whose gray folds, quick gleams of fire, like myriad serpent tongues are darting out. Around the guns of the battery, officers urging on the men, cannoniers [sic] springing to their work, wounded horses rearing and plunging, appear and disappear in the shifting smoke. Quickly the scene changes. On the left the smoke lifts up — rolls away to the right, and there, in battle array, are the long, gray lines of the enemy.[255]

As the 105th Ohio came up into position, the right of the line had fallen back. The guns of Parsons' battery stood alone on the hill—half of its guns silent; men and horses cut down by the enemy. A mounted aide pointed out the place the regiment was to occupy, as a team of terrified horses dragging a caisson galloped wildly through their line toward the rear.

The 105th Ohio passed through a rail fence and filed to the left, passing within twenty yards of the rear of Parsons' battery. The regiment continued to march until the right companies were beyond the shelter of the little knoll on which the battery stood. Once in position, Hall gave the command for the regiment to face the enemy. In the center of their line were the furled colors of the 101st Indiana Infantry. Advancing to the crest of this hill, the order came to open fire. "The order to open fire passes along the line, from company to company and soon the entire line is engaged — volley answers volley. As the lines of the enemy press closer."[256]

Lieutenant Cumings later recalled the scene:

> I commanded one section composed of two 12 pounders, and that day my section had the right of the battery and went into position at the right of the line just at the right of the position that the 105th Ohio soon took. Being on the right we were able to stay by our guns longer than the other detachments of the battery. The last gun fired from the battery was my right gun, which I fired with my own hands. General Terrill was with us, directing the working of the guns during most of the short engagement. The enemy took all our guns except one howitzer, which being in the rear did not have time to get into action.[257]

During the fighting about the battery, Private Hugh Lowry, a member of the 105th Ohio, won a compliment from his general. The young Ohio lad fired on the enemy's color bearer, the shot bringing both man and flag to the ground. General Terrill, then standing in the rear of the company, complimented him: "Well done boy."[258]

About 3:30 P.M., William became fearful that his men could not hold their position on Open Knob, and ordered Parsons to withdraw the battery. Within minutes, Maney's Confederates charged the battery. The Ohio correspondent described what happened next:

Lieutenant Charles C. Parsons, Terrill's friend and commander of the improvised battery (courtesy U.S.M.A. Archives).

> "Fix bayonets," the order comes from Gen. Terrill, himself, who is with us on the right.... Sharply the steel rattles and the glistening bayonets are set. Then comes the loud command, "Charge, don't let them take the battery!" The ranks spring forward right into that fearful storm of shot. Not a man falters— the living close over the dead, and with firm and steady step move on. New ranks of the enemy spring up — new vollies smite our advancing line. It falters— wavers— reels backward before that storm of lead, but does not break. Once more, led on by Gen. Terrill and Major Perkins, those brave men move forward against the foe, now swarming around the silenced guns. Louder rise the cheers of the enemy, —fiercer grows the decimating tempest. The line reels to and fro, unable to endure that awful storm of shot, yet unwilling to retreat. Useless, vain endeavor to drive back the veteran thousands of the enemy crowd-

ing on in all the confidence which success can give. The Gen'l. gives the command to fall back, and the 105th is driven from its first battle-field."[259]

At the moment the 105th Ohio was ordered to charge, Tourgée noted that William's "face was flushed with agony at the thought of losing the battery of which he was so proud."[260]

When the 105th Ohio reeled back from the Confederate onslaught, William finally accepted the futility of defending the guns, and gave the order to fall back. The men of Parsons' battery not killed or seriously wounded joined the retreat — all except the young lieutenant. Drawing his sword, Parsons stood alone amid the wreckage of his battery, prepared to give his life for it. William, who was close by, saw his dear friend standing in the face of the enemy, and had him forcibly removed.[261]

Before leaving the guns, according to one Ohio soldier, William "dismounted and sighted and fired one of the guns himself and then spiked it."[262] The general then followed his troops to some woods about fifty or sixty yards in the rear. Here, he attempted to rally his broken troops about a rail fence.[263]

About the time the men of Terrill's Brigade broke and retreated, William's horse fell dead. His command and dreams shattered, William was understandably depressed. An Ohio soldier recalled:

Rough Drawing of Parson's battery in action, showing the havoc it caused in the enemy's ranks. Drawing by Captain Robert B. Taylor. Diary of Captain Robert B. Taylor (Kentucky Historical Society).

> Slowly, at first, and with something like order, the hard fought [field] is yielded; but soon confused by the merciless fire of the pursuing enemy, and mingled with the broken ranks of an Ill. regiment, companies became scattered and order is lost.... General Terrill was conspicuous during the battle for that cool courage which distinguished him on the field of Shiloh. As we fell back down the hill, he remarked to those around him "General Jackson is dead, and I too must die."[264]

The shattered troops of Terrill's 33rd Brigade fell back to a cornfield, in the rear of the rail fence mentioned above. In the cornfield, William seated himself on a log, and was "the picture of utter woefulness."[265] Succeeding in rallying a few hundred men, William now moved to the right, giving Starkweather's men a clear field of fire. Colonel John Starkweather, of Rousseau's Division, had brought his troops into position in the rear of William's men before the attack began on Open Knob. Two batteries of artillery — commanded by Captains David C. Stone and Asahel K. Bush — occupied an elevation to the left of the Benton Road.

After bringing his men into position, Starkweather joined Generals McCook, Jackson and Terrill on Open Knob. While the officers were talking, Captain Stone observed Colonel John A. Wharton's cavalry moving about on the Benton Road. The captain opened fire upon them, firing fifteen or twenty well-placed rounds. From their position on Open Knob, the generals stopped what they were doing to admire the handling of Stone's guns.[266]

William conducted his few remaining troops into a position about two hundred yards behind Starkweather's right, and halted. Where, the shaken general wondered, was the remainder of his men? Finally, he concluded that his brigade had been wiped out. "He was very much depressed," wrote Tourgée, "thinking not of what his men had done, but of what he had failed to accomplish and of the stain he feared would fall upon his honor as a soldier."[267]

As the day ended, William regained some portion of his composure — perhaps his command had not been as badly shattered as he had first thought. "With reviving spirits," Albion W. Tourgée recalled, "Gen. Terrill's interest in the conflict which raged about him again awoke. Drawn as it seemed by an irresistible magnetism, he walked toward the battery now hotly engaged upon the opposite hill three hundred yards away. As he climbed the slope toward it, he was struck by a shell, and died almost before a friend could reach his side."[268]

The exact circumstances surrounding William's death are not clearly stated. Most scholars, says Kenneth W. Noe, have accepted Major James Connolly's account.[269] The Major, a member of the 123rd Illinois, wrote:

> General Terrell [sic], commanding our brigade was killed by a shell within 5 feet of me, and while he was giving me directions for rallying the men. I was the only one with him; I raised him to a sitting position, and saw that nearly his entire breast was torn away by the shell. He recognized me and his first words were: "Major do you think it is fatal?" I knew it must be, but to encourage him I answered: "Oh I hope not General." He then said: "My poor wife, my poor wife." He lived until 2 o'clock next morning.[270]

Captain Robert Taylor, of Garrard's detachment, tells a different story. He noted that sometime before William's death, he saw "our gallant Brigadier with his coat off, sleeves rolled up and working one of the two guns of the battery left, dealing death and destruction to the retreating enemy.... Now as I saw his manly form, busiest in this busy scene — manipulating the implements of the field gun with the skill and ease of an adept.... I looked upon this young chieftan [sic], after his brigade had been annihilated as he stood there in the ranks, whirling the rammer of a field gun around his head (with that peculiar grace only acquired by drill in the Artillery school) and with it driving his cartridge and canister far back into the barrels of the cannon."[271]

Not long after this, Taylor received a wound, and went to the hospital. After being treated, the doctors released him about midnight. Having to remain on the hospital grounds, Taylor sat down on the hospital steps. About half an hour later, he overhead one of the surgeons say that "General Terrill had just died."[272] Staggered by the news, Taylor at once spoke to the surgeon, asking him for news of the fallen general.

> He informed me that General Terrill had been struck on the breast with a shell, while he was working the guns of Parsons' Battery, about 6 o'clock in the afternoon; and that in the explosion of the shell, the entire left breast was torn from his

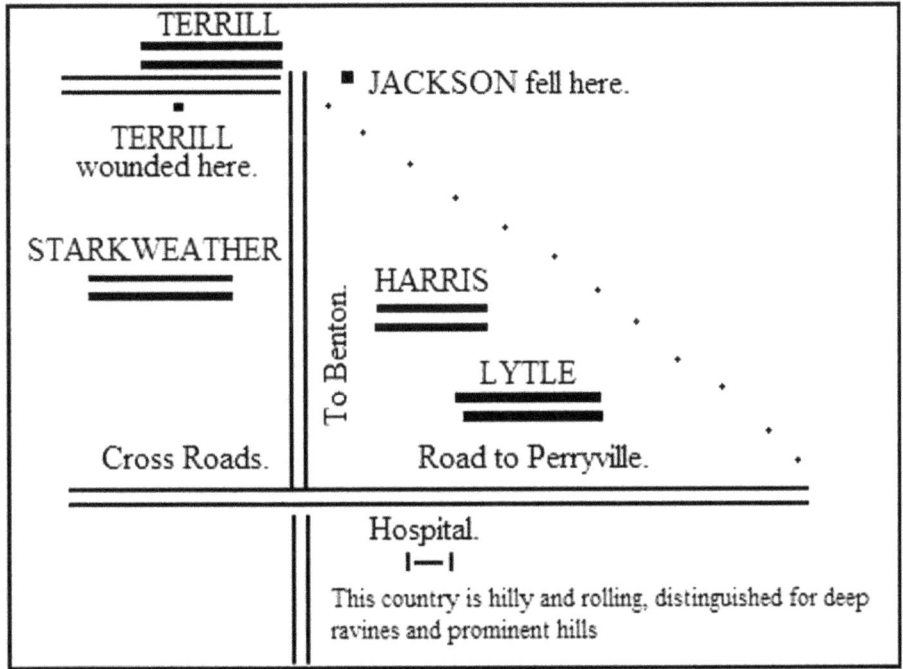

Detail map of Perryville, showing where Terrill fell (based on map in *Louisville Journal*, October 14, 1862).

body, that he had been brought to this hospital, and after lingering there died of his wounds but a few minutes since.[273]

Feeling compelled to look upon the shattered body of his friend and commander; the captain entered the hospital and sought out his body. "I approached the part of the building where his stalwart figure lay stretched upon the floor a shirt drawn around him to conceal his cruelly mutilated form."[274]

Taylor's account of William's death is strengthened by an account written by William Franklin Gore Shanks, who was at Perryville: "Terrill's horse was shot under him, and, being thus dismounted, and left without a command, he turned — the ruling passion strong in death — to the artillery, and assumed command of a couple of batteries fighting in General Rousseau's line. Thus returned to the arm of the service for which education and inclination adopted him, he did magnificent service. While thus engaged, and while in the act of sighting a gun of Bush's Indiana battery, he was mortally wounded, and died a few hours afterward, with a message to his wife unfinished on his lips."[275]

Another account of the battle, written by a member of the 105th Ohio (which the general called his favorite, because it had done its duty), noted that "he [Terrill] was with us during the fierce contest on the ridge, and with us when he fell. He was struck by the fragment of a shell, in the breast. As he was lying there, the blood flowing from his wound, Col. Monroe [123rd Illinois] riding up, said 'General are your hurt,' 'I am dying, sir,' was the reply."[276]

On the march to Perryville, William befriended the chaplain of the 121st Ohio Infantry. The chaplain, learning of the general's serious wound, went to his side. In the spring of 1863, he wrote:

> I hastened to visit him before he died, and if possible to render him some assistance. When I entered the room I found him lying upon a linen cot, and, as I approached his bed-side, he recognized me, and reached out his hand, and as he took my hand in his he said:—
>
> "Well, Chaplain, I am glad to see you," and, after talking with him a short time, he raised his voice and spoke in an audible tone, "God have mercy on my soul." Then adjusting the clothes about him, he said, "now let me rest."[277]

Captain John Calvin Hartzell recalled the general's death in his memoirs:

> "Here [behind Starkweather's line] Brigadier-General Correll [Terrill] was killed. His great, big, nice brigade had vanished, melted away. He had always hitherto been an artillery officer, and when the action commenced he forgot all about his infantry and rushed to the battle to fight it [the artillery]—so we were told. Anyway here he was mourning in a dazed helpless manner, and here he was killed in my presence—his whole right breast shot away, ribs and all. Our assistant surgeon, Dr. [Harvey S.] Taft, placed him in a sitting position with his back to a big rock, then his face turned blue and he joined the great pale army of the dead.[278]

Orderly Peter Fitzpatrick, in a letter to his sweetheart, wrote about the battle and the general:

You made a mistake when you thought I was on[e] of the men that fired the last gun in Chaplin Hills. But I was one of the two that fired the gun that Terrill was killed at for I was wounded about 2 o'clock and the battle lasted until dark. You must not think that I am brave, please. Fate has led me through the dangers of which I told you. For I can assure you that I didn't seek more of them. A great many these little excitements is over now since the General is dead.[279]

Now to examine these stories, aided by other data, to see which one is the most creditable. Bits and pieces of the truth, however, mingle throughout them. The accounts given by Tourgée and Hartzell indicate that William died on the field. The other accounts refute this. William was alive for several hours after being carried from the field.

The account given by Major Connolly is the simplest one. The one thing about his account that bothers historians is the fact that he claims to have been near General James S. Jackson when he was killed. Connolly says that William breathed his last about 2 A.M. on October 9. Every official document mentioning William's death records the date as October 8; therefore, it is unlikely that William died after midnight.

Captain Taylor's account is very detailed, but contains some obvious errors. He says that the shell fragments struck William about 6 P.M. General McCook, in his official report, notes the time at about 4 P.M. Like Connolly, Taylor places the death of his commander as occurring in the early hours of October 9. McCook reports Terrill died about 11 P.M. Evidently, there was some question in Washington about the time of William's death. On October 25, Major General Buell informed Adjutant General Lorenzo Thomas that William died on October 8 at 11 P.M.[280] Had William died after midnight, certainly Buell would have noted it in that telegram.

Taylor's account, however, does have a certain amount of credibility. He mentions that William had removed his jacket, and was working some guns when the fragments struck him. This would have required the general to remove his sword and revolver. Adjacent to the position of Stone's and Bush's batteries, on the right side of the Benton Road, stood the 121st Ohio Infantry. Charles Van Houten, a Sergeant in that regiment, picked up a sword on the battlefield and sent it to his wife. As it turned out, the sword belonged to General Terrill. For the sergeant to pick the sword up from the field, it had to have been removed at some point. The sword, however, could have been removed after William was wounded.

Another point in Taylor's account concerns William's working the artillery. Taylor says the guns belonged to Parsons' battery, but it is more likely the guns belonged to Bush's or Stone's batteries. Colonel Albert S. Hall, commanding the 105th Ohio, noted that the general was wounded while they were behind Bush's battery. Another account of the battle states that William was working a park of guns when he was wounded.[281] Given his love for artillery, it is certainly possible that William was working some of the guns. This fact is also borne out in Peter Fitzpatrick's letter.

It is generally accepted that William's dying words were of his wife. Private R. A. Kirk, a member of the 105th Ohio Infantry, noted that "Gen. Terrill lived long enough to know that the rebels were falling back. Said he, 'I die with victory in my heart: the rebels are retreating.'"[282] Kirk's account, however, appears to be fiction.

William was carried about two miles to the rear, and placed in the home of David Wilkerson, which the Northern troops used as a hospital.[283] Examination of his wound revealed that the fragment carried away a portion of his left lung. William, struggling for breath, told the surgeons and members of his staff to "carry me to Larz Anderson's house, in Cincinnati. Mrs. Anderson will take care of me."[284]

Probably the most reliable information about William's condition appears in the correspondence between W. S. Edwards and Professor A. D. Bache, of the U.S. Coast Survey. Edwards, writing on the night of October 9, informed Bache that William lived about four hours after receiving the wound, and that "the surgeon told him that he thought he would recover. He was struck in the left breast by a piece of shell that exploded in air, overhead, and his ribs mashed in, over his heart, his death resulted from internal hemorrhage."[285]

On the day after the battle of Perryville, Captain P. P. Oldershaw, Assistant Adjutant General of the 10th Division, took possession of the remains of Generals Jackson and Terrill, and Colonel Webster. The captain accompanied the bodies to Louisville. About 2 P.M. that day, W. S. Edwards, on his way to join William, met the procession and learned of his friend's death. Edwards returned to Louisville with the detail, where he relayed the sad intelligence to Professor Bache. In closing his letter, Edwards wrote:

> I shall proceed to Cincinnati with his body tomorrow.... I should think that he ought to be buried at West Point. He died as he had lived, a true soldier, without the fear of death before his eyes. In this city, although but little known personally, he seemed to be universally a favorite, and loud are the regrets expressed everywhere at his fall.[286]

William's remains arrived in Louisville about 9 o'clock on October 9, along with those of General Jackson and Colonel Webster. A brief notice copied from the *Louisville Democrat* of the 10th, read:

> The Gallant Dead.
> General James S. Jackson and General William Terrill, who gave their lives to the country, on the battle-field, near Perryville, on Wednesday, were widely known and loved in Kentucky. In the field, in the camp, and in "the battle's van," they were the champions of our cause. Their cool courage and daring knew no bounds. Gen. Jackson resigned his seat in Congress in the early stage of the rebellion, and returned to Kentucky, immediately raised a regiment of cavalry for the war. Terrill, on the plains of Shiloh, won immortal honor. Terrill's battery, and the work of death it done, are as familiar as household words.
> The bodies of Generals Jackson and Terrill reached our city last night, and were

taken to the Galt House. The body of Acting General Webster, also reached the city last night, *en route* to Ohio, for interment.[287]

A notice in the *Louisville Journal* noted: "Mrs. Terrell [Terrill], Gen. Terrell's widow, was in Cincinnati yesterday, at which point she received intelligence of the General's death."[288]

The *Berks & Schuylkill Journal* announced the general's death in Reading, Pennsylvania, on October 11, which noted that his family was residing in the city.

> The sad news in regard to one so highly esteemed in our midst, has cast a gloom over our whole city. Gen. Terrill was one of the bravest and most experienced officers in the service. He was a native of Virginia, but at the outbreak of the war, remained true to the Union cause. The loss of this gallant soldier and true patriot, at the outset of what promised to be a brilliant career, will be deeply mourned by all who knew and appreciated his worth.[289]

The *Louisville Journal* spoke of William in glowing terms: "Gen. Terrill has now fallen; he died in the holy cause to which he had devoted himself and he leaves behind him no nobler patriot or truer gentleman."[290]

Several days later, the *Louisville Journal* carried the following:

> Terrill is also dead, he who stood unharmed amid the shower of ball and shell at Shiloh, he who fought his battery there until every horse was killed, and but one man left to assist him in working his guns. He died like a soldier, standing by a cannon, and in the act of loading it he received a fatal wound. It is said that his brigade, which was composed of new troops, ran at the first fire, and left their General alone, when he went to Lieut. Parsons' battery, and assisted him in working his guns. If this is true, what infamy is black enough to heap upon them? Oh, what a coward is that man who turns his back upon his commander and his General, and ignominiously runs from the field![291]

This report and others like it brought a rebuttal from the men of the 105th Ohio. The correspondent of the *Western Reserve Chronicle* wrote:

> Let it [be] remembered, that three regiments of Terrill's brigade, bore alone and unaided, the determined onset of four times their number, of the choicest troops of Bragg's veteran army.... When it is said that the 105th gave way, and suffered Parsons' battery to be taken, let it be remembered that the regiment came on to the field and formed in line of battle, faced by the rear rank, under an incessant fire of musketry from four times their number, that the guns of the battery were already nearly silenced, and that in the face of that terrible fire, the 105th held its ground *until ordered by Gen. Terrill himself to fall back* and abandon a position which was no longer tenable.[292]

Despite the number of published accounts praising William's conduct, a closer examination of his performance at Perryville reveals serious flaws. Historian Stuart W. Sanders commented: "Had William Terrill survived the Battle of Perryville, I don't think that his performance here would have been well-respected or well-received by his commanding officers."[293]

One of the earliest printed accounts mentioning William's failure as a brigade commander appeared in 1866, written by William F. G. Shanks. He wrote: "I have elsewhere already noticed how Terrill, who, as a captain of artillery, gained a great reputation for his successful handling of his battery at Shiloh, and who was promoted to be a brigadier general of infantry, to utterly fail and throw away his young life in his chagrin and desperation."[294]

From the available evidence of William's conduct at Perryville, I believe that William was well aware of the errors he committed that day, and that it was far from what others expected of him.

The army sent William's remains to Cincinnati, Ohio, from Louisville by mail boat on the afternoon of October 11. Two days later, Major General Wright issued an order for the Quartermaster Department to "provide transportation, by express, from Cincinnati, O. to Reading, Penn. for the remains of the late Brigadier General Wm. R. Terrill, U.S. Vols., also transportation for Mr. W. S. Edwards, in charge of Gen'l. Terrill's remains."[295]

William was laid to rest on October 16, 1862, in a plot offered by Major James McKnight, in the Charles Evans Cemetery, in Reading, Pennsylvania. The *Berks & Schuylkill Journal* reported:

Funeral of Gen. Wm. R. Terrill.

"The remains of Brig. Gen. William R. Terrill, killed at the battle of Perryville, Ky., on the 8th instant, reached this city on Wednesday last, and were consigned to their final resting place in the Charles Evans Cemetery, on Thursday afternoon last. The funeral services were conducted in accordance with the Episcopal formula, in Christ Church, by the Rev. A. G. Cummins, the Rector, assisted by the Rev. J. Scarborough, of Poughkeepsie, N. Y., and the Reverend Mr. Tortat, Rector of St. Barnabas Church of this city. The sermon was preached by the Reverend Mr. Cummins, and was an eloquent tribute to the patriotism, bravery and Christian virtues of the deceased. Reverend Mr. Scarborough, Pastor of the church of which the deceased was for several years a parishioner, and who was enabled by that relation to know and appreciate his worth, closed with some touching remarks. The funeral cortege then moved from the church to the Cemetery, the following gentlemen acting as pall-bearers, viz:

Hon. John Banks,	Hon. J. Pringle Jones,
Hon. J. G. Jones,	Hon. Hiester Clymer,
Hon. W. M. Hiester,	John S. Richards, Esq.,
Isaac Eckert, Esq.,	Jos. L. Stichter, Esq.

The funeral was attended by the afflicted family of the deceased, who have resided in this city for some months past: by the Gen.'s Aids, who accompanied his body from the battle field to this place, and by all the officers and privates of the Army now in the city, including a number of convalescent soldiers from the Hospital, and a large concourse of soldiers. During the day all the flags of the city were draped in mourning and displayed at half mast. The principal places of business were closed, and the Court House bell as well as the several church bells in the city were tolled while the procession was moving, as a further token of respect. We have seldom seen the hearts of our citizens so deeply touched by any similar event. All felt that a true hero and patriot had passed from earth, and that in his untimely death at the onset of what promised to be a most brilliant career, the service, and the country which he honored, had sustained an irreparable loss.[296]

William's friend Edwards reported the ceremony to Professor Bache:

> The last sad duty is performed and Gen'l. Terrill's remains lie among strangers, but friends. We buried him here on last Friday. All the places of business were closed and the citizens did honor to his memory by attending his remains to the grave. Mrs. Henry takes the blow very severely and is unwilling that I should leave her at present.... After I retired to my room last night I rec'd a note from her in which she said "You *must* not leave us to morrow, remember that you are the last *tie to him*, when you leave that is severed, pity such desolation."[297]

The day following William's burial, his friends and pallbearers called upon the Reverend Cummins for a copy of the burial service. The Episcopal minister complied, with the simple request that address be published for private distribution among the friends of the deceased.[298]

A week or so later, Edwards was in New York. In reporting to Bache, Edwards confided: "It was a hard parting to leave Mrs. Henry & Mrs. Terrill, but I could do no good by remaining any longer, and every day made it more difficult to leave."[299]

In the sad days following the burial of William, Emily Terrill was faced with a decision — what to do with her husband's estate? On October 21, 1862, she wrote to the Registrar of Wills of Berks County, in Reading, Pennsylvania, renouncing and relinquishing her right to act as administrator of the estate. She requested that the court appoint her mother, Arietta L. Henry as administratrix.[300]

Days later, their friend Edwards wrote to Superintendent Bache, reporting their situation and asking for consideration. Edwards wrote:

> Mrs. Henry & Mrs. Terrill are desirous of obtaining writing this winter, in Washington, for the purpose of eking out their pittance. I took the liberty of assuring them of your cordial assistance, but at the same time represented to them that it was very doubtful as there are already so many ladies in and about Washington who support themselves in that way.[301]

Whether Emily and her mother gained employment for the winter is unknown. Emily, however, was living in Washington later in the year, when she applied for a pension from the government. Given Superintendent Bache's fondness of William, it is likely he did all he could to aid the ladies.

A lengthy obituary and biographical sketch of William appeared in the February 8, 1863, issue of the *New York Times*.

OBITUARY.
Tribute to the Late Gen. Wm. R. Terrill.

It will hereafter be our privilege and our duty faithfully to cherish the fame of those martyr-patriots who have sacrificed themselves that the nation might live. There was a modest and high-souled hero who laid down his life on the battle-field of Perryville, and whose career deserves to be held in loving memory. It is right that the purity of nature, the earnestness of principle and the endearing character of Gen. Terrill should be declared beyond the circle of his friends, for he now belongs to the nation in whose cause he so calmly and bravely died. Tried by the sternest and most painful tests he was found faithful among the faithless, bravest among the brave. This young soldier was no common man, for it is unfortunately a rare thing to find a life so entirely and yet gracefully subordinated to the highest principles of religious duty. Even now, when our noblest and bravest are falling like the leaves in Autumn, it is not intrusion to set forth for public consideration the facts of a life so worthy in its continuance and so noble in its close.

Born at Covington, Va., April 21, 1834, young Terrill went to West Point as a Cadet in 1849, and graduated in the Third Artillery in 1853. He was Acting Assistant Professor of Mathematics at the Military Academy in 1855-'6, and served against the Seminoles in Florida during the Winter of 1856, and the Summer of 1857. From 1858 to April, 1861, he was an assistant on the Coast Survey, and as such was employed in the office in the Hudson River triangulation, and as a chief of a party in the triangulation of Charlotte Harbor, Fla. In this capacity, his good judgment, industry and success amid many difficulties secured for him the high esteem of his chief, and of the many others who knew how well he discharged his duty.

It was while he was thus employed that the baleful fires of secession blazed out, confusing the weak and alluring the faithless. Be it remembered, to the honor of Gen. Terrill, that he never wavered from his patriotic duty; and though his heart was torn by the menace of a father's curse, and the powerful beseechings of family pleading, he held fast to what he felt was his sworn duty. Our fierce declaimers against the treason of those Southern army officers who resigned to enter the Confederate service, little realize the powerful motives at work where the ties of kindred, of home, of State, of all early associations, were drawn with intense energy to lead away from an allegiance too easily declared forfeit. It was a terrible ordeal, and those were truly moral heroes who defied all adjurations and passionate persuasions, and held with single heart to a sworn allegiance against all appeals of consanguinity and early friendship. It was not that the tender and awful voices of his child-home had lost their sway in Terrill's heart, for that was gentle and loving; but that he bowed himself humbly before the greater claims of plighted faith and patriotic duty. His nature and his life were truly religious, and this it was which held him firmly at his post. Noble and generous natures will honor him more for this religious loyalty, maintained at the cost of the dearest human ties, than even for the calm trust and brave patience which glorified his death.

He commanded temporarily the Twenty-fourth Pennsylvania Volunteers at Washington Arsenal, in May, 1861; was Acting Inspector-General of the Washington Department, in June, 1861; was appointed Captain Fifth Artillery, and commanded Battery H, Fifth Artillery, after July 1, 1861; was Commandant of Artillery at the Camp of Instruction, near Louisville, in November; was Chief of Artillery of the Second Division of the Army of the Ohio, from December, 1861 to June, 1862; was Gen. Nelson's Chief of Artillery for the defence of Cincinnati; was ordered to Lexington, and assisted in withdrawing our troops from that place; was appointed Brigadier-General early in September; was engaged in the defence of Louisville, and marching thence with his brigade was mortally wounded Oct. 8, 1862, at the battle of Chaplin's Hills or Perryville.

He was a truly skillful artillerist, and won solid titles to professional distinction by the singular efficiency which he gave to his battery in a short time. In the great and sanguinary battle of April 7, near Pittsburgh Landing, his services were very important, and even essential to saving the day. Gen. Nelson's report says: "This (Terrill's) battery was a host in itself. It consists of four 12-pounder brass guns, and two Parrott guns. Its fire was terrific. It was handled superbly. Wherever Capt. T. turned his battery, silence followed on the part of the enemy."

It is hardly needful here to recall the details of the battle of Perryville. Terrill's brigade of raw troops was crushed by an overwhelming concentration of Bragg's forces. While he, with sublime but vain courage, was striving to stay the disorderly retreat, a piece of shell struck him near the heart, inflicting a wound which soon proved fatal. He knew the deficiency of training in his brigade, and the evening before the fatal battle remarked that he expected to have to sacrifice his life in consequence. To the Chaplain's admonition that he should prepare for coming death, he replied, "I have been prepared to die for a long time." If to live a right and religious life is to be prepared, he was indeed ready.

Terrill was of good stature and well formed. His hair was flaxen and waving, his eyes a tender blue, his complexion rich, and his whole expression kind and gentle, but downright and decided. He had a winning frankness of manner, a steady cheerfulness under all circumstances, and a native cordiality which made it easy to like him. His intellect was clear, practical and judicious. His private life was exemplary; of his domestic life we may not speak, except to say that he was married to a daughter of the late Capt. Wm. S. Henry, of the army.

Many friends will cherish his memory all the more tenderly because his kindred disavow him, and because he died amid the wreck of an incoherent brigade, which he strove by hopeless and fruitless daring to reinstate. Could he have fallen directing the terrific fires of his splendid battery, it would have seemed kinder; but soldiers of duty such as he, die not for dramatic effect; they accept in patience the work assigned, dying unhonored martyrs if need be, well knowing that our Heavenly Father reads the inmost heart and gives eternal benediction to the self-denying and sincere. God be thanked for each noble soul which thus strengthens our faith in human nature, and let us not, amid the confusions of to-day, forget the sanctities of humanity which are now passing into history and which future generations of the good and wise will prize above all price. E. B. H.[302]

In Virginia, the *Staunton Spectator* reported on October 21:

> **Gen. Wm. R. Terrill, Killed.**— At the battle of Perryville in Kty., the Federal General Wm. R. Terrill was killed. He was a son of Wm. H. Terrill of Bath county, Va., and about 31 [sic] years of age. In speaking of him, a correspondent of the Lynchburg Republican says: He graduated at West Point in 1853 and was one year the senior of General J. E. B. Stuart. He was a good scholar and stood well in his class. After graduating he received the appointment of Assistant Professor of Mathematics, and then for some years was in the Coast Survey in Florida and elsewhere. He [Terrill] was a superior draughtsman and a fine officer. To the great mortification and chagrin of his father and brothers, he deliberately chose to remain and take sides with the enemies of his native State. He sleeps now in the warrior's grave, and I only regret that he could not have given his life in a better cause. He was an amiable, intelligent and courteous gentleman. How a native born Virginian could become a traitor to the South is a mystery I cannot solve.[303]

The Sword of General Terrill

About six months after William's death at Perryville, Captain Marshall B. Clason, of the 121st Ohio Infantry, wrote a letter to Brigadier General Jeremiah T. Boyle about the general's sword. Captain Clason stated "that Sergeant Chas. Van Housten [sic] of his company found the sword of the late Gen'l. Terrill the day after the battle of Chaplin Hills, Ky., and sent the same to his wife at Pleasant Township, Marion County, Ohio."[304] The captain informed General Boyle that he gave the information so "the sword may be sent to the widow of Gen'l. Terrill to whom it belongs"[305]

The authorities referred Captain Clason's letter to the U.S. Attorney for the Southern District of Ohio, at Cincinnati. The attorney responded on April 13, 1863, telling Boyle to place the matter in the hands of U.S. Marshal Earl Bill, and that Van Houten should be required to give up the sword.[306]

Major General A. E. Burnside, commanding officer of the Department of the Ohio, contacted Marshal Earl Bill in Cleveland. The marshal reported to General Burnside on April 18:

> I have the honor to acknowledge receipt, on the 15th inst., of the several papers forwarded from your Hd Quarters to me relative to the recovery of the Sword belonging to the late General Terrill, said to have been taken from the field of battle at Chaplin Hills whereon he received his mortal wounds; and it is with much pleasure in that I am able to inform you of the success attending my efforts for its recovery, made pursuant to your request.
>
> On the 16th inst, deeming the matter of a somewhat delicate nature, I proceeded in person to Marion County Ohio; and after having learned the place where Van Houten resides, called at his house in Pleasant township, some seven miles from Marion. Not finding Mrs. Van Houten at home, it was ascertained upon inquiring that a sword was in the house, which on being produced by some members of the family, and inspected, was found to bear upon the blade the following inscriptions: on one side "Gen. Boyle," and on the reverse, "To Gen. Terrill;" from which I was at no loss to determine that I had found the object of my search, and thereupon took possession of it, together with the scabbard in which it was found. Upon a close inspection the following additional inscription appears upon the *guard*: "C. Van Houten, Midletown, Marion Co. Ohio"—evidently engraved by Van Houten to perpetuate the evidence of his bravery in capturing the sword of his own slain General!
>
> Being ignorant of the residence of Gen T's. widow, I await your further order as to what disposition shall be made of the sword, now remaining in my hands.
>
> I hope it may not be out of place to remark that the actual expenses incurred by me in its recovery amount to the sum of $10.60. I take no account of my own time or services; and [should] it appear that the pecuniary circumstances of Gen. T's. family are such as would render a reimbursement of the above sum in the slightest degree inconvenient I should be very unwilling to accept anything on that score.[307]

The following month, Captain Clason commented on the affair. In a letter to his mother from Franklin, Tennessee, he wrote:

You know, by the papers, that I was instrumental in recovering the sword of Gen. Terrill who was killed at the Battle of Perryville. I wrote the letter which secured the recovery. The entire letter was published, and my name given. It occasioned considerable fluttering in certain quarters, and I anticipated trouble, and prepared for it.[308]

The sword evidently made its way back into the hands of General Terrill's widow. In 1898, the sword was part of the collection of the Ordnance Museum at West Point.[309] The sword remained in the museum collection until the 1960s (last inventoried in 1944), when it disappeared. It was dropped from the collection registers in 1980.[310]

Epilogue

The War Department officially recognized William as a Brigadier General of Volunteers on November 1, 1862. On December 23, 1862, President Lincoln nominated William to the Senate of the United States for appointment. The Senate failed to confirm his appointment, and the president nominated William again on February 27, 1863.

Again, the Senate failed to confirm his appointment. The president nominated him a third time on March 5, 1863, and this time the Senate confirmed the appointment on the 9th, as a token of the government's appreciation. The War Department issued William's commission as Brigadier General three days later, to rank from September 9, 1862. The Adjutant General's Office sent the commission to William's brother-in-law, Captain Guy V. Henry at Fort Hamilton, New York, on May 21, 1867. The present whereabouts of the commission is unknown.

A few days after Lincoln first nominated William to the Senate, Emily applied to the government for the benefits due her by act of Congress on July 24, 1862. She listed her residence as Washington, D.C., and gave her age as 22 years, adding that she had no children. She had to certify that she had not been involved in giving aid or abetment to the rebellion. The government granted the application for a pension on March 4, 1863, at the rate of $30 per month, to date from October 8, 1862.[311]

About a month after his burial, the first of three honors was bestowed upon William. Local officials named a camp for drafted soldiers located near Reading, Pennsylvania, Camp Terrill, in his honor. "Gen. Terrill, whose family resided in Virginia, being banished from his native home by his devotion to his country and her glorious old flag, voluntarily selected Reading, from all the loyal north, as his residence and that of his family; called it his home, and always so considered it, from the time he was first ordered here on the recruiting service. This compliment to our city, by a stranger, highly honored and esteemed, was fully appreciated; and it was deemed a fitting return to give his name to our Camp."[312]

The following month, the second honor was given at Munfordville, Kentucky. A fort, considered to be the "largest and the most heavily manned and gunned fort of the Munfordville defence [sic] system."[313] It is said that Fort Terrill and nearby Fort Willich was so strong that Confederate Cavalryman John Hunt Morgan never dared to attack them. A trench connecting the fortifications allowed a horseman to carry orders between the two positions.

The third honor was bestowed on May 30, 1863. By General Order, the War Department declared, "That the battery of field guns contiguous to and in advance of Fort Kearny be called Battery Terrill, after the late Brig. Gen. W. R. Terrill, who was killed at the Battle of Perryville, Ky., October 8, 1862."[314]

Although William left his battery in June 1862, its members did not soon forget him. A series of letters appeared in the *Toledo Commercial* in 1863, written by a soldier identified only as "Pork & Beans," which contained recollections of William. The first mention appears in the January 16, 1863 issue: "Terrill's old battery, commanded by the brave Captain Guenther, took on the field the flag of the 2d Arkansas Regiment and will retain it as a drop in the cup of revenge for the death of the brave General Terrill at Chaplin Heights."[315]

The second mention of William appeared on the anniversary of the "Bloody day at Shiloh," April 7:

> Brigadier William R. Terrill, than whom a braver man never breathed, who died at his post at Perryville, bravely fighting for his country. There is sadness in this camp to-day. He was the idol of his men; we speak of him in whispers. His memory is ours; we will in this ungodly struggle preserve his name, which he has left to his country without a blemish.... W. R. Terrill was the only one of a large and ancient Virginia family who stuck by the Constitution and [the] old Union. He knew no North, no South, no East, no West, nothing but the Union as it was, an uncompromising patriot, a brave soldier and a true and devout christian. May the memory of Brigadier General William Rufus Terrill be handed down to posterity, as [a] glorious example of valor and patriotism.[316]

In November 1864, William's family had his remains moved from Reading, Pennsylvania, to the cemetery at the U.S. Military Academy. He was buried in Section 26, Row A, Grave Number 5, on November 19, 1864. General George Cullum issued a circular, which read:

> The re-interment of the body of the late Brigadier General William R. Terrill, U.S. Vols. (Captain 5th U.S. Artillery) will take place this day at 2 P.M. from the Chapel.
> The Officers, Professors & Corps of Cadets at the Military Academy are afforded an opportunity to pay their tribute of respect to his memory.[317]

A small footstone bearing the inscription "W. R. Terrill," placed in 1939, marked his grave. Some years later, a tree limb fell on the marker, breaking it off at ground level. The stone marking the grave of his wife serves as the only marker for his grave.

Emily Henry Terrill lived in Washington, D.C., until March of 1865. That fall, she requested that the pension office send her benefit to her in New York.

In 1870, Emily was living in New York City with her mother and sister. Ten years later, Emily and her mother were living in Ossining, Westchester County, New York, having moved there about 1872.

Emily died in Sing Sing (now Ossining), New York at 9 A.M., February 18, 1884, of pneumonia and heart strain. She was buried with her husband in the West Point Cemetery on February 20, 1884.

>Funeral of
>Mrs. William R. Terrill
>The funeral of the late Emily D., widow of General Wm. R. Terrill, U.S.A., and daughter of the late Major W. S. Henry, U.S.A. took place last Wednesday morning in St. Paul's Church in this village. The remains were in a hard wood casket covered with black cloth, and a raised cross on the lid. The interment was at West Point Cemetery where [her] husband is buried. The attendance was very large.[318]

Gravestone of Emily Henry Terrill, U.S.M.A. Cemetery, West Point, New York. Although unmarked, General Terrill's remains were buried here in November 1864 (courtesy U.S.M.A. Archives).

Nearly fifty years after William's death, the courts in Washington, D.C., settled his estate. His widow, as previously mentioned, asked her mother to handle the settlement of the estate. Whatever the reason, Arietta L. Henry did not settle her son-in-law's estate. John Porterfield, a nephew, completed that task. In March 1911, the Superior Court of the District of Columbia appointed Porterfield as administrator of the estate. The court distributed the proceeds to his heirs in December 1912, the final action in settling the estate.[319] The case file cannot be located.

Chapter V

James Barbour Terrill

James Barbour Terrill
1838–1864

As William H. Terrill's legal practice expanded, so did his family responsibilities. Elizabeth delivered another son into the now male dominated household, on February 20, 1838. His parents named him James Barbour Terrill, in honor of the former governor of Virginia. Family members affectionately called him Jimmie while his schoolmates called him "Bath" Terrill.

James, along with a number of local boys, attended the "best primary schools" available at Warm Springs.[1] Following this, it appears that his father shipped James off to a boarding school, as he had the older children. James, however, attended a school near Salem, in Roanoke County, Virginia, rather than in Staunton like his siblings. He likely stayed with his brother George and his family while in school. James completed his studies there in late August 1854.[2]

Early in 1854, William H. Terrill wrote Colonel F. H. Smith, superintendent of the Virginia Military Institute at Lexington: "I think it probable I shall have to ask the admission of another of my son's at the Institute next summer."[3]

William made the formal request on October 11: "I shall send my son James over to you early next week to be enrolled as a Cadet of the Va. M. I., you must receive him as such ... James is in his 17th year and is a lad of excellent moral habits, with a capacity of the first order."[4]

James's military career got a late start on October 18, 1854, when he joined the Corps of Cadets as a pay cadet.[5]

The elder Terrill reported in early November:

> James, I understand is trying to do some thing at the Institute and looks quite military since he has been put in uniform. I hope he may not be unmindful of his duty but improve the opportunity he has of becoming a smart fellow. I fear he is too fond of company & of ease to distinguish himself in the way of learning.[6]

While it seems that James was adapting well to life at the Institute, he was less enthusiastic about the dining facilities. In a letter to John Allen Terrill, he commented: "We have to eat here what we can get & sometimes we cannot get that."[7]

As the end of his first year at VMI drew to a close, James buckled down and applied himself. "I have studied more in the last three weeks than I have done in twice that time ... I have studied incessantly."[8] The hard work paid off, and James finished his first year 10th out of 23 students. James' conduct, however, left something to be desired, having accumulated 101 demerits for the year.

Conduct, and particularly study habits, continued to be a problem for James. Colonel Smith addressed William H. Terrill on this matter on February 7, 1856, stating: "I find that your son has already 30 demerits for the month of Jany, and it is proper to caution him against the effect of his rapid increasing number. At this rate it would not take long to exceed the limit of the Regulations. He is now reciting to me and seems to be studying."[9]

On February 13, the elder Terrill weighed in upon the subject. In a letter to Colonel Smith, he wrote:

> You do not know, my Dear Sir, how I have suffered from my son's heedlessness.... I have written to him frequently upon the subject and so hoped he would become more circumspect in his deportment. I have made my last appeal and if he will not do better, I shall have to change his position by putting him to manual labor of some kind.[10]

At the end of the first quarter of 1856, Colonel Terrill received a progress report. Apparently, it was not a very good one, for it garnered this response:

> I am *truly distressed* to find that my son is doing *so badly*. I wrote to you to say that if he does not improve by the 1st day of January next, I shall then ask for permission to withdraw him from the Institute. It is a painful alternate but it *must* be met.[11]

James' difficulties became apparent after the year-end examinations in July 1856. He ranked 16th in a class of 21 cadets, and had accumulated 190 demerits for the year. A cadet faced dismissal if he had accumulated 100 demerits by January 1, or 200 before the end of the year.[12]

James commenced his third year at VMI and immediately encountered some difficulty. Less than two months into the new term he had trouble with mathematics, and his grades fell. He also repeated his earlier behavior in accumulating demerits; by December 1 he had received 71.

The January 1857 examinations revealed James' standing near the bottom of his class, and deficient in mathematics. Upon receiving the results of the January examinations, William H. Terrill wrote Colonel Smith on January 31:

> I had hoped that my son would have done better than it seems he has. *I have now no hopes of him*. I have exhausted every rational means to awaken him to a sense of

duty and have in vain endeavored to infuse into his mind some little ambition. I would appeal to you to use your influence to save him, but I feel persuaded you have already done your duty in that respect. You seem to think that his standing will be better at the next examination. I am admonished by the past that there is no hope for that. He is now in his twentieth year and his demerit and standing in his studies indicate a degree of *recklessness* that closes the door of hope. I cannot continue him longer at the Institute than the end of the present session unless there be *very soon* a *very decided change for the better*.[13]

This seemed to be a wake-up call for James. Colonel Smith reported to William H. Terrill in February that James was doing better since the examinations, and "is conscious of having provoked your displeasure with respect to habits of study and is anxious to redeem all those promises."[14]

James struggled through the final two years at VMI, graduating on July 5, 1858, ranking 16th in a class of 19 cadets.[15]

When James began his studies at Virginia Military Institute, it seemed that he would do well, ranking 10th at the end of his first term. However, with each passing term, his marks deteriorated. A possible explanation for this comes from Frederick County resident Samuel D. Buck, who would belong to James' regiment in the looming war. Buck mentioned that during the war James called upon him to look at some troops in the distance; the "Colonel" was near-sighted. This near-sightedness could well have been the cause of James' poor performance in the classroom. Nowhere do the records indicate when he first began to suffer the effects of vision loss, but perhaps it was after his first year at the Institute.

Sometime after graduation from the institute, Governor Henry A. Wise appointed James to the rank of major in the 5th Regiment Cavalry, Virginia Militia. He held this post until the Virginia Convention abolished all militia ranks above captain in late April 1861.

James next entered the Lexington Law School conducted by Judge John White Brockenbrough in 1859. This school later became the Law School of Washington and Lee University.

While at the law school, Henry Kyd Douglass asked his classmate James "Bath" Terrill about his former professor, Thomas J. Jackson. Terrill replied:

Prewar carte de visite (CDV) of James B. Terrill (courtesy Bath County Historical Society).

Old Jack is a character, genius or just a little crazy. He lives quietly and don't meddle. He's as systematic as a multiplication table and as full of military as a arsenal. Stiff, you see, never laughs, but as kind hearted as a woman — and by Jupiter, he teaches a nigger Sunday-school. But mind, if this John Brown business leads to war, he'll be heard from![16]

After graduating from Judge Brockenbrough's law school, James joined his father's practice at Warm Springs, Virginia. On May 16, 1860, the Bath County Courts admitted James to the bar, and allowed to practice in the county court. In the fall of 1860, James qualified in the county and circuit courts of Pocahontas County.

James was active in the local militia between 1859 and 1861. In Bath County the 81st Virginia Militia and the Bath Cavalry, 5th Regiment Cavalry, Virginia Militia held a general muster day near Warm Springs. As war loomed ever nearer, these musters became very important. One observer recalled seeing "'Jimmy' Terrill in full regimentals of VMI, galloping over the field, trying to whip into shape men who came down from neighboring coves and hollows, wearing coon skin caps and shouldering their muskets, which had previously been used only to provide meat for the family tables."[17]

James served on the staff of Brigadier General William H. Harman, who commanded the 13th Brigade of Virginia Militia. In December 1860, a newspaper article referred to James as holding the rank of lieutenant colonel.[18]

Upon being appointed to General Harman's staff, the *Staunton Vindicator* noted: "From the well known character of Mr. Terrill, it is unnecessary to suggest, that should his conduct on the battle field only half compare with his behavior on peaceful parade, the enemy had best look well to themselves."[19]

1861

In a February 1861 letter to his brother-in-law George A. Porterfield, James expressed his opinion on the current political situation:

> I am now perfectly indifferent as as [sic] to what course affairs may take (not through any rebellious motive but because every class of individuals are disposed to differ & wrangle. Anarchy I believe now even now is ringing and people of this ever happy & prosperous country must experience fully the horrors & ravages of a civil war before this or coming generations can appreciate the blessing that a Government confers. I care not whether it be a democracy or a monarchy so it confers law & order the effects for which governments are instilled it is far preferable to that state in which the lawless passions of men are unloosed. If bloodshed was all to be expected or dreaded in a state of anarchy men would soon learn to look quietly upon the tragedies that would be enacted, but that demoralization that must ensue from accustoming ones' self to such venues, must shock & paralyze every sense of virtue, this is all a reasoning & intelligent mind can expect from a disruption of our Government. No argument can be allowed in favor of such a suicidal course, all that can be asserted in justification of such a course, is what is conceived in prejudice & brought forth in passion.[20]

According to family lore, James was visiting relatives in the eastern part of the state when the Virginia State Convention adopted the Ordinance of Secession. He immediately went to Harpers Ferry and offered his services there, being one of the first Southern patriots who reached that point. As a graduate of the Virginia Military Institute, and considered a "very superior tactician," the commanding officer assigned James to duty drilling the officers and privates of the volunteer companies as they arrived.[21]

After several weeks of such work, he was relieved of duty in late April 1861, when the Virginia Convention abolished all militia ranks above captain. James went to Richmond, and there wrote his father's old friend, John Letcher, now governor of Virginia. In the letter, dated April [May] 5, James offered his services to the governor and to the commonwealth.[22]

> Having just been relieved from military duty at Harper's [sic] Ferry in [view] of the act of the Virginia Convention canceling all commissions previously held by Field Officers in the state, I deem it my duty to make a formal tender of my services in a military capacity to the Governor of the state.
>
> I will only say that I am a graduate of the Virginia Military [Institute], was Brigade Inspector of the 13th Brigade of Va. Militia & held the commission of Major of the 5th regiment of Virginia Cavalry & had been discharging the duties of a cavalry officer at Harper's [sic] Ferry from the time the place was [invested] by the Va. forces up to the time I was relieved from duty. With the greatest respect I will state that I prefer the volunteer service as it is a service with which I have been intimately connected since the reorganization of the volunteer system in the state & because I believe I could render at present more efficient service as a volunteer officer.[23]

James Barbour Terrill in militia uniform, about 1860 (courtesy Mercer Terrill Vaden).

The letter was endorsed on May 5, 1861 by John B. Baldwin: "I take pleasure in saying that Major Terrill bears the reputation in the Valley of being a competent & efficient officer—& that I believe he has the qualifications, as he shows the disposition, to do the state service."[24]

An interesting notice appeared in the *Lexington Gazette* on April 26, 1861, from J. W. Massie, the brigade inspector of the 13th Brigade. The notice read in part: "It is due to Lt. Col. James Barbour Terrill of Bath, that I should, in the name of the General commanding publically [sic] acknowledge the energetic and efficient services rendered by him as acting Brigade Inspector, at the last years trainings."25

No record confirming James' promotion to Lieutenant Colonel exists. It was either a very recent promotion or a temporary rank. It is likely that the latter is the case, for James only claims the rank of Major in his letter to Governor Letcher.

Just how James occupied himself during the time between tendering his services to Governor Letcher and the date of his commissioning is not known. It could be that he returned to Harpers Ferry to await Letcher's response. One source notes that Letcher appointed him to the rank of Major "without delay" and assigned him to duty with the 13th Virginia Infantry.26

On May 20, 1861, the Virginia authorities ordered James to report immediately to General Joseph E. Johnston, then commanding the troops at Harpers Ferry, for duty. Two days later, Governor Letcher nominated him to the Advisory Council for commissioning as Major of Volunteers. The confirmation came the following day.

The exact date that James joined his regiment is not stated. The Field and Staff Muster Roll for the period of April 17 to June 30, 1861, listed him as Major and present for duty. James later stated that he had been associated with the 13th Virginia Infantry since the last of May 1861. Records of the Confederate Paymaster, however, indicate that James received payment on June 29 for a period commencing April 23, 1861.

The 13th Virginia Infantry seems to have been the mother of generals. Its first colonel—Ambrose P. Hill—rose to the rank of general in late February 1862. James A. Walker was the second in May 1863, and James B. Terrill became the third in June 1864. The author of the sketch of James B. Terrill which appeared in the Virginia Volume of the *Confederate Military History* noted that he "would have worn higher distinction had his noble young life been longer spared."27

J. William Jones, in an article published in *The Southern Historical Society Papers*, referred to Terrill as "a brilliant graduate of the Virginia Military Institute, whose gallantry and skill won for him the Brigadier's wreath and stars."28 Of course this was written many years after the fact. Another comment, probably annotated soon after the war, stated, "Terrill apparently was a good and respected leader, but not entirely popular with the men of the 13th Virginia Infantry. They sometimes referred to him as 'Major Terrible.'"29

In early June, the 13th Virginia Infantry left Harpers Ferry and marched to Winchester. On June 15, Colonel Hill led his regiment and the 3rd Tennessee Infantry to Romney, in neighboring Hampshire County. The command made the forty-two mile march in two days, camping for the night along the way.

At Romney, Colonel Hill ordered Colonel John C. Vaughn (3rd Tennessee) to take two companies of his regiment and two companies of the 13th Virginia Infantry and march to New Creek Depot. Colonel Vaughn started at 8 P.M. on

June 18, and after a march of 18 miles, arrived near New Creek at 5 A.M. After routing a force of 250 Union soldiers, taking two pieces of artillery, a stand of colors, and destroying the 21st railroad bridge, he returned to Romney. Vaughn and his men reached Romney on the afternoon of the 19th.

Casualties on the expedition were light; one man of the 3rd Tennessee received a slight wound in the arm. The artillery pieces were loaded, but not fired. The enemy spiked the guns before abandoning them. Col. Vaughn reported that the loss of the enemy is not known, "but several were seen to fall."[30]

Colonel Angus McDonald's Cavalry relieved Hill's detachment, which left Romney on June 21, taking three days to reach Winchester. One diarist wrote of the march:

> The march back was much more severe than that to R[omney]. Under the com'd [command] of Maj. Terrill we had frequently to march eight miles thro' the hot sun without either resting or getting water, the dust being so thick that we could not see a man ten steps from us— In three days we reach our camp ground about five miles from W[inchester].[31]

It is likely that on this march James received the nickname of "Major Terrible."

The next significant event in the history of the 13th Virginia Infantry was the battle of First Manassas. The regiment commenced its march on July 18 for Manassas Junction, fording the Shenandoah River on the morning of July 19. Then moving by way of Ashby's Gap, the army arrived at Piedmont Station about midnight that night. Here they formed as a rear guard and waited impatiently as the remainder of the troops were shuttled to Manassas Junction. The long anticipated order to board the trains finally arrived at 4 P.M. July 20. Colonel Hill, with a portion of the men boarded one train, while Lieut. Col. Walker boarded another with the remainder of the men. Excitement turned to frustration as the men waited for the two trains to move to Manassas Junction.

The order to move finally came about 8 A.M. July 21, 1861. Derailments and rumors caused many delays during the journey to Manassas Junction. At one point, the men questioned the loyalty of the engineers.

About 4 P.M., the two trains arrived at Manassas Junction, and the sound of battle reached the ears of the eager soldiers. Upon arriving, the 13th Virginia Infantry took a position on the right, where they assisted in protecting the fords of Bull Run. To make matters worse, the two columns of the 13th Virginia Infantry became separated. Part spent the night near the McLean house, and the other part spent the night near Union Mills. The men of the 13th Virginia Infantry were disgusted over not being engaged in the battle, and felt deprived of the opportunity. Many of the soldiers blamed the lack of action on negligence.

On the 23rd, the reunited regiment moved to Fairfax Station, Virginia, where they performed picket duty on the Braddock Road. Here they remained for the duration of July and August. During this time, Major Terrill was in charge of coordinating the scouts and skirmishers of the 13th Virginia Infantry. In August, he assumed command of the regiment while Colonel Hill was absent sick.

On Sunday, the 25th of August, four companies of the 13th Virginia Infantry along with two guns of the Newtown Artillery, were detailed to assist Colonel J. E. B. Stuart in taking Mason's and Munson's Hills, in Northern Virginia. Major Terrill commanded the detachment from the 13th Virginia Infantry. After successfully taking Mason's Hill on the 26th, construction began on a line of fortifications. The 13th Virginia Infantry took part in the scouting and skirmishing, and was for three days without rations or blankets, suffering severely from the weather. During this time, they were in sight of the enemy's outposts and could plainly see the unfinished capitol dome in Washington, D.C.

James took the four companies of his regiment and moved toward Munson's Hill on August 27. After a slight skirmish, he took possession of Munson's Hill, and eight prisoners. In addition to the fighting on this hill, there was some sharp skirmishing on nearby Upton's Hill, in which the 13th Virginia Infantry suffered its first loss.

J. William Jones recalled the day's fighting:

> The day we captured Munson's hill, Major Terrill was sent with a detachment of the Thirteenth on a scout, during which we drove in the enemy's pickets, ate their smoking dinner, and pursued them back until they rallied on their reserve, and our gallant Major thought it would not be prudent to advance further. Accordingly we were moving back to our reserve when we met Stuart. "What is the matter? I hope you are not running from the Yankees," said the "gay cavalier." Major Terrill explained, and Stuart said, "That was all right, but the Maryland boys are coming, and I think we must go back and beat up the quarters of these people." Just then a scout rode up and informed him that the enemy were fully five thousand strong and had five pieces of artillery. (We numbered about five hundred). "Oh, no!" was the laughing reply, "you are romancing. But it does not matter how many they number. We can whip them anyway; and as for their artillery, the Southern Confederacy needs artillery, and we will just go and take possession of those pieces." Dismounting from his horse after our line of battle was formed, he took a musket and was among the foremost in the charge as we dashed forward and cleared the wood to and beyond the Loudoun and Hampshire Railroad, causing the long roll to beat and the troops to turn out for miles along General McClellan's front.[32]

Philip Edloe Jones, of the Louisa Blues (Company D), wrote his father of the exciting times. The August 31, 1861, letter reads very much like an account published in the *Richmond Dispatch*, signed "Louisa." There is a good chance that Jones was the author of that account.

Private Jones noted that the detachment marched with one day's rations about 6:30 A.M. on Sunday. After marching about ten miles, the men halted to rest at Annandale, Virginia. The men resumed the march at 1 P.M., and after going about 2 miles, halted on Chestnut Hill, on Captain Mason's farm. Here Colonel Stuart joined the infantrymen, and assumed command of the entire force.

Jones mentions in his letter that as they were working on the breastworks in front of Mason's house, the Yankees were firing at them from behind a schoolhouse in the nearby woods. To put an end to the threat, the Confederates burned the schoolhouse. Young Jones also related to his father the activities of August 27 near Upton's Hill and Bailey's Cross Roads, Virginia. He wrote that the column marched from Mason's Hill at about 8 A.M. After a slow, cautious march through the woods, taking an hour and a half, they reached the top of a hill overlooking Bailey's Cross Roads. The crossroads, nearly a mile away, was in the hands of a small force of Yankees.

While halted here, Major Terrill took two companies and proceeded to search the nearby house of Mr. Upton. They found no Yankees, but the unmistakable signs of their recent presence were plainly visible. The Northern troops left in such a hurry that they left their partially consumed breakfast behind.

Reinforcements soon arrived, and the Maryland Company of the 13th Virginia Infantry advanced toward the Loudoun and Hampshire Railroad. Encountering a force of the enemy, the Marylanders fell back with a loss of two men wounded. Having such a small force, James decided to fall back to the position on Munson's Hill. Almost at once, the retreating column met Stuart, who turned them around, telling them "it wd [would] *never do for us to run.*"[33]

Led by Stuart, the Confederates moved into the woods, advancing to the railroad. At that point, they charged across the tracks, driving the enemy back a short distance. The Northern men rallied briefly, only to fall back again in the face of Stuart's advance.

Here, Major Terrill made another impression on the men of the 13th Virginia Infantry. Private Jones wrote: "Our major showed a great deal of bravery & he raised himself in our estimation very much. I think he is most to rash."[34]

Two days later the 13th Virginia Infantry returned to Camp Blair, near Fairfax Station, Virginia. From that point, on August 31, a member of the regiment identified as "Louisa" contributed an account of the recent events to the *Richmond Dispatch*.

> At half-past three o'clock last Sunday morning, (the 25th,) four companies of our regiment, (the Montpelier Guards, Culpeper Minute Men, Lanier Guards and Louisa Blues,) received "marching orders," and accompanied by two pieces of Capt. Beckham's Newtown Artillery, were soon in motion for some point to us unknown. Arriving at Anandale [sic] — a little village on the turnpike leading from Alexandria to Fairfax Court House — we were joined by a small force of cavalry under Col. Stewart [Stuart], who took command of the whole expedition. After a short halt we took up the line of march for Mason's Hill, (the residence of Capt. Murray Mason, of the old U.S. Navy, but now in the Confederate service,) where the Federals had been posting their pickets and scouting parties. The Yankees took

to their heels on our approach and we quietly took possession of the hill — spending the remainder of the day and Monday in pretty sharp skirmishing with Yankee scouting parties, who frequently showed themselves at what they deemed a safe distance, and in throwing up entrenchments, lest we should be attacked by the greatly superior force which the enemy had within a mile of us. From this hill we could see very distinctly Washington and Alexandria, which were only about five miles distant, and our boys seemed to regret very much that it was not convenient for them to pay a visit to the two cities. By Tuesday morning we had pretty well finished the breastworks, and had gotten the Yankee scouts very shy, having killed several and taken one soldier and two citizens prisoners, so that our boys began to be a little impatient for another move. We were soon gratified; for having been reinforced by the Twentieth Georgia Regiment and the "Maryland Line," our four companies and two companies of Marylanders were ordered to take possession of Munson's Hill, situated a mile and a half off, and the residence of a notorious abolitionist, whose farm has been the headquarters of Yankee scouting parties. By filing around through some thick woods, we were enabled to come in between the Federal pickets on Munson's Hill and their camp at Bailey's Cross Roads, a mile distant, and although they made Bull Run time,[35] leaving behind overcoats, haversacks, &c., our boys succeeded in capturing eight prisoners and killing the horse from under their "field officer of the day" — probably wounding him very severely — without having a shot fired at us in return. We were halted for reinforcements as we were liable to be attacked at any moment by a superior force, and several companies from Fall's Church (of the 11th and 1st Virginia Regiments I believe,) pretty soon joined us. Leaving these to hold the hill our detachment (under Major Terrill and Major Johnson) was ordered to visit the house of the notorious Charles H. Upton and capture a company of Yankees whom we learned were quartered there and in another house close by. They were too fast for us, however, and we found only their uneaten dinner, with a number of haversacks, canteens, overcoats, &c., to tell of the haste in which they left. After spending an hour here quite pleasantly looking over abolition documents, &c., and eating some of the Hon. (?) Mr. Upton's nice peaches we were about returning to our comrades on Munson's Hill when our sentinels were fired upon by men concealed in a neighboring wood. Supposing that they were a party of our own men, Major Terrill, who in all these skirmishes acted with the most determined bravery, fearlessly exposing himself to the fire of the enemy, took five of his men and went across to the woods, calling out as he went that we were Confederate soldiers. His party being again fired on, however, they returned it, and sent back for our detachment to come up, with the intention of scouring the woods. Just then we learned from a scout that they were Georgians, who had mistaken us for Yankees — a compliment that we can forgive, as they were not near us — and that none of them were hurt. One of our party was slightly wounded. On our return to Upton's house, Major Terrill, with a small party of the Maryland Line, were scouting a piece of woods not far off, when they were fired on by a greatly superior force of the enemy, a private mortally wounded, and a Lieutenant slightly so. Being informed by a scout that the enemy were about three thousand strong, and had artillery, our officers deemed it prudent to fall back to the hill; but just then Col. Stewart [Stuart] came up, and learning the circumstances, immediately drew us up in line of battle, and ordered us to clear the woods. The scout remonstrated with him, "that they very greatly outnumbered us, and had artillery, while we had none." But the Colonel coolly replied: "We can whip them, and we will take their artillery—we need it, anyway. Forward, boys!" Our fellows were not slow to obey. Entering the woods we were fired upon and with a loud cheer we dashed on. Pretty soon we came to some very thick pines that it was very difficult to get through, and where it was impossible to preserve a regular line of battle, and here commenced what more nearly resembled a deer chase than a battle. The Yankees would "fire and fall back" on our approach and our boys, cheered on by our gallant leader, who, with musket in hand, gave us example as well as precept, rushed madly through the bushes, each man trying to get the first fire at the fleet-footed game. After running them some three quarters of a mile, we came to the Loudoun and Hampshire Railroad, on the opposite side of which the enemy raised a faint shout and made a feeble stand; but our boys boldly dashed across and soon had them in full retreat again. They halted at a fence some fifty yards beyond, from behind which they gave us a pretty severe volley, and then made good their retreat to camp. At their last fire two of our men (Robertson, of the Montpelier Guards, and Corporal Arnold, of the Lanier Guards) fell very severely wounded, and Private Sizer, of the Montpelier Guards, was unfortunately shot by one of our own men, so as to make the amputation of his leg necessary. We now returned to Munson's Hill and there followed another day of severe skirmishing, enlivened by the throwing of a few shot into Bailey's Cross Roads by a piece of the Washington Artillery, and throwing up breastworks, in which our detachment was largely relieved by the 3d Tennessee Regiment, Col. Kemper's 7th Virginia Regiment, and some companies from other regiments. Thursday morning we were ordered back to rejoin our regiment at Fairfax Station, and we marched the distance, 14 miles, through a drenching rain.[36]

James filed his official report of the fighting at Bailey's Cross Roads the same day. As far as is known, this is the only report written by James during the war. Any others were lost. He wrote:

> Fairfax Station, Army of the Potomac,
> August 31, 1861.
>
> To Col. A. P. Hill, Commanding Thirteenth Regiment Virginia Volunteers:
>
> Colonel,—I have the honor to submit the following report of an engagement with the Federal troops in the vicinity of Bailey's Cross Roads.
>
> On Sunday morning, August 25th, at 2 o'clock, A. M., I received from brigade headquarters an order from Gen. A. Elzey, to take four companies of the Thirteenth Infantry, accompanied by a section of Beckhams battery, to be commanded by Captain Beckham in person, the entire force to be under my command, and proceed to Anondale [Annandale] and there join Col. J. E. B. Stuart, of the First Cavalry, who would give me farther instructions.
>
> Upon arriving at Anondale, I joined Col. Stuart with his cavalry, who conducted my command, composed and officered as follows:
>
> Company A, Capt. Nalle; 1st Lieut. Cullen.
> Company B, 1st Lieut. Starke commanding.
> Company D, 1st Lieut. Winston command, 2d Lieut. Byrd, 3d Lieut. Hibbs.
> Company G, Capt. Hill.
>
> And one section of Beckham's battery, commanded by Capt. Beckham in person, to Mason's Hill, a eminence six miles from Alexandria, commanding a view of the Federal Capitol and all the principal points along the Potomac.

V — James Barbour Terrill

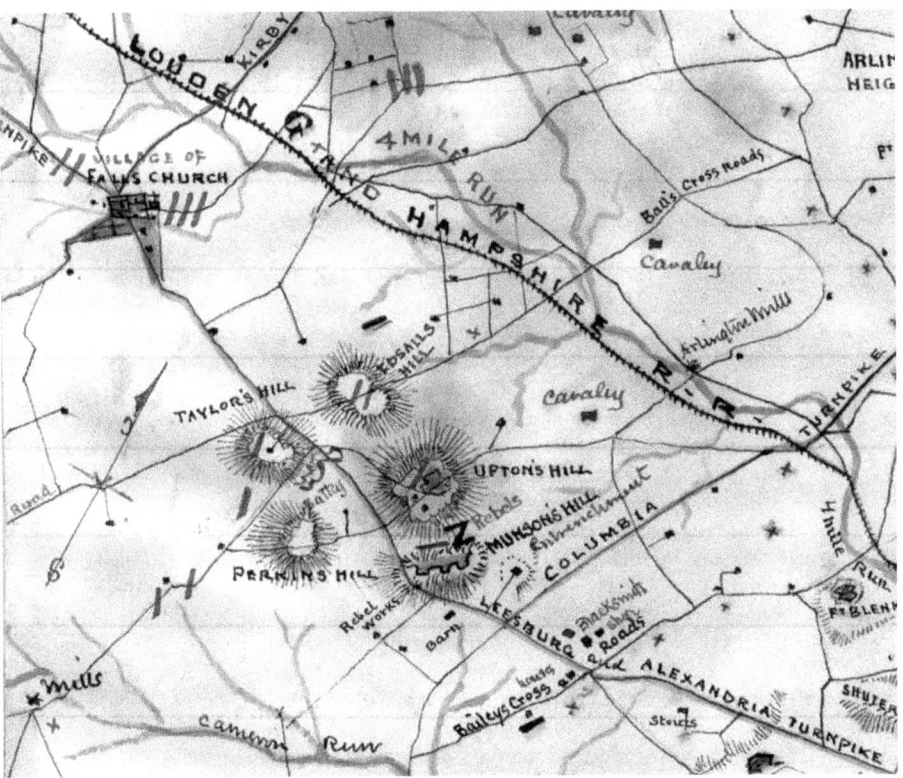

Map of Munson's Hill, Upton's Hill and Bailey's Cross Roads, Virginia. Detail of a map in Robert Knox Sneden Diaries (Virginia Historical Society, Richmond).

Almost immediately upon our arrival, a considerable force of Federal infantry and cavalry made their appearance in the road, about a quarter of a mile from the base of the hill. Col. Stuart directed me to attack them, and if possible cut off their retreat. I immediately proceeded with company G, Capt. Hill commanding. Not being familiar with the topography of the country, we unavoidably allowed ourselves to be discovered when within a few hundred yards of the enemy; the cavalry immediately fell back, the infantry retired to the woods, I ordered the company under my command to charge them on their right flank, which was promptly obeyed, ending in the loss of three killed and one prisoner on the side of the enemy.

About three A.M. the following day [Monday, August 26] my pickets were attacked — one horse shot in the knee being the only damage sustained on our side. At daylight the enemy opened a heavy fire upon my front and left flank. I immediately caused Captain Hill's company to be deployed as skirmishers at the base of the hill, with orders not to fire until the nearer approach of the enemy. A few sharp-shooters posted in the woods succeeded in killing several of the enemy, who, failing to ascertain our strength by drawing out my command, retired.

About four P.M. the same day I attacked with company B, (Culpeper Minute

Men), Lieut. Starke commanding, a company of U.S. Infantry, who were routed after heavy firing on both sides, with considerable loss on the part of the Federals. The enemy appeared greatly confused and astonished at the position we had taken, being almost surrounded by their camps.

On Tuesday [August 27] morning my entire command was relieved, and with two additional companies of the 1st Maryland Regiment, commanded by Major B. J. Johnson, the entire force commanded by Col. J. E. B. Stuart, advanced on Munson's hill, which was occupied by Federal troops, the attack on which, as well as on Upton's hill, still further in advance, was a complete success. The field officer of the day on the Federal side and a number of men were killed — six prisoners were taken. East of Upton's hill, near the Loudoun and Hampshire Railroad, whilst patrolling with a detachment of ten men from company I, 1st Maryland Regiment, commanded by Lt. Mitchell, I was attacked by about sixty of the enemy, who were under cover of the woods. By the first volley delivered, Lieut. Mitchell was severely wounded and private Fountaine killed by my side. I took the dead man's piece, and directed the rest of the party to fall upon the bank of the road and avail themselves of the cover of a few stunted bushes, from which position we returned their fire with great effect. The firing was kept up until the enemy were compelled to cease in order to bear off their dead and wounded. Nothing except the coolness of the men under my command prevented the entire detachment from being killed or captured. Colonel Stuart, coming up at the close of the action, directed me to have the wounded conveyed to Falls Church. In my absence, he made an attack with our entire force upon the enemy, who had been largely reinforced, routing them after a desperate fight, killing a large number. Colonel Stuart then ordered the entire command back to Munson's hill, where were kept active night and day to hold the position.

The killed and wounded of this command are as follows: Company A.— Killed — Private Robinson; wounded — Private Sizer, thigh amputated. Company G.— Corporal Arnold, mortally wounded; Private Hardigan, slightly wounded.

I cannot close this report without expressing to you my extreme gratification at the gallant and soldier-like conduct of every officer and private in the command. Constantly exposed to the fire of a superior force, without rations, lying out in a drenching rain without blankets or covering of any kind, they performed the most arduous and critical duties in a manner that argues well for the success of our cause.

With great respect, your ob't [obedient] serv't [servant],

J. Barbour Terrill,
Major 13th Infantry Va. Volunteers.
To Col. A. P. Hill, Commanding 13th Infantry.[37]

After the Confederates took Munson's Hill, Colonel J. E. B. Stuart with the 1st Virginia Cavalry occupied that position and picketed the surrounding area. Captain William Patrick's Valley Rangers covered the countryside between Munson's Hill and the Potomac River. Captain George R. Gaither's Maryland Company (Howard Dragoons) extended the line of pickets from the river to Lewinsville, in Fairfax County.

In early September 1861, the 13th Virginia Infantry returned to Munson's Hill to stand picket duty. They remained at that post until the 6th, and then

Lewinsville

In obedience of orders issued by General George B. McClellan, Colonel Isaac I. Stevens led a force of infantry, artillery and cavalry on a reconnaissance in force to the village of Lewinsville, Virginia, seven miles away from Chain Bridge. On the morning of September 11, 1861, a force consisting of just over 2,000 Union infantry, artillery, and cavalry left their camp near the Chain Bridge, on the Potomac River. The purpose of the movement was to make a reconnaissance in force to the vicinity of Lewinsville and examine the area for defensive positions.

As the Federals neared Lewinsville their advance guard commenced skirmishing with members of Captain Gaither's cavalry, numbering about fifty strong. As the Marylanders fell back before the overwhelming force, a courier dashed off to alert Colonel Stuart of the enemy advance.

Once in possession of the village, Colonel Stevens took steps to protect his position while First Lieutenant Orlando M. Poe of the Topographical Engineers was conducting the survey. Scouts, pickets, skirmishers and artillery covered all five roads converging at and near Lewinsville.

Learning of the advance about noon, Stuart wasted no time in responding. He quickly sent word to Major Terrill to form his battalion of the 13th Virginia Infantry, interrupting a regimental court-martial.[39] James joined Stuart with a force of 305 men.

Stuart also called for a section (2 guns) of Captain Thomas L. Rosser's Washington (New Orleans) Artillery. To this force, he added Captain Patrick's company of his own regiment. In all, Stuart's force numbered less than 525 men.

Stuart and his men marched through the fields and by-ways, avoiding the main roads by which the enemy expected them to advance. Stuart carefully moved his men into position on the enemy left and rear, moving his artillery to within 700 yards of the Federals before the enemy discovered them. Colonel Stuart sent James forward with a portion of his men to some woods at a turn in the road to see what lay beyond. Stuart later wrote: "This was admirably done, and the major soon reported to me that the enemy had a piece of artillery in position in the road just at Lewinsville; commanding our road."[40]

James informed Stuart of the location of the gun. Stuart directed him to post his riflemen to prevent the enemy from using the gun. If possible, he added, capture the gun. James deployed his men as skirmishers and took possession of the nearby thickets and a cornfield. From this position, the infantrymen kept up an incessant fire.

Lieutenant Poe completed the survey of a four square mile tract at Lewinsville by 3 P.M., and preparations to leave the village began. A body of rebel cavalry appeared in the direction of Falls Church, watching the Union

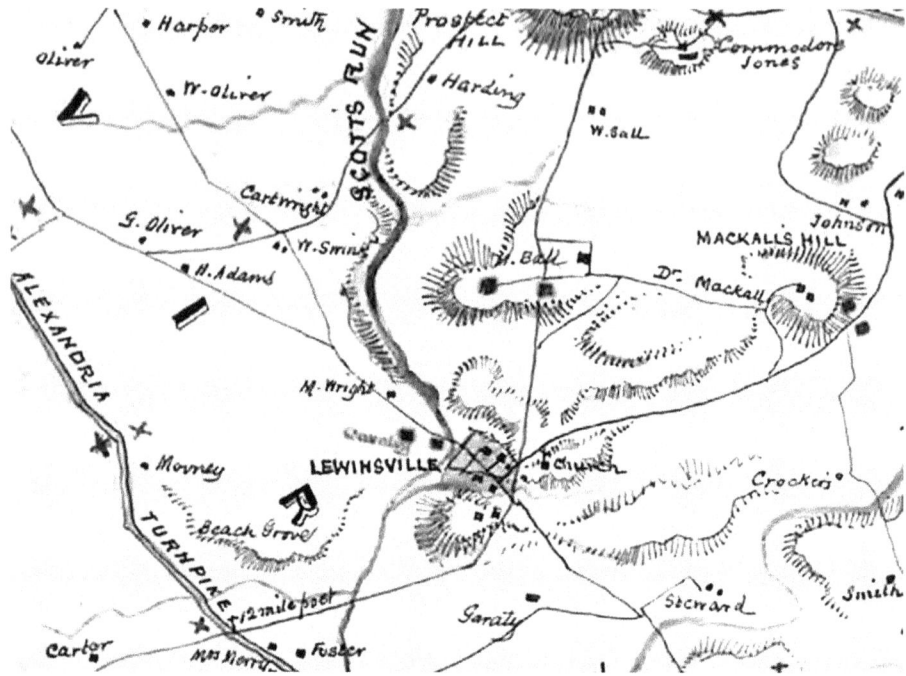

Map of Falls Church and vicinity of Lewinsville, Virginia. Detail of a map in Robert Knox Sneden Diaries. (Virginia Historical Society, Richmond).

army as the scouts, pickets and details withdrew. The object of the expedition accomplished, the Northern troops paid no attention to the presence of the Confederates. Besides, the cavalrymen were not trying to interfere.

As the Yankee force began marching out of the village, the Confederates suddenly opened fire from some woods and a cornfield on their right with artillery and muskets. The cavalry spotted earlier in the direction of Falls Church now attempted to flank the Union position.

Colonel Stevens ordered his men to form a line of battle, and directed them not to fire a shot until the rebels came out from their hiding place. Major Terrill's infantrymen did not leave their hiding places, other than to dart out, fire and then move back into cover. Their movements gave the Yankees the impression that a large force of infantry was moving against them.

Meanwhile, Captain Rosser's guns were rapidly firing on the Federal lines, firing more than a hundred rounds of shot and shell at the enemy. During this time, James took charge of some sharpshooters from Company I and "firing whenever a straggling Yankee showed his head."[41]

James and his men captured three men of the 19th Indiana Infantry at Lewinsville. His men took a sergeant and a private prisoner, and James personally captured a lieutenant.

Captain Charles Griffin, of Battery D, 5th U.S. Artillery, now brought his guns into action and began to return the Confederate fire. His gunners fired more than 50 rounds in the direction of the hidden Confederates, inflicting no damage.

An account of the fight at Lewinsville, published in the *Richmond Dispatch* on September 19, stated that as the skirmishers came out of the woods, Major Terrill loudly ordered his men to shoot down the cannoneers and the artillery horses. The Union artillery withdrew from the field after one of Terrill's men shot an artilleryman through the head.[42]

Hearing the firing from his camp near the Chain Bridge, Brigadier General William F. Smith gave orders for a large force to follow him, and hurried toward Lewinsville. Along the way, he encountered Captain Thaddeus P. Mott drilling the Third New York Battery, which he ordered to accompany him.

Upon his arrival at Lewinsville, Smith directed Captain Mott to engage the enemy with his 32-pounders. Mott quickly readied his guns and threw several shells in the direction of the Confederate cavalry. According to the Northern accounts, a single shell dispersed the horsemen.

Following Mott's firing on the cavalry, the entire Union force left the town. The cavalry of Colonel Stuart followed the Yankees, taking several prisoners along the way.

The only casualties in the fighting at Lewinsville were on the side of the Union, which had at least twenty-one men killed, wounded or captured. The Confederates suffered no known loss.

After re-establishing his picket line at Lewinsville, Stuart returned to Munson's Hill. The events of the day won much praise for Stuart and Terrill.

For its handsome conduct in the fighting at Lewinsville, the battalion of the 13th Virginia Infantry was highly complimented by General Joseph E. Johnston, the commander of the Army of the Potomac. General Johnston's comments, published in General Order No. 19, on September 12, 1861, read:

> The commanding general has great satisfaction in making known the excellent conduct of Col. J. E. B. Stuart, and of the other officers and men of his command, in the affair of Lewinsville, on the 11th instant, on which occasion Colonel Stuart, with Major Terrill's battalion (Thirteenth Virginia Volunteers), two field pieces of the Washington Artillery (Louisiana), under Captain Rosser and Lieutenant Slocomb, and Captain Patrick's company of cavalry (First Virginia), attacked and drove from that position in confusion three regiments of infantry, eight pieces of artillery, and a large body of cavalry, inflicting severe loss, but incurring none.[43]

While superior officers were complimenting James and the other officers for their actions at Lewinsville, others were voicing their dissatisfaction. Private Philip Edloe Jones, who had complimented Major Terrill weeks before, now criticized his commander. Jones wrote that after the action at Lewinsville, the Louisa Blues had to go out on picket duty that night in the rain. "You never saw such a *mad set* of fellow's in your life as we were ... we could have almost skinned [sic] old Major Terrel [sic], he certainly treated us very badly, & I hope we may never go under his command again."⁴⁴

The 13th Virginia Infantry spent the remainder of September in the performance of picket duty and operations in Northern Virginia. Early on September 19, General Joseph E. Johnston reviewed the regiment and expressed his appreciation of their excellent conduct during the recent operations. At 5 P.M., Lieutenant William W. Bird presented the regiment with a beautiful silk battle flag, sewn by Dolly Hill, Colonel A. P. Hill's wife. James accepted the flag on behalf of the regiment. The men loudly cheered and pledged to defend the banner to the last.⁴⁵

In a letter to cousin Cornelia H. Wise, James commented on the flag: "In virtue of the handsome flag Mrs. Hill presented us she is considered as second in command of the Regiment."⁴⁶

In mid–October the 13th Virginia Infantry left Fairfax Station and established a new camp near Centreville, christening it Camp Hill. The regiment remained here for some time, again performing picket duty. During October, while on his way to Richmond, William H. Terrill stopped at Centreville to visit with his son.⁴⁷

In early November, there was a chance for some excitement. The 13th Virginia Infantry, along with the 1st Georgia Infantry and 1st Maryland Infantry, accompanied Brigadier General J. E. B. Stuart to the vicinity of Pohick Church, at Lorton, Virginia, on the 10th. Stuart expected to surprise a detachment of Yankees at that place, but to their disappointment, the enemy was gone.

In mid–November, a letter requesting a promotion for James crossed the desk of Governor John Letcher. Doctor George Terrill, from his home in Mobile, Alabama, asked the governor to promote his nephew, Major James B. Terrill. "Major Terrill," the former Navy surgeon wrote, "has by his gallantry shown himself iminantly [sic] deserving of your favour"⁴⁸; His request was not acted upon by Governor Letcher.

The rest of November and the early part of December were spent performing picket duty near Centreville. Colonel Hill assigned James to duty with regimental court-martials on two occasions during November, serving as president of the court on at least one occasion.⁴⁹ At least once during November, James went out on outpost duty toward Alexandria. On December 19, the 13th Virginia Infantry moved to near Manassas Junction and established Camp Walker.

During the lull in action during November, James wrote his cousin Cornelia H. Wise, who lived at Bel Pre, in Culpeper County. It seems that James was feeling forgotten by his friends, and wrote:

> Your letter afforded me a great deal of pleasure especially as you are one of the very few of my friends who have given themselves the trouble to inquire after me since I have been in the "Army," not the fact has given me the least concern, but that I am not so intirely [sic] lost to the finer feelings of my nature as not to appreciate the remembrance of those whom I consider my friends.⁵⁰

Mary Jane Wise, Cornelia's mother, offered her home to her nephew should he become sick or wounded. James responded to her offer:

> Tell your "Ma" that I appreciate in the extreme her kind invitation to repair to her house in case I should be sick or wounded, but sincerely trust that the same Providence that has preserved me unscathed throughout the dangers & trials by which for six months I have been surrounded will guide me safely until the end, & that when I visit her it will be in the full health & vigor of manhood.[51]

Following his detail on outpost duty, James commented to Cornelia, "I have been living out doors so long that I am afraid I will never be able to reconcile the thought to myself of living in a house again."[52]

James left his regiment for a brief time during December, although there is no record of his taking a furlough. While absent from his regiment, he married Charlotte Eucebia Drewry of King William County, Virginia, the daughter of Captain Martin Drewry. The ceremony took place at the residence of the bride's father on December 12, 1861.[53] His best man was his old friend and classmate from the Virginia Military Institute, John Hyde Cameron. Also attending the joyous occasion was Philip M. Terrill, a paroled prisoner who traveled from Leetown to attend his brother's wedding.[54]

Charlotte Eucebia Drury, wife of James B. Terrill (courtesy Mercer Terrill Vaden).

By this time in his military career, James seems to have proven himself a competent officer, winning the confidence of both officers and men of the regiment. This feeling of confidence among his superiors only strengthened until his death. Charles D. Walker, in his biographical sketch of James for his book on the VMI alumni, writes:

> He acquired the reputation of being one of the bravest of the brave. His clarion voice, encouraging his men, was frequently heard above the din of battle; and when asked by his friends (as he frequently was) how it was that he acted so fearlessly in time of action, his reply invariably was, "I never think on such occasions of being killed."[55]

1862

The New Year brought to the men of the 13th Virginia Infantry more of the same — picket duty, drilling and monotony in camp. The officers, at least, received a break from the usual on February 25, 1862, when James and his fellow officers attended a grand military ball near Manassas. This may have been in celebration of Colonel A. P. Hill's promotion to Brigadier General, which occurred the following day.

Lieutenant Colonel James A. Walker now assumed command of the regiment, assisted by James. In early March, some skirmishing took place, after which the Confederate Army of the Potomac left the Manassas area and marched to Rappahannock Station. In late March and early April, the regiment was involved in some skirmishing along the Rappahannock River.

While James was involved with the day-to-day operations of his regiment, he was on the mind of his Union brother. From his camp near Columbia, Tennessee, on March 28, Captain William R. Terrill addressed a letter to Secretary of War Edwin M. Stanton concerning his family. Captain Terrill wrote (in part): "My brother James B. Terrill is a Major in the 13th Regiment Va. Vols. Any kindness that can be shown [him] should the fortunes of War bring [him] into our power, will be very thankfully received by me."[56]

From the Rappahannock River, the 13th Virginia Infantry accompanied the division of General Richard S. Ewell to Culpeper Court House, Gordonsville, Orange Court House and Liberty Mills during April 1862.

Between April 23 and 26, in compliance with the new Conscription Law enacted by the Confederate Congress, elections for company, battalion and regimental officers were held. Many strict disciplinarians or otherwise undesirable officers failed re-election. Would "Major Terrible" retain his position? When they tallied the results on April 26, the regiment had a new colonel and lieutenant colonel — James A. Walker and James B. Terrill. Apparently, James' gallant conduct and ability outweighed his reputation as "Major Terrible."[57]

Following the election of officers, Ewell's Division moved to Swift Run Gap, in the Shenandoah Valley, to take Jackson's place and keep an eye on Union forces near Harrisonburg. Jackson and his Valley Army first moved away from the valley, then taking the trains back to Staunton, moved his army to McDowell and Franklin. By the middle of May, Jackson had returned to the valley with Edward Johnson's command, and joined Ewell.

After Jackson's return, the Confederate forces began to move down the Shenandoah Valley. On May 23, Jackson's forces attacked the enemy at Front Royal, driving the enemy from the town, then moved toward Winchester. Two days later the Confederates engaged another Union force at Winchester, and drove them out of the town. During these operations, and those subsequently north of Winchester, the 13th Virginia Infantry seems to have played only a minor role. James was in command of the regiment much of this time, as Colonel Walker commanded Jackson's old brigade.

As Jackson moved up the valley before Fremont and Shields, the 13th Virginia Infantry served as the rear guard. Jackson and his men reached Harrisonburg on June 5, and by the 8th, the 13th Virginia Infantry was in position near the village of Cross Keys, in Rockingham County. A valley and creek lay before them, while woods lay on the left and right of their line.

During the morning of June 8, General Elzey ordered Colonel Walker to take the 13th Virginia Infantry and 25th Virginia Infantry to the Confederate right to prevent a flanking movement. Once in position, Colonel Walker ordered James to take two companies of the 13th Virginia Infantry and advance as skirmishers. With skirmishers thrown out, Colonel Walker followed with the two regiments. About 10 A.M., as James' skirmishers reached some woods near the Ever house, he discovered a large force of Fremont's command in his front.

Colonel Walker halted his men and reconnoitered the area, discovering that a battery of artillery in a wheat field about 400 yards away supported Fremont's men. Being in advance of Ewell's division, Colonel Walker pulled back a short distance to await reinforcements. As he was pulling back, he met General Isaac R. Trimble's brigade coming to his aid. Turning his men around, Colonel Walker placed his men on Trimble's right, and ordered James to again advance with his skirmishers. Before long, James's skirmishers encountered some Yankee skirmishers and drove them back, inflicting some loss.

Colonel Walker, imitating Terrill, posted his men under cover of the Ever house and barn. He remained here until Trimble ordered him to move farther to the right. Almost at once, a heavy fire of enemy musketry struck the 25th Virginia, which was on Colonel Walker's left. At the same time, the 13th Virginia Infantry discovered three Federal guns and three Federal regiments within 400 yards of their right.

The firing of the Northern cannon caused some brief confusion in the ranks, but the officers quickly restored order. The Confederates gallantly advanced to a fence, about fifty yards ahead. Colonel Walker wrote:

> I ordered the men to lie down and fire. This they did with such effect as to twice drive the enemy from one of their guns. The fire of the enemy was galling, and seeing no further good could be accomplished by remaining longer in my position, I moved again by the right flank to the cover of a wood and halted. About this time the enemy fell back and I was ordered to remain in my position.[58]

With the aid of reinforcements in mid-afternoon, Ewell drove Fremont's command back. General Trimble ordered Colonel Walker to hold his position on the right flank, and at sundown, ordered Walker to move to the left. At 10 P.M., the 13th Virginia Infantry returned to their camp, now under the command of Lieutenant Colonel Terrill, Walker being in command of the brigade.

The following day, the 13th Virginia Infantry marched toward Port Republic to take part in the battle at that place. The regiment, along with Colonel Walker's brigade, became lost in the impassible thickets and had to countermarch. Colonel Walker and his men arrived on the battlefield just as the Confederates captured the Union position. Colonel Walker's brigade pursued the retreating Federals for several miles, and then returned to the field for the night.

The fighting about Cross Keys and Port Republic took its toll on James. According to a sketch of James, he "was unable to accompany it [the regiment] by reason of an attack of sickness caused by physical prostration in the Port Republic engagements; he however, followed on in three or four days, but was too feeble to participate in the series of battles that occurred below Richmond, resulting in the utter defeat of the Federal Army."[59]

It seems that James missed all of the fighting about Richmond, just as the unknown biographer noted. Pay records indicate that James was paid at Staunton, Virginia, on June 30. The next pay period, July 31, showed him at Richmond, having joined the regiment sometime in July.

The next appearance of James in the record of the 13th Virginia Infantry, takes place in August 1862.

> His next participation with his "bloody Thirteenth" [so named because of its fighting ability] in conflict with arms was at Cedar Run, then at the Second Manassas, when at Fredericksburg, in December 1862, then at Winchester and Harper's Ferry and again at the second battle of Fredericksburg, in all of which series of battles he and his brave regiment were greatly distinguished.[60]

The 13th Virginia Infantry took part in the fighting at Cedar Mountain, near Culpeper Court House, on August 9. General Jubal A. Early, their new brigade commander, occupied an intersection that led to Madison Court House, throwing the 13th Virginia Infantry out on the left, near Major's schoolhouse. Following a brief artillery duel and an hour of quiet, General Early began to move on the left of the Culpeper Court House road. It was now about 2 P.M.

Crossing the road, General Early passed through some woods and behind a hill. The 13th Virginia Infantry moved into the woods as skirmishers, while the remainder of the brigade formed along a branch of Cedar Run, close to the road.

Lieutenant Colonel Terrill, commanding the left wing of the regiment, advanced into the woods. After going about 200 yards, James encountered a squadron of enemy cavalry and easily repulsed them. Not long afterward, the right wing encountered the enemy, who retired immediately to their main force. Colonel Walker halted the regiment until the remainder of the brigade arrived.

When the brigade was reformed, the 13th Virginia Infantry formed on the left of the line, supporting a battery of artillery. After the arrival of the Stonewall Brigade on Colonel Walker's left, the line moved forward to the crest of a hill and fired on some Federal infantry in a cornfield. The fighting became intense for several minutes, and then as the blue clad troops closed in, the brigades on Colonel Walker's left gave way. Panic stricken, several regiments on his right gave way, leaving only the 13th and 31st Regiments to hold back the enemy.

Quick to see the danger to an artillery piece to his right and front, Colonel Walker ordered both regiments forward to protect the gun until it could be removed. Within minutes, Colonel Walker realized that General Nathanial Banks had succeeded in flanking his position by moving through the woods. With no reinforcements in sight, Colonel Walker withdrew his men in good order as the Federals overran the position he had just abandoned, firing at close range.

After retiring 200 yards, Colonel Walker halted and rallied his men. About this time, General A. P. Hill arrived with fresh troops. Reinforced, the 13th Virginia Infantry now recaptured their former position from Banks' men, exchanging shots with still more Yankees in the cornfield. As Banks' line weakened and collapsed, the Confederates rushed forward with a shout and cleared the field of enemy infantry.

With victory within their reach, the Confederates were startled when a body of Yankee cavalry dashed through a wheat field along the Culpeper Court House road. Colonel Walker raised his sword with one hand, and lifted his hat with the other, bellowed, "Thirteenth, left wheel."[61] Moving at double quick, the 13th Virginia Infantry advanced to a fence to their left and front, and poured a devastating fire into the flank of the horsemen as they galloped up. The first volley downed so many horses and riders that the road was blocked, making the confused cavalrymen easy targets. Under fire from several directions, the Yankee horsemen withdrew, pursued only briefly by the Confederates. When the pursuit was broken off, Colonel Walker left James in command of the regiment, and reported to General Early.

The battle of Cedar Mountain was one of the crowning achievements of the 13th Virginia Infantry. Colonel Walker praised his men for their "bravery and disciplined valor."[62] General Early, the brigade commander, commented that Walker's men "are capital fighting men, their being none better in the army."[63]

General Early took note of James's actions in the battle of Cedar Mountain, citing him for "great gallantry"[64] in his report. In closing his report, General Early strongly recommended Colonel Walker's promotion to brigadier general, a step that General Ewell heartily seconded.

During the later part of August, James was again in command of the regiment, which now numbered less than 250 men.[65] James once again proved that he was a good officer at the battle of Second Manassas.

On August 27, General Early's brigade was ordered to take position in some pinewoods to cover other troops while they destroyed the railroad. A large Federal force approached during the afternoon, and in obedience to orders, the Confederates withdrew toward Manassas Junction. General Early's brigade remained behind to cover a bridge, then followed their retreating comrades. The 13th Virginia Infantry brought up the rear, checking the Union skirmishers.

At dawn on the 28th, General Early's men led the division as it marched across Blackburn's Ford and the stone bridge over Bull Run. They continued along the road and at last formed their line of battle in some woods. Moving later in the day, the brigade marched with other troops to rejoin the remainder of the division, now engaging the enemy. By the time General Early's men arrived, the fighting was over for the day.

On the 29th, the 13th and 31st Virginia Regiments were detached and sent into some woods east of the Warrenton Turnpike to observe Union troop movements. The men of the two regiments skirmished with the enemy periodically, until Longstreet's men relieved them and they rejoined the brigade. Late in the afternoon General Early's brigade, now strengthened by two additional regiments, marched to the aid of A. P. Hill's troops. Arriving at Hill's position, General Early ordered a charge and soon the Yankees were on the run. The Confederates pursued for several hundred yards, then lay on their weapons for the night along the railroad.

On the morning of August 30, the 13th Virginia Infantry came under fire from Federal sharpshooters. Later in day, General Early moved his brigade and formed along the railroad, posting three regiments in front and four in their rear. The 13th Virginia Infantry was among those posted in the rear. Following the repulse of a Federal force, the supporting regiments moved to the front line, taking the place of the original three who were now in pursuit of the enemy.

That evening General Early was ordered to join a major advance. After clearing some woods, he halted to allow another brigade to catch up. General Thomas J. "Stonewall" Jackson, eager to press forward, ordered General Early to investigate a report of Union activity on the left. James, with the 13th Virginia Infantry deployed in a skirmish line, crossed a railroad and entered a field. As darkness settled across the field, the skirmishers came under fire from a hill on their left. Being unable to distinguish friend from foe, a volunteer from the 44th Virginia scouted and discovered that it was friendly fire. There were no Union troops on the left. General Early's command returned to their former position and camped for the night.

General Early marched his brigade across Bull Run on the afternoon of August 31, turned to the left and followed a road that intersected with the Little River Turnpike. The next day, September 1, the Confederates again caught up with the Federals at Chantilly. The 13th Virginia Infantry was heavily engaged during the fighting that day, but James' role is unknown.

After the battle at Chantilly, command of the regiment fell to Captain Frank V. Winston, of Company D. Colonel Walker was in command of General Trimble's brigade; James was again absent sick, and Major John B. Sherrard was ready to resign. James was absent sick during the Antietam campaign, returning to the regiment sometime after that battle. James received a leave of absence of four days on a surgeon's certificate of disability a few days before the battle of Antietam.[66]

James next appears in the records on October 13, as a lieutenant colonel on a roster of General Early's Brigade, Ewell's Division. Thirteen days later, on the 26th, James signed a provision return as commander of the regiment.[67]

James's first child was born on October 31, 1862, at Bellevue, King William County, Virginia. Charlotte and James named the baby boy James Mercer Terrill.

After a period of rest, the 13th Virginia Infantry started marching about Northern Virginia on November 1, and went into camp near Winchester on November 14. A week later, the entire army began to move toward Fredericksburg, going into camp about a mile from Chancellorsville on November 30.

James Mercer Terrill, son of James and Charlotte Terrill (courtesy Mercer Terrill Vaden).

On the 12th of December, the 13th Virginia Infantry moved up to within five miles of Fredericksburg. The next day James and his men were engaged in the battle of Fredericksburg.

General Early, now commanding a division, posted his brigade in a second line of battle, supporting A. P. Hill's division. About half an hour into the engagement, Colonel Walker received orders to advance at double-quick, as the enemy had cut through the first line and were advancing. He moved his brigade forward and met the enemy near the middle of the woods, but they fell back as Walker arrived. The brigade pressed them, driving them across the railroad and into an open field. Colonel Walker halted and formed a line along the railroad, with no supporting troops on the left of his line. A large body of Federal infantry was seen moving across the railroad about 400 yards to his left, entering the woods.

Colonel Walker ordered James to deploy the 13th Virginia Infantry on the left flank, directing him to advance under cover of the timber and engage the enemy. Colonel Walker noted the promptness of the movement in his report. A brigade of Hill's division engaged the enemy in front at about the same time, and the enemy retreated. Colonel Walker held his position along the railroad until after dark, with no further incidents. After dark, Colonel Walker withdrew his command back into the woods about 150 yards, and went into camp. A strong picket force watched the railroad.

While engaged on the left flank about 3 P.M., Private Charles H. Sanner captured a Yankee captain and lieutenant. They surrendered their swords and side arms to James. The captain gave up a Colt revolver, commenting that it belonged to his wife, and asked James to present it to the bravest man in the regiment. James presented the revolver to Sanner.[68]

James had carried a heavy cavalry saber since the beginning of the war. During the war, he presented the saber to his cousin Cornelia H. Wise after finding a more suitable one. Perhaps one of the swords surrendered on December 13 served as the replacement.[69]

General Early remarked on the service of the 13th Virginia Infantry at Fredericksburg: "The 13th Regiment Virginia Infantry was never required to take a position that they did not take, or to hold one that they did not hold."[70]

The 13th Virginia Infantry remained in line of battle on December 14 and was held in reserve the following day. The fighting over, they moved to near Port Royal, Virginia, and went into camp, where they performed picket duty. On the 21st, the regiment went into winter camp, to await the arrival of spring.

1863

The 13th Virginia Infantry remained near Port Royal, Virginia, doing picket duty as required, until March 3, 1863, when they moved their camp about 12 miles. They established a new camp near Hamilton's Crossing, where the men resumed their duties of picket duty on the Rappahannock River and drilling.

Again James was absent on sick leave. A list of commissioned officers of General Early's brigade for the month of February 1863 indicates that James had been absent for 21 days out of the month, having left the regiment on the 6th.

The next record of James appears during April 1863. His name appears on a list of officers of Brigadier General William "Extra Billy" Smith's brigade as being present for duty, having been absent for eight days on sick leave. James returned to duty on April 9, following an extended sick leave.[71]

James and his regiment remained in camp near Hamilton's Crossing until late April. According to existing records, the Quartermaster issued James forage for two private horses, meaning he owned the horses, and was with his regiment.

The 13th Virginia Infantry was on picket duty when the enemy crossed the Rappahannock River in heavy force below their post at the mouth of Deep Run on April 29. They had a slight skirmish with the enemy during the morning. After being relieved later in the day, the 13th Virginia Infantry joined their brigade in the trenches above Hamilton's Crossing. They immediately helped construct some breastworks.

Disease was among the many dangers that faced soldiers in camp. During May 1863, a case of smallpox appeared in the camp of the 13th Virginia Infantry, when a soldier confined to the guard house contracted the disease.[72] The regimental surgeon recommended that the soldier's clothing be burned to prevent further spreading of the disease. James gave the necessary order, and directed the quartermaster to issue fresh clothing to the soldier. This action held the disease in check.

The first of May 1863 found the 13th Virginia Infantry in line of battle near Fredericksburg. The next night, the regiment marched seven miles toward Chancellorsville, then back to their former position near Fredericksburg.

At dawn on May 3, the 13th Virginia Infantry received orders to move forward as skirmishers, to occupy a position on a road held the previous day by the southern forces. Unknown to them, the Federals had moved forward and occupied the road. As they approached the road, and crossed an open field, the Federals started firing at them. The Federals were concealed behind the embankment along the road. Caught in the open, James sought protection for his men, and ordered them to construct a crude breastwork. Private Reuben M. Newman, 13th Virginia Infantry, recorded in his diary: "We protect ourselves by digging the dirt with our bayonets and throwing up mounds with our hands. It may be imagined we hugged mother earth pretty close."[73]

Considering his situation, James decided to change his tactics. Robert Catlett Cave, of the 13th Virginia Infantry, tells what happened next:

> At once, we saw that we must either fall back ourselves or drive them back. Our Colonel decided to do the latter, and ordered us to "charge." We dashed forward at full speed. The Federals greeted us with a volley which, as we were in open formation, did little damage; and then, realizing that we would be upon them before they could reload, took to their heels.
> As we neared the road, a battery posted in the field beyond, and until then hid from our view, opened on us with grapeshot. Luckily, the gunners had to aim a little high to clear the embankments, and most of their charges went over us, making a whirring and fluttering sound like that made by a flock of quail when rising from cover. They, however, killed several of our men and wounded others before we reached shelter. Then safely ensconced behind the embankments, we evened up matters by sending the artillerymen musket balls in return for the grapeshot they had sent us. When a number of them had fallen and they saw that they were completely at our mercy, they quickly limbered up and hurried away, taking their killed and wounded with them.[74]

Private Reuben M. Newman recorded his version of the charge in his diary:

> Col. Terrill ordered us to charge the enemy in the road, where they had two regiments and two batteries, one about four hundred yards beyond the other on the road to our left and enfilading it. Rather a formidable front for a Regiment of skirmishers deployed to charge but at the Colonel's command the 13th started forward at a double quick with a yell and drove the enemy from the road, killing and wounding a good many and made the cannoneers leave their guns for a short time,

but the regiment on our left failed to advance to our support as they should have done and both batteries opened a most terrific fire upon us, making the road unattainable for us.... We were ordered to fall back to our original position.... The 13th was highly complimented for its behavior in the charge.[75]

The 13th Virginia Infantry lost two men killed and seven wounded in the engagement. Late in the day, General Early withdrew his men and reformed after dark at the Cox house, beyond the Telegraph Road. Captain Samuel D. Buck, of Company H, recalled the events of the afternoon of May 3 around Fredericksburg:

> All was quiet until about the middle of the afternoon when Col. Terrill who was very near sighted came to where I was standing watching our flank, and asked me what was going on at the same time handing me his field glasses to look the field over. I did so and reported that the lawn in front of Stone House in our front was full of Yankee officers. He at once sent a courier back to report this fact and to order artillery to open on them. I knew this would bring on an engagement and got ready for it.... While the artillery fire was in progress Col. Terrill became very restless and again appealed to my better sight. After close examination I reported line of battle and several pieces of artillery in our front. We were well protected and from our position could look over an embankment in our front and see the enemy laying in the road not over a hundred yards to the left. Col. Terrill wanted the left thrown forward so as to get the same protection we had on the right. Had he seen as plainly as I the obstacle in his way, I feel sure he would not have undertaken to possess this road. As he did not he (rising to his full height) ordered the left forward. In their front, not over two hundred yards, lay a heavy line of battle while ours was only a heavy skirmish line. As soon as the men rose the enemy delivered a terrible volley and many of our poor fellows fell.[76]

Private Cave, one of Terrill's men, recalled the events in this way:

> A few minutes after the battery was driven from our front, I saw it, or another like it, wheeling into position on a slight elevation nearly a mile off to our left. The Federals were evidently getting ready to enfilade us; and, seeing that our Colonel was looking through his field-glasses at the movements of the enemy in front and had not noticed this menace to our flank, I called his attention to it. Walking out into the road to get a better view and make his own observations, he asked: "Where is the battery?" As I raised my hand to point it out, there was a puff of smoke; and, an instant later, a shell exploded almost directly over our heads. A large fragment of it struck the ground about five feet before us, and besprinkled us with the dirt of the road. "I see it, I see it," exclaimed the Colonel; and, turning to me, he ordered: "Run to the General, and tell him with my compliments, that it will be impossible to hold this position unless that battery can be silenced." I hurried away to our Brigadier, who was back on the railroad with the rest of the command; but, before I reached him, the commander of our artillery, sizing up the situation, opened on the battery and quickly silenced it.[77]

When Cave approached Brigadier General William Smith to deliver James' message, the general waved his hand, and shouted:

"Hurrah for the gallant 13th." ... When I [Cave] delivered the Colonel's message, he said: "Tell your Colonel his wishes were anticipated. Present my compliments and hearty congratulations to him and the brave men of his splendid regiment. I watched their brilliant and victorious charge with profound admiration, and I feel that it is truly a great honor to be in command of such men."[78]

On the morning of May 4, General Early led an attack resulting in the recapture of Marye's Heights. General Smith's brigade, to which the 13th Virginia Infantry belonged, supported the assault. General Smith then formed his brigade on the plain along the Orange Plank Road, at the Taylor house, just west of Marye's Heights. About noon, Smith's brigade advanced to test the Union position on the heights about a thousand yards away. The 13th Virginia Infantry assumed their usual position as skirmishers, in advance of the brigade.

Moving in single file, the regiment moved several hundred yards, across a level bottom with a stream passing through it, and reformed behind the stream's banks. This brought them midway to the Union position on the brow of a hill. Brush along the stream bank concealed the Confederates. James resumed the advance until striking the Federal line and breaking it. The Federals quickly rallied and drove the Confederates back. The Virginians rallied and charged the line again. This process was repeated five times, neither side willing to give up the ground.

General Smith sent the 58th Virginia to assist Terrill in taking this strong position. Other troops of Smith's brigade explored the weaker position to the left. The Federal artillery was able to concentrate their fire on the right, making the situation difficult for Terrill. After the fifth charge, Terrill fell back to the position of the 58th Virginia, and then withdrew a short distance. At the stream, James rallied his men and resumed firing for a short while, and then withdrew altogether.

Captain Buck recalled the fighting:

> Our brigade kept down the plank road until near the town [Chancellorsville] when we came in reach of the batteries at Falmouth which opened on us at once. To our left on a hill side, the enemy had formed. We waited a few minutes in the field at the left of the road when Gen. Early rode up and called for Col. Terrill and ordered him to take the "13th" and "feel" the enemy. We deployed as skirmishers very close, not over a foot apart. We knew what "feeling" meant as we had practiced this art very often. Gen. Smith asked Gen. Early to send his old regiment (a good one), 49th Virginia, as the "13th" had done duty on skirmish lines two days and a night but Gen. Early's confidence in Col. Terrill and his regiment was such as to cut all such claims short. "I prefer the Thirteenth," this ended the discussion and in a very few minutes we were moving upon the enemies works.[79]

Years later, Buck wrote about the incident for the *Confederate Veteran* magazine:

> Early put Col. Terrill again in front with the Thirteenth Virginia as skirmishers "to feel the enemy." The position they occupied was very strong. We made five dis-

tinct charges, and broke their lines every time, but could not hold them. From the plank road leading from Orange Courthouse to Fredericksburg, looking northwest, we could see plainly their lines on the hill protected by underbrush. To get to them we had to cross a bottom for fully a quarter of a mile, in the center of which there was a ditch several feet deep and a small stream of water, and on charging across this field the command had to jump this ditch or get down into it on one side and climb up on the other. When we got to this point we received a heavy volley from the enemy on the hill in front, which caused the men to take advantage of the protection thus afforded, and some time was lost in getting them forward. Col. Terrill led the charge, and as we dashed up the hill through the bushes a terrible fire met us from the woods held by the enemy; but on we went until within a few yards of the line, when they broke and fell back, but before we could get into the works another heavy line of skirmishers came up and drove us back. Five distinct charges were made by the regiment, and every time reinforcements came up in time to check us.... There was not a better regiment in the army than the Thirteenth Virginia. Gen. Lee said "It is the only regiment that never fails."[80]

General Early was now satisfied that only a stronger force could dislodge the enemy. After Smith's brigade rejoined the division, there was a long pause until evening, when Lee ordered a general attack. This attack forced the Union forces back across the Rappahannock River. During this action, James and the 13th Virginia Infantry remained in reserve, positioned to the left of Barksdale's men who occupied Marye's Heights.

The 13th Virginia Infantry spent May 5 in line of battle on Marye's Heights; however, the enemy had moved on. The next day, James moved his command back to Hamilton's Crossing, where they rested for the remainder of the month, reorganizing the regiment.

While others commended the 13th Virginia Infantry for their gallantry, James received severe criticism from within the ranks of his regiment. Lieutenant Wilson S. Newman, a member of Company A, wrote:

> Our Division had a great deal of hard work & hard fighting to do: but get credit for nothing as usual.... Col. Walker came back a day or two since & is in command of the regiment again. We are all very glad. Col. Terrill is not fit to command us in a fight. He ordered us to charge a battery well supported by infantry on Sunday & we did it in gallant style. [We] were complimented by old Early & all who saw it, but it was a very foolish thing. We had no support in half a mile of us & of course had to fall back—loosing several good men. Captain Fields among them—one of the bravest men I ever saw. Terrill is very anxious for promotion & would sacrifice the regiment to gratify his ambition.[81]

On the 15th of May, Colonel Walker was finally appointed to the rank of brigadier general, and assigned to command the original Stonewall Brigade. James replaced him as colonel of the regiment. The men of the 13th Virginia Infantry bid their former commander goodbye on the 21st by serenading Walker, which was followed by several speeches, including a farewell address by Walker.

Sometime in May 1863, the "battle worn—and bullet torn" flag of the 13th

Virginia Infantry was sent to Governor Letcher, to be "preserved in the archives of the State in memory of the bloody scenes through which it has been carried to honour [sic] & to victory."[82] Inscribed upon the flag were the names of fourteen battle honors.

Colonel S. Bassett French, aide-de-camp to the governor, informed Colonel Terrill that he would send a new flag as soon as possible. The governor, French wrote, has no doubt that the new flag "will be carried by your men with a determined purpose never to furl it while a vandal shall pollute our sacred soil with his accursed foot."[83] The new flag would be several months in arriving.

One of the first problems confronting James as colonel of the 13th Virginia Infantry, was an effort to have the regiment transferred to General J. E. B. Stuart's cavalry. Soon after the Chancellorsville campaign, the concept of converting the regiment to cavalry was proposed and met with Colonel Walker's approval. The men were enthusiastic at the idea, many recalling their service with Stuart during the early months of the war.

On May 17, the ordnance sergeant inventoried the regiment's weapons to ascertain how many were suitable for cavalry use. The men's excitement grew daily. A week later Stuart announced that the scarcity of horses was the only delay preventing the transfer.

Private Reuben M. Newman, 13th Virginia Infantry, wrote in his diary on May 23rd: "Our regiment has applied for a transfer to cavalry, having had experience enough in Infantry. Gen. Stuart is anxious to have us, so there is some chance for the transfer."[84]

General Stuart wrote to Colonel Terrill, requesting official action on the transfer. James received Stuart's request on May 30 and planned to write a protest to the secretary of war. That afternoon the regimental officers met and appointed a committee to speak to the colonel; however, their efforts to change his mind failed.

As to why James was so opposed to the transfer is a mystery. His opposition caused the exchange of many harsh words among the officers and men of his regiment. F. Stanley Russell offered his opinion in a letter to his father on June 1:

> There would have been no uncertainty about it had Col. Terrill and [General] Smith acted right, the application was sent back from the war department for remarks, Walker had already approved it, but when it came back, Walker had left us and Terrill opposed it, thinking I suppose that he would stand a better chance of being Brigadier by staying in the Infantry, the whole Regiment are down on him and say he will never be promoted by their good fighting. But the company officers are at work, and I believe with Lee, Hill and Stuart on our side, we will succeed despite Terrill's, Smith's and Early's endeavors to keep us in the Infantry.[85]

Had they known their colonel better, they would have seen that nothing was further from the truth. If anything, James opposed efforts to have him promoted above the rank of colonel. In one of his last letters to his father, James said, "he did not wish for his friends to press for his promotion for he would have as much honor dying a *Colonel* as a *General*."[86]

The disappointment of the men over the failed transfer to Stuart's command soon disappeared, as other concerns took its place. On May 27, Generals Robert E. Lee and A. P. Hill watched as General Ewell's division passed in review. Two days later, Ewell returned to duty, now commanding a corps. Smith's brigade, consisting of the 13th, 49th, 52nd and 58th Virginia Regiments, received welcome reinforcements when the 31st Virginia Infantry joined the command.

On the 4th of June 1863, the 13th Virginia Infantry was relieved from picket duty at Hamilton's Crossing and became a part of the march north. Their route took them through Spotsylvania Court House, Verdiersville, and Culpeper Court House, halting on the road to Sperryville on June 8. About 10 A.M. on June 9, as the sound of cannon rolled across the countryside from Kelly's Ford, James turned his men toward the sound, moving along the Orange and Alexandria Railroad. Within two miles of Brandy Station, Virginia, the Confederates formed a line of battle, but did not take part in the fighting. They returned to the Sperryville road the following day.

During the day, James took the opportunity to visit the Wise Family at Bel Pre, near Brandy Station. Mrs. Mary Jane Wise was his aunt, on his mother's side.[87]

The army resumed its march at 8 P.M., going by way of Gaines' Cross Roads, across the Blue Ridge at Chester Gap, and camped near Front Royal on June 12. The army arrived at Kernstown on June 13 and formed in line of battle. Soon afterward, they resumed the march toward Winchester. The 13th and 49th Virginia Infantry regiments led the advance that day and began skirmishing with the enemy near Winchester. That night, the men prepared for the coming battle.

The 13th Virginia Infantry formed in line on a ridge west of the Union fortifications, supporting General Hay's brigade. While moving into position, General Early called upon James for a detachment of twenty men to check the enemy's position. James quickly detached Company H, as it was composed of men from the Winchester area, and knew the countryside.

When Lieutenant Samuel D. Buck reached the top of the hill, fifty yards ahead of the skirmish line, he came into full view of the Union fortifications. The alert Yankees spotted him and sent a hail of bullets toward him. General Early, looking for himself, received a similar response. The general rode off, ordering the detachment to stand fast until relieved. As he left, he told them to listen for "my signal gun ... [then] you will see some fun."[88]

Thirty minutes later the signal guns sounded as promised. Company H joined in the firing, which continued for about half an hour, then watched the "grand spectacle."[89] To their right a large gray column, including the rest of the 13th Virginia Infantry, emerged from the woods, marching as if on parade. When they got close to the fortifications, they rushed them with a yell and took the position.

Daylight on June 15 revealed that General Robert H. Milroy's men had abandoned Winchester during the night. Aware of the possibility that Milroy would leave during the night, Ewell blocked their escape route and captured a large number of prisoners.

General Early ordered the 13th Virginia Infantry to remain in Winchester as the provost guard, with James to serve as the provost marshal. They were to protect private property and guard the spoils of war, including a supply train near the town. Three days later, General Early left Winchester, marching northward.

Major William W. Goldsborough, 2nd Maryland Infantry (Confederate), preceded James as provost marshal. During the fighting at Carter's Woods near Winchester on June 13, Surgeon Charles E. Goldsborough, 5th Maryland Infantry (Federal) was taken prisoner. Afterwards, the surgeon was taken before the provost marshal, Major Goldsborough — his brother.

Colonel Terrill relieved Major Goldsborough as provost marshal on June 16. Before leaving on his march into Pennsylvania, Major Goldsborough cautioned his brother not to speak to Colonel Terrill about General Terrill, who had been killed at Perryville the previous year.

Several days later, Surgeon Goldsborough joined Colonel Terrill for dinner. In the course of the meal the subject of the General William R. Terrill's death arose. The colonel expressed an interest in learning the details of his brother's death.

After Surgeon Charles E. Goldsborough reached Richmond, he learned some of the details of General William R. Terrill's death from his fellow prisoners. He wrote them down and sent them to James, but was never sure that the document reached its destination.[90]

David F. Riggs, in his book *13th Virginia Infantry*, wrote:

> The 13th Virginia lost little time in making itself at home. Abundant food and new clothes were welcomed by everyone, as were personal items. Even Terrill joined the methodical pillaging by taking a new pair of colonel's shoulder straps, and regimental headquarters were established in the court house square.[91]

James detailed the Orange County Company of the 13th Virginia Infantry as his bodyguard. Along with guarding their colonel, James ordered the men to keep watch over a large quantity of captured wine. This led to nightly toasts to General Milroy. The rest of the regiment, not having access to the wine cellar, had to settle for flat beer to make their toasts. These toasts were made whenever time permitted as they often stood watch and guard duty. Private Alexander Hunter recalled:

> These stores [including a lot of liquor] were placed under charge of the 13th, and in truth they kept them well. Especially faithful in seeing that none were wasted

was Company A, for the time Colonel Terrill's bodyguard. Theirs was only clerking duty, such as sorting the liquor, counting the stores (which had a lamentable way of getting mixed so as to require arranging every day), and attending the Colonel. The other nine companies had the watches, the details, and the guarding to do.[92]

After spending a week in camp at Winchester, James moved the regiment about a half mile outside the town. There he established a camp he named Fort Jackson on June 22. The men of the regiment did not meet the move with enthusiasm, many of them not wishing to leave their comfortable quarters in the town. To make matters worse, James ordered his men not to enter the town; however, he permitted the officers to remain. The men ignored the unpopular order, slipped into town, and usually returned to camp with some good thing to eat.

There was some excitement in camp on June 24 when a rumor circulated that the 13th Virginia Infantry would march on the following day to join the army its march to Pennsylvania. Once they learned that it was only rumor, and orders issued to remain on duty at Winchester, both citizen and soldier rejoiced.

Early in July, a reminder arrived that there was a war going on when a large group of Union prisoners passed through town from Gettysburg. On July 6, the townspeople and soldiers received another shock — word arrived that Lee had been defeated and his army was in retreat.

On July 20, General Robert E. Lee wrote Lieutenant General R. S. Ewell, suggesting that if he could spare Colonel Terrill from duty at Winchester, to send him to Front Royal to guard the pontoon bridge at that place. Lee left the bridge behind for Ewell's use in crossing the Shenandoah River.

While on duty at Winchester, the following incident involving Colonel Terrill occurred:

> In the evening Colonel Terrill, acting provost marshal, received orders to evacuate Winchester the next morning, and in accordance therewith he commanded his subordinates to make the necessary preparations.
>
> Those preparations consisted of a "secret" meeting in the provost marshal's office in the dead of night. As things progressed and many toasts were offered,

Colonel James Barbour Terrill, 13th Virginia Infantry, CSA (*The Confederate Soldier in the Civil War*).

A tremendous crash was heard and the door was burst in by the shock. Instantly the room was filled with soldiers with their guns at a charge, and behind them was the colonel. In a strange voice he cried: "Fire, men, fire!"

Paralyzed by the suddenness of the assault, not a man moved at first; but when the meaning of the order broke in on our astonished minds, we dropped flat on the floor with the simultaneous alacrity and crawled under the table with haste, all except one cool hand, who with a comprehensive sweep knocked the lights off the table and shrouded the place in utter darkness. Lying flat upon the floor, the crowd awaited developments.

After a while a light was struck, and behold, the group crouching on the ground and the guard gone! Had there ever been a guard or had it been all a dream? We rose and stared at one another in blank amazement, until Captain George returned with a solution of the mystery.

"The Colonel is very drunk," he said; "and having heard a noise in the office, he gathered a file of soldiers and broke open the door. Hardly knowing what he was saying, he ordered the guards to shoot, which of course they refused to do." As it was, with a glance they understood the condition of affairs, and went off laughing at our terror. The sudden darkness seemed to have sobered the Colonel, and he will apologize to you to-morrow, for I made him understand how he had compromised himself by being intoxicated and then ordering his escort not only to fire upon his own men but actually upon his own staff.[93]

Colonel G. C. Wharton's command relieved the 13th Virginia Infantry from provost duty at Winchester on July 23, and the regiment rejoined their division that evening. The regiment accompanied the division as it marched eastward, halting at last near Locust Dale, in the vicinity of Orange Court House on August 1.

The month of September brought two weeks of picket duty at Raccoon Ford and hours of drill by Colonel Terrill. "Terrill was garbed in a blue Union uniform (probably obtained from the spoils at Winchester) which led some men to smirk that he acted as if he preferred Yankee colors."[94]

On September 14, the 13th Virginia Infantry marched to Somerville Ford to meet a Federal movement in that area. The men remained in line of battle for several hours, taking artillery fire and skirmishing with the enemy, but no major engagement occurred. The two antagonists faced each other until the night of the 15th, when James received orders to move his regiment back about a mile and go into camp. Here they remained for several weeks.

Although A. P. Hill was no longer associated with the 13th Virginia Infantry, Mrs. Dolly Hill made another flag for the gallant regiment. The presentation took place on October 1, 1863, with James making the presentation and Lieutenant Wilson Newman receiving it on behalf of the regiment. As was customary, both parties offered short speeches.[95]

A week later, the picket duty along the Rapidan River abruptly ended. The army marched to turn General George Meade's right flank. By October 10, the army was near Madison Court House. The following day, General John Pegram assumed command of the brigade, and the march resumed to the Sperryville Pike. The 13th Virginia Infantry went into camp near Jeffersonton on the 12th.

The following day, the command moved to near Warrenton, Virginia. Marching at 4 A.M. on October 14, the 13th Virginia Infantry formed part of a force sent toward the Union right flank, as General Robert E. Rodes marched in Meade's front. After a march of nearly twenty miles, the regiment formed in line of battle near Bristoe Station about 5 P.M. The Confederates dodged an occasional shell, but this stopped as Meade withdrew. On the 15th, the 13th Virginia Infantry went to Manassas Junction to act as skirmishers. The men were excited at the prospect of meeting the enemy a third time on the field of Manassas. They were ready to show the Yankees that it would be best if they "never again to cross Bull Run."[96] The expected battle of 3rd Manassas did not materialize.

The men of the 13th Virginia Infantry spent the rest of October marching around the northern part of Virginia, often enduring pouring rain and performing picket duty. Rations were sparse, and in some cases the men had to sustain themselves on roasted acorns. A three-day break occurred near Brandy Station, and then the 13th Virginia Infantry moved to Bealeton Station, where they helped drive off some Union cavalry threatening the wagon train. With the threat to the wagon train gone, the men returned to camp.

On October 24, 1863, James' appointment as Colonel of the 13th Virginia Infantry became official. The government finally confirmed his rank, to date from May 15 of that year.[97]

On November 1, the division moved to a location near the railroad, about three miles above Brandy Station, Virginia, and went into camp on the farm of John Minor Botts. The soldiers received orders to build their winter quarters at that place. Terrill's men, however, were sent out on picket duty at Rappahannock Bridge. After two days, the men returned to camp. After a day's rest, they started on their winter huts on November 5.

New orders interrupted the work on the afternoon of November 7, when the brigade moved to the aid of troops under attack at the Rappahannock Bridge. After a ten-mile march, the brigade reached the bridge about dark and formed a line of battle along the Confederate side of the river. The brigades of Hays and Hoke formed on the opposite side of the river.

Soon after the arrival of Pegram's brigade, the Federals charged and captured a large number of the men of Hays' and Hoke's brigades. The 13th Virginia Infantry rushed into position to prevent the enemy from crossing the pontoon bridge. When the firing ceased, James' men moved down the hill and joined some Confederate artillery within fifty yards of the river and the bridge. They dug holes in the sandy soil for protection. About midnight, Pegram ordered the bridge burned.

On November 8, the 13th Virginia Infantry marched toward Culpeper Court House, formed in line of battle at an opporture spot and waited. No attack came, and after nightfall the men marched to camp at Somerville Ford, along the Rapidan River.

The regiment remained here for two weeks, during which time they began to build winter quarters. On November 25, the brigade received orders to prepare for action. The next day, Union troops crossed the Rapidan and attempted to turn Lee's right flank. That night, the 13th Virginia Infantry and Pegram's brigade stood picket at Robinson's Ford, while the remainder of the division marched down river.

The brigade was relieved on the morning of November 27 and joined the division at Mine Run about noon, taking a position about a mile west of Locust Grove. The 13th Virginia Infantry formed in line on the left of the Orange Turnpike near the Rowe farm. The regiment remained in reserve while their comrades constructed breastworks. That night, the 13th Virginia Infantry withdrew with the entire Confederate line almost a mile across Mine Run, and occupied a ridge.

On the 28th, Meade advanced to the stream, but made no effort to cross it. During a fierce artillery duel, the 13th Virginia Infantry moved forward as skirmishers in the rain. After nightfall, the regiment fell aback about a half mile. The 13th Virginia Infantry and Pegram's brigade formed the reserve on the 29th of November.

On November 30, the weather turned cold, freezing the ground. The 13th Virginia Infantry advanced as skirmishers and in the evening went to aid a portion of Hoke's line, which had broken. Ordered to support the demoralized skirmishers, James relieved them instead. Private Reuben Newman recorded in his diary that "our wise Col. relieves them instead. We are shelled furiously while getting into position, but no one hurt."[98] The 13th Virginia Infantry stayed out all night on picket duty in the cold.

December 1 was quiet and the 52nd Virginia relieved the 13th Virginia Infantry from picket duty. At 2 A.M. on December 2, Ewell's corps marched to relieve A. P. Hill's corps, which advanced against Meade, but found him gone. The 13th Virginia Infantry, along with other troops, followed the enemy to near Germanna Ford, and then returned to Mine Run for the night.

With the Federals gone, the 13th Virginia Infantry returned to Somerville Ford and resumed work on their winter quarters. With no expected active service until spring, many members of the regiment from the Orange and Culpepper companies left the regiment without permission to visit their homes. As Christmas drew closer, the remaining men became restless — anxious to go home. On December 23, in the midst of a snowstorm, more men from the Orange County company, as well as the Louisa County company started for home — without permission. Outraged, Colonel Terrill demanded that the company commanders furnish a list of the absent men.

The situation intensified that night. Orders arrived to be ready to march as a rumor indicated the Yankees were about to advance. As a result, no leaves were granted on Christmas day. Colonel Terrill and his subordinates lost the ability to control the men when someone brought in $300 worth of whiskey. One soldier noted that they were fast "becoming merry."[99]

Upon learning of the cancellation of the holiday leave, the men became furious, believing the rumored advance was only a tool used by the colonel to keep them in camp. Many of the men, if not all, left camp and went home.

By the 28th of December James had regained his composure and swore vengeance upon the rebellious companies, which were still absent. The following night, December 29th, most of the men returned to camp.

1864

The new year brought only more misery. Conditions in the camp of the 13th Virginia Infantry were bad, at best. Poor rations and cold conditions caused the men to grumble, and many gave up hope for their cause. It was amid these conditions that the government asked the men to re-enlist for the remainder of the war. Most of the 13th and 49th regiments expressed an interest, but only half of the other regiments in the brigade expressed an interest, explaining the poor response on dissatisfaction with their officers.

In the cold morning air of February 18, 1864, the officers formed the brigade before General Ewell. With much ceremony, General Pegram, Colonel Terrill and Colonel James H. Skinner made speeches, urging the men to do their duty and re-enlist. Following the speeches, the color bearers of each regiment stepped forward. General Pegram asked the men wishing to re-enlist to rally around the colors of their regiment, riding through the assembled crowd and urging them forward. An estimated 314 men of the 13th Virginia Infantry responded and re-enlisted. About thirty of the regiment did not answer the call.

Sometime following the re-enlistment of his men, James took another furlough, returning to duty on March 7. It was likely his last visit to his wife and infant son. His wife was expecting their second child.

A week later, on March 19, George Q. Peyton recorded the following incident in his diary:

> I saw a sight today that I never want to see again. A boy shot for desertion! We heard that his Reg't. refused to shoot. Gen. [Pegram] sent a note to Col. Terrell [sic] telling him to send a detail of 24 men. Col. T. sent back the inquiry what he wanted with them. Gen. P. sent back it was none of his business what he wanted them for. Col. T. then sent word that he would [not] send any men to shoot and that ended the correspondence.[100]

The Confederates spent the month of April 1864 preparing for the approaching spring campaign. The men drilled and the number of pickets increased to watch for expected movements in the Federal army. Excitement gripped the camp of the 13th Virginia Infantry. In the last known letter written by James, on April 19, he mentioned the expected battle to his brother George:

> You need not be surprised at any moment to hear of a collision between the two armies now confronting each other. Gen. Grant made a positive "change of front"

yesterday, it is presumed with a view of strengthening his right flank by covering the roads leading from Madison CH & using the commanding round at the base of the Blue ridge as a shoulder.... The soldiers of the army however regard the fact of Gen. Early's having donned his white hat & black plumes as the surest omen of a not far off Battle.[101]

The opening of the spring campaign came on May 3, a clear, sunny day. When the Army of Northern Virginia moved toward Mine Run the next day, the 13th Virginia Infantry remained behind to guard Somerville Ford. At about 11 P.M., the regiment was relieved and marched to join their comrades.

The unknown biographer of James wrote about the fighting during early May:

> Colonel Terrill and the invincible 13th were destined to immortalize themselves. At the Wilderness and Spottsylvania Court House they crowned themselves with glory.... After the first mentioned battle, they were in the front rank in the assault made upon the enemy to retake the position lost by the capture of General Edward Johnston's [Johnson's] Division. Colonel Terrill was among the first to mount the breastworks abandoned by the enemy.[102]

There was little rest for James and his men. The 13th Virginia Infantry received orders at 3 A.M. on May 5 to go back to Somerville Ford. A report had arrived indicating that the Federals were crossing there, and they were to investigate it. Arriving at the ford at sunrise, they found no trace of the enemy. The men deployed along the river and slept for a few hours. At noon, the regiment retraced their steps over the Orange Turnpike, finally catching up with the main army near Robinson's Tavern. They formed on the left of the turnpike, amid the distant sounds of a severe battle.

As Terrill's men advanced to meet the enemy, they soon found themselves within 200 yards of the Union army. "Soon the air was so thick with flying lead that Terrill's men were compelled to sit or lie on the ground for about twenty minutes until the firing ceased and permitted them to join the main line."[103]

In the dense, tangled woods, known as the Wilderness, the Confederates used the abundance of downed trees, stumps and dirt to construct a crude breastwork. When Grant's men approached, the Confederates opened fire on them, breaking the attack. Several times the enemy forces rallied and attacked, only to fall back again. After nightfall, occasional shots rang out as the men of the 13th Virginia Infantry searched for much needed equipment and supplies.

An account of the fighting at Spotsylvania Court House, written by Peyton and published in the *Confederate Veteran*, tells what happened that night:

> We lay down in front of the works and went to sleep. About ten o'clock we were suddenly roused by a terrific fire of musketry right in our faces. We jumped up and I took down the hill toward our breastworks. I was making two-forty time when I met the Colonel face to face. He had a cavalry saber about five feet long, and was waving it like a man mowing grass with a scythe blade. He made a motion at me and I went back and knelt down between two old fellows that did not run.[104]

The Federal forces in their front were gone at dawn on the morning of the 7th. About 7 A.M. James was ordered to move toward the enemy works. After marching about an hour, they rested for about two hours, listening to the sounds of the nearby fighting. At 10 A.M. a series of marches and countermarches occurred, but it would be about twenty-four hours before they would move with any purpose. Later in the evening, they reached Lee's new line near Spotsylvania Court House, and formed a part of the reserve.

On the morning of May 9, the 13th Virginia Infantry formed a line at a right angle to the main line and dug a trench to protect their right flank. About 4 P.M., James received orders to move to the front and form the advance. Once there, orders came to turn about and return to his former position. The Confederate position had a salient in the center, known as the Mule Shoe. James and the 13th Virginia Infantry remained in the reserve, near the Mule Shoe.

On the 10th of May, the Federals made a furious assault on the line, but it held. James and his men played a minor role as support for General Edward Johnson's men. They returned to camp about 11 P.M. that night.

The following day, May 11, the regiment took a position on the left side of the Mule Shoe, relieving General George Doles' brigade. After about thirty minutes, the regiment was relieved and took up a position in the rear, near the Harrison house.

As the men of the 13th Virginia Infantry prepared their breakfast on the morning of May 12 in the fog and light rain, a strange sound caught their attention. Within minutes, a brigade marched toward General Doles' position. Soon after its arrival, the men were astonished to see the guns on their left turn and fire across their rear. The men of the 13th Virginia Infantry became slightly confused, thinking that a mistake had been made. When ordered to the rear, their confusion increased. Near the Harrison house, they found themselves facing Generals Lee, Ewell and Gordon. Here they learned that their artillery had fired across their rear at a Union force that had penetrated the opposite side of the Mule Shoe.

The brigade quickly moved into some nearby pines, drove the enemy from them, and continued through some oaks and down a hill. Struggling through knee-deep mud, they climbed a hill bringing them to the captured breastworks, recently held by Johnson's division. Two solid lines of blue met them with a volley. Anticipating this fire, the men dropped to the ground, then quickly rose to their feet and charged. Much to their surprise, the Union troops fled, leaving the Confederates in possession of the extreme right of the line. This portion of the line would be forever known as the Bloody Angle. Despite being badly scattered, the men continued and recaptured the adjacent ditches.

The Federals quickly countered, attacking the thin Confederate line. They soon were in possession of the left side of the entrenchments and the Confederate line broke. The Confederate officers succeeded in rallying the men and attacked the Union line again, retaking the ditches. Seeing their desperation, General Ewell moved reinforcements to their aid.

Battle of Spotsylvania Court House

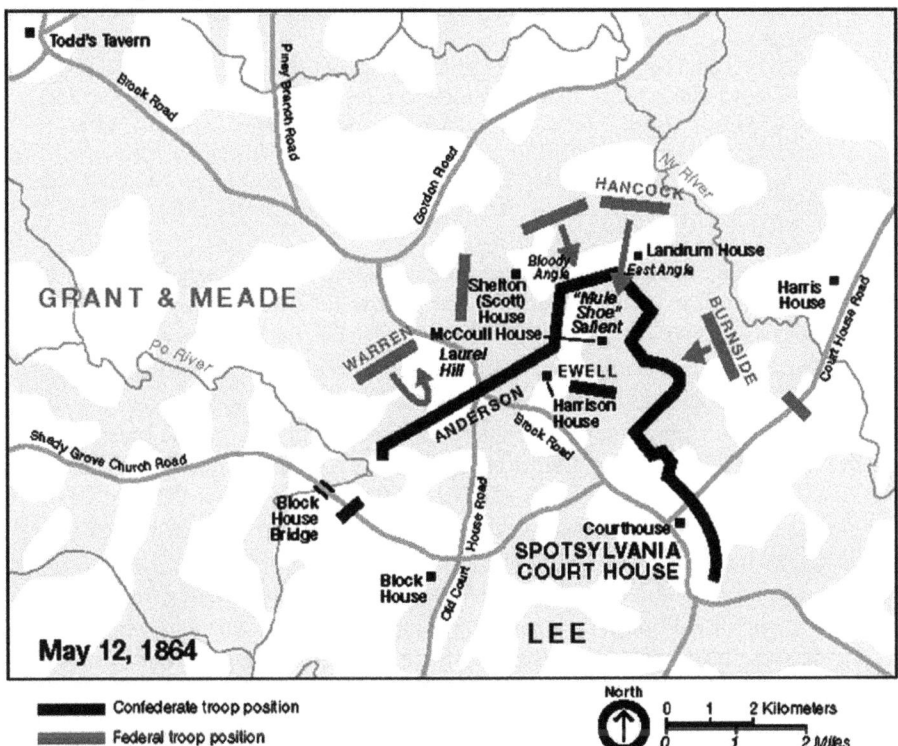

Map of Spotsylvania Court House, Virginia, May 12, 1864, showing the Mule Shoe and Bloody Angle (courtesy National Park Service).

In the fighting to regain the position lost by General Johnson's men, James took charge of an artillery piece. Private O. S. Fitzhugh, a member of Company D, 13th Virginia Infantry, recalled in 1903: "We went on to the third line of breastworks, where we found the ground strewed with dead men and horses. At this moment, Col. J. B. Terrell [sic], of my regiment, and Frank Hume, of Company A, commenced to fire a piece of artillery that had been captured from General Johnson."[105]

Darkness brought no relief. Pickets stood watch for a renewed attack and the men ordered not to sleep. The battle-weary soldiers often had to be awakened.

The following excerpt from the biography of James details the events of that miserable day.

> At the battle of Spotsylvania Court House on the 12th of May, when the leaden messengers of death were making dreadful havoc, he [James] sprang upon the hastily erected breastworks and whilst cheering and encouraging his men a ball

from the enemy struck the spur of his right foot and tore off the instep of his boot and although his coat was perforated by bullets, yet his life which then seemed a charmed one was only spared for a brief while longer.... Here he was joined by his Father [sic] who being around him and following him step by step to the Peninsula with a heart oppressed by the presentment that his earthly career would soon close, such was his intrepidity and total disregard of personal danger in time of battle, that the preservation of his life up to that period seemed miraculous. He always led his men and they followed with alacrity into the thickest of the fight. Wherever he led they followed and he was ever willing and anxious to lead where duty required.[106]

About dawn on the rainy morning of May 13, the brigade fell back and dug new fortifications. The dead of the brigade were buried on the 14th in graves two and a half feet deep. Starting on the 16th of May, the brigade served as skirmishers as the two armies faced each other. On the 18th, the fighting escalated and the Confederate skirmishers fell back.

The morning of the 19th revealed that the Union troops had pulled back from Ewell's corps, with the exception of the extreme right. General Ewell advanced, and once again his men came to the aid of Edward Johnson's division. About 10 P.M., the men received orders return to their original position. Exhausted, they reached their old camp about 2 A.M. on May 20.

May 20 was quiet, and the men of the 13th Virginia Infantry stood picket duty at the Bloody Angle. French born Chief Musician Henri Jean Mugler, on duty at the field hospital, noted that during the day Colonel Terrill "came in from the front to get some 'medicine' [whiskey]."[107]

On May 21, the 13th Virginia Infantry accompanied the brigade on a march through the woods, and in the afternoon emerged from the forest at Mud Tavern, on the Telegraph Road. After a brief halt, the march continued toward Richmond until about 10 P.M. Getting up at 3 A.M. on May 22, the army continued to Hanover Junction. During the evening, the 13th Virginia Infantry went out on picket duty along the North Anna River. The regiment remained in reserve for the next five days.

May 28 found the 13th Virginia Infantry in camp at Cold Harbor, near the scene of the fierce battle of 1862. The afternoon of the 29th brought some skirmishing in a wooded, swampy area, which lasted until the Yankees withdrew.

Following an afternoon march on May 30, the 13th Virginia Infantry began to dig new trenches. Before long orders interrupted the work for the entire brigade to move to the support of General Rodes, who was then engaged with the enemy. After a two mile march, the men halted near Bethesda Church, Virginia, and took shelter from the artillery fire behind a hill. Here they remained for several hours, then marched through some pines and made a charge. With a yell the Confederates advanced at a run for fifty yards under a hail of bullets and shells, jumped a fence, and entered a vegetable garden on the other side. A cabin was located in the center of the garden, and the Union breastworks were just beyond the dwelling. When the Confederates reached the cabin, the center of their line halted and confusion mounted as casualties increased, including a number of the officers.

The 13th Virginia Infantry, protected somewhat by the woods around them, did not halt at the cabin as the others did. Unaware for the moment of the others halting, the regiment continued to advance until the men realized their near isolation, and took cover in some trees. For an hour they remained here, constantly under fire. During this period a staff officer came to James, now suffering from an abdominal wound, informing him that he was to take command of the brigade.

As James moved through the vegetable garden and toward the cabin, it was the last time the regiment saw him alive. About 4 P.M., while leading the brigade against the enemy's fortifications, he was shot through the head, and died instantly. After dark the 13th Virginia Infantry fell back about a mile and camped for the night.

Despite the occasional bitterness expressed by the men of the 13th Virginia Infantry about their commander, James received positive appraisals as a combat officer from some of his critics. One soldier called him "one of the ablest tacticians in the Confederate army" while another conceded "no more gallant officer has laid down his life in our cause."[108]

Captain Samuel D. Buck, of Winchester, years later wrote of James:

> No more gallant spirit was offered to the cause than that of James B. Terrill. As a skirmish officer and a hard, close fighter, he had no superior and his equal was seldom found. As a regimental commander he was most efficient and much of the reputation of our command was due to his energy and discipline. Both Hill and Walker were, of course, fine officers, but were not so long in command of the regiment.[109]

George Q. Peyton recorded the day's events in his diary:

> We were ordered to the front to support Rodes, who had started an attack on the enemy's left flank. Marched about two miles and halted at Bethesda Church. Were ordered to get ready to charge. Advanced across a swamp and lay down under a hill to shelter us from the cannon balls which were coming pretty thick. Stayed here until nearly 6 PM when we were suddenly ordered forward. Advanced through a thick piece of pines, a hundred or so yards when we were ordered to charge.... We were met by a hail of cannon and rifle balls, although we could not see a single man. Ran about 50 yards and came to a fence, jumped over this into a truck-patch in the center of which was a cabin and just beyond the cabin were the enemy in breastworks, from which a cloud of smoke was flying. When we got to the cabin, the center of our line stopped. This created a confusion. The men all got mixed up, the officers all got killed or wounded. No orders were given to fall back and nearly the whole Brigade were killed or wounded. Ramseur was to blame for the whole thing, and ought to have been shot for the part he played in it. The 13th did not loose as many men as the others, because the woods in our part of the line went nearly to the Yankee breastworks. When the line stopped at the cabin, we went on

but seeing the line stop, we stopped and got behind trees. The Yankees had a battery on our right that enfiladed our whole line, so the trees did not help us much. We stayed here about an hour by which time near all the brigade were killed or wounded. Capt. Wilson, of Gen. Pegram's staff, came after Col. Terrill to take command of the Brigade, and the last we saw of him he was going through the truck-patch to the cabin. He was killed and all the other field officers were killed or wounded. He had just gotten his commission as Brig. Gen. for gallantry at Spotsylvania C.H.... All the blame for this affair was laid on Ramseur, who ordered the charge, without knowing anything about the ground or the force he was fighting.[110]

A brief notice appeared in the June 8 edition of the *Richmond Examiner* concerning James' death:

> We hear an affecting incident of the late fights around Richmond. At the time the battle was raging, Colonel [James B.] Terrill, of Bath county, Virginia, was observed to be acting with conspicuous gallantry, and, as a reward, he was instantly promoted; but before the news of his promotion could be got to him he was *dead!* His body was soon afterwards recovered by his distressed father on the battle field, but half covered by a few spade-fulls of dirt.[111]

The sketch of the life of James Barbour Terrill, most likely written by his father, tells of his last hours:

> It was ascertained that a portion of the enemy was in position near Bethesda Church, in the county of Hanover, in what force could not be ascertained as they were concealed behind their breast-works. In this state of the case General Ramsen [Ramseur] (who has since been killed and therefore we will tread lightly upon his ashes) in a vaporing manner proposed to General Early that he should permit him to take those breast-works, and upon repeating the proposition General Early, gave him permission to do so if he could and thereupon Pegram's Brigade and Ramsen's [Ramseur's] were ordered up and the assault commenced (the 13th formed a part of Pegram's brigade) in a few minutes the enemy opened a murderous war fire from their batteries in front and on the right flank of the assailants, who had to pass over an open field to reach the enemy's breast-works in front. Col. Willis, a brave young officer, who happened to be in command of Pegram's Brigade, in the absence of the General, soon fell. Col. Gibson, the officer next in rank assumed command of the brigade, and he too soon fell, Colonel Terrill just about this period was shot down, having received a mortal wound in the abdomen and while he was on his hands and feet struggling to rise the Adjutant of the brigade rode up to him saying "Col. Terrill, the Brigade is without a commander and it is your duty as the ranking officer to take command." Whereupon he rose to his feet, staggered along the line to his proper position and then flourishing his saber over his head, gave the command "Forward Men," and advanced but a short distance before he was killed, near the enemy's breast-works, by a bullet passing entirely through his head. Thus fell one of the bravest of the brave.
>
> Upon a post mortem examination made by the surgeons of the Brigade they decided that although the last wound caused instant death, that the first one was also necessarily mortal.
>
> His Father [sic] was near the battle-field at the time and heard with awful forebodings the battle strife and soon found that his worst fears were realized. The

enemy retained for a week afterward possession of the ground where he fell, at the expiration of which time Capt. Baughn of Culpepper County with a detachment of men, detailed for that purpose went upon the battleground and after a diligent search, succeeded with the assistance of Capt. A. L. Pitzer, (one of Gen. Early's aids,) in recovering his body, partially buried near the enemy's breast-works, and delivered it to his Father, who had it interred temporarily at the residence of Mr. Wm. Corvardin [Cowardin] below Mechanicsville, in Hanover County.[112]

Opposing the 13th Virginia Infantry and Pegram's Brigade at Bethesda Church that day was the Third Division of Brigadier General Samuel W. Crawford, part of Major General G. K. Warren's Fifth Corps. That night, May 30, Crawford reported the death of James to his superiors.

A detachment from the 13th Virginia Infantry was sent after nightfall to recover James' body but succeeded only in becoming prisoners. During the night, Union soldiers buried James on the battlefield, covering his body with a slight layer of sand. His body remained here for six days before being recovered. The body was taken to a field hospital for examination by the surgeons. They all agreed that the first wound to the body would have been mortal.[113]

President Jefferson Davis notified General Lee on May 31, 1864, that he had placed James' name in nomination to command Pegram's brigade, with the temporary rank of Brigadier General. Davis made the nomination under an act approved on May 30, 1864, and was to date from the date of confirmation. The Confederate Senate, which had to consent to all promotions, consented to the appointment the same day.

William H. Terrill wrote of James' death in a June 22 letter to former governor John Letcher:

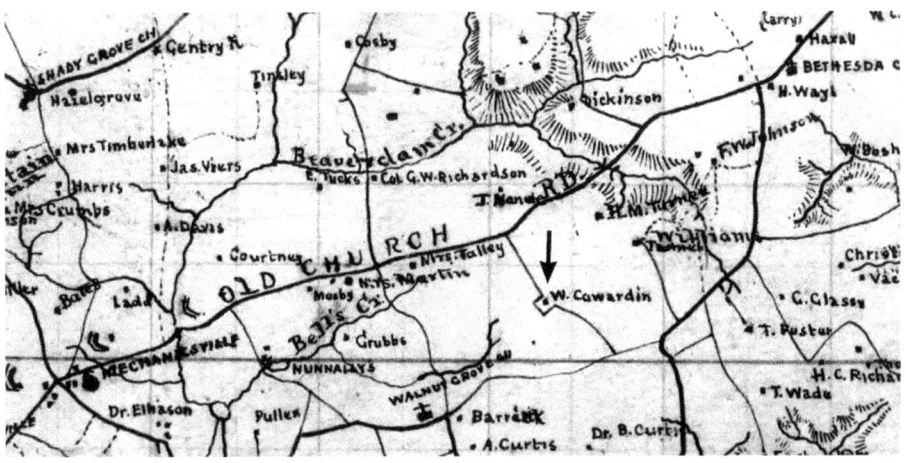

Map of the Mechanicsville area, showing the farm of W. Cowardin (see arrow), where James was buried by his father. Detail of [Map of Hanover County, Virginia] (courtesy Library of Congress, Geography and Map Division).

My gallant Boy met his destiny most gloriously and in a glorious cause. I hovered around him for four weeks, following him up day after day until he fell. He fell a matyr [martyr] to the cause in which he embarked as you know, as one of its earliest devotees. He fell mortally wounded at the head of the invincible *Thirteenth* but rose again as commander of his Brigade and whilst leading it upon the enemy's breastworks under a murderous fire of canister and grape shot, was shot through the head and died *instantly*. I succeeded in recovering his body after the lapse of seven days and had it interred.[114]

The following, brief obituary appeared in the July 22, 1864, issue of the *Lexington Gazette*.

Col. J. B. Terrill of the 13th Regiment of Virginia Volunteers, has been in service since the commencement of the war, and has proved himself a most gallant and efficient officer. No man has rendered better service, or has proved himself more devoted to the cause. He fell Monday last mortally wounded, and expired in a few hours afterward.

He was the son of William H. Terrill, Esq., of Bath county, and, graduated with great credit, at the Virginia Military Institute some years ago. He was brave, generous and chivalrous, and was greatly loved by his regiment. He leaves a wife and one child, and numerous friends, and relatives to lament his early death.[115]

Emily Barbour Terrill (Mrs. Henry Heth Vaden), born after James was killed (courtesy Mercer Terrill Vaden).

A short time after the publication of his obituary, Charlotte Terrill gave birth to her second child, a lovely daughter named Emily Barbour Terrill. Emily was born on August 8, at Oaklands, in Chesterfield County, Virginia.

A single piece of correspondence between the two surviving Terrill brothers (George wrote to Philip), dated August 31, 1864, reveals the following:

I have not had a line from Father since he left Richmond very shortly after poor James' death. I saw the notice in the newspaper of J's body having fallen into the hands of the enemy. I immediately went to Richd [Richmond] to try to recover it — before I reached there Father had succeeded in the recovery & had it buried about six miles out from the city. I accidentally met with Father, spent several hours in his company and then returned home.[116]

In January 1866, William H. Terrill wrote to his daughter Emily Porterfield, about James. He compared

James and his son-in-law, George A. Porterfield, in that both had suffered great injustices by the government. James "ought to have been a Major General long before he fell in battle."[117]

Charlotte Eucebia Drewry

Charlotte Eucebia Drewry, of King William County, Virginia, was born in April 1838, a daughter of Captain Martin Drewry and Mildred S. Fox. Her father was a veteran of the War of 1812, and a rather wealthy farmer. She married James Barbour Terrill at her father's residence on December 12, 1861.

Charlotte Drewry Terrill, now a widow with two small children, remarried at Bellevue, King William County, Virginia, on October 27, 1868, to Saint George Tucker Coalter. The Reverend John O. Turpin, who had married James and Charlotte in 1861, now performed the ceremony.

The 1870 Census placed the Terrill children at Beaver Dam Station, in Hanover County. The 1880 Census reveals that the Coalters were living in the Acquinton District of King William County. Both of the Terrill children are listed in the household.

Sometime in the early 1880s, James Mercer Terrill went to the New Mexico Territory. There he was shot and killed by a man named Andy McDonald on August 29, 1884.[118]

Emily Barbour Terrill married Henry Heth Vaden, of Chesterfield County, Virginia, and they had three children.[119] The Vadens lived in Richmond, where Emily died on March 31, 1943.

By 1900, Charlotte was once again a widow, her husband having died on August 28, 1897, at Bellevue, in King William County. She, two children, and a daughter-in-law moved to the Brookland District of Henrico County. Charlotte Terrill Coalter died in Richmond on February 12, 1916.

CHAPTER VI

Philip Mallory Terrill

Philip Mallory Terrill
1842–1864

As William H. Terrill settled into his role as prosecuting attorney for Bath and Pocahontas counties, Elizabeth delivered yet another son into the household on June 6, 1842. He would be their last child. They named the new arrival Philip Mallory Terrill, his middle name being the surname of his paternal great-grandmother.

When he was nine years of age, a debilitating illness struck Philip. His father spoke of the illness in a letter to his daughter Emily, on October 27, 1851:

"Poor little Philip is upon his feet at last, but he looks more like a spectre [sic] than a human being. He is but little more than a skeleton. He reaches out with difficulty to walk from his bed to the fire place. He was confined to his bed four weeks."[1]

Philip made a full recovery from his mysterious illness, although it was most likely the following spring before he was completely well. Between age nine and the time he was fourteen, Philip spent a great deal of time with Emily, and often suffered from some sickness or another.

Family recollections state that Philip attended a preparatory school operated by Gessner Harrison, near Charlottesville, before going to the University of Virginia.[2] No records support this story; however, he did attend a school called Brook Hill. The Brook Hill School was located near Charlottesville, and Philip attended it during the winter of 1858 and 1859. He was then nearly seventeen years old.

It seems that Philip was having difficulty in deciding what to do with his life. In a letter, written from Brook Hill School on October 9, 1858, Philip told the Rev. William T. Price of his uncertainty: "I am so ill prepared for the position which I am destined to fill that I feel as if I would wish to go back and be a child once again; there is one profession which seems to be marked out by providence for me, and that is the ministry."[3]

Philip began his studies at the University of Virginia in the fall of 1860. However, before the end of the term, the war interrupted his studies. In May 1861, he bid farewell to his classmates at the university and returned to Warm Springs. Back home, he turned his attentions to the army and assisted in raising a company of infantry in Bath County.

There is no direct mention in any of the Terrill family papers of Philip's reaction to his brother's decision to remain loyal to the Union. Philip, however, did correspond with his sister-in-law, Emily Henry Terrill. Inferring from this fact, he must not have shared his father's strong feelings about the disloyalty of his brother.

Philip received two commissions in the early part of June 1861. John Letcher, governor of Virginia and a close family friend, appointed him to the rank of 2nd Lieutenant in the 81st Regiment Virginia Militia on June 7, 1861. A week later, the governor promoted him to the rank of 1st Lieutenant, to date from June 6, 1861, Philip's nineteenth birthday.[4]

He enlisted for one year in the Bath Grays at Bath Court House (present-day Warm Springs) on June 6, 1861. The Bath Grays accompanied Brigadier General Robert S. Garnett to the relief of Philip's brother-in-law, Colonel George A. Porterfield. The Virginia troops, under Porterfield's command, had suffered a disastrous surprise and retreat at Philippi, Virginia, on the morning of June 3, 1861. This poorly armed and equipped force retreated to Huttonsville, in Randolph County, Virginia, where it awaited aid from the eastern part of the state.

Reaching Huttonsville on June 14, 1861, General Garnett quickly organized the companies into two regiments and a battalion. The Bath Grays became part of Colonel Porterfield's regiment, the 25th Virginia Infantry. General Garnett assigned Porterfield to duty at Beverly, Virginia, because of his handling of the Philippi affair. Physical command of the regiment fell to Lieutenant Colonel Jonathan McGee Heck, a native of Morgantown, Virginia.

The 25th Virginia Infantry was sent to occupy the important pass on Rich Mountain, through which the Staunton-Parkersburg Turnpike passed. The Virginians fortified an area on the western side of the moun-

Philip Mallory Terrill (*Bull Run to Bull Run*, by George Baylor).

tain, naming it Camp Garnett, in honor of their new commanding officer. The 20th Virginia Infantry, commanded by Lieutenant Colonel John Pegram, assisted them. Pegram assumed command of the position.

Captain William D. Ervin's horse threw him in early July, injuring him. Command of the Bath Grays then fell upon the shoulders of Lieutenant Philip M. Terrill.

Colonel Pegram was caught between two armies on July 11, 1861. Major General George B. McClellan brought a strong force to Pegram's front early in July. Part of this force, commanded by Brigadier General William S. Rosecrans, marched through the mountains and succeeded in getting into Pegram's rear.

After a heated fight on the summit of Rich Mountain on July 11, in the rear of Camp Garnett, Colonel Pegram sought to escape and join forces with General Garnett at Laurel Hill. As Pegram led his men through the dense wilderness on the night of July 11, the column broke apart. One part of the command managed to make its escape, while Pegram and the larger part became hopelessly lost. His men were tired and hungry, and the former U.S. officer felt there was only one answer to the situation.

The colonel called for a meeting of the officers on the evening of July 12 in which he proposed that they surrender themselves to McClellan's army. Captain John B. Moomau and Colonel Heck opposed the idea, believing that it was possible to traverse the wilderness via the Seneca Trail and reach safety in Pendleton County, Virginia. Pegram insisted that surrender was the only option left, and disregarded their advice. He should have listened to their wise council.

About midnight Pegram sent a messenger to Beverly, six miles away, with a note to General McClellan. Pegram wrote: "Owing to the reduced and almost famished condition of the force now here under my command, I am compelled to offer to surrender them to you as prisoners of war. I have only to ask that they receive at your hands such treatment as Northern prisoners have invariably received from the South."[5]

Between 7 and 8 o'clock on the morning of July 13, two officers brought McClellan's reply. The general agreed to accept Pegram, his officers and men as prisoners of war, and promised to treat everyone with due kindness.

Colonel Pegram now called upon his men to fall in, only then discovering that Captain Moomau and his company were missing. During the night, Captain Moomau spirited his company away, and after a grueling march through the mountainous wilderness, brought his men out safely to Monterey, in Highland County, Virginia.

With more than 600 officers and men, Pegram started for Beverly, meeting along the way several wagons loaded with hardtack for the hungry Confederates.

In Beverly, the Southern soldiers stacked their arms and without ceremony became prisoners of war. Most, if not all, had never fired a shot at an enemy.

Five companies, half of the 25th Virginia Infantry, became prisoners of war that day. Among them were Philip and the Bath Grays.

The Northern captors placed the enlisted men in comfortable quarters and issued rations to them. They allowed the officers, upon their parole of honor, to move freely about the town. Colonel Pegram, who was ill, took a room at the home of Jonathan Arnold, Thomas J. Jackson's brother-in-law. A number of the other officers took up residence in the local hotel.

General McClellan, on the morning of July 13, while waiting for Pegram and his men to arrive, contemplated a growing problem. Once Pegram arrived, he would have about a thousand prisoners to guard, feed and otherwise take care of. Unsure of what to do next, he wrote Colonel E. D. Townsend, the Assistant Adjutant General of the Union Army: "Please give me immediate instructions by telegraph as to the disposition to be made of officers and men taken prisoners of war."[6]

General Winfield Scott responded to McClellan's request on July 14. After extending his congratulations, he proceeded to give McClellan instructions on the disposition of the prisoners:

Discharge all your prisoners of war under the grade of commissioned officers who shall willingly take and subscribe a general oath in these terms:

> I swear (or affirm) that I will not take up arms against the United States or serve in any military capacity whatsoever against them until regularly discharged according to the usages of war from this obligation.

As to officers among your prisoners permit all to return to their homes who willingly sign a written general parole in these words:

> We and each of us for himself severally pledge our words of honor as officers and gentlemen that we will not again take up arms against the United States nor serve in any military capacity whatsoever against them until regularly discharged according to the usages of war from this obligation.[7]

General Scott continued, informing McClellan to withhold the privilege of parole from all prisoners that formerly belonged to the United States Army or Navy. These he directed to be sent to Fort McHenry, Maryland. Colonel Pegram, who had left the U.S. Army without submitting his resignation, was the only prisoner in McClellan's hands sent to Fort McHenry. The Union authorities later exchanged him. Later in the war, Pegram would command another of the Terrill brothers, as he became James' commanding officer.

Two days later, on the 16th, McClellan paroled the commissioned officers of Pegram's command and released them from custody. He paroled the enlisted men the following day. His company now released to return to their homes and await exchange, Philip had one last request of his former captors. He wrote:

> I have the honor to request that my company be permitted to make its way to their homes in the nearest route independent of the Regiment to which they are attached. We desire to follow a path leading through Pocahontas County departing

from the main road at Huntersville, thereby obviating a tedious march towards Staunton. If it pleases you to grant this request, rations for two days will be sufficient for us until we reach the neighborhood where we can obtain supplies from our friends residing in Pocahontas Co. My company was organized in Bath Co. and known as the "Bath Grays" belonging to Col. Heck's regiment — Hoping that this may meet your approbation.[8]

General McClellan approved Philip's request, and issued the following pass, mistakenly referring to him as Captain:

> Hd. Quarters Army of Occupation
> Western Virginia, Beverly, July 17/61.
>
> The members of the company known as "Bath Grays" commanded by Captain Philip M. Terrill, taken prisoner while bearing arms against the United States having been released upon parole of honor, are hereby permitted to go to Bath County, Virginia, and will be allowed to pass guards of this army, they may meet with in proceeding to their destination.[9]

Philip and his comrades from the Bath Grays made their way back to Bath County, where they resumed a somewhat normal life and awaited exchange. According to the practice during the early part of the war, both sides often released prisoners and allowed them to return to active duty.

Sometime in the late summer or early fall of 1861, Philip went to live with his sister Emily in Jefferson County. He went to Emily's to help care for the farm while her husband was absent in the Confederate Army.

In late November or early December, Philip left Elmwood on his way to King William County, below Richmond, to attend James' wedding. Along the way, he stopped briefly at Bel Pre, in Culpeper County to visit his Aunt Mary Jane Wise and her family. He wrote Emily on December 5, stating that he had arrived at the Wise home on the previous day. "Aunt Jane's family," he wrote, "were of course much surprised to see me, as they had heard nothing of James' intended marriage."[10]

After attending James' wedding in King William County on December 12, Philip remained in Richmond for a while. While there, he called upon Lieutenant William E. Merrill, a prisoner of war confined in a Richmond prison. The January 23, 1862, visit was for securing an exchange with Merrill. The following day, Merrill informed General Joseph G. Totten, commanding the U.S. Engineers, of the proposed arrangement.[11] The exchange, however, did not take place and Philip remained a paroled prisoner for another seven months. Resigned to his fate, Philip returned to Emily's home in Jefferson County, where he remained until the following August.

Apparently, not all of the Terrill family frowned upon William Rufus' decision to remain loyal to the United States. There was, it seems, some written communication between Emily and her brother William. A letter written by William Rufus Terrill to Secretary of War Edwin M. Stanton on March 28, 1862, evidences this.

My sister, the wife of Col. G. A. Porterfield lives near Leetown, Jefferson County, Virginia. My brother Captain Philip M. Terrill, (captured at Rich Mountain) a prisoner on parole is with her. About the 4th of March her stock was driven off her farm and when my brother went to Martinsburg to recover it, although he exhibited his parole he was thrown into the County Jail. He was released the next day. I beg that you will be kind enough to give Mrs. Porterfield a safeguard. She has a large family of small children, and all the property she claims is her own, for I know it was given her by my father.[12]

Philip left Elmwood again in the summer of 1862. From Charlottesville, on August 6, he wrote Confederate secretary of war George W. Randolph, asking about his exchange. He also asked if he was free to enlist in any branch of the service he wished to, as in the case of officers who failed to be re-elected in the re-organization of the forces. Secretary Randolph's response, if any, is missing.

Finally, on August 13, the U.S. authorities formally exchanged Philip and the other Rich Mountain prisoners at Aiken's Landing, Virginia. All were now free to return to the Confederate army.

To understand the ensuing events, it is necessary to examine several steps taken before their exchange. The first of these occurred about May 1, 1862, when Brigadier Edward Johnson reorganized the Army of the Northwest. At that time, the 25th Virginia Infantry consisted of five companies. There was a battalion in Johnson's command known as Hansbrough's Battalion (9th Battalion Virginia Infantry), consisting of four companies. In an effort to bring the 25th Virginia to full strength, Johnson ordered the consolidation of these two units. Still short a company, Johnson ordered the transfer of a company from the 31st Virginia Infantry to complete the reorganization of the 25th Virginia.

The Southern War Department did not recognize this consolidation, and as a result issued orders to dissolve it later in the year. Once again, the 25th Virginia consisted of six companies.

The second step came in May or June 1862, when the War Department issued an order discharging all paroled prisoners from the service of the Confederate States. The War Department revoked the order on July 31, 1862, too late to repair the damage already done. Many of the paroled prisoners followed the earlier order, and after their exchange enlisted in other companies.

Orders to reorganize the Rich Mountain prisoners came only a few days after their exchange. On August 23, the War Department issued an order to Captain J. B. Moomau and Lieutenant John T. Cowan, authorizing them to collect and reorganize the former prisoners of war into a battalion. In October, the secretary of war ordered Lieutenant Colonel A. C. Jones to assemble these same companies and reorganize the 25th Virginia Infantry. Colonel Jones, upon assuming command of these men at Warm Springs, noted that about fifty of the Bath Grays were there in camp, under the command of their First Lieutenant. The lieutenant was Philip M. Terrill. Soon after Jones arrived, a number of men deserted the camp and joined their former captain in General John D. Imboden's command.

To complicate matters even more, in November 1862, the Richmond authorities sent Colonel George H. Smith, commanding the 25th Virginia Infantry, to take charge of the Rich Mountain prisoners. The War Department authorized him to claim the soldiers and return them to the regiment. He met with little success, as Jones refused to turn the men over to him.

Tempers flared, and hard feelings arose between Jones, Moomau, Smith and Imboden. Letters of complaint quickly found their way to Richmond, and in December, they sent an officer to investigate the situation.

Eventually, the troops were left as they were. Captain William D. Ervin's Bath Grays remained a part of the 18th Virginia Cavalry. Lieutenant Colonel George W. Hansbrough's 9th Battalion remained a part of the 25th Virginia Infantry, and the remnants of the paroled prisoners collected by Jones, Moomau, Cowan and Smith filled out the ranks of the 62nd Virginia (Mounted) Infantry. The War Department appointed Colonel Smith to command the 62nd Virginia, and appointed a new commander for the 25th Virginia. The bulk of the former prisoners of war ended up in the command of Brigadier General John D. Imboden.

A biographical sketch stated that Philip "was ordered by the War Department to Warm Springs, to re-organize his old company. As all but 8 or 10 had joined other companies, he was allowed to return to the 12th Virginia Cavalry in the spring of 1863."[13]

The sketch is partly in error. Philip was not associated with the 12th Virginia Cavalry until September 1863. During the time between his exchange and going to Warm Springs to reorganize the Bath Grays, Philip volunteered to serve as one of General R. S. Ewell's bodyguards. At the beginning of the 2nd Manassas Battle in August 1862, Philip helped carry the wounded general from the field of Groveton.[14]

During the early months of 1863, Philip was carried on the rolls of Company A, 62nd Virginia (Mounted) Infantry as a first lieutenant. A muster roll of that company, dated February 28, 1863, noted that he was on leave until March 15.

Searching for another avenue to serve the Confederacy, Philip wrote the secretary of the treasury, C. G. Memminger on February 28, 1863. He applied for an appointment as a clerk in that department. He noted that the reorganization of his company had eliminated him from the service. His application was not processed.

Sometime prior to March 21, 1863, Philip submitted his resignation as 1st Lieutenant of the Bath Grays. Under the impression that the government was going to disband his company, he resigned his commission and expressed his desire to enlist in another arm of the service. Colonel George H. Smith, his commanding officer, approved the resignation and forwarded it to the War Department for action.[15]

On March 21, Philip wrote the Confederate Adjutant General, asking for the return of his resignation, if it was not too late. He stated that after submitting his resignation, he had learned that his company was not going to be disbanded after all. Three days later, Philip addressed a letter to Colonel Smith, expressing his desire to remain an officer in his regiment. Both Colonel Smith and General Imboden approved the request and forwarded it to the War Department.

Whether or not the Adjutant General's Office accepted or returned his resignation is not entirely clear. The April 30, 1863, roll of Company A, 62nd Virginia (Mounted) Infantry, listed Philip as being present for duty, and that he had not been re-elected to the position of first lieutenant. That being the case, the resignation must have been returned to Philip, and because of his not being re-elected, he was now free to enlist in any branch of service he wished to.

In June 1863, Colonel George H. Smith wrote a letter praising Philip and explaining his difficulties in the army. Smith wrote on June 22:

> It gives me pleasure to State that Mr. Phillip M. Terrill, late 1st Lieut. Co. A of this regiment, has acquitted himself while with the regiment as an intelligent & efficient officer & a most estimable gentleman. He leaves the regiment, (very much to the regret of his late associates) not being re-elected in the re-organization of his Co, which has lately been filled up by the transfer of a large majority of men from another county. The preference of his Co. for inferior men from their own county, while natural does not in any way affect Mr. Terrill's character as an efficient officer. It was very much regretted by his commanding officers.[16]

Brigadier General John D. Imboden added his approval to Smith's comments, stating simply, "I most cordially endorse & concur in what Col. Smith states above."[17]

Exactly how Philip spent the time between May and September 1863 is not fully known. Philip's uncle, David G. Wise, and his family had left their home (Bel Pre) near Brandy Station after the great cavalry battle was fought near there in June 1863. Being in poor health, Wise moved his family to Staunton, where he died on August 28. Philip remained at Bel Pre for a while, to keep an eye on the property for the Wise family. Released from his watchman's duties, Philip joined the army again.

Records of the 12th Virginia Cavalry indicate that Philip enlisted as a Private in Company B, at Brandy Station, Culpeper County, Virginia on September 1, 1863, to serve for a term of two years or the duration of the war. Company B, interestingly enough, was mostly composed of young men from Jefferson County — Philip likely knew many of them.

Philip's biographer, recounting his service in the 12th Virginia Cavalry, wrote simply, "He participated in the stirring scenes and battle's strife through which that gallant regiment passed while he was attached to it."[18]

Two-thirds of September passed without incident for the men of the 12th Virginia. On the morning of September 22, two cavalry divisions of General George Meade's army moved south toward the Confederate lines. Near Madison Court House, General John Buford's division split off and followed the Gordonsville Turnpike. General Judson Kilpatrick, commanding the second division, followed the Orange Court House Road.

To meet this threat, Major General J. E. B. Stuart, Philip's third cousin, moved northward with Wade Hampton's division of cavalry, which included Philip's regiment. At the small settlement of Jack's Shop, Stuart's men met Buford's division and quickly became engaged. As Stuart's horsemen swatted at the stronger foe, Kilpatrick's division moved into Stuart's rear, boxing them in, north and south.

General Stuart reacted quickly. He brought his artillery into play against both columns, while his cavalrymen charged front and rear. The brigade to which the 12th Regiment belonged was that day under the command of Colonel Oliver R. Funsten, a Clarke County physician turned soldier. Colonel Funsten moved his three regiments south on the Gordonsville Turnpike, passing through an open field, and into the woods beyond. His troopers smashed into Kilpatrick's advance brigade and swept it aside. Stuart quickly moved his division through this opening and moved back toward Liberty Mills, pursued by Buford and Kilpatrick. The pursuit was broken off near that point, as Stuart had moved to safety behind the lines of Confederate infantry at Liberty Mills.

Quiet descended upon the land once more, during which time many of the men received furloughs. Circumstances, however, soon caused the officers to recall the men.

Early in October, two corps of General Meade's Army of the Potomac left Virginia, thus reducing the force confronting General Robert E. Lee. Taking advantage of the more even odds, Lee led a fall offensive — turning the Federal right flank and getting into the rear of the Army of the Potomac.

To screen the movement from the Federals, Stuart sent Hampton's division to cover the right of the Confederate advance. At daybreak on October 10, Funsten's brigade left its comfortable camp near Madison Court House and moved out on the Sperryville Pike, headed toward Woodsville. The Bristoe Campaign was underway.

Despite their best efforts to remain under cover of the hills and woods, the Union cavalry soon discovered their movement and ascertained its intention. Meade pulled back from the Rappahannock, screening his movement with his cavalry. During the day, Company B of the 12th Regiment served as a bodyguard for Stuart, and occupied the advance of the column.[19]

On the morning of October 11, the Confederate advance came upon the 106th New York Infantry, in the rear of Meade's army, moving rapidly toward Culpeper. General Stuart immediately called for the nearest cavalry and ordered them to charge the enemy.

Colonel John Esten Cooke, an aide to Stuart, recalled the incident.

> Never had I seen him (Stuart) more excited. He was plainly on fire with the idea of capturing the whole party. The staff scattered to summon the cavalry, and soon a company came at full gallop. It was the "Jefferson Company," under that brave officer, Captain George Baylor. "Charge and cut them down," shouted Stuart, his drawn sword flashing as he forced his horse over fallen trees and debris of a great deserted camp. A fine spectacle followed. As the Federal infantry double-quicked up a slope, Baylor charged. As his men dared upon them, they suddenly halted, came to a front face, and the long line of gun barrels fell, as though they were parts of some glittering war machine. The muzzles spouted flame, and the cavalry received the fire at thirty yards. It seemed to check them, but it did not. They had come to an impassable ditch. In another moment the infantry broke, every man for himself, and, making a detour, the cavalry pursued and captured large numbers.[20]

Under normal circumstances, the Union fire should have decimated the ranks of the approaching cavalry. Fortunately for the advancing Confederates, a depression lay between them and the New Yorkers. At the moment the Northerners fired, Company B dropped into the depression, and the Minie balls passed over their heads.

General Stuart reported:

> This [his call] was gallantly responded to by a company of the Twelfth Virginia, under Lieutenant Baylor, and but for an impassable ditch these brave men would have ridden over the enemy and cut them down with the saber. They charged within 20 or 30 yards of the column and fired a volley into it, but were forced, from the nature of the ground, to retire, which was done without the loss of man or horse, although the enemy's fire was delivered almost in their faces. The enemy did not further contest the field. They broke and ran, dropping guns, knapsacks, and blankets, several of their number being captured.[21]

Making their way toward Fleetwood Hill, near Brandy Station, Stuart's men soon encountered more Union cavalrymen. Stuart reported:

> The Twelfth Virginia Cavalry, Lieutenant-Colonel Massie commanding, was at the head of the column, and being ordered to charge, did so in the most gallant manner, cutting off about 1,200 or 1,500 of the enemy, all of whom would have been killed or captured had not the headlong rapidity of the pursuit, added to the difficult character of the ground, so greatly extended the column as to impair for the moment its efficiency of action.[22]

Just as two North Carolina Regiments arrived to support the 12th Virginia, the enemy attacked them on their right. The Confederates broke and fled, despite the best efforts of Stuart and others to rally them. Fortunately, the 7th Virginia Cavalry arrived in time to drive off the attackers, and together the 7th and 12th moved to Brandy Station.

Charges and countercharges filled the remainder of the day. After dark, Stuart pulled back in the direction of Culpeper, while the Federals marched in the opposite direction. The second battle of Brandy Station was over.

On the morning of October 12, Stuart proceeded to protect the flank of Lee's infantry column, moving by Rixeyville toward Warrenton. Funsten's brigade occupied the front of General Ewell's column. When near Jeffersonton, the 11th Virginia Cavalry encountered the enemy's pickets and drove them in. It was discovered that approximately two regiments of cavalry were posted in the town, behind hills, fences and a stone wall enclosing a churchyard. The stronger force compelled the 11th Virginia Cavalry to fall back with a slight loss.

Colonel Funsten sent the 7th Virginia Cavalry to the left, while he proceeded with the 12th Virginia Cavalry to the right of the town. It was his intention to get behind the enemy and cut off their retreat. Lieutenant Baylor recalled:

> Reaching the road in the rear of Jeffersonton, Company B being in advance, we discovered a regiment of the enemy's led horses standing on the road leading to Jeffersonton, the men having gone forward and left them in charge of one man to each file of fours. A charge was ordered, meeting with little or no resistance and the rest of our regiment coming up, a large number of prisoners and horses were captured.[23]

The cavalrymen continued on to the Rappahannock River and Warrenton Springs, where Stuart intended to make his crossing. Reaching the crossing, the soldiers discovered a crude bridge, hardly more than a gangway of planks, across the river at this point.[24] To dispute their crossing, the Federals had deployed some artillery and dismounted cavalry near the banks of the river. Stuart ordered a force of dismounted men thrown against the defenders of the crossing, accompanied by some infantry and supported by artillery.

As this force futilely tried to force their way across the river, Stuart ordered Baylor to charge the enemy position. Lieutenant Baylor was a little reluctant to make the charge, but concluded, "a soldier's duty is to obey, do or die."[25] He later wrote:

> Assured that a bold front was half the battle, four brave men were placed in the rear of the company, with orders to shoot down the first man that fell back. Hearing the order, a member of the company plaintively remarked, "Well, boys, between death before and death behind, I will take death in front."[26]

General Stuart reported the results of the charge, stating that it "was gallantly done, Lieutenant Baylor's company leading, in face of heavy fire of sharpshooters. Such was the impetuosity of the charge that the enemy's sharpshooters who had not retired were speedily driven from their favorable position on the hills commanding the ford and a considerable number of them captured before they could escape."[27]

The Jefferson County soldiers had an audience on that October afternoon. Hundreds of infantrymen were watching the battle unfold before them. Among the observers were Generals Robert E. Lee, Stuart and R. S. Ewell. Baylor recalled the charge:

Down the road the company dashed amid a shower of bullets and reached the bridge over the river, to find the flooring torn up. Here we were forced to halt, face about and strike for a ford below. This movement was effected without faltering, and soon the river was crossed and the rifle-pits, with a large number of prisoners, in our possession.[28]

Major Henry McClellan, a member of Stuart's staff, called the fight "a gallant sight, [which] called forth wild huzzahs from the Confederate infantry." Baylor wrote that this was "the first and only occasion during the war, that I know or have heard of, where the infantry showed such appreciation of the cavalry."[29]

Perhaps most welcome of all was General Lee's token of appreciation. After the close of the Bristoe Campaign, Lee granted a ten-day furlough to the men of Company B for their gallantry at Warrenton Springs.

With a sufficient force of infantry now in place to hold the ford, Stuart ordered Funsten's and another brigade to advance to Warrenton. On their way to that place, the cavalrymen frequently skirmished with the enemy, finally going into camp that night at Warrenton.

On the morning of October 13, General Lee ordered Stuart to make a reconnaissance in the direction of Catlett's Station. At Auburn, Stuart posted Lomax's brigade as rear guard, and proceeded toward Catlett's Station with two brigades. After nightfall, Stuart learned that an enemy force occupied Auburn, again catching Stuart and his men between two Yankee columns.

Moving his command to the northern side of the road behind some hills, Stuart escaped detection. There, he put his guns into position, ready to fire, within three hundred yards of the enemy's line. The cavalrymen he held in close column, with strict orders to maintain silence. Everyone had an anxious night, each man expecting that the nearby enemy would discover him at any moment.

During the early part of the night, Stuart called upon Baylor for two volunteers to make their way through the lines and inform General Lee of their situation. These men, along with several others, all succeeded in making their way through the lines and reported to Lee. General Lee ordered troops to Stuart's aid, but they did not arrive in time to be of any assistance.

As day was breaking on the morning of October 14, Stuart realized that he must do something; else, the enemy would discover his men and destroy them. Baylor recalled what happened next:

> Orders were given to mount, our seven guns were advanced further on the brow of the hill, and all was ready for action. A few moments of suspense and our guns were raining canister upon the enemy, who, surprised, rushed in every direction. They soon, however, recovered from their fright, formed line of battle and began to move on our position, but, unable to stand the fire of our guns, gave way and disappeared behind the hills.[30]

About this time, an enemy force appeared on Stuart's left flank, the direction in which he hoped to make his escape. Stuart sent the 1st North Carolina

Cavalry out to meet this force, which succeeded in checking the enemy advance. Taking advantage of this temporary success, Stuart ordered his artillery and wagons to pass in rear of the enemy's position. He sent Companies B and I of the 12th Virginia Cavalry, under the command of Baylor, out on the road to Catlett's Station, to protect Stuart's left flank.

> Moving rapidly down to the point indicated, the squadron was formed across the road at the edge of a piece of woods, and the men directed to hold their fire until the enemy approached within thirty yards. We had not long to wait before the enemy's cavalry appeared in our front and, moving up to within 250 yards of our position, called to know what command we were. Having cautioned the men to remain quiet, no answer was given. Receiving no response, they moved cautiously about, gradually approaching nearer and nearer. After being detained by us for some time, they boldly moved a squadron forward, and when within thirty yards the order to fire was given, many saddles were emptied, and their squadron broke and fled in confusion.[31]

Baylor and his men now rejoined Stuart near Warrenton, where they received his congratulations.

On the 15th of October, Stuart moved Funsten's brigade toward Yates' Ford, near which the 12th Virginia engaged the enemy and drove them back. The following day, along with Hampton's division, the 12th Virginia Cavalry moved toward Groveton, skirmishing with the enemy, and drove them across Bull Run.

Determined to protect Washington, the Northern Army began to construct a line of entrenchments north of Bull Run. As a result, General Lee began a slow retreat. The Bristoe Campaign was drawing to a close.

The cavalry covered Lee's retreat down the Warrenton Pike, followed closely by Judson Kilpatrick's cavalry division. On October 19, Stuart and Kilpatrick clashed near Warrenton in a fight known as the Buckland Races. Following the fight, the 12th Virginia went into camp near Culpeper, where they began picketing the south bank of the Rappahannock.

Lieutenant Baylor noted the ensuing event in his recollections:

> On the morning after our return, Company B was agreeably surprised by an order from General Lee, received through General Stuart, granting the company a furlough of ten days, with permission to return to our homes in Jefferson [county], as a reward for gallant conduct at Warrenton Springs. A shout went up as we moved off for home, friends and relatives, and, notwithstanding the fact that those homes were with the Federal lines, no blockade was sufficient to keep us out, and the time was happily spent.[32]

Although Philip's home was in Bath County, he took the opportunity to visit his sister Emily in Jefferson County. He and his comrades returned to their regiment in Rappahannock County about the first of November.

About two weeks after their return, the brigade moved with Lee's army to the southern side of the Rapidan River. The brigade, now commanded by

Brigadier General Thomas L. Rosser, performed picket duty near Hamilton's Crossing.

In late November, Rosser's scouts reported a large force of Federal troops crossing the Rapidan at Germanna Ford, moving west on the Orange Plank Road. Evidently, General Meade was attempting to force Lee from his position along the Rapidan River.

Rosser moved his men to Todd's Tavern, at the southern end of the Wilderness. On the morning of November 27, he discovered the wagon trains of the Union First and Fifth Corps moving through the Wilderness on the Brock Road. Seizing the opportunity, Rosser struck. Baylor recalled:

> As we approached this road [Brock Road], the Twelfth regiment in front, Company B leading the advance, we rode into the wagon-train without opposition, and, turning to the right, moved some distance through the train before encountering any material force. On meeting a heavy infantry guard, a retreat was ordered, and we moved slowly back. We succeeded in destroying about 40 wagons and in bringing off about the same number, with seven ambulances, 230 mules and horses, and 95 prisoners.[33]

Following the day's work on the Brock Road, the brigade returned to Todd's Tavern and went into camp for the night.

The next day, the brigade moved along the Catharpin Road to Parker's Store, located on the Plank Road. Here they met a regiment of Northern cavalry and a brisk fight ensued. The 12th Virginia, along with the 35th Battalion, charged into the enemy, and "sweeping everything before them, killing, wounding, and capturing a large number and taking possession of their camp. They had just prepared breakfast. The coffee was smoking."[34]

A number of the Confederates proceeded to help themselves to the welcome meal, but not without cost. While taking their breakfast, the enemy suddenly charged upon them, taking many prisoners. A two-hour fight followed among the trees of the dense forest about Parker's Store. Finally, a North Carolina regiment arrived and drove the Federals back, leaving the position in Southern hands.

Toward the middle of December 1863, General Lee learned that several regiments of Yankee cavalry were moving from Winchester in the direction of Staunton. To counter the movement, Lee ordered Rosser's brigade to move into the Shenandoah Valley and cut off the retreat of the enemy.

Moving at dark on December 17, Rosser's men set out for the Valley. The next day brought misery in the form of a drenching rain, swollen streams and freezing conditions. The rain turned to sleet, increasing the suffering of man and beast. After capturing Sangster's Station, on the Manassas Gap Railroad, on the night of the 18th, Rosser and his weary men reached the vicinity of Upperville on the morning of December 19. There, he called a halt of an hour's duration, to allow the men and horses to rest and get something to eat. Pressing on, Rosser and his men arrived at Conrad's Store in Rockingham County, only to find that the enemy had escaped.

The commander allowed a rest of ten days at Mt. Jackson. The men shod and rested their horses, and enjoyed the Christmas holiday, as many of them were now close to their homes.

Only one letter between Emily Porterfield and Philip survives from 1863. Emily wrote her brother on December 18, informing him, "I have your clothes ready and wish you would come in for them, as I would not like to trust them in the care of any one going out."[35]

One additional bit of information can be learned from Emily's letter. It appears that Philip had a sweetheart in the Jefferson County area. Emily informed Philip: "I have not seen Lily since the receipt of your letter & consequently have not been able to deliver your message. She always seems pleased to hear from you. She told me to tell you that she cried because she missed seeing you when you were in last."[36]

As 1863 drew to a close, the men of Rosser's brigade were busy preparing for a new raid. General Lee needed meat for his hungry soldiers. Reports indicated that cattle could be found in the Patterson Creek Valley of Western Virginia. General Fitz Lee commanded the expedition, and set out to collect the cattle for the Confederacy.

On the second of January 1864, the raiders struck a wagon train in the South Branch Valley. They captured forty wagons loaded with ammunition, hides, and other stores. In addition, the raiders took 240 horses and mules, and 250 head of cattle. Moving to within a few miles of New Creek Station on the Baltimore and Ohio Railroad, a severe snowstorm hammered the Confederates, forcing them to return to the Shenandoah Valley.

It appears that Philip missed the excitement of this raid. Sometime in December 1863, the surgeon admitted him to the Staunton General Hospital for treatment of scabies. According to a hospital muster roll dated December 31, 1863, Philip was present at the hospital, and was improving.[37] He returned to his command sometime after January 13, 1864.

A second raid into West Virginia commenced in late January 1864, under the command of General Jubal A. Early. He ordered General Thomas's infantry brigade to accompany Rosser's cavalry brigade and McClanahan's battery back to the South Branch Valley. Arriving at Moorefield on the evening of January 29, General Early learned of a large Federal supply train moving from New Creek to Petersburg. The general ordered Rosser's cavalry to seize the prize.

Rosser and his men started out on the morning of the 30th, headed for a pass in the Patterson Creek Mountain. Near the pass, Rosser learned that huge amounts of downed timber choked the turnpike and 200 Union infantrymen protected the pass. They would have to literally cut their way through.

To protect the axmen, Rosser dismounted the 12th Virginia Cavalry and used them as sharpshooters to keep the Union infantrymen at bay. He sent the 1st Squadron (Baylor's) of the 12th Regiment to get behind the enemy's position.

Lieutenant Baylor's squadron succeeded in getting behind the enemy and attacked them at once. This finally dislodged the Union men, forcing them to pull back to their wagon train at Medley.

The wagon train, now aware of Rosser's presence, prepared for his attack. A thousand infantrymen protected the train of 95 wagons, parked on the road. Rosser again sent the 12th Regiment on a flanking movement, to get behind the wagon train.

After making a second frontal attack on the wagon train, the enemy began to slowly fall back. At about this time, the 12th Regiment appeared behind the enemy, and the retreat became a rush to safety.

The prize was a rich one. The wagons were loaded with corn, oats, bacon, rice, flour, beans, sugar, and coffee — in short, everything a hungry soldier needed for himself or his mount. In addition to these supplies, they captured 450 mules and 40 prisoners. Burning 40 of the wagons, Rosser's men brought the remainder back to the Shenandoah Valley. He arrived in the Valley on February 6, bringing with him over a thousand cattle and half as many sheep. This was only one of several successful raids into West Virginia carried out by Rosser in the coming year.

Sometime in January 1864, Philip wrote to his sister, probably soon after returning to his unit from Staunton. Only one page of the letter survives, in which Philip writes about idle time. He wrote that compared to "the hours that now hang so heavily on my hands with those spent so happily at Elmwood during the winter of 1862. You might infer that I am discontented with my lot — but such is not the case. I am cheerful & contented in the hope of a brighter & better day."[38]

Following their return to the Valley, the 12th Virginia Cavalry went into camp near Weyers Cave, between Staunton and Harrisonburg. The Kilpatrick-Dahlgren raid on Richmond broke the monotony of winter camp on the last day of February. Rosser's brigade started in pursuit about 8 p.m. on the 29th, marching across the Blue Ridge Mountains in a terrible ice storm, toward Charlottesville.

Onward they trudged, searching for their elusive enemy, reaching Spotsylvania Court House on March 3. Moving as far south as Hanover Junction on March 4, Rosser and his men found no trace of the raiders, so they returned to the Shenandoah Valley. The weary cavalrymen went into camp near Lexington, remaining there until the following month.

Because of the honors won on the field of battle during the previous year, Rosser's Brigade became known as the Laurel Brigade. Each man wore a badge of three laurel leaves on his hat, to let everyone know he was part of that honored brigade.

Philip, evidently on detached duty, was at Waynesboro, Virginia, on March 10, 1864. He took a spare moment to write to Emily Porterfield. The brief letter exhibited the change and depth of his feelings toward his enemies. He wrote

Emily that during "the first year of the war, I felt no animosity towards these vile beasts." He added, "I would give the last drop of my blood to see the Country rid of them finally & forever."[39]

Rejoining his regiment near the Natural Bridge, in Rockbridge County, Philip again wrote Emily. His April 10 letter was somewhat milder than the one written a month earlier. This time he gave her news of the family. Brother George and his family, he noted, are all well. Brother James had written George a long letter in which he spoke about the theory and practice of war. Philip said of his dear brother James: "I am afraid the Col's. vanity will be the death of him. He has two pets now — his Regiment & his "Boy." I sincerely hope that he may survive the war."[40]

With May came a new spring campaign. Generals U.S. Grant and Phil Sheridan now led the Union army against Richmond. The Laurel Brigade broke camp in Rockbridge County, and marched for eastern Virginia on May 1, arriving on General Lee's right flank three days later. Operating on the same ground where they fought the previous November, Rosser and his men quickly moved toward Todd's Tavern. The 1st Squadron of the 12th Regiment was in advance on that hot, spring day.

The Union forces had to maintain control of the intersection of the Catharpin and Brock Road at Todd's Tavern. Should they loose control of this vital point, Grant's army would be trapped in the Wilderness.

The first clash occurred eight miles west of the tavern, where the 1st Vermont Cavalry blocked Rosser's advance. General Rosser, who accompanied the advance, ordered the squadron to charge. Lieutenant Baylor recalled the charge:

> Off the squadron went, striking the enemy a blow which caused a panic and flight without much resistance. Rushing the advance back on its regiment, that also broke and joined in the retreat. Sabers were freely used on the retreating foe, and large numbers of them captured. Our advantage was pressed with vigor about two miles, when we ran into a brigade of the enemy drawn up to receive us, and so close was the pursuit that our front files passed through the enemy's line, with the fugitives, before the situation was realized.[41]

The Federal troops drove the Confederates back to Rosser's position. Both forces dismounted their regiments, and the fight continued in the thick pines bordering the Catharpin Road. After an hour, the Federals began to retreat. Rosser ordered his men to follow, but soon came under the fire of a Union battery, bringing his troops to a halt. Another charge became necessary.

Rosser's brigade, led by the 12th Virginia, rushed toward the Union position and eventually forced them to retire across the Po River. Throughout the remainder of the day, this scene repeated itself. The Union soldiers would retire and select a new position. This forced Rosser's cavalrymen to make another charge, at which point the Unionists would again retire. Nightfall found Rosser's Laurel Brigade on the western bank of the Po River, facing the divisions of James Wilson and Irvin Gregg.

The fight continued on May 6, both sides receiving heavy reinforcements. After a severe contest, which lasted all day, the Federals still maintained control of the vital intersection at Todd's Tavern. Among the handful of men from Company B, 12th Regiment wounded at Todd's Tavern that day was Philip Terrill. Only slightly wounded, it was enough to keep him out of service for a month or more. The regimental surgeon sent him to the Staunton General Hospital to recover.[42]

By early July, the Laurel Brigade was in camp on General Lee's right flank, on the Weldon Railroad, seven miles south of Petersburg. Here they remained during July and August, in relative peace, allowing the men to rest.

The next record of Philip places him near Stony Creek Depot, on the Weldon and Petersburg Railroad, in Surry County. He and a comrade had just returned to the regiment from the Shenandoah Valley. Whether he was just now returning from hospital, is unknown. Writing his sister on July 7, he informed her of his safe arrival at camp on the previous day, "after a journey of nine days of scorching sunshine & stifling dust, in a most lamentable state of exhaustion ... our horses wellnigh broken down. We could but feel bitter regret in leaving the Valley."[43]

Later that month, on the 31st, Philip again wrote Emily from his camp near Ream's Station, below Petersburg. He told her that other than being homesick, he was in good health.

> "We are all suffering intensely here," he wrote, "owing to the extreme heat & bad rations (corn bread made of unsifted meal) and everyone is praying for our command to be sent to Genl. Early's Army — but of that there is no probability & I fear I shall not revisit the Valley till the war ends, which God grant may be soon!"[44]

In early August, Hampton's division (including the Laurel Brigade) received orders to go to Culpeper and join General R. H. Anderson's command. After passing through Richmond, Hampton received a telegram recalling his division. The march back started at an early hour on the morning of August 14. On the following day, it joined General W. F. Lee's division at White's Tavern, eight miles below Richmond. After an engagement on the Charles City Road on August 18, Hampton returned to the vicinity of Ream's Station.

On the 23rd of August, Union infantry was discovered tearing up the track of the Weldon Railroad. That morning, Hampton's division met the Federal advance two miles west of Ream's Station at Monk's Neck Bridge, across Rowanty Creek. After a brief skirmish, the Federals withdrew to the station where they took up a position in some breastworks.

General Hampton now called for infantry support, intending to move against the Union position at Ream's Station. Part of General A. P. Hill's infantry corps arrived on the afternoon of August 25, and the attack began. The infantry occupied the left of the line, while Hampton's dismounted cavalry held the right. The 12th Virginia occupied the extreme right of the line that afternoon.

As the Confederates prepared to make the final push near sundown, the 12th Cavalry suddenly connected with the 12th Virginia Infantry. The infantry regiment, part of Hill's command, started out on the extreme left of the line, and in the course of the battle, advanced around the enemy's rear and met the Confederate right.

> When it was discovered there were two Twelfth Virginias side by side salutations were interchanged, and there was not a little bantering and boasting as to which of the two, the Twelfth Infantry or the Twelfth Cavalry, would be the first to reach and scale the ramparts in front of them. It was quite understood that there was to be a contest of valor, and bracing for the struggle, each regiment waited anxiously for the command to go forward.
> The two Twelfth regiments at the word "Charge!" went forward with noble rivalry, facing undaunted a heavy fire from the Federal artillery. For a brief space the race for glory was an even one; but, when near the works, the Twelfth Infantry halted to deliver its fire before rushing on. The Twelfth Cavalry never stopped, but with cocked pistols in hand, made straight for the breastworks, and leaping over them fairly won the race. The Federals fired one volley and, then throwing down their arms, fled precipitately.[45]

Three weeks of calm followed the battle of Ream's Station. Evidently, Philip's horse, which he reported as broken down in early July, did not get any better. On September 3, General Wade Hampton granted Philip a twenty-five day leave to procure a replacement. The order stated:

> The following members of Company B, 12th Regiment Virginia Cavalry, Rosser's Brigade, Hampton's Division, having given satisfactory evidence of their willingness and ability to procure horses in the place of those killed or lost, or rendered unserviceable in the service, will proceed, without delay, to their places of residence for that object, returning to their regiments within Twenty-five days, without fail.[46]

W. H. Taylor, Assistant Adjutant General for General Robert E. Lee, countersigned the order, effective on the 8th of September. On the reverse of the order, Lieutenant Baylor certified that Philip returned to duty on time, and brought with him a good horse.

On September 26, Rosser's Laurel Brigade received welcome news. The orders received directed them to return to the Shenandoah Valley. It was a homecoming of sorts for most of the men, as their homes lay in or near the Valley.

Their homecoming, however, was less than pleasant. Joining Jubal Early's command near Bridgewater on the evening of October 5, the men were distressed by the clouds of smoke that filled the air. Phil Sheridan and his soldiers were destroying the rich farms of the Shenandoah Valley.

The men of the Laurel Brigade, "blinded by rage at the sight of their ruined homes,"[47] pursued the Union rear guard vigorously. On the afternoon of October 7, the troopers caught up with the Union rear guard at Mill Creek. There the Confederates charged upon the rear of George Custer's division and shattered his line, forcing Custer to fall back to a hill near the main body of their army.

Rosser and his men crossed the stream and struck at Custer's force. "The Confederates, eager to get within sword range of the detested barn-burners, rode at them furiously. The Federals fought bravely, but could not withstand men who were seeking vengeance rather than victory."[48]

The Confederates continued to pursue the retreating Northern troops, until they reached Tom's Brook. Rosser, now far in advance of Early's infantry, suffered a severe defeat here on October 9.

Reforming his men, Rosser made another jab at Custer on October 16, but failed to surprise him. Following close on this attempt was the battle of Cedar Creek, which started out as a grand Confederate victory, but ended in a smashing defeat. General Early fell back to Fisher's Hill, and then continued on to New Market. Rosser's cavalry covered his rear, and formed their line near Stony Creek when Early finally halted. The next three weeks passed quietly, neither side attempting to strike the other.

In early November, on the 4th, Doctor George P. Terrill wrote Philip, expressing his fears for Philip's safety.

> I do most fervently pray that the same kind providence which has shielded you in the past from the missiles of the enemy and the diseases incident to exposure will continue to defend and preserve you in the future and that you may long live to enjoy the blessings of peace and independence.[49]

One can only guess whether Philip ever read these words—nine days later, he was dead.

The last known letter which Philip wrote to Emily was dated Camp of the 12th Va. Cavalry, Valley of Virginia, November 5, 1864. He wrote: "I have endured all manner of hardship & passed through many dangers since I saw you last. I have to thank a merciful God that I am still spared to enjoy the blessing of vigorous & unimpaired health."[50]

When Sheridan's forces fell back to a new position near Kernstown, Rosser and his men followed. On the 12th of November, at Cedar Creek, on the Back Road, they encountered a brigade of Custer's division. After a day of charges and countercharges, the Laurel Brigade fell back to Early's camp at Timberville.

During the final charge in the fighting near Middletown that November day, Philip was in the front ranks, where he fell mortally wounded. His comrades bore him from the field to the nearby house of a doctor. Along the way, Philip told one of his friends: "I am prepared to die and you must tell my father my last thoughts are of him."[51]

Lieutenant Baylor, in his recollections of the war, noted: "In this skirmish Company B lost Phil Terrill, killed; a soldier not only brave and courageous, but possessing many manly and social qualities."[52]

The esteem in which his comrades held Philip, as well as a glimpse of his character, appears in a biographical sketch of his life. Philip was "regarded by his companions in arms as a brave soldier and a perfect gentleman. He had no fondness for army life and its associations, his tastes were wholly different. A sense of duty always controlled his actions and conduct, inducing him to abandon his literary pursuits, of which he was passionately fond."[53]

Dr. J. H. Baldwin took Philip into his home and cared for him, but his wound was such that there was little the doctor could do. Philip clung to life until the following night, when he died.

Sometime after Philip's death, Doctor Baldwin wrote the following statement:

> Philip Terrill was wounded in the battle near my house on the 12th of November and died about 11 o'clock on the night of the 13th. Though he suffered much pain yet he bore his suffering with the fortitude of a soldier and maintained a firm composure of mind to the last. In sympathy for his fate we shed tears over his dying bed, and mourned the loss of one who appeared so noble in body and soul, and died a brave and glorious death for his country.
>
> J. H. Baldwin,
> Attending Physician.[54]

On November 24, 1864, while in Staunton, Virginia, William wrote to Major General Thomas L. Rosser, asking for news about his son.

> We are personally strangers to each other, but I trust you will pardon me for addressing you this letter when you shall have read it. I had a son, Philip M. Terrill, a private in the 12th Regiment of Virginia Cavalry, in your command who I understand was very badly wounded in an engagement with the public enemy on the 12 inst. but I have not heard from him since I beg of you the favour to inform me at your earliest convenience what has become of my brave boy.[55]

There is no record of Rosser's response to this father's plea. The old man made the painful journey to the Bath County Courthouse, where upon the pages of the Register of Deaths, he placed the name of his youngest son.

The following obituary appeared in one of Virginia's newspapers, announcing Philip's death.

> Obituary
> Killed in battle Nov. 12, 1864, near Middletown, in the 21st year of his age. His character was amiable, generous, and unselfish. He had the faculty of endearing himself to those who came within the sphere of his influence. A student at the University of Virginia when the war broke out, and though below the age, he buckled on his armor and joined the Confederate standard, bravely defending the freedom of his country till he fell among his comrades on the field. Gifted by nature with a high order of mind — indefatigable in the pursuit of knowledge, and possessing ample facilities of improvement — he had reached a high degree of cultivation in his studies. Shortly before receiving the mortal wound, he had united with a friend in prayer and afterwards requested him to say to his stricken father

(whose heart was already lacerated by the loss of two gallant sons) that he felt prepared and willing to die, and his last thought was of him.[56]

There is some speculation that Philip's death was the result of bold recklessness on his part. Some evidence in support of this appears in the biographical sketch of Philip's life: "For the last four or five months of his life he wielded the avenging saber, and wielded it with telling effect, with an arm nerved by the blood of his elder brother James, who fell upon the bloody field of Bethesda Church, on the 30th day of May 1864. They were devoted to each other."[57]

Philip must have had a premonition that he would fall in battle. Given the tone of his last letter to Emily, and comments made to one of the family servants. The last time that he visited home, he asked his favorite and trusted servant, "Lewis, take care of my father — I may never return."[58]

The final resting place of Philip Mallory Terrill, like many others, is unknown. The only clue to his burial indicates that he rests in the Shenandoah Valley — "kindly laid [in a grave] by the hands of weeping strangers."[59] Family members believe he is buried at Winchester.

Many years after the war his niece, Mrs. William Chase Morton, donated some of Philip's personal items and papers to The Museum of the Confederacy. The artifacts include his cartridge box (with his name and regiment, 62nd Virginia Infantry, written inside), wallet, tobacco bag, several Virginia buttons, a penholder and a bullet. Mrs. Morton also donated his commission as a 1st Lieutenant and a biographical sketch.

Appendix I: Address at the Burial of Brig. Gen. William R. Terrill

In Memoriam. Address at the Burial of Brig. Gen. William R. Terrill, October 16th, 1862, by the Rev. Alexander G. Cummins, in Christ Church, Reading, Pennsylvania.

Address.

"Ye shall die like men, and fall like one of the Princes.—Ps. LXXXII,7.

The Almighty Governor of the worlds, whose providence never faileth to order all things, both in heaven and earth, in His inscrutable wisdom has summoned to his Savior the soul of Brigadier-General William R. Terrill.

What mean these tokens of grief? these habiliments of mourning? Why do the people press into the courts of the Lord's sanctuary? Ah! they feel that one who was a man among men is dead; one who was a prince in battle, has fallen like one of the princes!

You are assembled to honor the memory of the heroic dead with hearts bowed in sorrow for the death of one who is lost not only to his family and relatives, but to you and to his country. Your loss, my friends, is indeed the nation's loss.

The country weeps with you to-day. Her heart bleeds for this her faithful son and brave defender, who lies cold in death, never more to unfurl her standard of freedom, — never more to plant her batteries against the ranks of invading enemies, or to marshal brigades on bloodstained fields for the nation's life and the nation's glory. You do well to weep for him: the country does well to weep. Ah! yes. We are gathered around the remains of a General who offered his body a willing sacrifice on the altar of his country. Nor only that; but a sacrifice which must have cost him a struggle in that manly heart of hearts, whose severity and duration could be realized only by one who should be placed in precisely similar circumstances.

General Terrill was a Virginian by birth. Among the hills of Virginia he received his early training from parents who loved him as the son of bright promise, and watched the progress of his studies and the unfolding of his intellect with unwonted parental solicitude. Finding that his mind turned with strong inclination to the military profession, they sent him to West Point. His career there distinguished him above his fellows; and his faithful habits of application to study, and the thoroughness of his acquirements, secured for him, at the end of the allotted term of study, the appointment of Assistant Professor in that institution. Although he received his professional education in the North, all his natural connections were with the South. At the age of not full twenty-eight years, when he was called upon to decide what should be his personal position toward the Government of the United States in its great crisis, he was young enough to be both impressible and impulsive; yet being morally mature above his years, he acted with sublime independence and patriotic devotion.

When the nation was first plunged into the fiery furnace of rebellion; when men's hearts were failing them for fear, in view of the mighty calamity which was rending society into fragments and ruthlessly severing the dearest ties of family and friendship; when men in the North were hurrying to their relatives in the South to fight against the flag which had protected them; and men in the South were banding together in solid masses to strike for what they called their liberty, and were branding all who clung to the Union as miscreants, General Terrill calmly surveyed the melancholy scene of desertion and treason, and firmly stood by the flag of his beloved country, which now infolds his body for the burial. His father urged him, with earnest and tearful entreaties, to join hands with his Southern relatives and friends. His ears were filled with the supplication of those most nearly allied to him, both in social and military bonds, at the South, and the most liberal offers of rank and position in the rebel army were made to him by men occupying high places, with many of whom he enjoyed intimacy and relationship. But notwithstanding all this pressure and temptation, he unfalteringly stood by the Union and the Constitution, resolved to die in their defense. Nothing could shake his lofty purpose. Nothing could swerve him from his conscientious duty. No rank or honor could tempt him from his allegiance. Like a rock, amid the lashings of the storm-tossed waves, he stood nobly by the old State ship, which was riding almost rudderless upon the angry sea of revolution. But the severest trial was to see the love of parents and friends changing into hatred. When they found that all their efforts were unavailing to win him to their cause, they not only fell off from him, but also banished him from their fellowship. In place of entreaties, they now hurled taunts and threats of the most stinging nature at him. But dauntless, he moved above them all. Was there no sacrifice? Was there not genuine patriotism?

I have said that General Terrill was a Virginian by birth. True; but the boundaries of no one State measured his patriotism. It extended from the mountains of Maine to the plains of Texas and the golden shores of California. He loved not Virginia alone, but his whole country. His heart could beat for every State; it had a chord for them all, which could vibrate for the weal or woe of each. His self-love was second to his love of country. It was first only as the poet has described it:

> Self-love but serves the virtuous mind to wake,
> As the small pebble stirs the peaceful lake;
> The centre moved, a circle straight succeeds,
> Another still, and still another spreads;
> Friend, parent, neighbor, first it will embrace,
> His country next, and next all human race.

The brave officer whose death we mourn, was well known to many of you, my brethren. Here in your streets you met and talked with him. You know what success attended his labors while recruiting as Captain in your midst. You saw his manly form and prince-like bearing. You looked upon the gallant Captain with pride. You had augured valiant service on the field of strife; and perhaps you prayed that it might be long-continued. Valiant service there was; but God decreed it to be not long-continued. To His will it is our part to bow in submission. And oh! why not? God holds in His hands the times and seasons. "He does not willingly afflict or grieve the children of men." "He hath done all things well."

And is there no consolation in the fact that the General died like a hero?

When engaged in the dreadful conflict which proved to be his last, the issue seemed to hang in awful doubt, and the soldiers of our army were holding back from the face of carnage, which shook the earth and scattered death; he advanced to the front, where the iron hail was falling in blasting showers, and with that calmness and self-possession so characteristic of his nature, cheered on his men, and then quietly went to the batteries to sight the pieces for more effective fire. Whilst there so engaged, a shell bursting in mid-air over his head sent a fragment of iron to his breast, and the brave General Terrill fell with a mortal wound. He fell "like one of the princes." The ambulance carried him from the field. With his faithful attendants around him he lingered for a short time, and then God took the soul of the hero to Himself. How are the mighty fallen, and the weapons of war perished!

General Terrill was no less a Christian than a patriot soldier. His eminent virtue endeared him to all who knew him. He lived in communion with the Episcopal Church, and was faithful in the discharge of all his religious duties. Indeed, his Christian life, for vigorous faith in salvation by Jesus Christ, for self-denial, and charity and zeal in the spread of the Gospel, was a beautiful pattern, in every way worthy of imitation both by the civilian and the soldier. He loved his Savior as much amid the stirring scenes of the camp as in the quiet retreat of home, and under the sweet influences of the family circle. He was a practical Christian, and made his religion felt by all those with whom he came into contact. The service of the Church, as contained in the Prayer-book, he was accustomed to read to his men on each Lord's day. Thus he never forgot the Captain of his salvation; but always endeavored to serve Him by his prayers and example.

The oath which bound him to serve his country he viewed as a high and holy thing, — as made unto God, and not with men. Whatever might have been his inclinations by nature, under the effectual guidance of Divine grace, he was so rooted and grounded in the principle of obedience to the powers constituted of God supreme, that he could not for a moment contemplate the violation of an obligation which, though assumed on earth, was witnessed to in heaven, without a shudder. Noble Christian was he when compared with many who cast off the same obligation without a scruple! If the pure principles of Christ's Gospel had ruled the hearts and minds of our earring brethren as his spirit was ruled, it is easy to see that there would have been no rebellion to quell, no war to wage, and no wounds of country to heal. We should cherish the memory of such an example, so notable for the love of country and the love of Christ. His is a rare example; and we should direct the eyes of young men, who are leaving home and its religious influences for the toils and turmoil of the campaigns of the army, to the pattern — the Christian pattern — which the life of General Terrill has wrought.

Life's loom stops only with death: it weaves through sleep. The pattern at sunset grows till sunrise. Death snaps the thread and cuts short the pattern. Let us trust that his shall increase, though he be dead, and increase till its counterpart shall be woven in the characters of many who have gone to the defense of justice and truth. And now let us go to the grave which shall receive all that embodied the virtues of the loving husband, the good and brave officer, the pure patriot, and the faithful Christian. He is now at rest. The sword is laid aside for the scepter of kingship with Christ. The word of command is merged in perfect obedience to God. We may not sorrow any more; "for if we believe that Jesus died and rose again, even so them also which sleep in Jesus will God bring with Him."

Appendix II:
Terrill Burial Monument Myth

Twenty-one years after the end of the Civil War, the following story appeared in *The State*, a Richmond newspaper.

> In Bath county, Virginia, there lives a very prominent family by the name of Terrill. Before the war it cut considerable of a swath in the social and political life of that section. The father brought the remains of his two gallant sons home and buried them on the farm, where both had spent their childhood days, and where they had grown to manhood, and there parted over a question of duty to State or nation. Both had laid down their lives for their sentiments. Between the simple graves of the two boys the father has erected a marble slab. A most touching inscription is cut in the white stone. It chides neither one. It expresses faith in the Creator and leaves Him to judge of his two heroes' conduct. It is a simple line and reads: "God only knows which one was right."[1]

This is the earliest known account of the burial of the Terrill brothers, and the monument erected to their memory. An earlier account, dated 1882, mentions only a Virginian burying his sons and erecting the monument.[2] The account did not mention any names.

This story, often repeated during the ensuing one hundred years, has appeared in print and on the World Wide Web. Several versions of the story appeared in the *National Geographic, Confederate Veteran,* and *The Saturday Evening Post*. The story has also been repeated in a number of books relating to the Civil War.

Who first penned these lines? This remains a mystery. The late Ezra Warner noted in a February 1954 letter, that the story was probably the "'brain-child' of a romantically inclined newspaperman of the day."[3] A recent biographical sketch of William R. Terrill attributes the story to "an unscrupulous war correspondent from Harper's Weekly."[4]

An undated and unidentified newspaper clipping found among the papers from the estate of Mrs. John (Ann) Porterfield, gives another account of the creation of the myth. An unknown writer noted that he had visited Warm Springs in 1918, looking for the graves and monument to the Terrill brothers. Not finding either, he visited attorney John W. Stephenson, and asked him about the monument.

Stephenson laughed and said the monument story had been created in his office during the 1890s. War correspondent and reporter Richard Harding Davis spent several summers at The Homestead while working for the *New York Herald*. One day he visited Stephenson, and the subject of the Terrill family came up. Upon learning the story of the two generals, Davis commented that "these two sons ought to have a monument." He then wrote a story for the *Herald*, creating the story of the Terrill monument. According to Davis, the monument took the shape of a cube, inscribed on opposing sides:

> Sacred to the Memory of William Rufus Terrill, Born _____, [sic] Brigadier General, U.S.A., Killed in Action at Perryville, October 8, 1862.
> Sacred to the Memory of James Barbour Terrill, Born _____, [sic] Brigadier General, C.S.A., Killed in Action at Bethesda Church, May 31, 1864.[5]

On an intervening face of the monument, appeared the phrase "God Knows Who Was Right."[6] Stephenson told his 1918 visitor that the monument never existed.

Terrill Hill historic marker near Warm Springs, Virginia. "Nearby is the site of Terrill Hill, home of the Terrill brothers of Bath County. Brigadier General William R. Terrill, a graduate of West Point, commanded a Union Brigade and was killed in the Battle of Perryville, Kentucky, October 8, 1862. His brother, Brigadier General James B. Terrill, a graduate of the Virginia Military Institute, served with General A.P. Hill's 13th Regiment, Virginia Infantry and died in the Battle of the Wilderness, May 31, 1864.* Legend says their father erected a monument to his sons with the inscription 'God alone knows which was right'." [*The paperwork announcing a promotion to brigadier general arrived just after his death.] (Author's photograph.)

During the early 1900s, and as late as the 1980s, many have looked for the fabled monument, but could not find it. Family members spent countless hours searching the hillsides about Warm Springs for the monument. They talked to the older residents of the area, who could not recall ever hearing that the two brothers were buried here, and had never seen any such monument. One elderly woman told them of two graves on the old Terrill property. It was determined that these graves were the final resting place of Jeremiah Morton Terrill and John Allen Terrill, and not the generals.

Taking into account the fact that no one at Warm Springs had ever seen the graves or the monument, they finally arrived at the conclusion that it simply did not exist. In addition, Colonel William H. Terrill was financially ruined by the war, and did have the resources to have the remains of his beloved sons brought back home. Neither did he have the means to erect a monument to their memory.

Chapter Notes

Chapter I

1. William's date of birth also appears as July 20, 1800. He is known to have had a brother and two sisters: George Terrill (1798–1893), Navy surgeon and businessman; Jane Terrill (1801–1867), who married George Mason Pilcher; and Sarah (Sara) Morton Terrill (1807–1849), who married John William Yancey.
2. Howard R. Hammond to author, July 8, 2007.
3. Evelyn Lee Moore, *The Terrill's of Bath*, unpublished typescript in author's possession; Reminiscences of Cornelia Heywood Wise Moore, Moore-Wise Family Papers, MS1361, Jones Memorial Library, Lynchburg, Va.
4. Superior Court Order Book, 1822–1830, Alleghany County Circuit Court, Covington, Va.
5. Elizabeth Pitzer was born in Botetourt County, Va., March 24, 1805.
6. Oren F. Morton. *A Centennial History of Alleghany County, Virginia* (Bridgewater, VA.: Carrier, 1970), p. 149.
7. Bath County Circuit Court Records, Warm Springs, Va.
8. William H. Terrill to Dr. George Morton, Charleston, Kanawha Co., Va., December 29, 1837. Papers of the Related Morton and Dickinson Families of Orange and Caroline Counties, Va., 1727–1978, Accession #9755a, Box 1, Folder Correspondence 1836–1837. Albert and Shirley Small Special Collections, University of Virginia Library, Charlottesville, Va. Hereafter cited as Morton-Dickinson Papers.
9. Evelyn Lee Moore correspondence with the author.
10. George Terrill to William H. Terrill, September 3, 1845. Terrill Papers, Bath County Historical Society, Warm Springs, Va. Hereafter cited as Terrill Papers, BCHS.
11. William H. Terrill to Emily C. Terrill, Warm Springs, December 5, 1845. Terrill Family Papers, Porterfield Estate, Bath County Historical Society, Warm Springs, Va. Hereafter cited as Terrill Family Papers, PE.
12. G. A. Porterfield to Mrs. Elizabeth Terrill, Buena Vista, 10th October 1847. Porterfield Family Papers, Jefferson County Historical Society, Charles Town, W. Va. George Porterfield refers to Sarah as "Mrs. McDaniel [McDannald]," indicating that she was married by this time. Hereafter cited as Porterfield Papers, JCHS.
13. Board of Visitors Records, Virginia Military Institute Archives, Lexington, Va.
14. Philip St. George Cooke (1808–1861), a graduate of West Point in 1832, became a planter in Virginia and Mississippi, and a Confederate Brigadier General.; Charles James Faulkner (1806–1884) in 1848 was a member of the Virginia House of Delegates, and in 1851 was elected to the House of Representatives in the U.S. Congress; John B. Floyd (1806–1863) in 1848 was a member of the Virginia Legislature, and in 1849 became governor of Virginia, and Secretary of War in 1857; George W. Mumford (Munford) served as secretary of the Commonwealth under Governor John Letcher, 1859 to 1863.
15. 1850 Census of the United States, Bath County, Va.; 1850 Slave Census of the United States, Bath County, Va. National Archives, Washington, D.C.
16. *Lexington Gazette*, August 29, 1850. Sarah's husband's name is spelled McDonald, but should be McDannald.
17. William H. Terrill to Emily Porterfield, Warm Springs, Va., October 27, 1851. Terrill Family Papers, PE.
18. Elizabeth Terrill to Martha Ann Smith, July 20, 1853. Typescript, Bath County Historical Society, Warm Springs, Va.

19. *Ibid.*
20. *Ibid.*
21. Evelyn Lee Moore correspondence with author.
22. Reminiscences of Cornelia H. Wise Moore, Moore–Wise Family Papers, MS1361, Jones Memorial Library, Lynchburg, Va.
23. William H. Terrill to John Allen Terrill, Warm Springs, November 10, 1855. Terrill Family Papers, PE.
24. Obituary of Elizabeth Pitzer Terrill, William T. Price Papers and Scrapbooks, Pocahontas County Historical Society, Marlinton, W. Va.; Death Records, Bath County Circuit Court, Warm Springs, Va.; Obituary of John Allen Terrill, Moore–Wise Family Papers, MS1361. Jones Memorial Library, Lynchburg, Va.
25. William H. Terrill to Dr. George Morton, Warm Springs, Va., February 7, 1858. Morton-Dickinson Papers, Box 1, Folder 1858–1875.
26. Philip M. Terrill to Emily Porterfield, February 7, 1858. Terrill Family Papers, PE.
27. William H. Terrill to Jane Pilcher, March 9, 1858. Terrill Family Papers, PE.
28. William H. Terrill to Emily Porterfield, Highland County, October 24, 1858. Terrill Family Papers, PE.
29. William H. Terrill to Emily Porterfield, Warm Springs, November 10, 1858. Terrill Family Papers, PE.
30. Marriage Record, Alleghany County Circuit Court, Covington, Va. Rachel Cameron Scott, daughter of James and R. Hamilton, was born in Bath County, Va., about 1807. She was first married to Dr. Andrew Moore Scott (1802–1839) on February 21, 1826, in Bath County, Va. Left with four daughters to raise, Rachel became a good businesswoman, and was prominent in the business and social circles of Covington. The Scotts and Terrills lived near each other on Bath Street (now Main Street) during the early 1830s. Rachel was a member of the First Presbyterian Church in Covington.
31. William R. Terrill to G. A. Porterfield, In Camp near Coxsackie, June 30, 1859. On the Hudson River doing Coast Survey duty. Terrill Family Papers, PE.
32. 1860 Slave Census of the United States, Bath County, Va., National Archives, Washington, D.C.
33. Poll Books, Bath County Circuit Court, Warm Springs, Va.
34. James B. Terrill to G. A. Porterfield, Warm Springs, Feb. 8, 1861. Terrill Family Papers, PE.
35. When tallied, the votes amounted to 132,201 in favor of secession, and 37,451 against secession.

36. Telegram, W. B. [H.] Terrill to Gov. Letcher, Staunton, April 22, 1861, Reel 4728, exposure 197–98. Virginia. Governor (1860–1864: Letcher). Executive papers of Governor John Letcher, 1859–1863. Accession 36787. State Government Records Collection, The Library of Virginia, Richmond, Va. 23219 Hereafter cited as Letcher Executive Papers.
37. *Bath County Historical Society Newsletter* 31, no. 2 (July 2001), p. 5.
38. C. B. Hopkins to President Davis, Healing Springs, Bath Co., Va., June 10, 1861. Letters Received by the Confederate Secretary of War, No. 1490. National Archives, Washington, D.C.
39. *Ibid.*
40. William H. Terrill to Gov. Letcher, Beverly, 24 June 1861. Letcher Executive Papers, Reel 4747, exposure 314.
41. County Court Orders, Bath County Circuit Court, Warm Springs, Va.
42. John Letcher to Jefferson Davis, February 11, 1862. Confederate Papers Relating to Citizens or Business Firms (M-346), William H. Terrill file, National Archives, Washington, D.C. Hereafter cited as Citizens Papers.
43. *Ibid.*
44. William H. Terrill to His Excellency President Davis, March 7, 1862. Citizens Papers
45. William R. Terrill to E. M. Stanton, March 28, 1862. Letters Received by the U.S. Secretary of War. National Archives, Washington, D.C.
46. Citizens Papers, William H. Terrill file.
47. "Col. William H. Terrill." *The Spirit of Jefferson*, Charles Town, W. Va., January 15, 1878.
48. John Letcher to Jefferson Davis, October 28, 1862. Citizens Papers, William H. Terrill file.
49. "To the Editors of the Enquirer," *Richmond Enquirer*, Richmond, Va., November 20, 1862. The corrections noted by Colonel Terrill appear in the section on General William R. Terrill.
50. The Reverend Price is mistaken in the statement that General W. R. Terrill was born in the home at Warm Springs. He was instead born in Covington, Virginia, and was raised at Rose Hill near Warm Springs, Virginia. William T. Price Papers, Pocahontas County Historical Society, Marlinton, W. Va.
51. "The Late Fight in Greenbrier." *Richmond Sentinel*, Richmond, Va., September 15, 1863.
52. William H. Terrill to John Letcher, Richmond, June 22, 1864. John Letcher Papers, 1790–1970, Virginia Historical Society Hereafter cited as Letcher Papers, VHS. The location of the grave is discussed further in the section on General James B. Terrill.
53. *Ibid.*

54. George B. Terrill to Philip M. Terrill, November 4, 1864. Terrill Family Papers, PE.
55. "Wm. H. Terrill, Esq." *Pocahontas Times*, Marlinton, W. Va., March 28, 1912.
56. William H. Terrill to Major General Thomas L. Rosser, November 24, 1864. Thomas L. Rosser Papers, 1860–1950, #1171, 1171a, 1171b, Albert and Shirley Small Special Collections, University of Virginia Library, Charlottesville, Va.
57. William H. Terrill to Emily Porterfield, January 15, 1865. Terrill Family Papers, PE.
58. *Ibid.*
59. *Ibid.*
60. *Ibid.*
61. *Ibid.*
62. William H. Terrill to A. D. Campbell, January 7, 1870. Terrill Papers, BCHS.
63. William H. Terrill to Emily Porterfield, January 15, 1865. Terrill Family Papers, PE.
64. "Ups and Downs of an Ex-Confederate Soldier" *Hampshire Review*, Romney, W. Va., Jan. 27, 1865.
65. William H. Terrill to Jeremiah Morton, Warm Springs, March 17, 1866. Morton-Halsey Collection, 1786–1938, Accession #3995, Box 1, Folder Jan–July 1866. Special Collections, Alderman Library, University of Virginia, Charlottesville, Va. Hereafter cited as Morton-Halsey Papers.
66. William H. Terrill to Emily Porterfield, January 8, 1866. Terrill Family Papers, PE.
67. William H. Terrill to Jeremiah Morton, Warm Springs, Va., March 17, 1866. Morton-Halsey Papers, Box 1, Folder Jan–July 1866.
68. Section 3, Fourteenth Amendment, Constitution of the United States.
69. William H. Terrill to Emily Porterfield, April 15, 1868. Terrill Family Papers, PE.
70. Evelyn Lee Moore, *The Terrill's of Bath*, unpublished typescript in possession of the author.
71. H. R. 1880, 40th Congress, 3d Session. Library of Congress, Washington, D.C.
72. Howard R. Hammond correspondence with author; Register of Communicants, Session Records, Vol. 1, Warm Springs Presbyterian Church, Warm Springs, Va.
73. Hustings—defined as a place where political campaign speeches are made.
74. "The Late Col. W. H. Terrill." *Spirit of Jefferson*, Charles Town, W. Va., December 25, 1877.

Chapter II

1. The uncle's name was Dr. George Terrill, with no middle name.
2. Record of Baptisms, Session Records, Volume I, Warm Springs Presbyterian Church, Warm Springs, Va.
3. The term Pay Cadet is used to identify those cadets not appointed by the governor and who had to pay tuition.
4. George Terrill to William H. Terrill, September 3, 1845. William H. Terrill Papers, Bath County Historical Society, Warm Springs, Va. Hereafter cited as Terrill Papers, BCCH.
5. William H. Terrill to Emily C. Terrill, Warm Springs, October 25, 1845. Terrill Family Papers, Porterfield Estate, Bath County Historical Society, Warm Springs, Va. Hereafter cited as Terrill Family Papers, PE.
6. Order Books, Virginia Military Institute Archives, Lexington, Va. Hereafter cited as VMI Archives.
7. Order Books, Order No. 40 and 41, VMI Archives.
8. Geo. P. Terrill, Rd. Pollard, and Benjamin F. Ficklin to His Excellency James K. Polk, Military Institute, Lexington, Va., Dec. 31st, 1847. Records of the Office of the Secretary of War, 1791–1947, Record Group 107, Entry 620, Applications for Appointment to Civilian or Military Positions, 1820–87.
9. F. H. Smith to William H. Terrill, April 12, 1848, Superintendents Outgoing Correspondence, Virginia Military Institute Archives, Lexington, Va. Hereafter cited as Superintendents Correspondence, VMI Archives.
10. F. H. Smith to William H. Terrill, June 10, 1848, Superintendents Correspondence, VMI Archives.
11. William H. Terrill to Colonel F. H. Smith, Warm Springs, January 24 (21), 1849. Superintendents Correspondence, VMI Archives.
12. Francis "Frank" Heath Terrill, born at Salem, February 27, 1854, attended the University of Virginia and the postgraduate course at Philadelphia as a physician; he began practice in 1873, and served in the U.S. Navy until 1884. He entered into private practice in San Francisco, California, where he died of smallpox in 1888. It is thought that he married, but did not have any children.
13. Elizabeth Dold Terrill married William T. Duncan on October 7, 1874, and lived in Denver, Colorado, where she died January 8, 1939. She gave birth to ten children, 8 of whom were living in 1900: George Terrill (1875–1929), Joseph Morton (1876–1918), Sarah Dold (1878–1966), Annalou (1881–1983), Jessie Wrok (1884–1884), Frances Heath Terrill (1885–?), Elizabeth McClanahan (1887–1977), William Emeric (1889–1890), Samuel Terrill (1891–1935), and Philip Kenneth (1896–1965).
14. William H. Terrill applied for appointment to the U.S. Military Academy, but was

unsuccessful. He became a traveling salesman and lived in New York City and Boston. He died in Detroit, Michigan, on March 17, 1932, and is buried in East Hill Cemetery, Salem, Va.

15. George Morton Terrill — born at Salem, on February 22, 1859, like his father, became a physician, attending Roanoke College and graduating from the University of Pennsylvania in 1883. Returning to Salem, he practiced here until 1885, when he moved to the Pacific Coast. He served in the U.S. Army as acting assistant surgeon in the Apache campaign of 1885 to 1886, and later served as brigade surgeon and Colonel of the 1st Regiment of Infantry, California National Guard, 1888 to 1898. He married Annie Marian Hutton in San Francisco in June 1899, but had no children. Annie Marian Terrill died in San Francisco on July 17, 1941, and George died on February 28, 1945.

16. William McCauley. *History of Roanoke County, Salem, Roanoke City, Virginia and Representative Citizens* (Chicago: Biographical, 1902), p. 148. Hereafter cited as McCauley.

17. Maria Louisa Terrill married James Morton Spencer, a Presbyterian minister. The Spencers lived in St. Louis, Missouri, where they raised their large family. Louisa died in St. Louis in 1900. Their children were Frank T., Mary S., James M. Jr., Sarah B., Lulu G., Frances B., Anna G., John G., Lillian and Elizabeth.

18. Notes regarding George Parker Terrill, Moore–Wise Family Papers, MS1361, Jones Memorial Library, Lynchburg, Va. Exactly what George's medical condition was is not known.

19. Officers of 157th Virginia Militia and Citizens of Roanoke to Governor Letcher, Salem, July 23, 1861, Reel 4751, exposure 164–167. Virginia. Governor (1860–1864: Letcher). Executive Papers of Governor John Letcher, 1859–1863. Accession 36787. State Government Records Collection, The Library of Virginia, Richmond, Va. Hereafter cited as Letcher Executive Papers.

20. *Ibid.*

21. George P. Terrill to Governor John Letcher, Salem, Reel 4751, exposure 49–50. Letcher Executive Papers.

22. Officers of 157th Virginia Militia and Citizens of Roanoke to Governor Letcher, Salem, July 23, 1861, Reel 4751, exposure 164–167. Letcher Executive Papers.

23. *Ibid.*

24. Janet B. Hewett, ed., *Supplement to the Official Records of the Union and Confederate Armies* (Wilmington, NC: Broadfoot, 1994), Vol. 73, p. 77–78.

25. McCauley, p. 147; Letters Received by the Confederate Secretary of War, M-437, Roll 106, 196-P-1863. National Archives, Washington, D.C.

26. Anna Carter Johnston Terrill married John E. Bushnell, a Lutheran minister, and lived at Luray and Blacksburg, Va., Oakland, California, and finally Detroit, Michigan, where she died July 21, 1953. She gave birth to seven children: George, Charles, Sarah, John Jr., William, Samuel, and Margaret. George E. Bushnell, her eldest son, became the chief justice of the Michigan Supreme Court.

27. Letcher Executive Papers, Reel No. 4779, exposure 247.

28. Darrell L. Collins. *General William Averell's Salem Raid: Breaking the Knoxville Supply Line* (Shippensburg, PA: Burd Street Press, 1998), p. 53. Hereafter cited as Collins.

29. United States War Department. *The War of the Rebellion: Official Records of the Union and Confederate Armies* (Washington, D.C.: Government Printing Office, 1880–1901), Vol. 29, p. 668. Hereafter cited as OR.

30. OR, Vol. 29, p. 668
31. *Ibid.*, part 2, p. 722–723
32. *Ibid.*, p. 712, p. 735
33. *Ibid.*, Vol. 30, part 4, p. 753.
34. *Ibid.*, Vol. 29, part 2, p. 796.
35. *Ibid.*, p. 797
36. *Ibid.*, p. 822
37. *Ibid.*, p. 827
38. *Ibid.*, p. 875
39. Collins, p. 53.
40. *Ibid.*, p. 54.

41. Jeffrey C. Weaver, *The Virginia Home Guards* (Lynchburg, VA: Howard, 1996), p. 108.

42. Samuel Miller Dold Terrill, like his father and brothers, followed the medical profession. At one time, he served as a surgeon on a Pacific Mail Line steamer. He married about 1898, while in Sacramento, California, then returned to Virginia. He practiced medicine in Shenandoah County (1900), Salem (1910), and by 1920 was back in San Francisco, California, where he died on August 2, 1943. He and his wife, Mabel, had four children: Samuel M., Lula (Leila) Belle, William H., and George S.

43. George P. Terrill to P. M. Terrill, Salem, November 4, 1864. Terrill Family Papers, PE.

44. George M. Pitzer and David E. Harris to Hon. J. C. Breckenridge, Secretary of War, March 27, 1865. George M. Pitzer file, Confederate Papers Relating to Citizens or Business Firms (M-346), National Archives, Washington, D.C.

45. McCauley, p. 148.

46. "Painful Accident," *The Salem Register*, Salem, Virginia, April 28, 1876.

47. His date of death is also reported as November 4, 1884; Obituary of George P. Terrill, Moore–Wise Family Papers, MS1361, Jones Memorial Library, Lynchburg, Va.

48. Obituary of George P. Terrill, Moore-Wise Family Papers, MS1361, Jones Memorial Library, Lynchburg, Va.
49. Obituary in possession of author.

Chapter III

1. Mrs. Maria Sheffey and the Rev. James McElroy, an Episcopal minister, established the Virginia Female Institute on January 1, 1844. This school became Stuart Hall in 1906. Tuition in 1845 amounted to about $125 per year.
2. William H. Terrill to Emily C. Terrill, Warm Springs, June 13, 1845. Terrill Family Papers, PE.
3. Frank B. Porterfield, *The Porterfields* (Roanoke, VA: Southeastern Press, 1985), p. 291-294.
4. William Terrill Porterfield, nicknamed "Willie," was killed by a playmate August 2, 1862, while playing with an "empty" gun.
5. Elizabeth Morton Porterfield, nicknamed "Bettie." According to a letter written by Elizabeth Terrill, her name was Mary Elizabeth. She married Henry Harrison Cooke, October 2, 1877. Children: Emily Terrill Cooke (1878-1916), Edward Esten Cooke (1880-1926), Elizabeth M. Cooke (1885-1885). Elizabeth died April 1, 1885; Elizabeth Terrill to Martha Ann Smith, July 20, 1853, (typescript), William H. Terrill Papers, Bath County Historical Society, Warm Springs, Va.
6. Emily C. Porterfield to John Allen Terrill, Elmwood, February 3, 1856. Terrill Family Papers, PE.
7. There is no time frame associated with this incident. Elizabeth Jackson Morton related the story to the author in February 1978. Bettie was born in 1853; William Rufus graduated from West Point in 1853, and was killed in October 1862. The visit undoubtedly took place in the late 1850s.
8. John Allen Terrill to Emily C. Porterfield, Bleak House, Oct. 6, 1857. Terrill Family Papers, PE.
9. John Moler Porterfield was also known as John Allen Porterfield, and is listed as such in the 1860 Census of Jefferson County, Virginia. He married Anna L. Green, August 8 or 9, 1876. Children: John Terrill Porterfield (1879-1938), Claibourne Porterfield (1881-1923), Philip Terrill Porterfield (1886-1954), and Mary McDonald Porterfield. John died January 25, 1938.
10. Emily C. Porterfield to John Allen Terrill, Elmwood, February 3, 1856. Terrill Family Papers, PE.
11. George Terrill Porterfield married Susan E. Simmons. Children: George Terrill Porterfield (1886-1963), James Simmons Porterfield (1888-1940), Emily Porterfield (1890-1964). George died Sept. 2, 1907.
12. Mary Jane Porterfield was born at Charles Town, Va. She married her cousin, William Chase Morton, son of General Jackson Morton and Elizabeth Archer. She had one child, Elizabeth Jackson Morton, of Richmond, who died on December 24, 1988. Mary Jane donated a framed photograph of her grandfather (William H. Terrill) to the Bath County Circuit Court. She also donated some personal items of her uncle Philip M. Terrill to The Museum of the Confederacy, in Richmond. Mary died March 20, 1939.
13. Charles Alexander Porterfield applied for appointment to the U.S. Military Academy, but was unsuccessful. He married Katherine Knox Taylor in 1891. Children: George Alexander Porterfield (1892-1931), Charles Porterfield (1894-____), James Knox Taylor Porterfield (1897-____), John Porterfield (1916-____). Charles died in 1936.
14. George A. Porterfield to E. C. Porterfield, Hd. Qrs. Va. Forces, near Grafton, Va., May 18, 1861. Abraham Lincoln Papers, Library of Congress, Washington, D.C.
15. William R. Terrill to Edwin M. Stanton, Camp Stanton, Opposite Columbia, Tennessee, March 28, 1862. File T-241, Letters Received by the U.S. Secretary of War, National Archives, Washington, D.C.; the land on which Emily and George lived was purchased by George; the livestock, or property was given to Emily and George by William H. Terrill.
16. Emily D. Terrill to Emily Porterfield, Reading, Pa., July 17, 1862. Terrill Family Papers, PE.
17. Elizabeth Jackson Morton, letter to the author, May 23, 1978.
18. A. S. Dandrich to Edmond Pendleton, August 3, 1862. Terrill Family Papers, PE.
19. Attachment to letter of A. S. Dandrich to Edmond Pendleton, August 3, 1862. Terrill Family Papers, PE.
20. Emily Porterfield to General R. H. Milroy, June 6, 1863. Terrill Family Papers, PE.
21. *Ibid.*
22. *Ibid.*; The letter which Emily refers to was written in March 1862.
23. Arietta L. Henry was the mother of Emily D. Henry, who married William Rufus Terrill.
24. Arietta L. Henry to E. M. Stanton, Reading, Berks Co., Penna., Nov. 30, 1863. File H-30, Letters Received by the U.S. Secretary of War. National Archives, Washington, D.C.
25. Letter to Mrs. A. S. [L.] Henry, Washington, D.C., December 7, 1863. Terrill Family Papers, PE.

26. Rob. S. Rogers to Wm. M. Berne, Head Quarters 2d Brig., 1st Div., D'p't. W. Va., Martinsburg, Va., Dec. 24th, 1863. Provost Marshal's Letters Received, National Archives, Washington, D.C.
27. Brig. Gen. E. M. Canby to Mrs. Arietta Henry, WD, WC, Jany. 9, 1864. Terrill Family Papers, PE.; copy also in National Archives, Washington, D.C.
28. Emily C. C. Terrill to Brig. Gen. [Jeremiah] Sullivan, Near Leetown, Jeffn. Co., Va., Jan. 2d, 1864. Provost Marshals File, M-345, Roll 220. National Archives, Washington, D.C.
29. Ibid.
30. Jr. C. Sullivan to Captain _____, Head Quarters 1st Div., Dept. Western Virginia, Harpers Ferry, Jany. 8, 1864. M-345, Roll 220, Union Provost Marshals' File of Papers Relating to Individual Citizens, National Archives, Washington, D.C.
31. Brig. Gen. E. M. Canby to "Madam" [Mrs. A. S. Henry], January 9, 1864. Terrill Family Papers, PE.
32. Emily C. Porterfield to E. M. Canby, Near Kearneysville, Jefferson Co., Va., Jan. 23d, 1864. M-567, File P-102, Letters Received by the Office of the Adjutant General, National Archives, Washington, D.C.
33. Jas. Barbour Terrill to P. M. Terrill, December 15, 1863. Terrill Family Papers, PE.
34. Emily C. Porterfield to Philip M. Terrill, Elmwood, December 18, 1863. Moore–Wise Family Papers, MS1361, Jones Memorial Library, Lynchburg, Va.
35. Related to the author by Barbara Porterfield, Charles Town, W. Va.
36. Emily C. Porterfield to E. M. Canby, Near Kearneysville, Va., March 26th, 1864. M-567, File 348-P-1864, Letters Received by the Office of the Adjutant General, National Archives, Washington, D.C.
37. Emily Serena Porterfield, also as Mary Serena. She married George Washington on February 16, 1886, the last Washington to be born at the ancestral home at Mount Vernon. His father, John Augustine Washington, was killed in Randolph County in the fall of 1861. Children: Richard Blackburn Washington (1887–1898), Louisa Fontaine Washington (1889–1898). Emily Serena died November 10, 1944.
38. P. M. Terrill to Emily Porterfield, July 31, 1864. Terrill Family Papers, PE.
39. Reminiscences of Cornelia H. Wise Moore. Moore–Wise Family Papers, MS1361, Jones Memorial Library, Lynchburg, Va.
40. Ibid.
41. Ibid.
42. Probably Colonel James N. Schoonmaker, commanding a brigade in General Averell's division.
43. Reminiscences of Cornelia H. Wise Moore. Moore–Wise Family Papers, MS1361, Jones Memorial Library, Lynchburg, Va.
44. Katherine "Kate" Seton Porterfield was most likely named for Kate Seton Henry, sister of Emily D. Henry, who married William R. Terrill. She died October 20, 1926, and is buried in Green Hill Cemetery, Martinsburg, WV.
45. Elizabeth Jackson Morton, letter to author, May 23, 1978.
46. Obituary of Emily Terrill Porterfield, courtesy of Elizabeth Jackson Morton, Richmond, Va., copy in possession of author.
47. Letter of Francis H. Smith, Va. Military Institute, Feb. 7th, 1843. Porterfield Family Papers, Jefferson County Historical Society, Charles Town, W. Va. Hereafter cited as Porterfield Papers.
48. Letter of C. Crozet, Jan. 24, 1843, Cadet Application File, National Archives, Washington, D.C.
49. U.S. Military Academy Cadet Application Papers, 1805–1866. M-688, Roll 148, George A. Porterfield File, National Archives, Washington, D.C.
50. Mexican War Pension Record, George A. Porterfield, National Archives, Washington, D.C.
51. Compiled Service Record, Mexican War, 1st Virginia Regiment, George A. Porterfield. National Archives, Washington, D.C.; The actual enlistment most likely took place sometime after the 16th, since Governor William Smith did not receive the request until November 18.
52. John Francis Hamtramck—born in Fort Wayne, Indiana, in 1798; graduated in 1819 from the U.S. Military Academy; died at Shepherdstown, Virginia on April 21, 1858.
53. "Swords For The Volunteer Officers." *Richmond Whig*, Richmond, Va., February 19, 1847.
54. G. A. Porterfield to Mother, Camargo, March 28, 1847. Porterfield Papers; the sword is indeed a beautiful piece of workmanship by the Ames Manufacturing Company. The sword, minus its scabbard, is now on display in the Jefferson County Museum in Charles Town, W. Va., as is the letter of presentation.
55. G. A. Porterfield to Mother, Camargo, March 28, 1847. Porterfield Papers.
56. Aztec Club of 1847: History of its Founding. www.aztecclub.com/history.htm. George, in his duties as Adjutant General, preserved a large amount of historic material, which was later given to the Aztec Club.
57. George A. Porterfield to Captain Anderson, Charles Town, W. Va., December 10, 1903. Alumni Biographical File, VMI Archives.
58. William H. Terrill to Col. F. H. Smith,

Notes — Chapter III

Warm Springs, December 3, 1857. Superintendents Correspondence, VMI Archives.

59. Col. F. H. Smith to W. H. Terrill, Virginia Mil. Institute, Decr. 7, 1857. Superintendents Correspondence, VMI Archives.

60. H. W. Benham to Hon. Lewis Cass, New York, Aug 2 1858. Porterfield Papers.

61. A. D. Bache to Hon. Lewis Cass, Washington, March 2, 1859, RG23 — Records of the Coast and Geodetic Survey, M642, Roll 200. National Archives, Washington, D.C.

62. Steve French, "Porterfield never recovers after Philippi," *The Washington Times*, Washington, D.C., June 14, 2003: H. W. Flournoy, *Calendar of Virginia State Papers and Other Manuscripts from January 1, 1836, to April 15, 1869; Preserved in the Capitol at Richmond* (Richmond: n.p., 1893), Vol. 11, p. 180.

63. Compiled Service Records, 25th Virginia Infantry, File of George A. Porterfield, National Archives, Washington, D.C.

64. Petition of Officers for the assignment of Col. Porterfield to be given command of troops from Berkeley County, Virginia, April 25, 1861. Virginia. Governor (1860–1864: Letcher). Executive Papers of Governor John Letcher, 1859–1863. Accession 36787. State Government Records Collection, The Library of Virginia, Richmond, Va. Hereafter cited as Letcher Executive Papers.

65. George A. Porterfield to Col. Frances H. Smith, Harper's Ferry, April 29, 1861. Superintendents Correspondence, VMI Archives.

66. Ibid.

67. John M. Brooks to Col. Geo. A. Porterfield, Hd. Qrs. Va. Forces, Richmond, May 3, 1861. Records of the Virginia Forces, National Archives, Washington, D.C.

68. R. E. Lee to Col. George A. Porterfield, Head Qrs. Va. Forces, Richmond, May 4, 1861. Records of the Virginia Forces, National Archives, Washington, D.C.; OR, Series 1, Volume 2, pages 802–3.

69. G. A. Porterfield to Col. F. H. Smith, Elmwood, May 9–61, Superintendents Correspondence, VMI Archives.

70. R. E. Lee to Hon. James Mason, Headquarters Virginia Forces, Richmond, Va., May 24, 1861; OR, Series 1, Volume 2, page 860.

71. Geo. A. Porterfield to Col. R. S. Garnett, Grafton, Va., May 14, 1861. OR, Series 1, Volume 2, page 843.

72. George A. Porterfield to Col. Garnett, Grafton, Va., May 16, 1861. OR, Series 1, Volume 2, page 855.

73. Ibid.

74. R. E. Lee to George A. Porterfield, Head Quarters Va. Forces, Richmond, Va., May 19, 1861. Records of the Virginia Forces, National Archives, Washington, D.C.

75. G. A. Porterfield to E. C. Porterfield, Hd. Qrs. Va. Forces, near Grafton, Va., May 18, 1861. Abraham Lincoln Papers, Library of Congress, Washington, D.C.

76. R. E. Lee to Col. Geo. A. Porterfield, Head Qrs. Va. Forces, Richmond, May 24, 1861. Records of the Virginia Forces, National Archives, Washington, D.C.; OR, Series 1, Volume 2, pages 873–4. Several companies from the Staunton vicinity joined Porterfield in late May 1861. The company sent from Harpers Ferry apparently never joined Porterfield.

77. "The War in Western Virginia: Letcher's Bridge Burning Order," *New York Times*, June 10, 1861.

78. Ibid.

79. George A. Porterfield to Col. R. S. Garnett, Headquarters Virginia Forces, Grafton, May 25, 1861. OR, Series I, Vol. 51, part 2, p. 109.

80. R. E. Lee to Col. George A. Porterfield, Headquarters Virginia Forces, Richmond, Va., May 27, 1861. OR, Series 1, Vol. 2, page 884.

81. G. A. Porterfield to Col. R. S. Garnett, Headquarters of Virginia Forces, Philippi, Va., May 29, 1861. OR, Series 1, Vol. 2, pages 51–52.

82. "Proclamation Of A Rebel Leader," *New York Times*, June 13, 1861.

83. G. A. Porterfield to Hon. Jno. Letcher, Philippi, Va., May 31st, 1861. Letcher Executive Papers, reel 4745, exposure 442–443.

84. John A. McNeel. "Famous Retreat From Philippi," *Richmond Times-Dispatch*, November 4, 1906.

85. Testimony of Col. George W. Hansbrough, Court of Inquiry Record, Compiled Service Record, 25th Virginia Infantry, File of George A. Porterfield, National Archives, Washington, D.C.

86. Ibid.

87. Hu Maxwell. *History of Barbour County, West Virginia: from its earliest exploration and settlement to the present time* (Morgantown, WV: Acme, 1899), p. 250–1, George A. Porterfield to Hu Maxwell, Charlestown, W. Va., Aug. 12, 1899.

88. Maj. D. B. Stewart. "Battle of Philippi Recounted," *Confederate Veteran* 13, no. 3 (March 1910), p. 116–118. Hereafter cited as Stewart.

89. Fritz Hasselberger, *Yanks From the South: The First Land Campaign of the Civil War: Rich Mountain, West Virginia* (Baltimore: Past Glories, 1987), p. 45. Hereafter cited as Hasselberger.

90. Hasselberger, p. 49.

91. Ibid.

92. Stewart, p. 116–118.

93. Ibid.

94. "The Affair at Phillippa," *Staunton Spectator*, June 11, 1861.

95. Testimony of Captain B. J. Jordan, Court of Inquiry Record, Compiled Service Record, 25th Virginia Infantry, File of George A. Porterfield, National Archives, Washington, D.C.
96. H. W. Benham, "Recollections of West Virginia Campaign, with 'The Three Months Troops,' May, June, and July, 1861. By an Engineer Officer," *Old and New*, June 1873, p. 678. Hereafter cited as Benham.
97. Ibid.
98. Ibid.
99. Letter to Mrs. E. C. Porterfield, Hd. Qrs. Va. Forces, near Grafton, Va., May 18, 1861. Abraham Lincoln Papers, Library of Congress. This letter was most likely singled out because of content regarding the political climate in northwestern Virginia.
100. "Battle of Philippi: An Account of the Wounding of Gen. B. F. Kelley by an Eye-Witness," National Tribune, Washington, D.C., May 12, 1892.
101. "The War in Western Virginia: Letcher's Bridge Burning Order," *Daily Evening Bulletin*, June 7, 1861.
102. Letter from Adjutant John A. Stein, *The Daily Courier*, an unknown Indiana newspaper, not dated.
103. J. N. Potts, "Personal Recollections of the War," *The Baptist Banner*, August 9, 1893.
104. J. N. Potts, "Recollections of the War Between The United States and The Confederate States of America (That 'Storm Cradled Nation That Fell.')," *Randolph Enterprise*, September 21, 1922. Hereafter cited as Potts.
105. J. H. Cammack, "An Added Chapter of Recollections," *The Baptist Banner*, October 4, 1893.
106. David Poe, *Personal Reminiscences of the Civil War* (Buckhannon, WV: Upshur Republican Print, 1911), p. 5.
107. M. G. Harman to Gov. Letcher or Genl. Lee, By Telegraph, Staunton, Va., June 6th [1861]. Letcher Executive Papers, reel 4745, exposure 204.
108. M. G. Harman to R. E. Lee, Headquarters Virginia Forces, Staunton, Va., June 6, 1861, OR, Series 1, Vol. 2, p. 69–70.
109. Lieut. Normount to Governor Letcher, By Telegraph From Staunton, Rec'd Richmond June 6th, 1861. Letcher Executive Papers, reel 4745, exposure 179.
110. M. G. Harman to George A. Porterfield, Headquarters Virginia Forces, Staunton, Va., June 6, 1861. OR, Series 1, Vol. 2, p. 69.
111. Geo. A. Porterfield to Col. R. S. Garnett, Headquarters of Virginia Forces, Huttonsville, Va., June 9, 1861. OR, Series 1, Vol. 2, p. 70.
112. Ibid.

113. C. B. Hopkins to President Jefferson Davis, Healing Springs, Bath Co., Va., June 10, 1861. Letters Received by the Confederate Secretary of War, No. 1490, National Archives, Washington, D.C.
114. Geo. A. Porterfield to Col. R. S. Garnett, Headquarters of Virginia Forces, Randolph County, Va., June 11, 1861, OR, Series 1, Vol. 2, p. 70.
115. J. M. Heck to Maj. M. G. Harman, Hevener's Store, June 11th, 1861. Letcher Executive Papers, reel 4745, exposure 520–521.
116. R. E. Lee to Col. George A. Porterfield, Headquarters Virginia Forces, Richmond, Va., June 13, 1861. OR, Series 1, Vol. 2, p. 71–2.
117. General Orders No. 24, Headquarters Virginia Forces, Richmond, Va., June 1, 1861. OR, Vol. 51, Part 2, p. 123.
118. "A Narrative of the Service of Colonel Geo. A. Porterfield in Northwestern Virginia in 1861–2," *Southern Historical Society Papers*, Vol. 16 (1888), p. 82–91, hereafter cited as SHSP; George A. Porterfield to Major R. W. Hunter, Charles Town, W. Va., June 1908, Department of Military Affairs, Library of Virginia, Richmond, Va.
119. Order and Letter Book of George A. Porterfield, Porterfield Papers.
120. George A. Porterfield to Col. F. H. Smith, Beverly, Va., June 26th, 1861. Superintendents Correspondence, VMI Archives, Lexington, Va.
121. OR, Vol. 2, pages 72–4.
122. Ibid.
123. Ibid.
124. George A. Porterfield to Col. F. H. Smith, Beverly, Va., June 26, 1861. Superintendents Correspondence, VMI Archives, Lexington, Va.; Letcher Executive Papers, Roll 4748, exposure 389.
125. Granville D. Hall, *Lee's Invasion of Northwest Virginia in 1861* (Chicago: Mayer & Miller, 1911), p. 156.
126. Potts, *Randolph Enterprise*, January 25, 1923.
127. "The Killing of John A. Washington," *The Indiana True Republican*, October 10, 1861.
128. Clifford Dowdy, ed., *The Wartime Papers of R. E. Lee* (New York: Bramhall House, 1961), p. 76.
129. "A Washington Made A Priest," *The Star and Sentinel*, June 19, 1920.
130. George A. Porterfield to General Robert E. Lee, Huntersville, Va., November 3, 1861. Records of the Virginia Forces, M-998, National Archives, Washington, D.C.
131. SHSP, 82–91.
132. P. B. Duffy & other officers to Hon. J. P. Benjamin, Camp Alleghany, Jan. 7th, 1862. File 9270, Letters Received by the Confederate

Secretary of War, National Archives, Washington, D.C.

133. G. A. Porterfield to John Letcher, Staunton, Va., December 14, 1861. Letcher Executive Papers, Reel 4759, exposure 363. The petition, signed by thirteen officers of the 31st Virginia Infantry, requested General W. W. Loring to assign Porterfield to command the regiment. The petition was dated Alleghany Top, and was written in November 1861. Reel 4759, exposure 364, Letcher Executive Papers.

134. Richard L. Armstrong, *Jackson's Valley Campaign: The Battle of McDowell* (Lynchburg, VA: Howard, 1990), p. 22–23. Hereafter cited as *Battle of McDowell*.

135. *Ibid.*, p. 24; OR, Vol. 12, part I, p. 487. Baldwin, during much of the winter, had been absent, serving in the Virginia House of Representatives. He returned to his regiment (52nd Virginia Infantry) by April 22.

136. Jed Hotchkiss Papers, Library of Congress, Washington, D.C.

137. SHSP, 82–91.

138. Edward Johnson to Geo. W. Randolph, Camp Valley Mills, May 1, 1862, CSR, George A. Porterfield, 25th Virginia Infantry, National Archives, Washington, D.C.

139. SHSP, 82–91.; George A. Porterfield to A. R. Botler, Staunton, May 8, 1862, CSR, George A. Porterfield, 25th Virginia Infantry, National Archives, Washington, D.C.

140. George A. Porterfield to Major R. W. Hunter, Charles Town, W. Va., June [no day], 1908, Dept. of Military Affairs, Library of Virginia.

141. George A. Porterfield to Maj. Gen. John E. Wool, Jefferson Co., Va., August 9, 1862. CSR, George A. Porterfield, 25th Virginia Infantry.

142. The Register of Deaths in the Jefferson County Court House lists the cause of death as pneumonia.

143. "Col. George A. Porterfield Dead," *Farmers Advocate*, March 1, 1919, in Alumni Biographical File, George A. Porterfield, VMI Archives.

Chapter IV

1. His date of birth appears as April 20 in a letter written by his father in 1848, seeking his appointment to the U.S. Military Academy. The April 21 date is the one generally accepted as his actual date of birth.

2. William H. Terrill to Gen. Totten, Warm Springs, Bath County, Va., December 23, 1848. Cadet Application Papers, 1814–1866, William R. Terrill File, Records of the Adjutant General's Office, 1780s–1917, National Archives, Washington, D.C. Hereafter cited as Cadet Application Papers, WRT.

3. "Obituary: Tribute to the Late Gen. Wm. R. Terrill," *New York Times*, New York, February 8, 1863.

4. William R. Terrill to the Secretary of War, Warm Springs, Va., April 9, 1849. Cadet Application Papers, WRT.

5. Peter W. Houck, ed., *Duty, Honor, Country: The Diary and Biography of General William P. Craighill: Cadet at West Point, 1849–1853* (Lynchburg, VA: Warwick House, 1993), entry for June 16, 1849, p. 82, hereafter cited as Craighill Diary. A Descriptive List of Cadets indicates that William reported to the academy on June 1, 1849 (Descriptive Lists—Alphabetical List of New Cadets for 1849, USMA Archives). According to Academy Regulations (1839), new cadets were to report between June 1 and June 20.

6. List of Candidates for Admission into the [U.S.] Military Academy, B-4404, examined June 24, 1849. Records Relating to the U.S. Military Academy, Records of the Adjutant General's Office, 1780s–1917, Record Group 94, National Archives, Washington, D.C. The vaccination mark mentioned was for smallpox, developed by English physician Edward Jenner in 1796.

7. William R. Terrill to Emily C. Porterfield, West Point, October 15, 1849. Terrill Family Papers, PE.

8. William R. Terrill to Emily Porterfield, West Point, January 20, 1850. Terrill Family Papers, PE.

9. Cadet Warrant, July 1, 1849, Cadet Application Papers, WRT.

10. Henry Brewerton to Brig. Genl. Jos. G. Totten, U.S. Military Academy, West Point, N.Y., Sept. 30, 1851, Excuse of William R. Terrill, West Point, N.Y., September 9, 1851, (enclosed with No. 5438). Letters Received, USMA.

11. *Ibid.*

12. *Ibid.*

13. B. R. Alden to The Adjt. Mil. Acady, Hd. Qrs. Corps of Cadets, West Point, N.Y., Sept. 15th, 1851, enclosed with Henry Brewerton to Brig. Genl. Jos. G. Totten, U.S. Military Academy, West Point, N.Y., Sept. 30, 1851, No. 5438. Letters Received, USMA; Sheridan, in his Memoirs, said that an officer broke up the fight. Philip Henry Sheridan, *Personal Memoirs of P. H. Sheridan, General, United States Army* (New York: Webster, 1888), Vol. 1, p. 11.

14. Orders, December 4, 1851, Post Order Book No. 3, p. 623, USMA Archives; Register of Delinquencies, 1849–1853, USMA Archives.

15. Monthly Class Reports and Conduct Rolls, 1831–1866, November 1851. Records Re-

lating to the U.S. Military Academy, Records of the Adjutant General's Office, 1780s–1917, Record Group 94, National Archives, Washington, D.C. Hereafter cited as Monthly Class Reports.

16. Adele H. Mitchell, ed., *The Letters of Major General James E. B. Stuart* (Richmond, VA: Stuart-Mosby Historical Society, 1990), James E. B. Stuart to George Hairston, U.S. Military Academy, West Point, New York, Christmas Day, 1851, p. 43.

17. William R. Terrill to John A. Terrill, Fort Hamilton, N.Y., April 9, 1856. Terrill Family Papers, PE.

18. Cadet Wm. R. Terrill to Col. Samuel Cooper, West Point, N.Y., June 16th, 1853. Applications for Promotion, USMA Archives

19. Special Order No. 46, Headquarters of the Army, New York, May 26, 1855. Special Orders, HQ Army; Post Returns, Fort Hamilton, N.Y., June–July 1855, Returns From U.S. Military Posts, 1800–1916, Roll 442, M-617, Records of the Adjutant General's office, 1780s–1917, Record Group 94, National Archives, Washington, D.C.

20. Special Order No. 157, War Department, Adjutant General's Office, August 24, 1855. Special Orders Issued, Records of the Adjutant General's Office, 1780s–1917, Record Group 94, National Archives, Washington, D.C.

21. J. B. Terrill to John A. Terrill, VMI, December 2, 1855. Terrill Family Papers, PE.

22. William R. Terrill to G. A. Porterfield, Fort Mackinac, Mich., not dated. Terrill Family Papers, PE.

23. T. Williams to L. Thomas, Fort Mackinac, Mich., Oct. 12, 1856. Letters Received, HQ Army.

24. Robert Garth Scott, ed., *Forgotten Valor: The Memoirs, Journals & Civil War Letters of Orlando B. Wilcox* (Kent, OH: Kent State University Press, 1999), p. 208. Hereafter cited as *Forgotten Valor*.

25. *Forgotten Valor*, p. 209

26. *Ibid*.

27. *Ibid*., p. 209–10; Hottentot is the name given to a South African tribe; Hottentot Village refers to a group of crude shelters.

28. *Ibid*., p. 211

29. *Ibid*., p. 213

30. Records of Fort Kissimmee, Florida. Department of Florida, Records of U.S. Army Continental Commands, 1821–1920, Record Group 393, National Archives, Washington, D.C. Hereafter Cited as Department of Florida.

31. Records of Events, Battery L, 4th U.S. Artillery, March–April 1857. Muster Rolls of Regular Army Units, Records of the Adjutant General's Office, 1780s–1917, Record Group 94, National Archives, Washington, D.C. Hereafter cited as Record of Events, Battery L, 4th Artillery.

32. Thos. A. McParlin to W. H. McParlin, Encampment Fort Kissimmee, Fla., Sunday Morning, August 9, 1857. Special Collections, Guy Weatherly Collection of McParlin Family Papers, August 9, 1857, MdHR MSA SC 595-B3-F86. Courtesy of the Maryland State Archives.

33. William R. Terrill to Professor [A. D.] Bache, Fort Kissimmee, Fla., August 29," 1857. Correspondence of A. D. Bache, Superintendent of the Coast and Geodetic Survey, 1843–1865 (M-642), Records of the Coast and Geodetic Survey, Record Group 23, National Archives, Washington, D.C. Hereafter cited as Coast Survey Records.

34. A. D. Bache to Wm. R. Terrill, Bangor, Me., Sept. 30, 1857. Coast Survey Records.

35. Record of Events, Battery L, 4th Artillery, September–October 1857.

36. Emily C. Porterfield to Elizabeth Terrill, Washington, December 20, 1857. Terrill Family Papers, PE; filial — the relationship between a child and a parent.

37. William Seton Henry (1816–1851) and Arietta Livingston Thompson (1818–1886) were married on March 9, 1837, in New Orleans, Louisiana. Their children were Guy Vernon Henry (1839–1899), who graduated from the military academy in 1861, and served in the Charles Town area during 1863; Emily Drennen Henry (1840–1884); Emmett Henry; and Kate (Katherine) Seton Henry. Note that March 9 was the date that Major Henry was buried at West Point; it was his wedding anniversary, the date of Guy Vernon Henry's birth, and the date of Emily's wedding in 1858.

38. [A. D. Bache] to Howell Cobb, Coast Survey Office, March 10, 1858. Coast Survey Records.

39. The letter of Mrs. Henry to the secretary of war, mentioned in the Register of Letters Received, was not found in the files at the National Archives.

40. Special Orders No. 40, War Department, Adjutant General's Office, Washington, March 17, 1858. Special Orders Issued, Adjutant General; William R. Terrill to Howell Cobb, Washington City, March 17th, 1858. Coast Survey Records.

41. [A. D. Bache] to Wm. R. Terrill. C. S. Office, March 19, 1858. Coast Survey Records.

42. National Oceanic and Atmospheric Administration. *The Hassler Legacy: Ferdinand Rudolph Hassler and the United States Coast Survey*. www.lib.noaa.gov/edocs/HASSLER1.htm.

43. Virginia Congressmen to John B. Floyd, Washington, D.C., April 18, 1860. Letters Received, Adjutant General.

Notes — Chapter IV

44. A. D. Bache to W. R. Terrill, C. S. Office, April 27, 1860. Coast Survey Records.
45. A. D. Bache to W. R. Terrill, C. S. Office, Jan. 9, 1861. Coast Survey Records.
46. William R. Terrill to A. D. Bache, New York, April 20, 1861. Coast Survey Records.
47. William R. Terrill to A. D. Bache, Tampa, Fla., January 20, 1861. Coast Survey Records.
48. William R. Terrill to A. D. Bache, Tampa, Fla., January 28, 1861. Coast Survey Records.
49. A. D. Bache to W. R. Terrill, C. S. Office, Jany. 31, 1861. Coast Survey Records.
50. [A. D. Bache] to W. R. Terrill, C. S. Office, Feb. 5, 1861. Coast Survey Records.
51. William R. Terrill to A. D. Bache, Charlotte Harbor, Fla., February 27, 1861. Coast Survey Records.
52. Tortugas, Spanish for sea turtles, is a cluster of seven islands, and has been a national park since 1992.
53. William R. Terrill to William H. Terrill, March 9, 1861, written from the island of Tortugas. Terrill Family Papers, PE.
54. William R. Terrill to A. D. Bache, U.S. Mail Steamer *Quaker City*, Near Sandy Hook, March 29, 1861. Coast Survey Records.
55. A. D. Bache to W. R. Terrill, C. S. Office, April 27, 1861. Coast Survey Records.
56. A. D. B[ache] to S. P. Chase, Coast Survey Office, May 9, 1861. Coast Survey Records.
57. Evelyn Lee Moore. *The Terrill's of Bath*, unpublished typescript in author's possession.
58. "The American Nation: Lives of her Fallen and Brave Living Heroes," Part 18, p. 430. Owen D. Young Library, Canton, NY. Judging from the content of William H. Terrill's letter to his son, where he speaks of William Rufus' loyalty to his oath indicates that the Constitution story was contained in either the April 29 or May 7 letter to his father.
59. "Brigadier General William R. Terrill..." *Louisville Daily Journal*, Louisville, Ky., October 11, 1862.
60. "To the Editors of the Enquirer." *Richmond Enquirer*, November 20, 1862.
61. Francis Darr to Emily Porterfield, October 12, 1862. Porterfield Family Papers, Jefferson County Historical Society, Charles Town, W. Va.
62. Your Father [William H. Terrill] to [William R. Terrill], Bath Co., Virg., May 15, [1861]. Alexander Dallas Bache Papers, USMA Archives.
63. A. D. Bache to Colonel [G. W.] Cullum, Capitol Hill, May 20, 1861. Alexander Dallas Bache Papers, USMA Archives.
64. Special Orders No. 137, Head Qrs. Dept. of Washington, Washington, D.C., June 11, 1861. Special Orders Issued, Department of Washington, 1860-1861. Records of U.S. Army Continental Commands, 1821-1920, Record Group 393. National Archives, Washington, D.C.
65. Albert Baker Pitzer (1821-1891), youngest brother of Elizabeth Pitzer Terrill, who was then serving in Company B, 2nd Virginia Cavalry, CSA.
66. Wm. R. Terrill to Andrew Johnson, Harrisburg, Pa., July 3d, 1861. The Andrew Johnson Papers, Series #1, (Microfilm), University Library, Texas Tech University, Lubbock, Tx.
67. "Captain William R. Terrill...," *Berks & Schuylkill Journal*, Reading, Pa., July 13, 1861.
68. William R. Terrill to T. W. Sherman, Reading, Pa., July 9, 1861. Letters Received, 5th U.S. Artillery, Records of United States Regular Army Mobile Units, 1821-1942, Record Group 391, National Archives, Washington, D.C. Hereafter cited as Letters Received, 5th U.S. Artillery); The recruiting office was located at present day 522 Penn Street, Reading, PA. ("General William Rufus Terrill: The Civil War Officer that Reading Adopted." by Gary L. Shugar, *Historical Review of Berks County* 71, no. 3 (Summer 2006) p. 111-114.)
69. Wm. R. Terrill to The Acting Adjutant 5th Regt. U.S. Artillery, Reading, Pa., July 20, 1861. Letters Received, 5th U.S. Artillery.
70. W. R. Terrill to Lt. H. DuPont, Reading, Pa., July 30, 1861. Letters Received, 5th U.S. Artillery.
71. Wm. R. Terrill to Professor A. D. Bache, Reading, Pa., August 6th, 1861. Reel No. 3, Document No. 1875-1876, A. D. Bache Papers, Manuscript Division, Library of Congress. Hereafter cited as Bache Papers.
72. *Ibid.*
73. *Ibid.*
74. Wm. R. Terrill to Lt. Henry DuPont, Reading, Pa., Aug. 8, 1861. Letters Received, 5th U.S. Artillery.
75. William R. Terrill to Maj. Gen. [G. B.] McClellan, Telegram dated Reading, Pa., August 17, 1861. Telegrams Collected by the Secretary of War (unbound), 1860-1870 (M-504), Records of the Office of the Secretary of War, Record Group 107, National Archives, Washington, D.C.
76. "Recruiting for the war...," *Berks & Schuylkill Journal*, Reading, Pa., August 17, 1861.
77. William R. Terrill to L. Thomas, Reading, Pa., Aug. 26, 1861. File T-267, Letters Received, Adjutant General
78. General Order No. 233, War Department, Adjutant General's Office, Washington, D.C., August 29, 1861. Orders Received, 1861-1865, 5th U.S. Artillery, p. 6, Records of United States Regular Army Mobile Units, 1821-1942, Record Group 391, National Archives, Wash-

ington, D.C.; Regimental Orders No. 42, Headquarters 5th Reg't Artillery, Harrisburg, Penn., September 2, 1861. Regimental Order Book, 5th U.S. Artillery, 1861–1862, p. 25, Records of United States Regular Army Mobile Units, 1821–1942, Record Group 391, National Archives, Washington, D.C.
79. "Off For The War," *Berks & Schuylkill Journal*, September 7, 1861
80. "Who Wants to Enlist?" *Reading Daily Times*, September 3, 1861.
81. *Louisville Journal*, September 13, 1861.
82. *Louisville Journal,* September 17, 1861.
83. "From Capt. Terrill's Company," *Berks & Schuylkill Journal*, September 21, 1861
84. Wm. R. Terrill to Brig. Genl. Ripley, New Port Barracks, Ky., Sept. 12, 1861. Letters Received, Records of the Office of the Chief of Ordnance, Record Group 156, National Archives, Washington, D.C. Hereafter cited as Letters Received, Ordnance.
85. Wm. R. Terrill to Brig. Gen'l Ripley, New Port Bks., Ky., September 27, 1861. Letters Received, Ordnance.
86. Wm. R. Terrill to Brig. Genl. Ripley, New Port Bks., Ky., October 7, 1861. Letters Received, Ordnance.
87. "Loyality of Slaves," *Staunton Spectator*, Staunton, Virginia, September 24, 1861.
88. Wm. R. Terrill to L. Thomas, New Port, Ky., Oct. 4, 1861. File T-375, Letters Received, Adjutant General.
89. Telegram to Capt. Seymour, National Telegraph Line, Washington, October 12th, 1861. Orders Received, 5th U.S. Artillery.
90. Lieut. V. H. Stone to Capt. T. Seymour, Newport Barracks, Ky., Oct. 19th, 1861. Letters Received, 5th U.S. Artillery.
91. "Newport News. Artillery Drill." *Cincinnati Enquirer*, October 2, 1861.
92. Wm. R. Terrill to Prof. A. D. Bache, Middletown, Ohio, October 13, 1861. Reel No. 3, Document No. 1995–1998. Bache Papers.
93. *Ibid*. William is mistaken on several points. Philip was a lieutenant, not a captain. Col. Porterfield, though reported wounded in the newspapers, escaped physical injury at Philippi, Virginia, on June 3, 1861. Dr. George P. Terrill was in command of the local militia and home guards during the war.
94. Record of Events, September–October 1861, Muster Rolls, 5th U.S. Artillery, Battery H, Records of the Adjutant General's Office, 1780s–1917, Record Group 94, National Archives, Washington, D.C. Hereafter cited as Record of Events, Battery H, 5th U.S. Artillery.
95. J. F. Mohr to Dear Brother, Carthage, Oct. 31/61. James F. Mohr Letters, The Filson Historical Society, Louisville, Ky. Hereafter cited as Mohr Letters.

96. J. F. Mohr to Dear Brother, Camp Monroe, Nov. 5/61. Mohr Letters
97. Register of Letters Received, Sept. 1861–Jan. 1862, Departments of Cumberland and Ohio, Records of U.S. Army Continental Commands, 1821–1920, National Archives, Washington, D.C. Hereafter cited as Departments of Cumberland and Ohio.
98. William R. Terrill to L. Thomas, New Port Bks., Ky., November 10, 1861. Letters Received, Adjutant General.
99. James F. Mohr to Dear Brother, Camp Monroe, November 18/61. Mohr Letters
100. C. C. Gilbert to Jas. B. Fry, Louisville, Ky., Nov. 25, 1861. Letters Received, Departments of Cumberland and Ohio.
101. Samuel Cordell Frey, Alfred Sperry and Perez G. Clark. *Battery D, First Ohio Veteran Volunteer Light Artillery: Its Military History, 1861–1865* (Oil City, PA: Derrick, 1908), page 20. Hereafter cited as Battery D.
102. *Ibid.*, p. 24.
103. *Ibid.*, p. 26.
104. James F. Mohr to Dear Brother, Camp Monroe, November 9/61. Mohr Letters.
105. J. H. Gilman to Jas. B. Fry, Head Quarters Dept. of the Ohio, Louisville, Ky., Dec. 2nd, 1861. Letters Received, Departments of Cumberland and Ohio.
106. Inspection Report, Major Jno. Buford, Louisville, Ky., Jan. 1st, 1862. Letters Received, Departments of Cumberland and Ohio.
107. Philip M. Terrill to Emily C. Porterfield, Bel Pre, Culpeper Co., Va., December 7, 1861. Terrill Family Papers, PE.
108. William R. Terrill to Professor A. D. Bache, Camp Gilbert, Ky., near Louisville, Dec. 16, 1861. Reel No. 3, Document No. 2129. Bache Papers.
109. William Sumner Dodge, *History of the Old Second Division, Army of the Cumberland* (Chicago: Church & Goodman, 1864), p. 115. Hereafter cited as Dodge.
110. Richard J. Staats, *A Grassroots History of the American Civil War. Volume III: Captain Cotter's Battery* (Bowie, MD: Heritage Books, 2002), p. 46. Hereafter cited as Cotter's Battery; VOL. 967 A. S. Bloomfield Civil War Letters [transcription], Letter to Father, 10 March 1862: Ohio Historical Society. Bloomfield was mistaken about Terrill being engaged at First Bull Run—it was another battery of the 5th U.S. Artillery. He was also mistaken about the time of Cotter's trial. Cotter was tried in mid–January and cashiered.
111. Cotter's Battery, p. 46; VOL. 967 A. S. Bloomfield Civil War Letters [transcription], Letter to Father, 10 March 1862: Ohio Historical Society.
112. Proceedings of a General Court Mar-

Notes — Chapter IV

tial ... Captain C. S. Cotter, File NN-3816. Records of the Office of the Judge Advocate General (Army), Court-Martial Case Files, 1809–1894, Record Group 153, National Archives, Washington, D.C. Hereafter cited as Court Martial of C. S. Cotter.

113. *Ibid.*
114. *Ibid.*
115. *Ibid.*
116. Cotter's Battery, p. 48; Special Orders No. 86, War Department, Adjutant General's Office, Washington, April 19, 1862. Compiled Military Service Record of Charles S. Cotter, Company A, 1st Ohio Light Artillery, Records of the Adjutant General's Office, 1780s–1917, Record Group 94, National Archives, Washington, D.C.
117. Cotter's Battery, p. 48.
118. "Letter from Kentucky," *Berks & Schuylkill Journal*, February 15, 1862
119. General Felix K. Zollicoffer, a Confederate General, had been killed days before at the battle of Mill Spring, Kentucky. Lieutenant Bailie Peyton, Jr., was killed during the same battle.
120. Wm. R. Terrill to D. McCook, Head Qrs. Light Arty. Brigade, Camp Wood, Ky., 10 PM, Jan. 31st, 1861 [1862]. Letters and Reports Received, 1862–65, Department and Army of the Ohio, Records of U.S. Army Continental Commands, 1821–1920, Record Group 393, National Archives, Washington, D.C.
121. Wm. R. Terrill to Hon. Gov. Letcher, Camp Wood, Munfordville, Ky., Jan. 30th, 1862. Civil War Collection 4, box 1, folder 6, Special Collections Research Center, Morris Library, Southern Illinois University at Carbondale, Carbondale, Ill.
122. Mark W. Johnson. *That Body of Brave Men: The U.S. Regular Infantry and the Civil War in the Wes.* (Cambridge, MA: Da Capo Press, 2003), p. 88–9. Hereafter cited as Johnson.
123. *Ibid.*, p. 88; [Peter Fitzpatrick] to Bridget, Nashville, Tennessee, September 9, 1862. Fitzpatrick Letters, Stones River National Battlefield Park, Murfreesboro, Tn. Hereafter cited as Fitzpatrick Letters.
124. "Letter from Tennessee." *Berks & Schuylkill Journal*, March 22, 1862.
125. Endorsement on Inspection Report, Brigadier General D.C. Buell, Headquarters Department of Ohio, March 14, 1862. Endorsement Sent, Mar. 1862–June 1865, Department of the Cumberland and Division and Department of Tennessee, Records of U.S. Army Continental Commands, 1821–1920, Record Group 393, National Archives, Washington, D.C.
126. Wm. R. Terrill to Jas. B. Fry, Camp Andy Johnson, near Nashville, Tenn., March 10," 1862. Letters Received, Adjutant General.
127. Johnson, p. 92; [Peter Fitzpatrick] to Bridget, Nashville, Tennessee, September 9, 1862, Fitzpatrick Letters.
128. William R. Terrill to Edwin M. Stanton, Camp Stanton, Opposite Columbia, Tennessee, March 28," 1862. File T-241, Letters Received, Adjutant General.
129. Wm. R. Terrill to Professor [A. D. Bache], General Grants Hd. Qrs., Savannah, Tenn., Midnight April 6, 1862. Reel No. 4, Document No. 2365. Bache Papers. Dr. Dallas Bache was a nephew of Professor Bache.
130. R. U. Johnson, and C. C. Buel, eds., *Battles and Leaders of the Civil War* (New York: T. Yoseloff, 1956), Vol. 3, Notes of a Staff Officer at Perryville, p. 61. Hereafter cited as *Battles and Leaders.*
131. Johnson, p. 111
132. *Ibid.*
133. E. Hannaford, *The Story of a Regiment: A History of the Campaigns and Associations In The Field, of The Sixth Regiment Ohio Volunteer Infantry* (Cincinnati: Published by the Author, 1868), p. 266. Hereafter cited as Hannaford.
134. *Battles and Leaders*, Vol. 2, p. 593.
135. "Battle of Pittsburg [Landing]." *Berks & Schuylkill Journal*, April 19, 1862.
136. Johnson, p. 112; [Peter Fitzpatrick] to Bridget, Nashville, Tennessee, September 9, 1862, Fitzpatrick Letters.
137. Johnson, p. 112–3; The article was probably written by one of the Anderson brothers from Cincinnati. Given the fact that Lieutenant William P. Anderson became William's Adjutant General later in the fall, he may have been the author of the article.
138. J. F. Mohr to Dear Brother, Pittsburg Landing, April 10/62, Mohr Letters.
139. Hannaford, p. 267
140. "Terrill's Battery at Pittsburg Landing." *Berks & Schuylkill Journal*, April 26, 1862.
141. A Staff Officer, "The Second Division at Shiloh," *Harper's New Monthly Magazine* 28, (December 1863 to May 1864), p. 832.
142. Johnson, p. 114; [Peter Fitzpatrick] to Bridget, Nashville, Tennessee, September 9, 1862, Fitzpatrick Letters.
143. [James F. Mohr] to Dear Brother, Camp near Corinth, May 12/62, Mohr Letters.
144. One of these batteries has been identified as Harper's Jefferson Mississippi Battery (*Shiloh: Bloody April*, by Wiley Sword, p. 394.)
145. Report of Capt. William R. Terrill, Fifth U.S. Artillery, Chief of Artillery, Second Division, Battle of Pittsburg Landing, or Shiloh, Tenn., OR, Vol. 10, Part 1, p. 321–323.
146. Died of wounds received in battle, April 7, 1862.

147. Report of Captain William R. Terrill, Battery H, 5th U.S. Artillery, Battle Ground, of Pittsburg Landing, April 8th, 1862. Letters Received, Entry 252, Box 1, Records of United States Regular Army Mobile Units, 1821–1942, Record Group 391, National Archives, Washington, D.C.
148. Record of Events, March–April 1862, Battery H, 5th U.S. Artillery.
149. Report of Brigadier General William Nelson, U.S. Army, commanding Fourth Division, Battle of Pittsburg Landing, or Shiloh, Tenn., OR, Vol. 10, Part 1, p. 325
150. William Nelson to Commanding Officer of the 5th Regt. U.S. Artillery, Head Quarters 4th Division, Army of the Ohio, Field of Shiloh, April 16, 1862. Letters Received, 5th U.S. Artillery.
151. OR, Vol. 10, Part 1, p. 295–6.
152. OR, Vol. 10, Part 1, p. 304.
153. Dodge, p. 208.
154. Cotter's Battery, p. 54–5; VOL. 967 A. S. Bloomfield Civil War Letters [transcription], Letter to Father and Mother, 20 April 1862: Ohio Historical Society.
155. VOL. 967 A. S. Bloomfield Civil War Letters [transcription], Letter to Father and Mother, 20 April 1862: Ohio Historical Society.
156. OR, Vol. 10, Part 1, p. 301.
157. "Captain Terrill at the Battle of Pittsburg." *Weekly Patriot and Union*, May 8, 1862.
158. J. F. Mohr to Dear Brother, Pittsburg Landing, April 10/62. Mohr Letters.
159. The names of the men who came forward first to help Terrill were H. Petty; James Moore; H. Herman; R. G. Delaney; B. P. Critchell; H. Walter Wilson; W. W. Paddock; J. A. Cushing; K. N. Cowing; C. Roth. Hannaford, p. 268.
160. Sam S. Harris to George S. Garner, Corinth, April 18, 1862. OR, Series 2, Vol. 3, p. 849.
161. "Letter from Camp Shiloh — The Pea Ridge Reconnaissance in Force," *Semi-Weekly Dispatch*, May 6, 1862.
162. Robert G. Athearn, ed., *Soldier In The West — The Civil War Letters of Alfred Lacey Hough*, (Philadelphia: University of Pennsylvania Press, 1957), p. 73.
163. Record of Events, May–June 1862, Battery H, 5th U.S. Artillery.
164. Special Order No. 81, Headquarters Dept. of the Ohio, Nashville, Tenn., June 19th, 1862. Special Orders, Nov. 1861–June 1862, Departments of Cumberland and Ohio, Records of U.S. Army Continental Commands, 1821–1920, Record Group 393, National Archives, Washington, D.C.
165. Louvall H. Rousseau to Hon. E. M. Stanton, Washington City, June 30, 1862. File R-968, Letters Received, Secretary of War.
166. "Brigadier-General Terrell [sic]," *Berks & Schuylkill Journal*, December 6, 1862
167. William R. Terrill to O. D. Greene, Cincinnati, Ohio, July 14, 1862. File T-429, Letters Received, Adjutant General
168. Parotid Gland — a salivary gland situated on each side of the face, below and in front of the ear; when infected, more commonly known as mumps.
169. Certificate of Jno. Moore, Surg., U.S.A., Cincinnati, Ohio, July 28, 1862. File T-435, Letters Received, Adjutant General.
170. Emily D. Terrill to Emily C. Porterfield, Mansion House, Reading, Pa., July 17, 1862. Terrill Family Papers, PE.
171. Wm. R. Terrill to The Adjutant General, U.S. Army, Reading, Penn., Aug. 4, 1862. File T-435, Letters Received, Adjutant General.
172. "Serenade to Capt. Terrell [sic]," *Reading Daily Times*, August 6, 1862
173. Pension Record of James H. Reed, 5th U.S. Artillery, National Archives; 1st Lieut. F. L. Guenther to Lieutenant H. A. DuPont, Head Quarters, Battery "H" 5th Artillery, Camp near Battle Creek, Tenn., August 3, 1862, Letters Received, 5th U.S. Artillery.
174. OR, Vol. 16, part 2, p. 449.
175. *Ibid.*, p. 987.
176. *Ibid.*
177. OR, Vol. 16, part 1, p. 908.
178. *Ibid.*
179. F.B. James, "Perryville and the Kentucky Campaign of 1862," in Military Order of the Loyal Legion of the United States, Ohio Commandery, *Sketches of War History, 1861–1865* (Cincinnati: Clarke, 1903), Vol. V, p. 161.
180. OR, Vol. 16, part 2, p. 485.
181. Charles I. Switzer, ed., *Ohio Volunteer: The Childhood and Civil War Memoirs of Captain John Calvin Hartzell, OVI* (Athens, OH: Ohio University Press, 2005), p. 93. Hereafter cited as *Ohio Volunteer*.
182. "A Merited Promotion," *Reading Daily Times*, September 5, 1862.
183. General Order No. 1, Head Qrs. Light Brigade, Army of Kentucky, Sept. 6, 1862. Regimental Letter, Endorsement, Order and Misc. Book, 105th Ohio Volunteer Infantry, Volunteer Records, Records of the Adjutant General's Office, 1780s–1917, Record Group 94, National Archives, Washington, D.C. Hereafter cited as Regimental Records, 105th Ohio Infantry.
184. General Orders No. 2, Head Qrs. Light Brigade, Army of Kentucky, Sept. 6, 1862. Regimental Records, 105th Ohio Infantry.
185. General Orders No. 3, Headquarters Light Brigade, Army of Kentucky, September 6, 1862. Regimental Records, 105th Ohio Infantry.

186. Wm. R. Terrill to L. Thomas, Head Qrs. Light Brigade, Army of Kentucky, Sept. 6th, 1862. File A-348, Letters Received, Adjutant General.
187. H. W. Hallek to Hon. E. M. Stanton, Head Quarters of the Army, Washington, Sept. 7th/62. File H-490, Letters Received, Secretary of War.
188. Endorsement by Adjutant General, September 22, 1862 on 525-T-1862, Endorsements, 1851–70, Adjutant General.
189. OR, Vol. 16, part 2, p. 498.
190. Edwin M. Stanton to Brig. Gen. Wm. R. Terrill, War Department, Washington, September 9, 1862. Pension Record of William R. Terrill, National Archives, Washington, D.C.
191. Wm. R. Terrill to L. Thomas, Louisville, Ky., Sept. 9th, 1862. File T-572, Letters Received, Adjutant General.
192. General Orders No. 12, Headquarters Light Brigade, Army of Kentucky, September 21, 1862; General Orders No. 15, Headquarters Light Brigade, Army of Kentucky, September 23, 1862; Regimental Records, 105th Ohio Infantry.
193. Telegram — A. D. Bache to William R. Terrill, Philadelphia, September 22, 1862. Coast Survey Records.
194. A. D. Bache to W. S. Edwards, Philadelphia, Sept. 24, 1862. Coast Survey Records.
195. W. S. Edwards to A. D. Bache, New York City, Sept. 28th, 1862. Coast Survey Records.
196. A. D. Bache to W. S. Edwards, Philadelphia, Sept. 28, 1862. Coast Survey Records.
197. Peter Fitzpatrick to Brigit, November 15, 1862, Nashville. Fitzpatrick Letters, courtesy of Mark W. Johnson.
198. Johnson, p. 226
199. Albion W. Tourgée, *The Story of a Thousand, Being a history of the service of the 105th Ohio Volunteer Infantry, in the war for the union from August 21, 1862 to June 6, 1865* (Buffalo: S. McGerald & Son, 1896), p. 101. Hereafter cited as Tourgée.
200. "Editorial Correspondence. Head Quarters 123d Illinois Regiment." *Matoon Gazette Weekly*, October 18, 1862.
201. Tourgée, p. 100; Tourgée is mistaken in his account about William's father being a member of the clergy — he was instead an attorney. Also, Tourgée's account has William receiving the Bible before graduation from the military academy instead after graduation. The soldier-turned-writer called the story a "pretty one, and it might well be true."
202. *Ibid.*
203. J. H. Gilman to J. B. Fry, Head Quarters Army of the Ohio, Louisville, Ky., Sept. 30, 1862. Letters Received, Departments of Cumberland and Ohio; Lieutenant Henry Harrison Cumings, a member of the battery, claimed that the company consisted of eight guns — 5 Napoleons, 1 three inch rifled Parrott, and 2 twelve-pounder howitzers. The two howitzers must have been added after the date of the inspection. The Rev. Jason N. Fradenburgh, *In Memoriam — Henry Harrison Cumings, Charlotte J. Cumings* (Oil City, PA: Derrick, 1913 [1914]), p. 39. Hereafter cited as Fradenburgh.
204. Fradenburgh, p. 44
205. U.S. Senate. Talton T. Davis, Committee on Military Affairs (to accompany S. 2371). (S. Report No. 1193). Washington: Government Printing Office, 1900. Hereafter cited as Senate Report No. 1193.
206. "From Louisville." *Cincinnati Daily Gazette*, September 17, 1862.
207. J. G. Crawford to "Dear Lizzy," Camp Buel near Louisville, Ky., Sept. 17th, 1862. Elizabeth Ethel Parker Bascom, ed., *"Dear Lizzie:" Letters written by James "Jimmy" Garvin Crawford to his sweetheart Martha Elizabeth "Lizzie" Wilson while he was in the Federal Army during the War between the States, 1862–1865* (Ridgewood, NY: Bascom, 1978), p. 23. Hereafter cited as Crawford.
208. Loren J. Morse, ed. and comp., *Civil War Diaries and Letters of Bliss Morse* (Wagoner, OK: Loren J. Morse, 1985), entry dated Louisville, Ky., Sunday [September] 28 [1862], p. 29. Hereafter cited as Morse.
209. Crawford, p. 24.
210. J. of the Blacksheep. *Perryville 2001: 105th Ohio — Day by day.* Letter of John C. Hathaway, Company E, 105th Ohio Volunteer Infantry, p. 8, www.ezboard.com. Accessed in 2001; removed from the Internet..
211. James Glauser, transcriber, *The Civil War Diary of Private Josiah Ayre.* Typescript dated about 1975, Cleveland Public Library, Cleveland, Ohio, p. 5.
212. James Lee McDonough, *War in Kentucky: From Shiloh to Perryville* (Knoxville: University of Tennessee Press, 1994), p. 279. Hereafter cited as McDonough.
213. McDonough, p. 279
214. *Ibid.*
215. Crawford, p. 143.
216. Tourgée, p. 102
217. *Ibid.*
218. *Ibid.* This comment leads me to believe that it was the colors of the 101st Indiana Infantry, detailed to guard the division train and not engaged in the battle at Perryville.
219. Special Orders No. 64, Headquarters Light Brigade, Army of Kentucky, September 24th, 1862. Order Books, Company A, 123rd Illinois Infantry, Volunteer Records, Records

of the Adjutant General's Office, 1780s–1917, Record Group 94, National Archives, Washington, D.C.
220. Transcript of Diary of John Fritz, Co. D, 101st Regiment [Indiana Infantry], entry for September 26, 1862, William Henry Smith Library, Indiana Historical Society, Indianapolis, Indiana.
221. "Editorial Correspondence. Head Quarters 123d Illinois Regiment." *Matoon Gazette Weekly*, October 18, 1862.
222. Bianca Morse Federico and Betty Louise Wright, *Civil War: The Letters of John Holbrook Morse, 1861–1865* (Washington, D.C.: Federico, 1975), p. 58. Hereafter cited as *John Holbrook Morse*.
223. William R. Terrill to General _____, Head Qrs. Light Brigade, Louisville, September 27th, 1862. File of Francis L. Guenther, National Archives, Washington, D.C.; copy courtesy of Mark W. Johnson.
224. Morse, letter dated Sunday, [September] 28, Louisville, Ky., p. 29
225. Johnson, p. 83
226. Joseph P. Fried, "How One Union General Murdered Another," *Civil War Times Illustrated* 1, no. 3 (June 1962), p. 16.
227. Tourgée, p. 113
228. "Battle of Chaplin Hills—From the 105th Regiment." *The Western Reserve Chronicle*, November 12, 1862.
229. Hambleton Tapp, ed., "The Battle of Perryville, October 8, 1862, as Described in the Diary of Captain Robert B. Taylor," in *The Register of the Kentucky Historical Society* 60, no. 4 (October 1962): 259. Hereafter cited as Taylor.
230. "History of the 101st Regiment of Volunteer Infantry of Indiana." By Levi P. Fodrea, Official Historian of the Regiment. Annotated and Emendated by Hugh Anthony Maker. (Indiana Collection). Indiana State Library, Indianapolis, Indiana.
231. W. S. Edwards to A. D. Bache, Louisville, Ky., Oct. 8, 1862. Coast Survey Records.
232. Taylor, p. 268–9
233. *Sheridan the Inevitable*, p. 80; CWTI, February 1975, page 16–18. It is said that this meeting between Sheridan and Terrill took place on the night before the battle, but this is not so. A considerable distance separated Sheridan and Terrill at that time. (Roy Morris, Jr., *Sheridan: The Life and Wars of General Phil Sheridan*, p. 93.)
234. "Obituary. Tribute to the Late Gen. Wm. R. Terrill," *New York Times*, February 8, 1863.
235. Stuart W. Sanders, "The 1862 Kentucky Campaign and the Battle of Perryville," *Blue & Gray Magazine* 22, no. 5 (Holiday 2005), p. 12.

236. "Battle of Chaplin Hills—From the 105th Regiment." *The Western Reserve Chronicle*, November 12, 1862.
237. Samuel M. Starling to his daughters, Head Quarters U.S. Forces, Bowling Green, Ky., November 16, 1862. Lewis-Starling Collection, Manuscripts, Kentucky Building, Western Kentucky University, Bowling Green, Ky. Copy provided by Perryville Battlefield State Historic Park, Perryville, Ky. Hereafter cited as Starling letter.
238. Ibid.
239. Kenneth W. Noe, *Perryville: This Grand Havoc of Battle* (Lexington: University Press of Kentucky, 2001), p. 186, hereafter cited as Noe; Shelby Foote, *The Civil War: A Narrative* (New York: Random House, 1958), p. 735.
240. Tourgée, p. 116.
241. Taylor, p. 274.
242. "The Battle Of Chaplin's Hills," *New York Herald*, October 15, 1862.
243. Starling letter.
244. Fradenburgh, p. 44–5.
245. Tourgée, p. 119.
246. "Battle of Chaplin Hills—From the 105th Regiment." *The Western Reserve Chronicle*, November 12, 1862.
247. Ibid.
248. "The Battle of Chaplin's Hills." *New York Herald*, October 15, 1862.
249. Fradenburgh, p. 44–5.
250. Tourgée, p. 119.
251. "Editorial Correspondence. Headquarters 123d Reg. Ill. Vol." *Mattoon Gazette Weekly*, November 22, 1862.
252. Ibid.
253. Ibid.
254. "The Battle of Chaplin's Hills." *New York Herald*, October 15, 1862.
255. "From the 105th." *Western Reserve Chronicle*, Warren, Ohio, November 12, 1862.
256. Ibid.
257. Fradenburgh, p. 43.
258. "From the 105th," *Western Reserve Chronicle*, November 12, 1862.
259. Ibid.
260. Tourgée, p. 121.
261. Eugene C. Tidball, "Duty, Honor, County, and Skullduggery: Lincoln's Secretary of War Meddles at West Point," *Civil War History* 45 (March 1999): 1–27.
262. John Holbrook Morse, p. 63–65.
263. Noe, page 211.
264. "From the 105th," *Western Reserve Chronicle*, November 12, 1862.
265. Tourgée, p. 146.
266. Noe, 190–1.
267. Tourgée, p. 125–126.
268. Ibid., p. 126.
269. Noe, p. 257

Notes — Chapter IV

270. Paul M. Angle, ed., *Three Years in the Army of the Cumberland. The Letters and Diary of Major James A. Connolly*. Civil War Centennial Series (Bloomington: Indiana University Press, 1959), p. 21. Hereafter cited as Connolly.
271. Taylor, p. 277
272. Taylor, p. 278
273. Taylor, p. 278–9
274. Taylor, p. 279
275. William Franklin Gore Shanks, *Personal Recollections of Distinguished Generals* (New York: Harper & Brothers, 1866), p. 137. Hereafter cited as Shanks.
276. "From the 105th," *Western Reserve Chronicle*, November 12, 1862
277. "Recollections of the Late Brigadier-General Terrill." *Philadelphia Inquirer*, May 15, 1863.
278. Ohio Volunteer, p. 97. Other accounts state he was struck in the left breast by a shell fragment.
279. Peter Fitzpatrick to Brigit, Nashville, December the 5th/1862. Fitzpatrick Letters, courtesy of Mark W. Johnson.
280. Telegram, D.C. Buell to L. Thomas, Louisville, [October] 25th. Letters Received, Adjutant General.
281. "The Perryville Fight." *Louisville Journal*, October 11, 1862. "Park" is another term for a battery of artillery.
282. "The Battle of Chaplin Hills." *Mahoning Register*, November 13, 1862. Kirk adds that the words are "strangely" like the dying words of the heroic Wolfe, who also died just as it was known that his arms were triumphant. Coincidence — or did Kirk take poetic license?
283. Noe, p. 257; "Funeral of Gen. Wm. R. Terrill," *Berks & Schuylkill Journal*, October 18, 1862.
284. "Brigadier-General Terrell," *Berks & Schuylkill Journal*, December 6, 1862.
285. W. S. Edwards to A. D. Bache, Louisville, Ky., Oct. 8 [9], 1862. Coast Survey Records.
286. *Ibid*.
287. "The Gallant Dead," *Cincinnati Commercial*, October 13, 1862.
288. "The remains of Generals...," *Louisville Daily Journal*, October 11, 1862.
289. "Gen. William R. Terrill Killed," *Berks & Schuylkill Journal*, October 11, 1862.
290. "Brigadier General William R. Terrill," *Louisville Daily Journal*, October 11, 1862.
291. "The Battle of Chaplin — Movements of Generals Crittenden, Sheridan, and Mitchel." *Louisville Journal*, October 16, 1862.
292. "From the 105th," *Western Reserve Chronicle*, November 12, 1862.
293. Stuart W. Sanders to author, e-mail letter dated January 4, 2001.
294. Shanks, p. 146.

295. Special Order No. 62, Headquarters, Department of the Ohio, Cincinnati, Ohio, October 13th, 1862. Special Orders, Aug. 1862–Apr. 1864, Department of the Ohio.
296. "Funeral of Gen. Wm. R. Terrill." *Berks & Schuylkill Journal*, October 18, 1862. The men chosen to be pallbearers were: John Banks, lawyer and former congressman; J. Glancy Jones, lawyer and former congressman; J. Pringle Jones, lawyer and judge; Hiester Clymer, state senator; William M. Hiester, lawyer and former state senator; John S. Richards, lawyer and former editor of the *Berks and Schuykill Journal*; Isaac Eckert, owner of Clay Furnace and president of Farmer's Bank and Leesport Iron Company; and Joseph L. Stichter, former partner in the hardware business with James McKnight before McKnight left for the army. *Historical Review of Berks County*, Summer 2006.
297. W. S. Edwards to A. D. Bache, Mansion House, Reading, Pa., [Oct. 1862]. Coast Survey Records.
298. The Rev. Alexander G. Cummins, "*In Memoriam. Address at the Burial of Brig. Gen. William R. Terrill, October 16th, 1862, by Rev. Alexander G. Cummins, in Christ Church, Reading* (Philadelphia: C. Sherman & Sons, Printers, 1862).
299. W. S. Edwards to A. D. Bache, N.Y., Oct. 29th [1862]. Coast Survey Records.
300. Emily D. Terrill to the Registrar of Wills of Berks County, Pa., Reading, October 21, 1862. Copy courtesy of Gary L. Shugar.
301. W. S. Edwards to A. D. Bache, Haddam, Conn., November 4th, 1862. Coast Survey Records.
302. "Obituary. Tribute to the Late Gen. Wm. R. Terrill." *New York Times*, February 8, 1863. The identity of "E. B. H." remains unknown.
303. "Gen. Wm. R. Terrill, Killed," *Staunton Spectator*, October 21, 1862.
304. M. B. Clason to J. T. Boyle, Franklin, Tennessee, April 2, 1863. Register of Letters Received, Aug. 1862–Apr. 1864, Department of the Ohio, 1862–64.
305. *Ibid*.
306. F. Ball to _____, Office Dist. Atty., U.S., Southern Dist. of Ohio, Cincinnati, Ohio, April 13, 1863. Register of Letters Received, Aug. 1862–Apr. 1864, Department of the Ohio, 1862–64.
307. Earl Bill to A. E. Burnside, United States Marshal's Office, Northern District of Ohio, Cleveland, April 18, 1863. File B-117, "Generals' Papers and Books," Records of the Adjutant General's Office, 1780s–1917, Record Group 94, National Archives, Washington, D.C.

308. M. B. Clason to My Dear Mother, Franklin, Tenn., May 22, 1863. Letters of Captain Marshall B. Clason, 121st Ohio Infantry. www.1210vi.org/13.shtml. 2000. Now removed from the Internet.
309. John T. Thompson, *A Descriptive Catalogue of the Ordnance Museum, Department of Ordnance and Gunnery, U.S. Military Academy* (West Point, NY: U.S. Military Academy Press, 1898), p. 153.
310. E-mail from Les Jensen, curator of arms and armor, West Point Museum, to author, June 5, 2008.
311. Pension Record, Emily D. Terrill, widow of Brigadier General William R. Terrill.
312. "Camp Terrill," *Reading Daily Times*, November 17, 1862.
313. Description of Fort Terrill, Munfordville, Kentucky, from Harry H. Wilson; notes of a conversation between Betty Turner, owner of the fort, in the 1970s, and the author.
314. OR, Vol. 25, Part 2, p. 568–569.
315. "From Nashville. Incidents of the Battle," *Toledo Commercial*, January 16, 1863. Courtesy of Mark W. Johnson.
316. "From the Army of the Cumberland," *Toledo Commercial*, April 14, 1863. Courtesy of Mark W. Johnson.
317. Post Order Book No. 6, page 289, USMA Archives.; Circular, Head Quarters, Military Academy, West Point, N.Y. November 19, 1864, copy courtesy of Gary L. Shugar, Reading, Pa.
318. "Funeral of Mrs. William R. Terrill," *Democratic Register*, February 23, 1884.
319. Docket Book, 1911–1912, Probate Division, Superior Court, District of Columbia (Washington, D.C.). The case file is missing.

Chapter V

1. Charles D. Walker. *Memorial, Virginia Military Institute: Biographical sketches of the graduates and eleves of the Virginia Military Institute who fell during the war between the states* (Philadelphia: Lippincott, 1875), p. 512. Hereafter cited as Walker.
2. George P. Terrill to John Allen Terrill, Salem, Va., August 24, 1854. Terrill Family Papers, PE.
3. William H. Terrill to F. H. Smith, February 22, 1854. Superintendents Correspondence, VMI Archives.
4. William H. Terrill to F. H. Smith, October 11, 1854. Superintendents Correspondence, VMI Archives.
5. The cost of a pay cadet at VMI in 1854 was about $300 and about $347 in 1858.
6. William H. Terrill to John Allen Terrill, Warm Springs, November 9, 1854. Terrill Family Papers, PE.
7. James B. Terrill to John A. Terrill, February 12, 1855. Terrill Family Papers, PE. Meals were prepared from a supply of apples, bacon, beef, coffee, corn, eggs, molasses, potatoes, and rice, along with various spices and tea.
8. James B. Terrill to John A. Terrill, May 10, 1855. Terrill Family Papers, PE.
9. F. H. Smith to W. H. Terrill, February 7, 1856. Superintendents Correspondence, VMI Archives.
10. William H. Terrill to Col. F. H. Smith, February 13, 1856. Superintendents Correspondence, VMI Archives.
11. William H. Terrill to Col. F. H. Smith, [April] 1856 (undated). Superintendents Correspondence, VMI Archives.
12. E-mail from Diane B. Jacob, VMI Archives, to the author April 11, 2005.
13. William H. Terrill to Col. F. H. Smith, January 31, 1857. Superintendents Correspondence, VMI Archives.
14. F. H. Smith to William H. Terrill, February 2, 1857. Superintendents Correspondence, VMI Archives.
15. Merit Roll, July 5, 1858. VMI Archives.
16. Henry Kyd Douglas. *I Rode with Stonewall* (Greenwich, CT.: Fawcett, 1961), p. 225.
17. Evelyn Lee Moore, "A Few Notes About Germantown, Va.," unpublished article, author's collection.
18. "Grand Military and Civil Ball," *Staunton Spectator*, December 25, 1860; Notice in *Staunton Vindicator*, April 30, 1859.
19. Notice in *Staunton Vindicator*, April 30, 1859.
20. James B. Terrill to G. A. Porterfield, February 8, 1861. Terrill Family Papers, PE.
21. Sketch of James Barbour Terrill, courtesy of Mercer Terrill Vaden, Richmond, Va., 1977 Hereafter cited as Sketch of James Barbour Terrill; Walker, p. 512–513.
22. James B. Terrill to Gov. John Letcher, April 5, 1861, VMI Archives. The letter, clearly dated April 5, 1861, carries an endorsement dated May 5 by John B. Baldwin. Because of this endorsement and the fact that James states he has been in service at Harpers Ferry, and was relieved of duty by an act of the Virginia Convention, the proper date of the letter should be May 5, 1861.
23. Ibid.
24. Ibid.
25. "13th Brigade — Training of Officers of:" *Lexington Gazette*, April 26, 1861.
26. Walker, p. 513.
27. Clement A. Evans, dd., *Confederate Military History* (Wilmington, NC: Broadfoot, 1987–1989), Virginia Volume, p. 125.

Notes — Chapter V

28. J. Wm. Jones, "Reminiscences of the Army of Northern Virginia, or the Boys in Gray, as I saw them from Harper's Ferry in 1861 to Appomattox Courthouse in 1865," *Southern Historical Society Papers* 9 (1881): p. 92. Hereafter cited as Jones, SHSP.

29. Zephaniah Turner Ross, *A Different Window ... a different victory. The Civil War Records. Diaries and Letters of Zephaniah Turner Ross, Captain, Company B, 13th Virginia Infantry Regiment, May, 1863–September, 1864* (Orange, VA: Orange County Historical Society, 1999), p. 184. Hereafter cited as Ross.

30. OR, Vol. 2, p. 131.

31. Diary kept by James Stanley Newman, Gordonsville Grays, Co. C, 13th Va. Inf. Eleanor S. Brockenbrough Library, The Museum of the Confederacy, Richmond, Va., typescript, p. 5. Hereafter cited as J. S. Newman Diary.

32. Jones, SHSP 9, p. 131.

33. P. Edloe Jones to My dear Pa, Camp Fairfax, August 31, 1861. Jones Family Papers, 1853–1908, Accession #13407, Special Collections, Alderman Library, University of Virginia, Charlottesville, Va. Hereafter cited as Jones Family Papers.

34. Ibid.

35. Bull Run Time—meaning to run, as the Northern troops fled at the first battle of Bull Run in July 1861.

36. "The taking of Mason's and Munson's hills." *Richmond Dispatch*, September 7, 1861.

37. "Major Terrill's Official Report of Skirmishes Near Alexandria," *Richmond Whig*, September 14, 1861.

38. Companies B, C, F, G, H and I all contributed to the force sent to Lewinsville.

39. Order Book, Order No. 58, September 10, 1861, court to convene on Sept. 11. A. P. Hill Papers, Virginia Historical Society, Richmond, Va.

40. OR, Vol. 5, p. 183.

41. Ibid., p. 184.

42. The casualty lists do not show any of the artillerymen killed or wounded at Lewinsville.

43. OR, Vol. 5, 181–2.

44. P. E. Jones to his mother, Camp Blair, Sept. 17th/61. Jones Family Papers.

45. "From the 13th Virginia Infantry," *Richmond Daily Dispatch*, September 23, 1861.

46. J. Barbour Terrill to Cornelia H. Wise, Head Quarters 13th Inf., Near Centreville, November 4th, 1861. Copies in possession of the author, provided by Evelyn Lee Moore.

47. J. Barbour Terrill to Cornelia H. Wise, In Camp near Centreville, November 15th, 1861. Copies in possession of the author, provided by Evelyn Lee Moore.

48. George Terrill to John Letcher, Mobile, Alabama, 13th November 1861, Reel 4768, exposure 213–214. Virginia. Governor (1860–1864: Letcher). Executive Papers of Governor John Letcher, 1859–1863. Accession 36787. State Government Records Collection, The Library of Virginia, Richmond, Va. Hereafter cited as Letcher Executive Papers.

49. Order Book, A. P. Hill Papers, Virginia Historical Society, Richmond, Va.; Terrill Letters, Copies in possession of the author, provided by Evelyn Lee Moore.

50. J. Barbour Terrill to Cornelia H. Wise, Head Quarters 13th Inf., Near Centreville, November 4th, 1861. Copies in possession of the author, provided by Evelyn Lee Moore.

51. Ibid.

52. J. Barbour Terrill to Cornelia H. Wise, In Camp near Centreville, November 15th, 1861. Copies in possession of the author, provided by Evelyn Lee Moore.

53. "Married," *Richmond Whig*, December 31, 1861. The bride's name was spelled Drury, and James' residence was given as Manassas.

54. John Hyde Cameron Recollections, Alumni Biographical File, VMI Archives; Philip M. Terrill to Emily C. Porterfield, December 5, 1861. Terrill Family Papers, PE.

55. Walker, p. 513.

56. William R. Terrill to Edwin M. Stanton, Camp Stanton, Opposite Columbia, Tennessee, March 28, 1862. File T-241, Letters Received, Adjutant General.

57. Although elected to the position of lieutenant colonel on April 26, the date of his appointment is given as April 15, 1862.

58. OR, Vol. 12, part 1, p. 792.

59. Sketch of James Barbour Terrill

60. Sketch of James Barbour Terrill; the Thirteenth Virginia earned the nickname "Bloody Thirteenth" because of the hard fighting its men had done.

61. David F. Riggs, *13th Virginia Infantry* (Lynchburg, VA: Howard, 1988), p. 20. Hereafter cited as Riggs.

62. OR, Vol. 12, part 2, p. 235.

63. Ibid., p. 232.

64. Ibid., p. 232.

65. Provision returns, August 23–29, 1862, 13th Virginia Infantry. The Lomax-Early Papers, MS 1354, H. Furlong Baldwin Library, Maryland Historical Society, Baltimore, MD.

66. Special Order No. 272, HQ Valley District, Sept. 24, 1862. Section 19, Jubal Anderson Early Papers, Virginia Historical Society, Richmond, Va.

67. Provision returns, 13th Virginia Infantry. The Lomax-Early Papers, MS 1354, H. Furlong Baldwin Library, Maryland Historical Society, Baltimore, MD.

68. George H.T. Greer, "All thoughts are ab-

sorbed in the War," *Civil War Times Illustrated* 17 (December 1978), p. 34.

69. Cornelia H. Wise Moore Recollections, Moore-Wise Family Papers, MS 1361, Jones Memorial Library, Lynchburg, Va.

70. Walker, p. 514.

71. Compiled Service Record, James B. Terrill, 13th Virginia Infantry. National Archives, Washington, D.C. Hereafter cited as CSR, James B. Terrill; Reuben Manning Newman Civil War [Diary], 1862–1867 (Accession #4261), Albert and Shirley Small Special Collections, University of Virginia Library, Charlottesville, Va. Hereafter cited as R. M. Newman Diary.

72. Ross, p. 26.

73. R. M. Newman Diary, May 3.

74. Walbrook D. Swank, *Raw Pork and Hardtack: A Civil War Memoir From Manassas to Appomattox* (Shippensburg, PA: Burd Street Press, 1996), p. 39. Hereafter cited as *Raw Pork and Hardtack*.

75. R. M. Newman Diary, May 3.

76. Capt. Samuel D. Buck. *With the old Confeds: Actual Experiences of a Captain in the Line* (Baltimore: Houck, 1925; Reprinted, Gaithersburg, MD: Butternut Press, 1893), p. 78–79. Hereafter cited as Buck. A slightly different account by Buck appears in the *Confederate Veteran* 13, no. 1 (January 1905), p. 20–22.

77. *Raw Pork and Hardtack*, p. 40–41.

78. *Ibid.*

79. Buck, p. 81.

80. S.D. Buck, "Thirteenth Virginia at Fredericksburg," *Confederate Veteran* 13, no. 1 (January 1905), p. 21.

81. W. S. Newman to "My Dear Wife," Camp 13th Va. Vols., May 9th, 1863. Newman-Henshaw Family Papers (Mss. A N556 2), The Filson Historical Society, Louisville, Ky.

82. S. Bassett French to Colonel J. B. Terrill, Executive Department Va., Richmond, May 26, 1863. Letcher Executive Papers, reel 4778, frame 202–3.

83. *Ibid.*

84. R. M. Newman Diary, May 23.

85. Douglas Carroll, MD, ed., *The Letters of F. Stanley Russell* (Baltimore: Harrod, 1963), p. 20–21.

86. Sketch of James B. Terrill

87. Diary of Fannie Wise Rixey, June 9, 1863. Notes courtesy of Evelyn Lee Moore.

88. Riggs, p. 35.

89. *Ibid.*

90. "Gen. Wm. R. Terrill," *National Tribune*, March 23, 1893.

91. Riggs, p. 35.

92. Alexander Hunter, "Thirteenth Virginia Infantry — Humor," *Confederate Veteran* 16, no. 7 (July 1908), p. 339–342.

93. *Ibid..*

94. Riggs, p. 37.

95. R. M. Newman, October 1, 1863

96. Riggs, p. 38.

97. CSR, James B. Terrill. Other documents show that it was in mid–December before the appointment was officially made. He was confirmed by the Confederate government on February 16, 1864, accepting it on March 28, 1864.

98. R. M. Newman, Nov. 30, 1863.

99. Riggs, p. 41.

100. Walbrook D. Swank, *Stonewall Jackson's Foot Cavalry: Company A, 13th Virginia Infantry* (Shippensburg, PA: Burd Street Press, 2001), p. 18. Hereafter cited as Swank.

101. J. Barbour Terrill to George [P. Terrill], Hd. Quarters 13th Va. Inf., April 19th, 1864. Frederick M. Dearborn collection of military and political Americana, Part II: The Civil War and the Confederacy, MS Am 1649.24, Houghton Library, Harvard University, Cambridge, Mass., by permission of the Houghton Library, Harvard University.

102. Sketch of James B. Terrill.

103. Riggs, p. 45.

104. George Q. Peyton, "Pegram's Brigade at Spotsylvania," *Confederate Veteran* 38, no. 2 (February 1930), p. 59.

105. "Lee to the Rear," *Richmond Times Dispatch*, July 12, 1903.

106. Sketch of James B. Terrill.

107. Riggs, p. 50.

108. Riggs, p. 51.

109. Buck, p. 19.

110. Swank, p. 56–57.

111. "We hear an affecting incident...," *Richmond Examiner*, June 8, 1864.

112. Sketch of James B. Terrill.

113. Walker, p. 515; burial reported by Major General G. K. Warren at 10:15 A.M., May 31st, 1864, OR, Vol. 36, p. 390.

114. William H. Terrill to John Letcher, Richmond, June 22, 1864. Letcher Papers.

115. "Col. J. B. Terrill...," *Lexington Gazette*, Lexington, Va., July 22, 1864.

116. George P. Terrill to Philip M. Terrill, August 31, 1864, Terrill Family Papers, PE.

117. William H. Terrill to Emily Porterfield, January 8, 1866. Terrill Family Papers, PE.

118. *Richmond Dispatch*, Richmond, Va., September 6, 1884.

119. The children were: Mercer Terrill Vaden (1896–1985), Thomas B. Vaden (about 1900–1992), and Charlotte D. Vaden (1901–1999), who married a man by the name of Warwick.

Chapter VI

1. William H. Terrill to Emily C. Porterfield, Warm Springs, October 27, 1851. Terrill Family Papers, PE.
2. "The Terrill's of Bath," unpublished typescript by Evelyn Lee Moore, in author's possession.
3. Philip M. Terrill to W. T. Price, Brook Hill School, October 9, 1858. William T. Price Papers, Pocahontas County Historical Society, Marlinton, W. Va.
4. Commission dated June 7, 1861, Bath County Historical Society, Warm Springs, Va., and commission dated June 13, 1861, Eleanor S. Brockenbrough Library, The Museum of the Confederacy, Richmond, Va.
5. OR, Vol. 2, p. 266–67.
6. OR, Series 2, Vol. 3, p. 9.
7. OR, Series 2, Vol. 3, p. 9–10.
8. Phil M. Terrill to Major General McClelland [sic], [July 17, 1861], George B. McClellan Papers, Reel 9, Library of Congress, Washington, D.C.
9. Pass issued Philip M. Terrill, July 17, 1861. George B. McClellan Papers, Reel 9, Library of Congress, Washington, D.C.
10. Philip M. Terrill to Emily C. Porterfield, December 5, 1861. Terrill Family Papers, PE.
11. OR, Series 2, Vol. 3, p. 213.
12. William R. Terrill to Edwin M. Stanton, Camp Stanton, Opposite Columbia, Tennessee, March 28, 1862. File T-241, Letters Received, Secretary of War.
13. Sketch of Philip Mallory Terrill, Eleanor S. Brockenbrough Library, The Museum of the Confederacy, Richmond, Va. Hereafter cited as Sketch of Philip Mallory Terrill.
14. Ibid.
15. The actual letter of resignation is lost.
16. Letter of George H. Smith, June 22, 1863. Terrill Family Papers, PE.
17. Ibid.
18. Sketch of Philip Mallory Terrill.
19. George Baylor, *Bull Run to Bull Run: Four Years in the Army of Northern Virginia* (Richmond, VA: Johnson, 1900), p. 140. Hereafter cited as Baylor.
20. Ibid., p. 141.
21. OR, Vol. 29, Part 1, p. 441.
22. Ibid., p. 443.
23. Baylor, p. 144.
24. Dennis E. Frye, *12th Virginia Cavalry* (Lynchburg, VA: Howard, 1988), p. 51. Hereafter cited as Frye.
25. Baylor, p. 145.
26. Ibid.
27. OR, Vol. 29, part 1, p. 445.
28. Baylor, p. 145.
29. Frye, p. 52.
30. Baylor, p. 149.
31. Ibid.
32. Ibid., p. 154.
33. Ibid., p. 155–156.
34. Ibid., p. 156.
35. Emily C. Porterfield to Philip M. Terrill, Elmwood, December 18, 1863. Moore-Wise Family Papers, MS1361, Jones Memorial Library, Lynchburg, Va.
36. Ibid.
37. CSR, Philip M. Terrill, Company B, 12th Virginia Cavalry, National Archives, Washington, D.C.
38. Philip M. Terrill to Emily C. Porterfield, undated page, most likely written in January 1864. Terrill Family Papers, PE.
39. Philip M. Terrill to Emily C. Porterfield, Waynesboro, Va., March 10, 1864. Terrill Family Papers, PE.
40. Philip M. Terrill to Emily C. Porterfield, Camp of 12th Va. Cavalry Near Natural Bridge, April 10, 1864. Terrill Family Papers, PE. This quote refers to James and his son James Mercer Terrill.
41. Baylor, p. 173.
42. Sketch of Philip Mallory Terrill.
43. Philip M. Terrill to Emily Porterfield, Camp of Rosser's Brigade near Stony Creek Depot, Weldon & Petersburg R. R., Surry Co., July 7, 1864. Terrill Family Papers, PE.
44. Philip M. Terrill to Emily Porterfield, Camp of Rosser's Brigade, Reams' Station, July 31, 1864. Terrill Family Papers, PE.
45. William N. McDonald, *Laurel Brigade, Originally Ashby's Cavalry* (Arlington, VA: Beatty, 1969), p. 273–4. Hereafter cited as McDonald.
46. General Order, Headquarters Cavalry Corps, September 3, 1864. Terrill Family Papers, PE.
47. Frye, p. 74.
48. McDonald, p. 303.
49. George P. Terrill to Philip M. Terrill, Salem, November 4, 1864. Terrill Family Papers, PE.
50. Philip M. Terril to Emily C. Porterfield, Camp of the 12th Va. Cav., Valley of Virginia, November 5, 1864. Terrill Family Papers, PE.
51. Sketch of Philip Mallory Terrill.
52. Baylor, p. 222.
53. Sketch of Philip Mallory Terrill.
54. Statement of Dr. J. H. Baldwin, Terrill Family Papers, PE.
55. William H. Terrill to Maj. Genl. Rosser, Staunton, November 24, 1864. Rosser Papers, Alderman Library, University of Virginia.
56. Moore-Wise Family Papers, MS1361, Jones Memorial Library, Lynchburg, Va.
57. Sketch of Philip Mallory Terrill.

58. *Ibid.*
59. *Ibid.*

Appendix II

1. The Taylor Family, The State, Richmond, September 2, 1886.
2. "Congress and Its Work," The New York Times, April 28, 1882.
3. Letter of Ezra J. Warner to Mrs. Maurice Moore, Douglas, Arizona, February 22, 1954. Ezra J. Warner research collection on Civil War generals, 1952–1968, James Barbour Terrill File, Chicago Historical Society, Chicago, Illinois.
4. "About William R. Terrill," http://tripatlas.com/William_R._Terrill. Accessed January 28, 2008.
5. "Information On Burial Of Two Civil War Generals Is Revealed In A Letter Here." Undated, unidenti?ed newspaper clipping, Terrill Family Papers, Porter?eld Estate, Bath County Historical Society, Warm Springs, Va. Hereafter cited as Information On Burial, BCHS.
6. Information On Burial, BCHS.

Bibliography

Manuscripts and Public Records

Alleghany County Circuit Court, Covington, VA.
    Superior Court Order Book, 1822–1830.
    Chancery Records.
    Marriage Records.
Bath County Circuit Court, Warm Springs, VA.
    Law Order Books.
    Will and Inventory Book.
    Chancery Records.
    County Court Order Books.
    Deed Book 9.
    Register of Deaths.
    Photograph of William H. Terrill.
    Land Books, 1838–1890.
Bath County Historical Society, Warm Springs, VA.
    Terrill Family Papers, Porterfield Estate.
    Papers of William H. Terrill.
    James B. Terrill Letter, October 15, 1856.
    Commission of Philip M. Terrill, June 7, 1861.
    Terrill Family Photographs.
    Photograph of old Bath County Courthouse and Jail.
Chicago Historical Society, Chicago.
    Ezra J. Warner research collection on Civil War generals, 1952–1968 (James B. Terrill File; William R. Terrill File).
Cincinnati Historical Society, Cincinnati, OH.
    Special Orders, Army of the Ohio, Second Division (fUS8AC).
Cleveland Public Library, Cleveland, OH.
    The Civil War Diary of Private Josiah Ayre (transcribed by James Glauser, 1975).
Don C. Terrill, Alexandria, VA.
    Terrill Society of America — Descendents of William Henry Terrill.
Eleanor S. Brockenbrough Library, Museum of the Confederacy, Richmond, VA.
    Diary kept by James Stanley Newman, Co. C, 13th Va. Inf. (typescript).
    Philip Mallory Terrill Papers and Artifacts.
Filson Historical Society, Louisville, KY.
    James F. Mohr Letters.
    Newman — Henshaw Family Papers.
First Presbyterian Church, Covington, VA.
    Session Records.
Gary L. Shugar, Reading, PA.
    William R. Terrill File.
Houghton Library, Harvard University, Cambridge, MA.
    James Barbour Terrill, letter to George P. Terrill, April 19, 1864, with letter to Charles Colcock Jones from William H. Terrill. Frederick M. Dearborn Collection of Military and Political Americana, Part II: The Civil War and the Confederacy, MS Am 1649.24 (939). By permission of the Houghton Library, Harvard University.
Howard Revercomb Hammond, Greenville, SC.
    Terrill — Scott Correspondence.
Indiana Historical Society, Indianapolis.
    Transcript of Diary of John Fritz, Co. D, 101st Regiment Indiana Infantry.
Indiana State Library, Indianapolis.
    History of the 101st Regiment of Volunteer Infantry of Indiana. By Levi P. Fodrea, official historian of regiment. Annotated and emendated by Hugh Anthony Maker.
Jeannette Grosvenor, Chardon, OH.
    Letters of John C. Hathaway, Company E, 105th Ohio Infantry.

Jefferson County Court House, Charles Town, WV.
    County Court Office: Register of Deaths; Register of Marriages.
Jefferson County Historical Society, Charles Town, WV.
    Porterfield Family Papers.
    Photograph of George A. Porterfield.
    Mexican War Sword of George A. Porterfield.
    Sword Presentation letter from the City of Richmond, 1847.
Jones Memorial Library, Lynchburg, VA.
    Moore—Wise Family Papers, 1850–1980 (MS-1361).
Kentucky Historical Society, Frankfort, KY.
    Captain Robert B. Taylor Diaries.
Library of Congress, Washington, D.C.
    Abraham Lincoln Papers—G. A. Porterfield Letter (online).
    Picket Papers—Roll 65—Pay voucher for Lt. Col. J. B. Terrill, August 30, 1862.
    Papers of George B. McClellan (Microfilm).
    Papers of Jedediah Hotchkiss (Microfilm).
    Photograph of William Rufus Terrill, before 1862.
    A. D. Bache Papers (Microfilm).
    Photograph of Alexander McD. McCook.
    Photograph of Alexander D. Bache.
    Photograph of Charles S. Cotter.
    Map of Hanover County, Virginia
Library of Virginia, Richmond, VA.
    Pitzer—Martin Papers (Acc. 40344).
    Department of Military Affairs Papers (Acc. 27684).
    Executive Papers of Governor John Letcher, 1859–1863 (Acc. 36787).
    J. Stanley Newman Diary (Acc. 24035).
Maryland Historical Society, Baltimore.
    Lomax-Early Papers, Provision Returns, 13th Virginia Infantry (Ms. 1354).
Maryland State Archives, Annapolis.
    Guy Weatherly Collection of McParlin Family Papers (MSA SC 595).
National Archives and Records Service, Washington, D.C.
    RG—23—Records of the Coast and Geodetic Survey: Correspondence of A. D. Bache, Superintendent of the Coast and Geodetic Survey, 1843–1865 (M-642).
    RG-92—Records of the Quartermaster General's Office: Register of Letters Received; Letters Received; Clothing & Equipage Letters Received; Monthly Forage Reports; Consolidated Quartermasters File.
    RG-94—Records of the Adjutant General's Office, 1780s–1917: Letters Received by the Office of the Adjutant General, 1822–1860 (M-567); Letters Sent by the Office of the Adjutant General (M-565); Endorsements 1851–1870 (E-295); Compiled Service Records of Volunteer Soldiers Who Served During the Mexican War in Organizations from the State of Virginia (First Virginia Volunteers [George A. Porterfield File]); U.S. Pension Records—Mexican War (George A. Porterfield File); U.S. Pension Records—Civil War (William R. Terrill File; James H. Reed File)
    Records Relating to the U.S. Military Academy: U.S. Military Academy Cadet Application Papers, 1805–1866 (M-688) (William R. Terrill; George A. Porterfield; Guy V. Henry); Letters Received Regarding Military Academy (E-234); Letters Sent Regarding Military Academy (M-91); Monthly Class Reports and Conduct Rolls (E-232).
    Returns from U.S. Military Posts, 1800–1916 (M-617): West Point, NY; Fort Columbus, NY; Fort Hamilton, NY; Fort Mackinac, MI; Fort Deynaud, FL; Fort McRay, FL; Fort Kissimmee, FL; Fort Leavenworth, KS.
    Returns of Regular U.S. Artillery Units (M-727): 3rd U.S. Artillery; 4th U.S. Artillery; 5th U.S. Artillery.
    Muster Rolls of Regular Army Organizations, 1784–1912: Battery L, 3rd U.S. Artillery; Battery C, E, & L, 4th U.S. Artillery; Battery H, 5th U.S. Artillery.
    Field Records of Hospital Records, 1821–1912 (E-544): New York (United States Military Academy, West Point [#606–609]).
    Letters of Army Appointments (E-314).
    Senate Rolls
    Register of Letters Received (M-711).
    General Orders Issued.
    Special Orders Issued.
    Records of the Recruiting Service, Letters Sent.
    Reports of the Recruiting Service, 1856; 1861 (E-481).
    Army Registers of Appointments, 1848–1855.
    "Generals' Papers and Books" (E-159, Box 14).
    Historical & Alphabetical Registry of Commissioned Officers of the Line of the Army, 1853.
    Register of Army Commissions.

Station Book for Officers and Regiments of Artillery, Cavalry and Infantry of the Regular Army. 1861–1862.

Monthly Statements, 5th Artillery.

Register of Requisitions on the Secretary of War for funds to conduct the Recruiting Service.

Letters Sent Relating to Nominations in the Army, 1837–76 (E-294).

Compiled Military Service Records of Volunteers Who Served in Union Organizations from the State of Ohio: 1st Regiment Ohio Light Artillery (Charles A. [S] Cotter, Company A).

Records Relating to Volunteers and Volunteer Organizations, Civil War: Illinois (123rd Illinois Infantry [Order Books, Company A]); Indiana (101st Indiana Infantry [Order Books]); Ohio (105th Ohio Infantry [Regimental Letter, Endorsement, Order and Misc. Book]).

RG—99—Records of the Paymaster Generals Office: Register of Letters Received; Pay Records of William R. Terrill, Vol. 11, p. 394–95 (E-53).

RG-107—Records of the Office of the Secretary of War: Letters Received by the Secretary of War (M-619); Letters Sent by the Secretary of War, Relating to Military Affairs, 1800–1889 (M-6); Orders and Endorsements Sent by the Secretary of War, 1846–1870 (M-444); Applications for Appointment (Civilian) (G. A. Porterfield File); Applications for Appointment (Army) (William R. Terrill File); Telegrams Collected by the Office of the Secretary of War (unbound), 1860–1870 (M-504); Applications for Appointment to Civilian or Military Positions, 1820–87.

RG-108—Records of the Headquarters of the Army: Special Orders Issued; Letters Sent by the Headquarters of the Army (Main Series) (M-857); Letters Received; Register of Letters Received; Endorsements and Memorandum Sent.

RG—109—Records of the Confederate States of America: Compiled Service Records of Confederate Soldiers Who Served in Organizations from the State of Virginia (M-324) (157th Virginia Militia, George P. Terrill File; 25th Virginia Infantry, George A. Porterfield File; 25th Virginia Infantry, Philip M. Terrill File; 13th Virginia Infantry, James B. Terrill File; 62nd Virginia Infantry (Mounted), Philip M. Terrill File; 12th Virginia Cavalry, Philip M. Terrill File); Compiled Service Records of Confederate General and Staff Officers, and Nonregimental Enlisted Men (M-331): George P. Terrill File; James B. Terrill File; Confederate Papers Relating to Citizens or Business Firms (M-346): George M. Pitzer File; William H. Terrill File; Warm Springs Turnpike Company File (George A. Porterfield File; Emily C. Porterfield File); Letters Received by the Confederate Secretary of War (M-437); Letters Received by the Confederate Adjutant and Inspector General (M-474); Records of the Virginia Forces (M-998); Union Provost Marshals' File of Papers Relating to Individual Citizens (M-345).

RG-153—Records of the Office of the Judge Advocate General (Army): Court-Martial Case Files, 1809–1894, File NN-3816.

RG-156—Records of the Office of the Chief of Ordnance: Letters Sent (E-3); Letters Received (E-21).

RG-192—Records of the Office of the Commissary General of Subsistence: Letters Received; Letters Sent; Subsistence Officers; Record of Officers Rendering Returns of Provisions & Property, 1861–1867; Provision Book; Expenditure of Appropriation for Subsistence for the Fiscal Year, ending June 1857.

RG-217—Records of the Accounting Officers of the Department of the Treasury: Misc. Letters Sent by the 3rd Auditors Office; Letters Sent by the 2nd Auditors Office; Report Books, 2nd Auditors Office; Report Books, 3rd Auditors Office; War Requisition Books; Credit Requisitions; Records of Certificates Paid by the Second Auditor of the Treasury Department

RG-391—Records of United States Regular Army Mobile Units, 1821–1942: 5th U.S. Artillery (Letters Received, 1861–1862 [E-252]; Regimental Order Book, 1861–1862 [E-253]; Descriptive Books, 1857–1863; Letters Sent; Orders Received, 1861–1865 [E-254]).

RG-393—Records of U.S. Army Continental Commands, 1821–1920: Department of the Cumberland and Division and Department of Tennessee (Endorsements Sent [E-871]; Letters Received [E-877]; Letters Received [E-878]; Endorsements Sent, Mar.

1862–June 1865 [E-911]; Letters ... [E-920]; Orders... [E-944]; Special Orders, Nov. 1861–June 1862 [E-890]); Army of the Cumberland (General Orders, 2nd Division [E-6465]; Letters... [E-3491]); Department of Washington (Special Orders Issued [E-5367]; Register of Letters Received [E-5363]; Endorsements Sent [E-5366]; Endorsements [E-5362]; Register of Officers [E-5368]); Department of the Ohio, 1862–4 (General Orders [E-6540]; Register of Letters Received, Aug. 1862–Apr. 1864 [E-3489]; Special Orders, Aug. 1862–Apr. 1864 [E-3494]; Department of the East (Special Orders; Register of Letters Received; Letters Received); Department of Florida (Orders and Special Orders Issued [E-1627]; Letters Sent [E-1640]; Special Orders; Letters Received [E-1623]; Records of Fort Kissimmee); 1st District of Florida (Register of Letters Received); Troops Serving in Kansas (Special Orders Issued); Department and Army of the Ohio (Letters and Reports Received, 1862–65 [E-3541]).
RG — 418 — Records of St. Elizabeths Hospital: Records of Medical Records Branch (E-66) (Katherine Mackey, File #12116, Box 241; Katherine Mackey, File #11870, Box 229).

Ohio Historical Society, Columbus, Ohio
Letters Received by the Governor and Adjutant General, Series 147; Vol. 967
A. S. Bloomfield Civil War Letters (transcriptions).

Perryville State Historical Site, Perryville, KY
Civil War: The Letters of John Holbrook Morse, 1861–1865. Edited by Biznca Morse Federico and Betty Louise Wright. Washington, D.C., 1975.

Pocahontas County Courthouse, Marlinton, WV.
Circuit Court Office: Common Law Order Books.
County Court: County Court Order Books.

Pocahontas County Historical Society, Marlinton, WV.
William T. Price Papers and Scrapbooks.

Porterfield Family Information.
Mr. & Mrs. Philip T. Porterfield, III, Charles Town, WV.

Public Records
1830–1930 Census Records of the United States.
1850–1860 Slave Schedule of the United States.

Rockbridge County Court House, Lexington, VA.
Marriage Records.

St. Lawrence University, Owen D. Young Library, Canton, New York.
William B. Goodrich Collection 1853–1898 — Mss. 056.
The American Nation: Lives of her Fallen and Brave Living Heroes, Part 18, p. 430.

Sally Mead, Basin, WY.
Genealogical Records— George P. Terrill.

Special Collections Research Center, Morris Library, Southern Illinois University at Carbondale, Carbondale, IL.
Civil War Collection 4: William R. Terrill Letter, Jan. 30, 1862 — box 1, folder 6.

Stones River National Battlefield Park, Murfreesboro, TN.
Letters of Peter Fitzpatrick, Battery H, 5th U.S. Artillery.

Superior Court, District of Columbia, Washington, D.C.
Probate Division: Docket Book, 1911–1912.

Terrill Family Collection, Richard L. Armstrong, Hot Springs, VA.
Obituaries of William H. Terrill.
Sketch of Warm Springs, VA, 1859, Evelyn Lee Moore.
Evelyn Lee Moore Correspondence with author.
"The Terrill's of Bath," by Evelyn Lee Moore.
Notes of a telephone conversation with Miss Elizabeth Jackson Morton, February 27, 1978.
Sketch of James Barbour Terrill — Mercer Terrill Vaden.
Photograph of James Barbour Terrill — Mercer Terrill Vaden.
"A Few Notes About Germantown, Va." by Miss Evelyn L. Moore.
Letters of James B. Terrill to Cornelia H. Wise —from Evelyn L. Moore.
"Reminiscences of Cornelia H. Wise Moore."— notes provided by Evelyn L. Moore.
Correspondence with various Terrill Relatives.
Photograph of Charlotte E. Drury Terrill — Mercer Terrill Vaden.
Photograph of Emily Barbour Terrill — Mercer Terrill Vaden.
Photograph of James Mercer Terrill — Mercer Terrill Vaden.
Photographs of Emily C. C. Terrill — Miss Elizabeth Jackson Morton.

Bibliography

Photograph of Emily D. Henry Terrill — Evelyn Lee Moore.
Photographs of William R. Terrill — Evelyn Lee Moore.
Photograph of John Allen Terrill — Miss Elizabeth Jackson Morton.
Photograph of Elizabeth "Betty" Porterfield — Miss Elizabeth Jackson Morton.
Photograph of William H. Terrill — Elizabeth P. Terrill Gravestone.
Photograph of George P. Terrill — Sarah B. Terrill Gravestone.
Texas Tech University Library, Lubbock, Texas.
The Andrew Johnson Papers (Microfilm).
Thomas, Anne Terrill (Mrs. Arthur), Pennsburg, PA.
Records of the Terrill and related families.
Photograph of George P. Terrill.
Correspondence with the author.
United States Military Academy Archives, West Point, NY.
Alexander Dallas Bache Papers.
Cullum File #1594, William R. Terrill, Class of 1853.
Register of Punishment, No. 2, Sept. 1847–Oct. 1857.
Register of Delinquencies, Volume 5, 1846–1852.
Register of Delinquencies, Volume 6, 1852–1856.
Post Order Books, 1851–53; 1856; 1864.
Superintendent's Letter Book, 1856.
Superintendent's Letter Book No. 2 and No. 3.
Letters Received by the Adjutant.
Applications for Promotion.
Treasurers Records, 1849–1853.
Descriptive Lists — Alphabetical List of New Cadets for 1849.
Vertical File, William R. Terrill (1853).
Photograph of Cadets George Crook, Philip Sheridan, and John Nugen.
Photograph of General William R. Terrill, USMA Class of 1853.
Early Photographs of U.S. Military Academy.
Photograph of Charles C. Parsons.
Photograph of Emily H. Terrill — William R. Terrill Gravestone.
United States Army Military History Institute, Carlisle, PA (The Army Heritage and Education Center).
Brian Pohanka Photograph Collection: Photograph of General William R. Terrill.
Massachusetts Commandery, Military Order of the Loyal Legion: Photographs of William R. Terrill.
University of Virginia (Alderman Library), Charlottesville, VA.
Albert and Shirley Small Special Collections Library: Thomas L. Rosser, Papers, 1860–1950, Accession #1171, 1171-a, 1171-b; Reuben Manning Newman Civil War [Diary], 1862–1867, Accession #4261; Papers of the Related Morton and Dickinson Families of Orange and Caroline Counties, VA, 1727–1978, Accession #9755–9775-b; Morton Family Material Concerning, 1792, Accession #4065.
Special Collections: Morton — Halsey Collection, 1786–1938, Accession #3995; Jones Family Papers, 1853–1908, Accession #13407.
Alumni Catalogue.
Virginia Historical Society, Richmond, VA.
John Letcher Papers (Mss1 L5684 a FA2).
Jubal Anderson Early Papers (Mss3: Ea 7642).
A. P. Hill Papers, Order Book (Mss1 H5503 a).
Confederate States of America, Department of Henrico (Mss3 C7604 a 14–253).
Faulkner Family Papers (Mss1 F2735 a FA2).
Robert Knox Sneden Diaries (Mss5: 7 Sn237: U).
Virginia Military Institute Archives, Lexington, VA.
Alumni Biographical Files: George P. Terrill, Class of 1849; George A. Porterfield, Class of 1844: James B. Terrill, Class of 1858; John Hyde Cameron, Class of 1857.
Superintendents Correspondence — Incoming and Outgoing.
Board of Visitor's Records.
Andrew Cameron Lewis Gatewood Papers.
Letter of James B. Terrill, Richmond, April 5th, 1861 (Mss. 00161).
Reports of VMI — Document No. 11 — April 28, 1855.
VMI Order Books, 1846–1857.
Merit Rolls, 1855–1858.
Personal Accounts, 1847–1849.
Stonewall Jackson Papers (Mss. 00102).
Photograph of George A. Porterfield, c. 1895 (Class of 1844).
Photograph of General Francis H. Smith, 1862.
Warm Springs Presbyterian Church, Warm Springs, VA.
Session Records.
Western Kentucky University, Bowling Green, KY

Lewis—Starling Collection: Letter of Samuel M. Starling (copy courtesy Perryville Battlefield Park).

Wilson, Harry H., Munfordville, KY. Information Regarding Fort Terrill.

Articles

"At Rose Hill..." *Lexington Gazette,* Lexington, VA, August 29, 1850.

"Attention Volunteers!" *Richmond Enquirer,* Richmond, VA, November 21, 1846.

Barnett, James. "Munfordville in the Civil War." *The Register of the Kentucky Historical Society* 69, no. 4, October 1971: 339–361.

"The Battle of Chaplin Hills." *Louisville Daily Journal,* Louisville, KY, October 14, 1862.

"The Battle of Chaplin Hills." *Mahoning Register,* Youngstown, OH, November 13, 1862.

"Battle of Chaplin Hills—From the 105th Regiment." *Western Reserve Chronicle,* Warren, OH, November 12, 1862.

"The Battle of Chaplin—Movements of Generals Crittenden, Sheridan, and Mitchel." *Louisville Journal,* Louisville, KY, October 16, 1862.

"The Battle of Chaplin's Hills." *The New York Herald,* New York, October 15, 1862.

"Battle of Philippi: An Account of the Wounding of Gen. B. F. Kelley by an Eye-Witness." *National Tribune,* Washington, D.C., May 12, 1892.

"Battle of Pittsburg [Landing]." *Berks & Schuylkill Journal,* Reading, PA, April 19, 1862.

Benham, H. W. "Recollections of West Virginia Campaign, with 'The Three Months Troops.' May, June and July, 1861. By an Engineer Officer." *Old and New* (June 1873): 677–678.

Bidgood, Joseph V. "List of General Officers and Their Staffs in the Confederate Army, Furnished By Virginia, As Far As I Have Been Able to Get Them." *Southern Historical Society Papers* 38, (1910): 156–183.

"Brigadier-General Terrell [*sic*]." *Berks & Schuylkill Journal,* Reading, PA, December 6, 1862.

"Brigadier General William R. Terrill..." *Louisville Daily Journal,* Louisville, KY, October 11, 1862.

Brock, R. A., ed. "A Narrative of the Service of Colonel Geo. A. Porterfield in Northwestern Virginia in 1861–'2." *Southern Historical Society Papers* 16 (1888): 82–91.

Buck, Capt. S. D. "Thirteenth Virginia at Fredericksburg." *Confederate Veteran* 13, no. 1 (July 1905): 20–22.

Cammack, J.H. "An Added Chapter of Recollections." *The Baptist Banner,* Huntington, WV, October 4, 1893.

"Camp Terrill." *Reading Daily Times,* Reading, PA, November 17, 1862.

"Capt. Terrill, ..." *Reading Daily Times,* Reading, PA, April 29, 1862.

"Captain Terrill at the Battle of Pittsburg." *Weekly Patriot and Union,* Harrisburg, PA, May 8, 1862.

"Captain William R. Terrill, ..." *Berks & Schuylkill Journal,* Reading, PA, July 13, 1861.

Christian, Colonel C. B. "The Battle at Bethesda Church." *Southern Historical Society Papers* 33 (1905).

"Circumstances of the Death of John A. Washington." *Daily Courier,* Zanesville, OH, September 25, 1861.

"The Civil War: Brother against Brother." *The Saturday Evening Post* 234, no. 15 (April 15, 1961), p. 103.

"Col. G. A. Porterfield Dead." *The Washington Post,* Washington, D.C., February 28, 1919.

"Col. George A. Porterfield Dies in his 97th Year." *Spirit of Jefferson,* Charlestown, Jefferson County, WV, March 4, 1919.

"Col. J. B. Terrill." *Lexington Gazette,* Lexington, VA, July 22, 1864.

"Col. William H. Terrill." *Spirit of Jefferson,* Charlestown, Jefferson County, WV, January 15, 1878.

"Died: At the Battle of Perryville, ..." *Reading Daily Times,* Reading, PA, October 17, 1862.

"Editorial Correspondence. Head Quarters 123d Illinois Regiment." *Mattoon Gazette Weekly,* Mattoon, IL, October 18, 1862.

"Editorial Correspondence. Headquarters 123d Reg. Ill. Vol." *Mattoon Gazette Weekly,* Mattoon, IL, November 22, 1862.

French, Steve. "Porterfield Never Recovers After Philippi." *The Washington Times,* Washington, D.C., June 14, 2003.

"From Capt. Terrill's Company." *Berks & Schuylkill Journal,* Reading, PA, September 21, 1861.

"From Gen. Taylor's Army." *Martinsburg Gazette,* Martinsburg, VA, October 14, 1847.

"From Louisville." *Cincinnati Daily Gazette,* Cincinnati, OH, September 17, 1862.

"From Nashville." *Toledo Commercial,* Toledo, OH, January 16, 1863.

"From the 105th." *Western Reserve Chronicle,* Warren, OH, November 12, 1862.

"From the 105th Regiment. They are now in Louisville, Ky." *Mahoning Herald,* Canfield, OH, September 18, 1862.

"From the 13th Virginia Infantry." *Richmond Daily Dispatch,* Richmond, VA, September 23, 1861.

"From the Army of the Cumberland." *Toledo Commercial,* Toledo, OH, April 14, 1863.

Bibliography

"The funeral of a brave man..." *Reading Daily Times*, Reading, PA, October 16, 1862.
"Funeral of Gen. Wm. R. Terrill." *Berks & Schuylkill Journal*, Reading, PA, October 18, 1862.
"Funeral of Mrs. William R. Terrill." *Democratic Register*, Sing Sing, NY, February 23, 1884.
"Further From the Battle at Perryville — Five Federal Generals Killed — Another Battle at Chaplins Creek." *Lynchburg Virginian*, Lynchburg, VA, October 15, 1862.
"The Gallant Dead." *Cincinnati Commercial*, Cincinnati, October 13, 1862.
"Gen. Wm. R. Terrill." *National Tribune*, Washington, D.C., March 23, 1893.
"Gen. Wm. R. Terrill, Killed." *Staunton Spectator*, Staunton, VA, October 21, 1862.
"Gen. William R. Terrill Killed." *Berks & Schuylkill Journal*, Reading, PA, October 11, 1862.
Gilbert, C. C. "Bragg's Invasion of Kentucky." *Southern Bivouac* 1 (October 1885), p. 298.
"Grand Military and Civil Ball." *Staunton Spectator*, Staunton, VA, December 25, 1860.
Greer, George H. T. "All Thoughts are Absorbed in the War." *Civil War Times Illustrated* 17, no. 8 (December 1978), p. 34.
Hillard, James M. "'You Are Strangely Deluded': General William Terrill." *Civil War Times Illustrated* 13, no. 10 (February 1975): 12–18.
"The Honor Roll of the University of Virginia." *Southern Historical Society Papers* 33, (1905): 55.
Hunter, Alexander. "Thirteenth Virginia Infantry — Humor." *Confederate Veteran* 16, no. 7 (July 1908): 339–342.
"In Memory of General Terrill, who fell in the Battle of Chaplin Hills." *Mahoning Register*, Youngstown, OH, December 4, 1862.
Johnson, General B. T. "Memoir of First Maryland Regiment." *Southern Historical Society Paper*, 9 (1881).
Jones, J. Wm. "Reminiscences of the Army of Northern Virginia, or the Boys in Gray, as I Saw Them from Harper's Ferry in 1861 to Appomattox Courthouse in 1865." *Southern Historical Society Papers* 9, (1881): 92, 131.
"The Killing of John A. Washington." *The Indiana True Republican*, Centreville, Wayne County, IN, October 10, 1861.
"The Late Col. W. H. Terrill." *Spirit of Jefferson*, Charlestown, Jefferson County, WV, December 25, 1877.
"The Late Fight in Greenbrier." *Richmond Sentinel*, Richmond, VA, September 15, 1863.
"The Late General Terrill." *National Intelligencer*, Washington, D.C., October 22, 1862.
"Lee to the Rear." *Richmond Times Dispatch*, Richmond, VA, July 12, 1903.
"Letter from Kentucky." *Berks & Schuylkill Journal*, Reading, PA, February 15, 1862.
"Letter from Adjutant John A. Stein." *The Daily Courier*, undated clipping from an Indiana newspaper, author's collection.
"Letter from Camp Shiloh — The Pea Ridge Reconnaissance in Force." *Semi-Weekly Dispatch*, Franklin, PA, May 6, 1862.
"Letter from Tennessee." *Berks & Schuylkill Journal*, Reading, PA, March 22, 1862.
"Loyality of Slaves." *Staunton Spectator*, Staunton, VA, September 24, 1861.
"Major Terrill's Official Report of Skirmishes Near Alexandria." *Richmond Whig*, Richmond, VA, September 14, 1861.
"Married." *Richmond Whig*, Richmond, VA, December 31, 1861.
"The May Campaign in Virginia." *Atlantic Monthly*, 14, no. 81, (July 1864), p. 124–132.
"A Merited Promotion." *Reading Daily Times*, Reading, PA, September 5, 1862.
Military Order of the Loyal Legion of the United States, Ohio Commandery. "Perryville and the Kentucky Campaign of 1862." *Sketches of War History, 1861–1865*. Vol. 5, p. 161. Cincinnati: Robert Clarke.
"Mrs. George A. Porterfield." *Spirit of Jefferson*, Charlestown, Jefferson County, WV, June 4, 1906.
"Newport News. Artillery Drill." *Cincinnati Enquirer*, Cincinnati, October 2, 1862.
"Newport News. Gone Into Camp." *Cincinnati Enquirer*, Cincinnati, October 4, 1862.
Notice in *Staunton Vindicator*, Staunton, VA, April 30, 1859.
"Official Information" *Confederate Veteran* 34, no. 6 (June 1926): 223.
"Obituary [Brig. Gen. William R. Terrill]." *Frank Leslie's Illustrated News*, New York, October 25, 1862, page 67.
"Obituary. Tribute to the Late Gen. Wm. R. Terrill." *New York Times*, New York, February 8, 1863, p. 3.
"Off for the War." *Berks & Schuylkill Journal*, Reading, PA, September 7, 1861.
"Old Berks at Pittsburg Landing." *Berks & Schuylkill Journal*, Reading, PA, April 19, 1862.
"The 105th Regiment." *Western Reserve Chronicle*, Warren, OH, October 22, 1862.
Ossad, Steven L. "The Terrill Boys Fought for Different Causes, but Found Unity under a Common Grave." *America's Civil War* 19, no. 4 (September 2006): 17–18; 20.
"Paging Through the Past." *Bath County Historical Society Newsletter* 31, no. 2 (July 2001): 5.
"Painful Accident." *The Salem Register*, Salem, VA, April 28, 1876.
"The Perryville Fight." *Louisville Daily Journal*, Louisville, KY, October 11, 1862.

Peyton, George Q. "Pegram's Brigade at Spotsylvania." *Confederate Veteran* 38, no. 2 (February 1930): 58–62.

Potts, J.N. "Personal Recollections of the War." *The Baptist Banner*, Huntington, WV, August 9, 1893.

Potts, J.N., late Adjutant, 18th Virginia Cavalry, C. S. A. "Recollections of the War Between The United States and The Confederate States of America (That 'Storm Cradled Nation that Fell.')." *Randolph Enterprise*, Elkins, WV, September 21, 1922.

"Proclamation of a Rebel Leader." *New York Times*, New York, June 13, 1861.

"Recollections of the Late Brigadier-General Terrill." *Philadelphia Inquirer*, Philadelphia, May 15, 1863.

"Recruiting for the Fifth." *Berks & Schuylkill Journal*, Reading, PA, July 13, 1861.

"Recruiting for the war..." *Berks & Schuylkill Journal*, Reading, PA, August 17, 1861, p. 2, col. 4.

"The remains of Generals..." *Louisville Daily Journal*, Louisville, KY, October 11, 1862.

Sanders, Stuart W. "The 1862 Kentucky Campaign and The Battle of Perryville." *Blue & Gray Magazine* 22, no. 5 (Holiday 2005).

"Serenade to Capt. Terrell [sic]." *Reading Daily Times*, Reading, PA, August 6, 1862.

Shugar, Gary L. "General William Rufus Terrill: The Civil War Officer that Reading Adopted." *Historical Review of Berks County* 71, no. 3 (Summer 2006): 111–114.

_____. "The 167th Pennsylvania: Civil War's Only All-Berks Regiment." *Historical Review of Berks County* 65, no. 3 (2000): 112.

"Sketches of Killed and Wounded Officers: Sketch of General Terrill." *The New York Herald*, New York, October 11, 1862.

A Staff Officer. "The Second Division at Shiloh." *Harper's New Monthly Magazine* 28, (December 1863–May 1864), [1864]: 828–833.

Steiner, Paul E. "Medical-Military Studies on the Civil War. 11. Brigadier General William R. Terrill, U.S.V., and Brigadier General James B. Terrill, C.S.A." *Military Medicine* 131, no. 2 (February 1966): 178–183.

Stewart, Maj. D. B. "Battle of Philippi Recounted." *Confederate Veteran* 13, no. 3 (March 1910), 116–118.

"Swords for the Volunteer Officers." *Richmond Whig*, Richmond, VA, February 19, 1847.

"The Taking of Mason's and Munson's Hills." *Richmond Dispatch*, Richmond, VA, September 7, 1861.

Tapp, Hambleton, ed. "The Battle of Perryville, October 8, 1862, as Described in the Diary of Captain Robert B. Taylor." *The Register of the Kentucky Historical Society* 60, no. 4 (October 1962): 255.

"The Taylor Family." *The State*, Richmond, VA, September 2, 1886.

"Terrill's Battery at Pittsburg Landing." *Berks & Schuylkill Journal*, Reading, PA, April 26, 1862.

"Terrill's Brigade." *Louisville Daily Journal*, Louisville, KY, October 23, 1862.

"Terrill's Brigade at Perryville." *National Tribune*, Washington, D.C., June 14, 1906.

"13th Brigade — Training of Officers of." *Lexington Gazette*, Lexington, VA, April 26, 1861.

"Thirteenth Virginia at Fredericksburg." *Confederate Veteran* 13, no. 1 (January 1905): 20–22.

"To the Editors of the Enquirer." *Richmond Enquirer*, Richmond, VA, November 20, 1862.

"Ups and Downs of an Ex-Confederate Soldier in the Years 1861–1865." *Hampshire Review*, Romney, WV, March 15–May 17, 1905.

"A Veteran of Two Wars." *Confederate Veteran* 22, no. 8, (August 1914): 359.

"Volunteers from Richmond." *Richmond Whig*, Richmond, VA, May 19, 1846.

"Volunteer Meeting." *Richmond Whig*, Richmond, VA, May 19, 1846.

"The War in Western Virginia: Letcher's Bridge Burning Order." *Daily Evening Bulletin*, Philadelphia, June 7, 1861. [Also in *New York Times*, June 10, 1861].

"A Washington Made a Priest." *The Star and Sentinel*, Gettysburg, PA, June 19, 1920.

"We hear an affecting incident..." *Richmond Examiner*, Richmond, VA, June 8, 1864.

"Who Wants to Enlist?" *Reading Daily Times*, Reading, PA, September 3, 1861.

"Wm. H. Terrell, Esq." *The Pocahontas Times*, Marlinton, WV, March 28, 1912, p. 1.

"Yesterday's *Republican*..." *Richmond Whig*, Richmond, VA, February 19, 1847.

Published and Online Works

"About William R. Terrill." http://tripatlas.com/William_R._Terrill. Last viewed January 28, 2008.

Angle, Paul M., ed. *Three Years in the Army of the Cumberland. The Letters and Diary of Major James A. Connolly*. Civil War Centennial Series, Bloomington: Indiana University Press, 1959.

Armstrong, Richard L. *Jackson's Valley Campaign: Battle of McDowell*. Lynchburg, VA: Howard, 1990.

Athearn, Robert G., ed. *Soldier In The West: The Civil War Letters of Alfred Lacey Hough*. Philadelphia: University of Pennsylvania Press, 1957.

Atkinson, George Wesley. *Prominent Men of West Virginia*. Wheeling, WV: Callin, 1890.

Bibliography

Aztec Club of 1847. *Aztec Club of 1847: History of its Founding.* www.aztecclub.com/history.htm 2006. Accessed 28 August 2000.

Bascom, Elizabeth Ethel Parker. *"Dear Lizzie": Letters Written by James "Jimmy" Garvin Crawford to his sweetheart Martha Elizabeth "Lizzie" Wilson while he was in the Federal Army during the War between the States, 1862–1865.* Ridgewood, NY: Bascom, 1978.

Baylor, George. *Bull Run to Bull Run: Four Years in the Army of Northern Virginia.* Richmond, VA: Johnson, 1900.

Biographical Directory of the United States Congress: 1774–Present. http://bioguide.congress.gov/scripts/biodisplay.pl?index. 2007.

Boatner, Mark Mayo, III. *The Civil War Dictionary.* 4th ed. New York: McKay, 1966.

Bohannon, Keith S. *The Giles, Alleghany and Jackson Artillery.* Lynchburg, VA: Howard, 1990.

Boney, F. N. *John Letcher of Virginia: The story of Virginia's Civil War Governor.* University, Alabama: University of Alabama Press, 1966.

Boyle, J.T. *Telegram to President Lincoln, Oct. 12th, 1862.* http://memory.loc.gov/mss/mall/189/1898800/001.gif—1898800/002.gif 2005.

Brock, R. A. *Hardesty's Historical and Geographical Encyclopedia, Illustrated: Roanoke and Montgomery County Edition.* New York: Hardesty, 1884.

Buck, Capt. Samuel D. *With the Old Confeds: Actual Experiences of a Captain in the Line.* Baltimore: Houck, 1925. Reprinted, Gaithersburg, MD: Butternut Press, 1983.

Burr, Frank A., and Richard J. Hinton. *"Little Phil" and His Troopers: The Life of Gen. Philip H. Sheridan.* Providence, RI: Reid, 1888.

Bushong, Millard Kessler. *Historic Jefferson County.* Boyce, VA: Carr, 1972.

Cappon, Lester J. *Virginia Newspapers 1821–1935.* New York: Appleton-Century, 1936.

Carroll, Douglas, ed. *The Letters of F. Stanley Russell.* Baltimore: Harrod, 1963.

Clason, Marshall B. *Clason's Letters.* www.12lovi.org/letters121.shtml. Accessed December 25, 2000; no longer on the Internet.

Cocke, Ellen M., comp. *Some Fox Trails in Old Virginia: John Fox of King William County. Ancestors, Descendants, Near Kin.* Richmond, VA: Dietz Press, 1939.

Collins, Darrell L. *General William Averell's Salem Raid: Breaking the Knoxville Supply Line.* Shippensburg, PA: Burd Street Press, 1998.

Comstock, Jim, ed. *West Virginia Heritage Encyclopedia.* Vol. 18. Richwood, WV: Comstock, 1974.

Cooper, Col. William. *One Hundred Years at V.M.I.* Vol. 1. Richmond, VA: Garrett and Massie, 1939.

Cullum, George Washington. *Biographical Register of the Officers and Graduates of the U.S. Military Academy.* Vol. 2. New York: Van Nostrand, 1868.

Cummins, Rev. Alexander G. In Memoriam. Address at the Burial of Brig. Gen. William R. Terrill, October 16th, 1862, by the Rev. Alexander G. Cummins, in Christ Church, Reading. Philadelphia: C. Sherman & Son, Printers. 1862. Copy provided by Miss Mercer Terrill Vaden, Richmond, VA, granddaughter of James B. Terrill.

Darlington, William Aubrey. *Sheridan.* New York: Macmillan, 1933.

Davis, Gen. Henry Eugene. *General Sheridan.* New York: Appleton, 1918.

Dodge, William Sumner. *History of the Old Second Division, Army of the Cumberland.* Chicago: Church & Goodman, 1864.

Douglas, Henry Kyd. *I Rode With Stonewall.* Greenwich, CT: Fawcett, 1961.

Dowdy, Clifford, ed. *The Wartime Papers of R. E. Lee.* New York: Bramhall House, 1961.

Engle, Stephen D. *Don Carlos Buell: Most Promising of All.* Chapel Hill: University of North Carolina Press, 1999.

Evans, Clement A., ed. *Confederate Military History.* Wilmington, NC: Broadfoot, 1987–1989.

Executive Documents Printed By Order of The Senate of the United States, During the First Session of the Thirty-Second Congress, 1851-2. Vol. I. Washington: Printed by A. Boyd Hamilton, 1852.

Federico, Bianca Morse, and Betty Louise Wright, eds. *Civil War: The Letters of John Holbrook Morse, 1861–1865.* Washington, D.C.: Federico, 1975.

Flournoy, H. W. *Calendar of Virginia State Papers and Other Manuscripts from January 1, 1836 to April 15, 1869; Preserved in the Capitol at Richmond.* Vol. 11. Richmond: n.p., 1869.

Foote, Shelby. *The Civil War: A Narrative.* New York: Random House, 1958.

Fradenburgh, Rev. Jason N. *In Memoriam — Henry Harrison Cumings, Charlotte J. Cumings.* Oil City, PA: Derrick, 1913 (1914).

Frey, Samuel Cordell, Alfred Sperry and Perez G. Clark. *Battery D, First Ohio Veteran Volunteer Light Artillery: It's Military History, 1861–1865.* Oil City, PA: Derrick, 1908.

Frost, Lawrence A. *The Phil Sheridan Album: A Pictorial Biography of Philip Henry Sheridan.* Seattle: Superior, 1968.

Fry, James B. *Military Miscellanies.* New York: Brentano's, 1889.

Frye, Dennis E. *12th Virginia Cavalry.* Lynchburg, VA: Howard, 1988.

Gwin, Hugh S. *Historically Speaking: True Tales of Bath County, Virginia*. Warm Springs, VA: Bath County Historical Society, 2001.

Hale, Laura Virginia, and Stanley S. Phillips. *History of the Forty-Ninth Virginia Infantry, C.S.A.: "Extra Billy Smith's Boys."* Lanham, MD: Phillips, 1981.

Hall, Granville D. *Lee's Invasion of Northwest Virginia in 1861.* Chicago: Mayer & Miller, 1911.

Hannaford, E. *The Story of a Regiment: A History of the Campaign and Associations In The Field, of The Sixth Regiment Ohio Volunteer Infantry*. Cincinnati: Published by the Author, 1868.

Hansen, R.B. *Field Artillery Battery Positions and Duties*. www.cwartillery.org/hansen.html. Accessed in 2006.

Hasselberger, Fritz. *Yanks from the South: The First Land Campaign of the Civil War: Rich Mountain, West Virginia*. Baltimore: Past Glories, 1987.

Herbesheimer, Joseph. *Sheridan*. Cambridge: Riverside Press, 1931.

Hewett, Janet B., ed. *Supplement to the Official Records of the Union and Confederate Armies*. Wilmington, NC: Broadfoot, 1994.

Houck, Peter W., ed. *Duty, Honor, Country: The Diary and Biography of General William P. Craighill: Cadet at West Point, 1849–1853*. Lynchburg, VA: Warwick House, 1993.

Hughes, Nathaniel Cheairs, Jr., and Gordon D. Whitney. *Jefferson Davis in Blue: The Life of Sherman's Relentless Warrior*. Baton Rouge: Louisiana State University Press, 2002.

Hughes, Nicky and Susan Hughes. *Brief Narrative History of the 7th Kentucky Volunteer Inf.* www.7thkentucky.org/modules/smartsection/item.php?itemid=2. Accessed in 2006.

Hunter, Alfred, comp. *The Washington and Georgetown Directory, Strangers' Guidebook for Washington, and Congressional and Clerks' Register*. Washington: Kirkwood & McGill, 1853.

Irvine, Leigh H., ed. *History of the New California: Its Resources and People*, Chicago: Lewis, 1905.

J. of the Blacksheep. *Perryville 2001: 105th Ohio — Day by day*. www.ezboard.com. Accessed in 2001; removed from the Internet.

Johnson, Mark W. *That Body of Brave Men: The U.S. Regular Infantry and the Civil War in the West*. Cambridge, MA: Da Capo Press, 2003.

Johnson, R. U., and C. C. Buel, eds. *Battles and Leaders of the Civil War*. New York: T. Yoseloff, 1956.

Krick, Robert E. L. *Staff Officers in Gray: A Biographical Register of the Staff Officers in the Army of Northern Virginia*. Chapel Hill and London: University of North Carolina Press, 2003.

Lee, Robert E., [Jr.] *Recollections and Letters of General Robert E. Lee*. Garden City, NY: Garden City Publishing, 1924.

Lesser, W. Hunter. *Rebels at the Gate: Lee and McClellan on the Front Line of a Nation Divided*. Naperville, IL: Sourcebooks, 2004.

Lewis Publishing Company. *The Bay of San Francisco*. Chicago: Lewis, 1892.

Long, E. B., and Barbara Long. *The Civil War Day by Day: An Almanac 1861–1865*. Garden City, NY: Doubleday, 1971.

McAllister, J. Gray. *Sketch of Captain Thompson McAllister, Civilian, Soldier, Christian*. Petersburg, VA: Fenn & Owen, 1896.

McCartney, Clarence Edward. *Grant and His Generals*. New York: McBride, 1953.

McCauley, William. *History of Roanoke County, Salem, Roanoke City, Virginia, and Representative Citizens*. Chicago: Biographical, 1902.

McDonald, William N. *Laurel Brigade, Originally Ashby's Cavalry*. Arlington, VA: Beatty, 1969.

McDonough, James Lee. *War in Kentucky: from Shiloh to Perryville*. Knoxville: University of Tennessee Press, 1994.

Maxwell, Hu. *History of Barbour County, West Virginia: From its Earliest Exploration and Settlement to the Present Time*. Morgantown, WV: Acme, 1899.

Message from the President of the United States, to the Two Houses of Congress, at the Commencement of the Second Session of the Thirty-First Congress. Part II. Washington: Printed for the Senate, 1850.

Metheny, Constance Corley, and Eliza Warwick Wise. *Bath County Marriage Bonds and Minister's Returns, 1791–1853*. Warm Springs, VA: Bath County Historical Society, 1978.

Military Essays and Recollections: Papers Read Before the Commandery of the State of Illinois, Military Order of the Loyal Legion of the United States. Volume II. Chicago: McClurg, 1894.

Miller, Thomas Condit, and Hu Maxwell. *West Virginia and Its People*. New York: Lewis, 1913.

Mitchell, Adele H., ed. *The Letters of Major General James E. B. Stuart*. Richmond, VA: Stuart-Mosby Historical Society, 1990.

Morris, Roy, Jr. *Sheridan: The Life and Wars of General Phil Sheridan*. New York: Crown, 1992.

Morton, Oren F. *A Centennial History of Alleghany County, Virginia*. Bridgewater, VA: Carrier, 1970.

_____. *A History of Highland County, Virginia*. Monterey, VA: Morton, 1911.

Morse, Loren J., ed. and comp. *Civil War Diaries and Letters of Bliss Morse.* Wagoner, OK: Loren J. Morse, 1985.

National Cyclopedia of American Biography. Vol. 9. New York: White, 1907.

National Oceanic and Atmospheric Administration. *The Hassler Legacy: Ferdinand Rudolph Hassler and the United States Coast Survey.* June 18, 2001. www.lib.noaa.gov/edocs/HASSLER1.htm. Accessed in 2006.

National Park Service. *Dry Tortugas.* www.nps/gov/drto/. Accessed in 2005.

Ness, George T., Jr. *Battery B, 4th U.S. Light Artillery — The Regular Army Artillery on the Eve of the Civil War.* Baltimore: Toomey Press, 1990.

Noe, Kenneth W. *Perryville: This Grand Havoc of Battle.* Lexington: University Press of Kentucky, c. 2001.

Norris, J. E., ed. *History of the Lower Shenandoah Valley.* Chicago: Warner, 1890.

O'Connor, Richard. *Hood: Cavalier General.* New York: Prentice Hall, 1949.

_____. *Sheridan the Inevitable.* Indianapolis: Bobbs-Merrill, 1953.

Paine, Lincoln Paxton. *Ships of the World: An Historical Encyclopedia.* New York: Houghton Mifflin, 1997.

Poe, Captain David. *Personal Reminiscences of the Civil War.* Buckhannon, WV: Upshur Republican Print, 1911.

Porterfield, Frank B. *The Porterfields.* Roanoke, VA: Southeastern Press, 1985.

Powell, Colonel Wm. H. *List of Officers of the Army of the United States from 1779 to 1900.* New York: Hamersly, 1900.

Rectors of the University of Virginia. *Manual of the Board of Visitors of the University of Virginia. 1998.* Charlottesville: University Press of Virginia, 1998.

Reed, Maj. D. W., comp. *Shiloh National Military Park Commission. The Battle of Shiloh.* Washington, D.C.: Government Printing Office, 1903.

Regulations Established For The Organization and Government of the Military Academy, at West Point, New York, by order of The President of the United States, to which is added The Regulations for the Internal Police of the Institution, with An Appendix, containing the rules and articles of war, and extracts from the general regulations of the army, applicable to the academy. New York: Wiley & Putnam, 1839.

Riggs, David F. *13th Virginia Infantry.* Lynchburg, VA: Howard, 1988.

Robertson, James I., Jr., ed. *Proceedings of the Advisory Council of the State of Virginia April 21–June 19, 1861.* Richmond: Virginia State Library, 1977.

Rodenbough, Theo. F., and William L. Haskin, eds. *The Army of the United States: Historical Sketches of Staff and Line with Portraits of Generals-in-Chief.* New York: Maynard, Merrill, 1896.

Ross, Zephaniah Turner. *A Different Window... a different victory. The Civil War Records. Diaries and Letters of Zephaniah Turner Ross, Captain, Company B, 13th Virginia Infantry Regiment, May, 1863–September, 1864.* Orange, VA: Orange County Historical Society, 1999.

Rowell, John W. *Yankee Artillerymen: Through the Civil War with Eli Lilly's Indiana Battery.* Knoxville: University of Tennessee Press, 1975.

_____. *Yankee Cavalrymen: Through the Civil War with the Ninth Pennsylvania Cavalry.* Knoxville: University of Tennessee Press, 1971.

Samuel, Kathleen (Boone). *A Civil War Marriage in Virginia; reminiscences of letters collected by Carrie Esther Spencer, Bernard Samuels, Walter Berry Samuels, the three surviving children.* Boyce, VA: Carr, 1956.

Scott, Robert Garth, ed. *Forgotten Valor: The Memoirs, Journals & Civil War Letters of Orlando B. Wilcox.* Kent, OH: Kent State University Press, 1999.

Scott, W. W. *A History of Orange County.* Richmond, VA: Waddy, 1907.

Shanks, William Franklin Gore. *Personal Recollections of Distinguished Generals.* New York: Harper & Brothers, 1866.

Sheridan, Philip Henry. *Personal Memoirs of P. H. Sheridan, General, United States Army.* New York: Webster, 1888.

Smith, Dave. *The Battle of Perryville, October 8, 1862. Battle chronology.* www.members.aol.com/jfepperson/Perryville.html. Accessed in 2006.

Staats, Richard J. *A Grassroots History of the American Civil War. Volume III: Captain Cotter's Battery.* Bowie, MD: Heritage Books, 2002.

Summers, Festus P., ed. *A Borderland Confederate.* Pittsburgh: University of Pittsburgh Press, 1962.

Surgeon-General's Office. *The Medical and Surgical History of the War of the Rebellion. (1861–65).* Washington: Government Printing Office, 1875.

Swank, Walbrook D. *Stonewall Jackson's Foot Cavalry: Company A, 13th Virginia Infantry.* Shippensburg, PA: Burd Street Press, 2001.

_____. *Raw Pork and Hardtack: A Civil War Memoir From Manassas to Appomattox.* Shippensburg, PA: Burd Street Press, 1996.

Switzer, Charles I., ed. *Ohio Volunteer: The Childhood and Civil War Memoirs of Captain*

John Calvin Hartzell, OVI. Athens: Ohio University Press, 2005.

Sword, Wiley. *Shiloh: Bloody April.* New York: Morrow, 1974.

TenBrink, Charles. *The Civil War Artillery Page.* http:\\www.cwartillery.org/artillery.html. (October 31, 2000). Last viewed September 20, 2007.

Tenney, W. J. *The Military and Naval History of the Rebellion in the United States with Biographical Sketches of Deceased Officers.* New York: Appleton, 1865.

Thompson, John T. *A Descriptive Catalogue of the Ordnance Museum, Department of Ordnance and Gunnery, U.S. Military Academy.* West Point, NY: U.S. Military Academy Press, 1898.

Tourgée, Albion W. *The Story of a Thousand, Being a history of the service of the 105th Ohio Volunteer Infantry, in the war for the Union from August 21, 1862, to June 6, 1865.* Buffalo: Gerald & Son, 1896.

Tyler, Lyon Gardiner, LLD, ed. *Encyclopedia of Virginia Biography.* New York: Lewis, 1915.

The Union Army: A History of Military Affairs in the Loyal States 1861–65 — Records of the Regiments in the Union Army — Cyclopedia of Battles — Memoirs of Commanders and Soldiers. Madison, WI: Federal, 1908.

United States Adjutant Generals Office. *Official Army Register for....* Washington: Government Printing Office, 1854–1863.

U.S. Government. *Journal of the Congress of the Confederate States of America, 1861–1865.* Washington D.C.: Government Printing Office, 1904.

_____. Report of the Superintendent of the Coast Survey, showing the Progress of the Survey During the year 1862. Washington, D.C.: Government Printing Office, 1864.

U.S. Interior Department. *Register of Officers and Agents, Civil, Military, and Navel in the Service of the United States, on the Thirtieth September, 1861.* Washington, D.C.: Government Printing Office, 1862.

U.S. Military Academy. *Official Register of Officers and Cadets of the U.S. Military Academy, West Point, New York — June 1850.* New York: Wright, 1850.

_____. *Official Register of Officers and Cadets of the U.S. Military Academy, West Point, New York — June 1851.* New York: Burroughs, 1851.

_____. *Official Register of Officers and Cadets of the U.S. Military Academy, West Point, New York — June 1852.* New York: Burroughs, 1852.

_____. *Official Register of Officers and Cadets of the U.S. Military Academy, West Point, New York — June 1853.* New York: Burroughs, 1853.

U.S. Senate. *Talton T. Davis. (Senate Report No. 1193).* Washington, D.C.: Government Printing Office, 1900.

United States War Department. *War of the Rebellion: Official Records of the Union and Confederate Armies.* Washington, D.C.: Government Printing Office, 1880–1901.

VanHorne, Thomas B. *History of the Army of the Cumberland.* Cincinnati: Clarke, 1875.

Walker, Charles D. *Memorial, Virginia Military Institute: biographical sketches of the graduates and eleves of the Virginia Military Institute who fell during the war between the states.* Philadelphia: Lippincott, 1875.

Wallace, Lee A., Jr. *A Guide to Virginia Military Organizations 1861–1865.* Lynchburg, VA: Howard, 1986.

Warner, Ezra. *Generals in Blue: Lives of the Union Commanders.* Baton Rouge: Louisiana State University Press, 1964.

_____. *Generals in Gray: Lives of the Confederate Commanders.* Baton Rouge: Louisiana State University Press, 1959.

Washington and Lee University. *Alumni Directory, 1749–1888.* Lexington, VA: Washington and Lee University, 1888.

Weaver, Jeffery C. *The Virginia Home Guards.* Lynchburg, VA: Howard, 1996.

Welsh, Jack D., MD. *Medical Histories of Union Generals.* Kent, OH: Kent State University Press, 1996.

Wilson, James Grant, and John Fiske. *Appleton's Cyclopaedia of American Biography.* Volume 6. New York: Appleton, 1889.

Wise, Jennings C. *The Military History of The Virginia Military Institute.* Lynchburg, VA: Bell, 1915.

Index

Numbers in ***bold italics*** indicate pages with illustrations.

Alden, Capt. B.R. 89, 90
Alexandria, Va. 180–182, 188
Alleghany Co., Va. 9, 10, 16, 19, 28, 40, 44
Allen, Alexander 133
Anderson, Larz 137, 162
Anderson, Lt. Col. Nicholas 129, 132
Anderson, Gen. R.H. 235
Anderson, Robert 110, 114
Anderson, William P. 137, 140–142
Annandale, Va. 179, 180, 182
Archy (slave) 28
Arkansas Troops: Infantry 122; 2nd Infantry 170
Arnold, Jonathan 221
Augusta Co., Va. 40, 112
Averell, William Woods 23, 41–43, 54, 55
Ayre, Josiah 145

Bache, Alexander Dallas 61, 96–***99***, 100, 102–104, 106–108, 113, 118, 126, 142, 143, 149, 162, 165
Bache, Dr. Dallas 126, 132
Bagley, Lt. 95
Bailey's Cross Roads, Va. 180–182, ***183***
Baldwin, Briscoe G. 36
Baldwin, Dr. J.H. 238
Baldwin, James W. 36
Baldwin, Mr. & Mrs. John B. 47
Baldwin, John Brown 81, 176
Baltimore & Ohio Railroad 48, 64, 66, 232
Banks, John 164
Banks, Maj. Gen. Nathaniel 51, 82, 193
Barbour Co., (W) Va. 63, 66
Bate, Judge D.W. 87
Bath Co., Va. 1, 2, 10–35, 40, 44, 49, 74, 112, 214, 216, 218, 219, 222, 230
Bath Court House, Va. ***14***, 20, 47, 219, 238; *see also* Warm Springs, Va.
Battery Terrill, Washington, DC 170

Battles: Bethesda Church 1, 23, 212–***215***, 239; Brandy Station 202, 225, 227; Buckland Races 230; Cedar Creek 237; Cedar Mountain 193; Cedar Run 192; Chancellorsville, Va. 195, 197, 199, 201; Chantilly 194; Cold Harbor 212; Corricks Ford 77; Cross Keys 191, 192; Fredericksburg 192, 195–198, 200; Gettysburg 204; Jack's Shop 226; Jeffersonton 228; 1st Manassas 178; 2nd Manassas 192–194, 224; Mill Creek 236, 237; Parker's Store 231; Patterson's Creek 232; Perryville 1, 23, 35, 51, 146, 148–***151***, 152–***159***, 160–170; Philippi 20, 66–***69***, 70–73, 75–78, 113, 219; Pittsburg Landing 126, 127, 131–3, 136, 141, 142 (*see also* Shiloh, Tn.); Port Republic 192; Ream's Station 235, 236; Rich Mountain 2, 39, 49, 75, 77, 80, 113, 219, 220, 223, 224; Richmond, Ky. 138, 140, 145; Sangster's Station 231; Shiloh, Tn. 1, 35, 126–***128***, 134, 136–139, 158, 163, 170 (*see also* Pittsburg Landing); South Branch Valley 232; Spottsylvania Court House 209–***211***, 233; Todd's Tavern 231, 234, 235; Tom's Brook 237; Wilderness 209, 234, 235
Baughn, Capt. 215
Baylor, George 227–234, 236, 237
Beauregard, Gen. P.G.T. 126, 127, 130
Benham, Henry W. 61, 71, 72
Berkeley Co., (W) Va. 48, 57, 58, 60, 61, 83
Beverly, (W) Va. 21, 49, 62–66, 70, 72, 74–77, 219–222
Bickel, Daniel C. 110, 121, 130
Bill, Earl 168
Bird, Lt. William W. 188
Bland, Dr. William J. 21
Bloomfield, Alpheus 118, 119, 134
Bloomfield, Ky. 149
Bogges, Capt. 63
Botetourt Co., Va. 10, 40

283

Botts, John Minor 206
Bowling Green, Ky. 123, 124
Boyle, Jeremiah T. 168
Bragg, Gen. Braxton 136, 138, 147, 148, 163
Brewerton, Henry 89
Bridgewater, Va. 236
Brockenbrough, John W. 21
Brockenbrough, John White 174, 175
Brodie, Corp. 131
Bruffey, Dr. J.W. 44
Buck, Samuel D. 174, 198, 199, 202, 213
Buell, Don Carlos 114, 115, 123-125, 127, 134, 135, 137, 138, 147, 148, 150, 161
Buford, John 117, 125, 226
Burnside, Maj. Gen. A.E. 168
Bush, Asahel K. 158, 160
Bushnell, Mrs. J.E. 46

Cameron, John Hyde 189
Cameron, Simon 103
Cammock, John Henry 73
Camp Andy Johnson, Tn. 124
Camp Buckner 40
Camp Garnett, Va. 220
Camp Gilbert, Ky. 115, 116, 118
Camp Jenkins, Ky. 115, 116
Camp Larkin Smith, Va. 58
Camp Stanton, Tn. 125
Camp Terrill, Ky. 146
Camp Terrill, Pa. 169
Camp Wood, Ky. 118
Canby, Brig. Gen. E.M. 53, 54
Carrington, Edward C., Jr. 58, 83
Carroll, James 133
Carroll, John T. 131
Carthage, O. 111, 113, 114
Castle, Frederick 133
Cave, Robert Catlett 197-199
Centreville, Va. 188
Charlotte Harbor, Fl 94, 99, 100-*101*, 102
Charlottesville, Va. 218, 223
Chase, Capt. 72
Chase, S.P. 103
Chenowith, Lt. 64, 70
Chrisman, Capt. Lewis 144, 151
Cincinnati, O. 110, 111, 136-138, 140, 141, 162-164
Clason, Marshall B. 168
Clymer, Hiester 164
Coalter, Saint George Tucker 217
Cobb, Howell 97, 98
Cochran, Capt. John, Jr. 142
Coleman, John 148
Columbia, Tn. 125
Confederate troops: Signal Corps 27
Connolly, Maj. James 158, 161
Cooke, Giles B. 41
Cooke, Henry H. 50
Cooke, John Esten 227
Cooke, Philip St. George 14

Cooper, Samuel 75, 81, 90, 100
Corinth, Miss. 136
Corley, James L. 76
Cotter, Charles S. 118-*120*
Covington, Ky. 111
Covington, Va. 9, 10, 18, 19, 30, 44, 47, 85
Cowan, John T. 223, 234
Cowan, Maj. 65
Cowardin, William *215*
Craig Co., Va. 40
Craighill, William P. 86
Crawford, James G. 145, 146
Crawford, Samuel W. 215
Crittenden, Thomas L. 148
Crook, George *88*
Crozet, Claudius 57
Cruft, Brig. Gen. Charles 138, 140
Cullum, George W. 106, 170
Culpeper Co., Va. 117, 222, 225
Cumings, Henry Harrison 144, 153, 154, 156
Cummings, Rev. A.G. 164, 165
Cunningham, Daniel 133
Custer, George A. 237

Dandrich, A.S. 50
Darr, Francis 105
Davis, Jefferson 20-22, 39, 74, 104, 105, 215
Davis, Brig. Gen. Jefferson C. (US) 147, 148
Davis, Sgt. 131
DeLagnal, Julius A. 76
Devine, Bernard 133
Dold, Samuel Miller 38
Dold, Sarah Brent 38, 41, 44-46; *see also* Dole, Miss
Dold, William 44
Dole, Miss 15; *see also* Dold, Sarah Brent
Doles, George 210
Douglas, Henry Kyd 174
Drewry, Charlotte Eucebia *189*, 217; *see also* Terrill, Charlotte
Drewry, Martin 189, 217
Dublin, Va. 43
Duffy, James 133
Duncan, Mrs. Wm. 46
Dunn, Corp. Robert 133
DuPont, H.A. 109

Early, Jubal A. 54, 192-196, 198-200, 202, 203, 209, 214, 215, 232, 235-237
Ebersole, John 133
Echols, John 42
Eckert, Isaac 164
Edwards, William S. 142, 143, 149, 162, 164, 165
Egan, Sgt. 131
Elzey, Brig. Gen. Arnold 1, 22, 33, 182, 191
Ervin, Corp 131
Ervin, William D. 220, 224
Ewell, Richard S. 190, 191, 193, 195, 202-204, 207, 208, 210, 212, 224, 228

Fairfax Station, Va. 179, 180, 182, 188
Falls Church, Va. 184, 185, *186*
Falmouth, Va. 199
Farmville, Va. 9
Faulkner, Charles James 14
Fauntleroy, Thomas Turner 73, 74
Ficklin, Benjamin 37
Fitzhugh, O.S. 211
Fitzpatrick, Peter 123–125, 129, 130, 143, 160, 161
Florida troops: Felix Robertson's Battery 127
Floyd, John B. 14, 99
Fort Bassinger, Fl. 96
Fort Brooke, Fl. 96
Fort Center, Fl. 95
Fort Denaud, Fl. 94, 95
Fort Hamilton, NY 91, 169
Fort Independence, Boston 92
Fort Kissimmee, Fl. 95, 96
Fort Leavenworth, KT 96, 97
Fort Mackinac, MI 92
Fort McHenry, Md. 221
Fort McRae, Fl. 95
Fort Myers, Fl. 94, 95
Fort Terrill, Ky. 170
Fort Willich, Ky. 170
Foster, C.W. 139
Fox, Mildred S. 217
French, S. Bassett 201
Fristoe, Edward T. 37
Front Royal, Va. 190, 202, 204
Fry, Capt. 132
Funsten, Oliver R. 226, 228–230

Gaither, George R. 184, 185
Garnett, Robert S. 40, 74–78, 219, 220
Garrard, Col. 148
Georgia troops: 1st Infantry 188; 12th Infantry 81; 20th Infantry 181
Gibson, Capt. 94
Gibson, Col. 214
Gilbert, Charles C. 115, 139–141, 145, 148
Gilman, J.H. 116, 117, 135, 144
Goff, David 62–64
Goldsborough, Charles E. 203
Goldsborough, William W. 203
Gordon, John B. 210
Grafton, (W) Va. 62–68, 70, 71, 78
Grant, U.S. 123, 126, 208, 209, 234
Greenbrier Co., (W) Va. 15, 16, 28, 41, 42
Gregg, Irvin 234
Griffin, Capt. Charles 187
Guenther, Francis L. 107, 114, 116, 131, 132, 138, 147, 170

Haines, Benjamin M. 27
Hall, Albert S. 146, 154, 155, 161
Halleck, Henry W. 123, 141, 142
Hamilton's Crossing, Va. 196, 200, 202, 231
Hampton, Wade 226, 230, 235, 236

Hamtramck, John Francis 58, 71
Hannah, Mrs. 44
Hansbrough, Lt. Col. George W. 43, 68, 70, 80, 224
Hardee, Gen. 136
Harman, Michael G. 39, 40, 73, 74
Harman, William H. 175
Harper, Kenton 61, 62
Harpers Ferry, (W) Va. 48, 52, 53, 176, 177, 192
Harris, David E. 43
Harris, Leonard 152, 153
Harris, Lt. Sam 135
Harrison, Gessner 218
Harrison Co., (W) Va. 63
Hartzell, John Calvin 140, 160, 161
Hathaway, John C. 145
Hawkins, Wilson T. 89
Hawthorne, Col. 122
Hazen, William B. 129
Healing Springs, Va. 20, 74
Heck, Jonathan McGee 65, 75, 219, 220, 222
Henry, Arietta Livingston 48, 52–54, 97, 98, 106, 108, 165
Henry, Emily Drennen *97*; *see also* Terrill, Emily H.
Henry, Guy V. 114, 169
Henry, Kate Seton 55
Henry, Major William S. 97
Heth, Henry 40
Hiester, W.M. 164
Highland Co., Va. 16, 18, 28, 68, 75, 220
Hill, Mrs. A.P. (Dolly) 117, 188, 205
Hill, Ambrose P. 177–179, 182, 184, 188, 190, 193–195, 201, 202, 205, 207, 213, 235, 236
Hindman, Gen. 122
Hoblitzell, Lt. W.T. 127, 131
Hodegon, Henry C. 142
Hooker, Joseph 146
Hopkins, Charles B. 20, 21, 74
Horse Cave, Ky. 121, 122
Houghton, R.W. 154, 155
Hume, Frank 211
Hunt, G.G. 140
Hunter, Alexander 203
Huntersville, (W) Va. 80, 222
Huntington, Lt. 142
Huntsville, Ala. 136
Huttonsville, (W) Va. 75, 219

Illinois troops: 80th Infantry 143–146; 123rd Infantry 143, 144, 146, 152–155, 158, 160
Imboden, John D. 224, 225
Indiana troops: 7th Infantry 72; 17th Infantry 79; 19th Infantry 186; 101st Infantry 143, 151, 155

Jackson, James S. 138, 140, 142, 145, 148, 150, 152, 153, 155, 158, 161, 162
Jackson, Thomas J. 62, 64, 80, 81, 174, 190, 191, 194, 221

James, F.B. 139
Jefferson Co., (W) Va. 48, 61, 72, 79, 82, 113, 125, 222, 223, 225, 228, 230, 232
Johnson, Andrew 107
Johnson, Major B.J. 184
Johnson, Edward 81, 82, 190, 209–212, 223
Johnson, Gen. R.W. 121, 122
Johnston, Albert Sidney 118, 126
Johnston, Joseph E. 66, 113, 177, 187, 188
Johnston, Robert 71
Jones, A.C. 223, 224
Jones, J.G. 164
Jones, J. Pringle 164
Jones, J. William 177, 179
Jones, Philip Edloe 179, 180, 187
Jones, Maj. Gen. Samuel 42, 43
Jordan, Capt. B.J. 70, 71

Kanawha Co., (W) Va. 10
Kelly, Patrick 133
Kelly's Ford, Va. 202
Kentucky troops (US): 7th Infantry 144; 10th Cavalry 142; 14th Infantry 142; 23rd Infantry 144
Kernstown, Va. 237
Kilpatrick, Judson 226, 230
King William Co., Va. 222
Kirk, R.A. 162
Konkle, A.J. 116

Landon, G.H. 43
Lane, D.M. 51
Laurel Brigade 233–237
Lee, Gen. Fitzhugh 78, 79, 232
Lee, Gen. Robert E. 9, 62–65, 73–81, 90, 200–202, 207, 210, 216, 226, 228–232, 234–236
Lee, Gen. W.F. 235
Letcher, John 9, 20–*21*, 23, 40, 61, 62, 64, 67, 73, 77, 79, 99, 113, 122, 176, 177, 178, 201, 215, 219
Lewinsville, Va. 184–*186*, 187
Lewis (slave) 16, 239
Lewis, Capt. John V. 142
Lewisburg, (W) Va. 40, 42
Lexington, Ky. 138–140, 147, 148
Lexington, Va. 15, 38, 44, 46, 47, 57, 172
Liberty, Va. 43
Lincoln, Abraham 48, 100, 104, 120, 121, 141, 169
Litchfield, Connely T. 86
Lockwood, Stanley 145, 146
Long, John H. 133
Longstreet, Gen. James 194
Looper, William 112
Loring, William Wing 77, 78, 80
Loudoun & Hampshire Railroad 179, 180, 182, 184
Louisiana troops: Washington Artillery 182, 185, 187; 1st Cavalry 125

Louisville, Ky. 110, 115, 116, 118, 136, 137, 139, 140, 142, 143–146, 148, 149, 162, 164
Lowry, Hugh 156
Ludlow, Israel 107, 119, 129, 131
Lynch, Corp. 131
Lynchburg, Va. 43

Mackville, Ky. 149
Manassas Gap Railroad 231
Maney, George 153, 154, 156
Manson, Mahlon D. 138
Mansfield, Joseph K. 106, 107
Marshall, John 132
Martinsburg, (W) Va. 48, 50–52, 54, 56, 58, 60, 84, 125, 223
Maryland troops (CS): Howard Dragoons 184; Maryland Line 181; 1st Infantry 184, 188; 2nd Regiment 203
Maryland troops (US): 5th Infantry 203
Mason, James 63
Mason, James M. 99
Mason, Capt. Murray 180
Mason's Hill, Va. 179, 180, 182
Massie, Lt. Col. 227
Massie, J.W. 176
Maubeck, Sgt. 131
Mayo, Joseph 21
Mayse, George 15, 23, 112
McAllister, William M. 30
McChesney, Dr. Alexander G. 17
McClellan, George B. 49, 66, 71, 109, 179, 185, 220–222
McClellan, Henry 229
McCook, Alexander McDonald 114, 118, *119*, 123, 125, 127, 131, 132, 134–136, 148, 150–152, 158, 161
McCook, Capt. Daniel 133
McDannald, Charles T. 14, 15
McDannald, Sarah Jane 14; *see also* Terrill, Sarah Jane
McDannald, William H. 13–15
McFadden, Elizabeth 38
McFarden, Martin 133
McKnight, James 164
McParlin, Dr. Thomas A. *95*, 96
McWhorter, Judge 34
Meade, George G. 205–207, 226, 231
Mechanicsville, Va. *215*
Memminger, C.G. 224
Merrill, William E. 222
Metcalf, Sgt. Richard 129, 131, 133
Metzgar, George 133
Mexican War 58–60, 83
Michigan troops: 6th Cavalry 54
Middletown, O. 113
Middletown, Va. 237, 238
Milroy, Robert H. 51, 203
Missouri troops (CS) 130
Moffett, George H. 31
Mohr, James F. 114, 116, 129, 130, 135

Index

Monterey, Va. 220
Moomau, John B. 220, 223, 224
Moore, Cornelia H. 9, 16; see also Wise, Cornelia H.
Moore, John 137
Morris, Thomas A. 71
Morse, Bliss 147
Morse, John Holbrook 147
Morton, Dr. George 10, 17
Morton, Jackson 21
Morton, Jane 9
Morton, Jeremiah 28, 30
Morton, Mrs. W. Chase 57, 84, 239
Mott, Thaddeus P. 187
Mugler, Henry Jean 212
Mulhall, John 133
Mumford, George W. 14
Munford, Carlton R. 58
Munfordville, Ky. 116, 118, 121, 169, 170
Munson's Hill, Va. 179–181, *183*, 184, 185, 187

Nashville, Tn. 123–125
Nelson, William "Bull" 127, 130–132, 134, 138–141, 145, 147, 148
New Creek Depot (Station), (W) Va. 177, 178, 232
New York troops: 3rd Battery 187; 106th Infantry 226
Newman, Reuben M. 197, 201, 207
Newman, Lt. Wilson S. 200, 205
Newport, Ky. 111, 113
Newport Barracks, Ky. 109, 110, 112, 113
Newton, Capt. 122
Nichols, Lt. T.J. 140, 142
Noakes, Thomas 51–53
Normount, Lt. 73
North Carolina Troops 227, 231; 1st Cavalry 229, 230
Nugen, John *88*

Ohio troops: Battery A 118, 134; Battery D 116; Cotter's Battery 121, 124; Konkle's Battery 121; 1st Ohio Light Artillery; 6th Infantry 129, 130, 132, 137, 140; 24th Infantry 132; 105th Infantry 140, 142–148, 151, 153–157, 160–163; 121st Infantry 160, 161, 168
Oldershaw, P.P. 162
Orange & Alexandria Railroad 202
Orange Co., Va. 9, 31

Parsons, Charles C. 140, 142, 144, 151–153, *156*, 163
Patrick, William 184, 185, 187
Pegram, John 76, 77, 80, 205–208, 214, 215, 220, 221
Pendleton, Edmond 50, 51
Pendleton Co., (W) Va. 220
Pennsylvania troops: 12th Infantry 50; 25th Infantry 108
Pensacola, Fl. 13

Pettigrew, Mr. 33
Peyton, Lt. Bailie 121
Peyton, George Q. 208, 209, 213
Philadelphia, Pa. 38
Phillips, Lewis A. 68, 70
Pierce, Franklin 91
Pilcher, Jane 17
Pitzer, Capt. A.L 215
Pitzer, Elizabeth 10; see also Terrill, Elizabeth
Pitzer, George M. 43
Pitzer, Mary Jane 11, 18, 29; see also Wise, Mary Jane
Pocahontas Co., (W) Va. 13, 16, 28, 31, 34, 42, 80, 175, 218, 221, 222
Poe, David 73
Poe, Orlando M. 185
Polk, James K. 37
Pollard, Richard 37
Port Royal, Va. 196
Porterfield, Charles Alexander 48, 84
Porterfield, Elizabeth Morton 48, *50*; see also Porterfield, Mary Elizabeth
Porterfield, Emily Serena 54, 79, 83
Porterfield, Emily Terrill 14, 15, 17, 18, 25, 27, 29, 39, Porterfield, Mary Elizabeth
Porterfield, Emily Terrill 14, 15, 17, 18, 25, 27, 29, 39, 48–*49*, *55*, *56*, 57, 60–83, 87, 97, 117, 125, 126, 137, 216, 218, 222, 223, 230, 232–235, 237; see also Terrill, Emily Cornelia Clay
Porterfield, George 55
Porterfield, George Alexander 2, 18–21, 31, 35, 39, 47–*49*, 50–*59*, 60–*82*, 83, 84, 92, 113, 125, 175, 217, 219, 223
Porterfield, George Terrill 48
Porterfield, John Moler 48, 55, 84, 171
Porterfield, Katherine Seton 55
Porterfield, Mary Elizabeth 15; see also Porterfield, Elizabeth Morton
Porterfield, Mary Jane 48
Porterfield, Mary Tabb 57
Porterfield, William Terrill 48, 50, 56, 83
Potts, James N. 72, 78
Powers, Pike 85
Preston, John T.L. 57
Preston, William B. 85
Price, Rev. William T. 23, 67, 68, 218

Ramseur, Stephen 213, 214
Randolph, George W. 22, 223
Randolph Co., (W) Va. 16, 49, 219
Reading, Pa. 50, 107, 108, 110, 113, 137, 138, 163–165, 169
Reed, Sgt. James H. 133, 138
Reynolds, Gen. 141
Richards, Archibald T. 21
Richards, John S. 164
Richmond, Va. 10, 16, 19, 21–24, 33, 41, 50, 57–59, 64, 76–78, 113, 117, 125, 192, 212, 214, 216, 222, 224, 234, 235

Ripley, Gen. 111
Rittenhouse, Benjamin Franklin 107, 110, 132
Roanoke Co., Va. 39–43, 172
Roberson, Corp. 131
Roberts, George E. 37
Roberts, Col. Joseph 95
Robertson, Capt. Felix 127
Robertson, Henry H. 19
Rockbridge Co., Va. 40, 234
Rockingham Co., Va. 231
Rodes, Robert E. 206, 212, 213
Rogers, Col. R.S. 52
Romney, (W) Va. 177, 178
Rosecrans, William S. 117, 220
Rosser, Thomas L. 24, 25, 35, 185–187, 231–234, 236–238
Rousseau, Louvall H. 118, 123, 136, 148, 152, 153, 160
Russell, F. Stanley 201

Salem, Va. 15, 38, 39, 40–45, 113
Sanner, Charles H. 196
Savannah, Tn. 126, 131
Scarborough, Rev. J. 164
Schoonmaker, Col. 55
Scott, Rachel Hamilton 18; *see also* Terrill, Rachel
Scott, Winfield 92, 100, 103, 104, 106, 107, 221
Shanks, William F.G. 160, 164
Shaw, B.C. 72
Shenandoah Co., Va. 24
Sheridan, Phillip H. **88**, 89, 150, 234, 236, 237
Sherman, Col. T.W. 107, 108, 112
Sherman, William T. 114
Sherrard, Maj. John B. 194, 195
Sill, Joshua W. 148
Sitlington, Thomas 19
Skinner, James H. 208
Smith, Edmond Kirby 138, 139, 147, 148
Smith, Francis H. 37, **38**, 57, 58, 60, 62, 76, 77, 172–174
Smith, George H. 224, 225
Smith, Martha Ann Pitzer 15
Smith, William "Extra Billy" 13, 21, 31, 58, 196, 198–202
Smith, William F. 187
Smyser, Jacob H. 107, 114, 131, 132
Snodgrass, Anne Porterfield 50
Solomon, Owen Fort 86
Spencer, Mrs. J.M. 45
Spencer, Rev. J.M. 45
Spratt, Mr. 89
Stanton, Edwin M. 22, 49, 51, 126, 136, 141, 190, 222
Starkweather, John 158
Starling, Samuel M. 152, 153
Staunton, Va. 20, 21, 24, 25, 39, 40, 47, 54, 64, 73, 74, 80, 81, 85, 167, 172, 192, 222, 225, 231, 232, 235, 238
Stevens, Isaac I 185, 186

Stewart, Major D.B. 68, 70, 71
Stichter, Jos. L. 164
Stone, David C. 158
Stone, Lt. V.H. 112
Stringfellow, Charles S. 42
Stuart, Alexander H.H. 122
Stuart, James E.B. 9, 90, 167, 179–185, 187, 188, 201, 202, 226–230
Sullivan, Jeremiah C. 51–54
Surry Co., Va. 235

Tabb Family 50
Taft, Dr. Harvey S. 142, 160
Taliaferro, William B. 76
Taylor, Robert B. 148, 149, 153, 157, 159–161
Taylor, W.H. 236
Taylor, Zachary 85
Taylor Co., (W) Va. 63, 73
Taylorsville, Ky. 148, 149
Tennessee troops (CS): 3rd Infantry 177, 178, 182
Tennessee troops (US): 3rd Infantry 144
Terrill, Anna Carter Johnston 41
Terrill, Charlotte 195, 216, 217; *see also* Drewry, Charlotte E.
Terrill, Elizabeth **11**, **15**–17, 30, 31, 36, 47, 172, 218; *see also* Pitzer, Elizabeth
Terrill, Elizabeth Dold 39
Terrill, Emily Barbour **216**; *see also* Vaden, Emily T.
Terrill, Emily Cornelia Clay 2, 10, 13, 47–57, 60; *see also* Porterfield, Emily T.
Terrill, Emily Henry 50, 54, 55, 137, 163, 165, 168–171, 219; *see also* Henry, Emily Drennen
Terrill, Francis Heath 39, 45
Terrill, Dr. George 10, **12**, 13, 36, 113, 188
Terrill, George Morton 39, 45, 46
Terrill, George Parker 2, 10, 13, 15, 23, 25, 36, **37**, 38–46, 113, 172, 208, 216, 234, 237
Terrill, James Barbour 1, 2, 13, 17–19, 23, 24, 27, 35, 39, 50, 53, 62, 113, 117, 125, 172–**174**, 175, **176**, 177–**204**, 205–217, 221, 222, 234, 239
Terrill, James Mercer **195**, 217
Terrill, Jeremiah Morton 9, 10, 17
Terrill, John Allen 9, 13, 16, **17**, 48, 90, 173
Terrill, Maria Louisa 39
Terrill, Philip Mallory 1, 13, 17, 18, 24, 25, 27, 35, 39, 43, 49, 50, 53, 54, 75, 113, 117, 122, 125, 189, 216, 218, **219**–239
Terrill, Rachel 27, 30; *see also* Scott, Rachel Hamilton
Terrill, Samuel Miller Dold 43, 46
Terrill, Sarah Jane 9, 10, 13; *see also* McDannald, Sarah Jane
Terrill, William H. 39, 46
Terrill, William Henry 1, 2, 9, **10**, **11**–**26**, 27, **28**, **29**, **30**–36, 38, 44, 47, 55, 60, 74, 85, 102, 105, 112, 113, 125, 167, 172–174, 188, 212, 214–216, 218, 238

Index

Terrill, William, Jr. 9
Terrill, William Rufus 1, 2, 10, 15, 17, 18, 20, 22, 23, 25, 36, 29, 48, 49, 51–55, 85–*91*, *92*–97, *98*–102, *103*–111, *112*–114, *115*–117, *118*–171, 190, 203, 222
Texas troops (CS): Texas Rangers 122, 124
Third Seminole War 92–96
Thomas, Gen. 232
Thomas, Lorenzo 112, 141, 161
Thompson, Capt. 63
Thompson, W. Smith 97
Tolles, Wm. R. 140, 142
Tompkins, Daniel D. 97
Tortat, Rev. 164
Totten, Joseph G. 85, 89, 222
Tourgée, Albion W. 143, 144, 148, 152, 153, 157, 158, 161
Townsend, Col. E.D. 221
Trimble, Isaac R. 191, 194
Turner, Capt. 122
Tuttle, Lt. William R. 142

U.S. Coast Survey 20, 48, 60, 61, 77, 96–100, 102–104, 106, 126, 142, 143
U.S. Military Academy *see* West Point, NY (USMA)
U.S. troops: Battery D 187; Battery H 1, 104–171; Garrard's Detachment 142, 148, 152–154, 159; Mendenhal's Battery 130; 3rd Artillery 90; 3rd Infantry 97; 4th Artillery 91, 92, 94, 96, 99, 103, 106, 140, 142; 4th Cavalry 140; 5th Artillery
U.S. Volunteers: Parson's Battery 143, 152–*157*, 161, 163; Terrill's Guards & Scouts 144, 145, 151
Upton, Charles H. 181
Upton's Hill, Va. 179, 180, *183*, 184

Vaden, Henry Heth 216, 217
VanHouten, Charles 161, 168
Vaughn, Col. John C. 177, 178
Virginia & Tennessee Railroad 41
Virginia Home Guards 41–43
Virginia militia: 5th Regiment Cavalry 174–176; 13th Brigade 175, 176; 67th Regiment 61, 62; 81st Regiment 175, 219; 157th Regiment 39–41
Virginia troops: Angus McDonald's Cavalry (7th Regiment) 178, 227, 228; Bath Cavalry 20, 21, 175; Bath Grays 75, 219–224 (1st Cavalry 182, 184, 186; 11th Cavalry 228; 18th Cavalry 224; 44th Infantry 194; 49th Infantry 202, 208; 52nd Infantry 202, 207; 58th Infantry 199, 202; Hansbrough's Battalion Infantry [9th Battalion] 80, 81, 223, 224); Lynchburg Lee Artillery 81; McClanahan's Battery 232; New Market (8th Star) Artillery 81; Newtown Artillery 179, 182 (7th Infantry 182; 12th Cavalry 24, 224–228, 230–238; 13th Infantry 27, 50, 125, 177–216; 20th Infantry 220; 25th Infantry 75, 77, 80–82, 191, 219, 221, 223, 224; 35th Battalion Cavalry 231; 62nd Mounted Infantry 224, 225, 239)
Virginia troops (Mexican War): 1st Infantry 58; Richmond Grays 59; Richmond Rangers 58, 59; Virginia Military Institute 13, 35–38, 44, 57, 58, 60, 62, 172–174, 176, 177, 189, 216

Walker, James A. 177, 178, 190–196, 200, 201, 213
Warm Springs, Va. 11, 13, 17, 18, 20, 23, 25, 30, 31, 41, 44, 49, 60, 97, 172, 175, 219, 223, 224
Warren, G.K. 215
Washington, George 79
Washington, Mrs. George 84
Washington, John Augustine 78, 79
Washington, D.C. 15, 33, 48, 54, 60, 97, 98, 102, 104, 108, 113, 114, 117, 120, 169, 170, 171, 179, 181
Waynesboro, Va. 233
Webster, Col. George 150–152, 162, 163
Weldon & Petersburg Railroad 235
West Point, NY (USMA) 15, 23, 57, 58, 85, *86*–91, 144, 162, 170, 171
Wharton, Col. G.C. 205
Wharton, John A. 158
White Sulphur Springs, (W) Va. 15, 41
Wilcox, Orlando B. 94, 95
Wiley, Col. W.J. 65
Wilkinson, David 162
Williams, Beverly D. 152
Williams, Capt. 92
Willis, Edward 214
Wills, Annie Smith Scott 30
Wilson, James 234
Winchester, Va. 2, 24, 25, 81, 177, 178, 190, 195, 202–205, 231, 239
Winfree, Christopher V. 36
Winston, Capt. Frank V. 194
Wise, Cornelia H. 55, 188, 189, 196; *see also* Moore, Cornelia H.
Wise, David G. 11, 225
Wise, Henry A. 174
Wise, Mary Jane 104, 189, 202, 222; *see also* Pitzer, Mary Jane
Wise Family 55, 117, 202
Woodstock, Va. 24
Wool, John E. 60, 82, 83
Woolworth, Col. 54
Wright, Horaito G. 91, 138–142, 164
Wright, J. Montgomery 127
Wright, M.W. 140

Zollicoffer, Felix K. 121

www.ingramcontent.com/pod-product-compliance
Ingram Content Group UK Ltd.
Pitfield, Milton Keynes, MK11 3LW, UK
UKHW041927140426
5217IPUK00014B/344